WITHDRAWN
FROM COLLECTION
VANCOUVER PUBLIC LIBRARY

Praise for *mySAP Toolbag for Performance Tuning and Stress Testing*

"A good book for people who deal with SAP systems for a living. I haven't read another book like this. It's technical but it's also an entertaining read. A pleasant departure from the norm."

—David C. Gilliland, S⁓⁓⁓⁓ ⁓⁓⁓⁓⁓⁓⁓⁓ ⁓⁓⁓⁓⁓⁓⁓ merica, Inc.

"Clearly, this book could be used as an ⁓⁓⁓⁓⁓⁓⁓⁓⁓⁓⁓⁓⁓⁓⁓⁓⁓⁓ ⁓⁓ could help a company like mine perfect perfo⁓⁓⁓⁓⁓⁓⁓⁓⁓⁓⁓⁓⁓ ⁓⁓andards."

—Dennis Prince, SAP Developm⁓⁓ ⁓⁓⁓⁓⁓⁓ ⁓⁓ecialist, Hewlett-Packard

"SAP optimization is one of those subjects that developers struggle to find time for and managers don't know is necessary. Presenting the value of the process up front serves to give the developer ammunition to win time for optimization and the manager an education in the value and necessity of optimization. Even if the manager types don't read past chapter 3, George's job is done. They should be convinced that someone technical in their IT department needs to be reading this book."

—Crew Reynolds, Software Development Manager, Daydots

"[This book features] good discussion on performance tuning the mySAP suite that no other books have so far. This is the perfect book for SAP Stress Test Project Managers, SAP Stress Test Project Teams, SAP Basis Administrators, Oracle DBAs, Unix Administrators managing SAP systems, and project implementation teams. Those who stress test their systems with the help of this book will have significant returns."

—Sanjoy Rath, SAP Consultant

Hewlett-Packard® Professional Books

HP-UX

Cooper/Moore	HP-UX 11i Internals
Fernandez	Configuring CDE
Madell	Disk and File Management Tasks on HP-UX
Olker	Optimizing NFS Performance
Poniatowski	HP-UX 11i Virtual Partitions
Poniatowski	HP-UX 11i System Administration Handbook and Toolkit, Second Edition
Poniatowski	The HP-UX 11.x System Administration Handbook and Toolkit
Poniatowski	HP-UX 11.x System Administration "How To" Book
Poniatowski	HP-UX 10.x System Administration "How To" Book
Poniatowski	HP-UX System Administration Handbook and Toolkit
Poniatowski	Learning the HP-UX Operating System
Rehman	HP-UX CSA: Official Study Guide and Desk Reference
Sauers/Ruemmler/Weygant	HP-UX 11i Tuning and Performance
Weygant	Clusters for High Availability, Second Edition
Wong	HP-UX 11i Security

UNIX, LINUX, WINDOWS, AND MPE I/X

Mosberger/Eranian	IA-64 Linux Kernel
Poniatowski	UNIX User's Handbook, Second Edition
Stone/Symons	UNIX Fault Management

COMPUTER ARCHITECTURE

Evans/Trimper	Itanium Architecture for Programmers
Kane	PA-RISC 2.0 Architecture
Markstein	IA-64 and Elementary Functions

NETWORKING/COMMUNICATIONS

Blommers	Architecting Enterprise Solutions with UNIX Networking
Blommers	OpenView Network Node Manager
Blommers	Practical Planning for Network Growth
Brans	Mobilize Your Enterprise
Cook	Building Enterprise Information Architecture
Lucke	Designing and Implementing Computer Workgroups
Lund	Integrating UNIX and PC Network Operating Systems

SECURITY

Bruce	Security in Distributed Computing
Mao	Modern Cryptography: Theory and Practice
Pearson et al.	Trusted Computing Platforms
Pipkin	Halting the Hacker, Second Edition
Pipkin	Information Security

WEB/INTERNET CONCEPTS AND PROGRAMMING

Amor	E-business (R)evolution, Second Edition
Apte/Mehta	UDDI
Chatterjee/Webber	Developing Enterprise Web Services: An Architect's Guide
Kumar	J2EE Security for Servlets, EJBs, and Web Services
Mowbrey/Werry	Online Communities
Tapadiya	.NET Programming

OTHER PROGRAMMING

Blinn	Portable Shell Programming
Caruso	Power Programming in HP OpenView
Chaudhri	Object Databases in Practice
Chew	The Java/C++ Cross Reference Handbook
Grady	Practical Software Metrics for Project Management and Process Improvement
Grady	Software Metrics
Grady	Successful Software Process Improvement
Lewis	The Art and Science of Smalltalk
Lichtenbelt	Introduction to Volume Rendering
Little/Maron/Pavlik	Java Transaction Processing
Mellquist	SNMP++
Mikkelsen	Practical Software Configuration Management
Norton	Thread Time
Tapadiya	COM+ Programming
Yuan	Windows 2000 GDI Programming

STORAGE

Thornburgh	Fibre Channel for Mass Storage
Thornburgh/Schoenborn	Storage Area Networks
Todman	Designing Data Warehouses

IT/IS

Anderson	mySAP Tool Bag for Performance Tuning and Stress Testing
Missbach/Hoffman	SAP Hardware Solutions

IMAGE PROCESSING

Crane	A Simplified Approach to Image Processing
Gann	Desktop Scanners

MY**SAP** TOOLBAG
FOR PERFORMANCE TUNING
AND STRESS TESTING

George W. Anderson

Prentice Hall PTR
Upper Saddle River, New Jersey 07450
http://www.phptr.com

Library of Congress Cataloging-in-Publication Data

Anderson, George W.
    MySAP toolbag for performance tuning and stress testing / George W. Anderson.
            p. cm. – (Hewlett-Packard professional books)
    Includes index.
    ISBN 0-13-144852-8 (paper)
    1. mySAP.com 2. Business—Computer programs. 3. Industrial management—Computer
    programs. I. Title. II. Series.

    HF5548.4.R2A528 2004
    658'.00285'5376—dc22

                                                2004040061

Editorial/production supervision: *BooksCraft, Inc., Indianapolis, IN*
Cover design director: *Jerry Votta*
Cover designer: *Nina Scuderi*
Art director: *Gail Cocker-Bogusz*
Executive editor: *Jill Harry*
Editorial assistant: *Noreen Regina*
Marketing manager: *Robin O'Brien*
HP Books publisher: *William Carver*

© 2004 by Hewlett-Packard Development Company, L.P.

Prentice Hall books are widely used by corporations and government agencies for training, marketing, and resale.

PRENTICE
HALL
PTR   For information regarding corporate and government bulk discounts please contact:
Corporate and Government Sales (800) 382-3419 or corpsales@pearsontechgroup.com

Company and product names mentioned herein are the trademarks or registered trademarks of their respective owners.

All rights reserved. No part of this book may be reproduced, in any form or by any means, without permission in writing from the publisher.

Printed in the United States of America
First printing.

ISBN 0-13-144852-8

Pearson Education LTD.
Pearson Education Australia PTY, Limited
Pearson Education Singapore, Pte. Ltd.
Pearson Education North Asia Ltd.
Pearson Education Canada, Ltd.
Pearson Educación de Mexico, S.A. de C.V.
Pearson Education—Japan
Pearson Education Malaysia, Pte. Ltd.

16 JUN 2005

Contents

Preface

This book is about a whole lot more than performance tuning and testing. It's about saving and making money—your company's money, your own customer's budget dollars left on the negotiating or purchasing table, and even your personal funds. By getting the most up front out of your infrastructure investment in SAP, and continuing to reap the benefits of a well-oiled and well-performing machine over time, the dollars will accumulate quickly. How? Simple—by keeping your SAP Business Warehouse users well informed, your SAP Customer Relationship ManagementCRM team highly productive, and your R/3 users anything but idle. In turn, your company will reap the benefits of rapid access to information, increased sales per customer, and more—saving and making not only money, but jobs and careers as well.

This book is also about managing the risk inherent to the single most important thing that makes tuning and testing so critical: change. The manner in which change is handled—or how your company verifies that a change to its mission-critical SAP systems will not significantly impact the performance or availability of those same systems—has the power to turn average good companies into great ones. Of course, the converse is true as well. That is, for centuries unmanaged change has left behind in its footprints a broad wake of destruction, squashing and consuming otherwise successful entities while sparing only the adaptable. Certainly, once-great companies and institutions have risen and fallen over seemingly less important matters.

Fortunately, given the past, it only follows that the opportunity for greatness is just as promising—simply take a look at the Global 2000, and it should be self-evident that companies with their arms around change thrive even in the midst of great difficulties. The best of these companies embrace testing beliefs and employ tuning processes similar to those I will discuss here, taking a holistic view of their SAP and other enterprise systems to maximize performance, minimize service disruptions, and ultimately mitigate the risk of change. Indeed, that's the real reason behind why I wrote this book before you—to provide a blueprint or roadmap of sorts, such that we can survive, even thrive, rather than unwittingly perish as victims of change.

Acknowledgments

The word *change* brings to my mind thoughts of performing system upgrades, managing and installing SAP support packages, and applying patches and fixes. I think about all that is at stake—the performance and availability of a system and its capability of supporting the labor and livelihood of thousands of people—and take my work and that of my team very seriously. But the thought of change evokes other, more personal, feelings as well. I'm talking about the lifelong and eternal changes oneself can realize, changes made possible through our Father in Heaven and His son. No, I'm not a minister or pastor or priest. I'm simply a person like so many others that chose for years to do things my way, and then one day *got it*, and chose instead to try to do things God's way.

With that, it almost goes without saying that I wish to acknowledge the role Jesus has played in my life, making it possible for me to write this book by virtue of the family and job He blessed me with; the clients He provided, which in turn afforded the experience reflected herein; and the means to make all of this possible without sacrificing too much time away from my family. Naturally, a huge thanks goes to my family as well—my children, Phillip, Ashley, and Meagan, and especially my wife and best friend, Michelle. To my many customers across North America, particularly my favorite clients in Houston, Cleveland, Austin, Cranston, and Rochester, thank you for the opportunities to work together and learn from one another. To my SAP colleagues at HP, SAP, Microsoft, Oracle, Capgemini, and elsewhere, thank you for your unwavering support and friendship over the years. And to my testing partners and peers at AutoTester, Compuware, Mercury Interactive, SAP, Microsoft, and so many others, my thankful appreciation for your assistance and generosity. Finally, to my close friends, church family, and others with whom I work and serve every day, thank you—I am forever grateful for your guidance, accountability, and friendship.

Introduction

Welcome to *mySAP Toolbag for Performance Tuning and Stress Testing: A Technology Stack Approach!* Over the course of these 15 chapters, we will walk through everything necessary to plan for, staff, develop, test, execute, and evaluate the results of stress testing (sometimes called load or performance testing) so as to ultimately tune and optimize your SAP systems for the best performance possible. SAP stands for Systems, Applications, and Products in Data Processing, an acronym better known for including all of the very capable albeit expensive software applications developed by SAP AG, one of the largest software companies in the world. By defining concrete success criteria that reflect what good performance means to *you and the users of your particular SAP systems,* and then leveraging the right tools for the job at hand, you will be well positioned to test and tune the impact of everything from replacing your core R/3 Enterprise solution's disk subsystem, to analyzing the impact that new NetWeaver-enabled complex business processes have across multiple mySAP components in your growing enterprise. Because my experience is entrenched in the real world of SAP deployments, infrastructure upgrades, and ongoing support, you will benefit not only from my years of lessons "learned the hard way," but also from my hands-on experience with the tools and approaches commonly used to test and tune, along with what I consider to be "best practices" in performance tuning and stress testing that I have developed along the way.

1.1.   Why I Wrote This Book

Before we begin, though, you may be curious as to why I chose to write a book that focuses on methodical and recurring stress testing as a means to achieve lasting SAP performance. Certainly other approaches are common; for example, a number of excellent texts, articles, and whitepapers have been published that focus on tuning SAP systems at an application layer or in terms of various hardware and database components. In my eyes, however, these otherwise good resources fall short in two critical ways:

- They tend to address only a layer or two of the SAP technology stack; thus, only a small piece of the whole performance-tuning picture is ever presented in great detail. And, by looking at SAP performance tuning less than holistically, I believe these resources leave their readers with less than what is truly required to get the most out of an SAP system.

- More important, the bulk of SAP tuning today is performed reactively and somewhat blindly, rather than proactively and with confidence. Why? Because without both a real and a repeatable load on your system, it's next to impossible to tune your production system intelligently. Instead, as is common at so many SAP shops, performance-impacting changes are crammed into a small window of downtime without understanding the full impact that the changes invite when the system is *running under load.* Without the benefit of load testing, the shop's greatest realistic hope is that the new change will not totally destroy end-user response times or batch processing/reporting throughput. And, if these SAP shops are lucky, performance might wind up improving. Maybe.

To this last point, even if you are lucky enough to improve your overall performance, it's likely that the gain will be short-lived, since an SAP system is rarely static for long—mySAP components and their infrastructural underpinnings change constantly, both functionally and technically. What worked well a few months ago may result in less than adequate performance in the near future. Thus, if you take the traditional approach to tuning, and do so reactively, you'll never find yourself completely out of the woods. Instead, every few months you will face new performance holes from which to dig yourself out, and ever-shrinking downtime windows in which to do this.

No one who subscribes to reactive tuning is exempt from this "digging yourself out of a hole" fate. In fact, no SAP customer is exempt from performance tuning, period. Like I mentioned, ever-changing SAP system landscapes make tuning a fact of life. Even in cases where you might "pay as you go," and forfeit extra dollars to an outsourcing provider for increased computing capacity during peak processing periods, you'll still want to tune at some level; not doing so simply costs money, too—the same budget money you tried to save by embracing a pay-as-you-go model in the first place.

Performance issues do not simply manifest themselves up front, to be taken care of quickly after being easily identified, and never seen again. In the last 7 years of my own SAP basis and project management experience, I've seen performance issues crop up mere days before Go-Live in new implementations, both before and after functional upgrades and technology refreshes, and at the most inopportune times, such as after a change was introduced into a production system without the benefit of thoroughly load testing the change prior to promoting it. It's not that performance tuning was ignored or put off—on the contrary, usually many of these last-minute issues were simply the result of 11th-hour functional changes or the result of misunderstanding how the updated system behaved under load. But, without exception, my customers who embraced stress testing prior to Go-Live, and as a business-as-usual practice during an SAP system's lifecycle, fared better than their less proactive counterparts. The experiences that I've gained supporting all of these accounts—my own SAP customers—will be passed on to you.

1.1.1. Common Perceptions against Stress Testing and Tuning in the Real World

My goal in writing this book is actually pretty simple, if not on the verge of being too idealistic. I hope to merely change the way in which you think of performance tuning your core SAP and mySAP solutions, and then walk you through how to do so as cheaply and simply as possible using a variety of situation-specific stress testing tools and approaches. What you do with this information—whether you wish to proactively or reactively tune your systems—is of course up to you! But before we get ahead of ourselves, it's only fair to warn you that you may encounter these top commonly perceived reasons to forgo stress testing:

- After broaching the subject of stress testing at many a SAP customer site, I've been told over and over again that it was already done, and the tests were successful. A bit of prodding, though, often uncovers what amounts to a fairly weak stress-testing execution plan. For example, one of my customers thought running a couple of hard-hitting batch processes would prove his system was robustly configured. Another thought 50 concurrent users would be adequate to simulate what would eventually be 500 concurrent users and a large overlapping nightly batch workload. And many more have insisted over the years that having some of the team log in to the development or test system and execute a number of key transactions placed enough load on the system—a system configured nothing like production, mind you—to make an informed Go-Live or post-SAP Migration decision.
- At the other end of the spectrum, more than a few of my customers have been bold enough to say that they have performed such extensive functional testing (typically single-user testing, discussed at length in the next chapter) that the need for dedicated "expensive" stress testing is simply a waste of time. Along the same lines, technical teams responsible for SAP Basis and Database Administration (DBA) functions have prematurely blessed their particular solution stacks prior to executing real-world stress tests under the assumption that everything was configured correctly.
- Perhaps the most common excuse when it comes to skipping stress testing involves time: no one has it, no one can make it, time costs money, and so on. True, time is a scarce resource that must be carefully managed even in the best of worlds. But forgoing stress testing because of a lack of time seems to me a sure-fire way of spending plenty of time later chasing down and rectifying performance problems. Indeed, a system's basic availability is put at risk as well when performance issues get out of control!
- Money, or lack thereof, is another big excuse handed down from information technology (IT) management teams to the people responsible for supporting a particular SAP solution. As we'll see later, however, it can become very expensive, very quickly, to skip stress testing.
- Finally, the fact that a well-conceived stress test requires knowledge of stress testing, along with the knowledge of how to use a particular test tool or approach, creates a

problem; organizations uncomfortable climbing a relatively steep but potentially very focused learning curve will naturally shy away. Similarly, organizations acclimated to stress testing but unfamiliar with a particular tool set, approach, or method may tend to back away from new forms of testing and tuning as well.

1.2.   How I Wrote This Book

The foundation of this text stems from years of hands-on performance tuning, stress testing, and generally supporting hundreds of SAP customer systems, ranging from Hewlett-Packard (HP)– and Compaq-based solutions, to platforms developed by Digital, IBM, Dell, EMC, Data General, and a few others. From an SAP product perspective, most of my experience has been with R/3, Business Information Warehouse (BW), Enterprise Buyer Pro (SRM/EBP), Advanced Planner and Optimizer (APO), and Internet Transaction Server (ITS), although I've also worked closely with Workplace, Enterprise Portal (EP), Customer Relationship Management (CRM), and, to a lesser extent, Product Lifecycle Management (PLM), Strategic Enterprise Management (SEM), and, most recently, SAP's Exchange Infrastructure (XI) and Master Data Management (MDM) products. With some notable exceptions, most of my stress-testing expertise was borne of the need to optimize R/3-, BW-, EBP-, and ITS-based solutions. In supporting these mission-critical systems over the years, I've developed close relationships with many of my customers, to the point where I could actually have made use of many of their nonproduction systems to help me put together this book.

For purposes of this book, however, I wanted a complete and fairly static environment that was not only available to me 24/7 (because that's how I tend to write—a paragraph here, a figure there—around the clock) but also one that could be re-created by you assuming you would eventually desire to see firsthand how a particular tool set, utility, or approach works in the real world. Thus, I created something of a custom home-based SAP technical sandbox to fulfill both of these needs in the following manner:

- My "core" system is a workhorse SAP R/3 4.6C IDES system, running on Windows 2000 and Oracle 8.1.7—a very "mainstream" product (despite the aging database release!) today and likely for the next year or so.
- I also performed a fresh install of an "empty" BW 3.0B system on SQL Server 2000, thus giving me both a different database flavor and a mySAP component based on SAP's Web Application Server.
- I then added a CRM 3.0A system to the mix, also running on SQL Server 2000. As one of the fastest growing SAP products out there today, it makes sense to give it a home in my own sandbox.
- Finally, I installed two instances of SAP's Internet Transaction Server, to facilitate end-user testing via the SAP HTML "WebGUI" in addition to SAP's more traditional user interfaces, all of which I'll cover in detail later.

Note the variety in terms of the underlying database and SAP application layers. I could have chosen to introduce even more variety from an Operating System (OS) perspective, in the

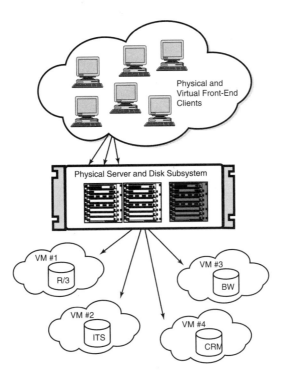

Figure 1–1 By using VMware's GSX product, I was able to assemble a very complex testing environment quickly, at minimal cost, leveraging a single HP ProLiant to load four "guest" virtual machines, each executing a different SAP component or product.

form of a Linux-based solution, but, at the end of the day, I felt more comfortable standardizing on Windows—it was just easy, too. I also standardized on a single hardware platform. Why? Even though I'm a senior consultant in a large hardware- and services-centric organization, and have access to pretty much any hardware and software I could ever want, I no longer have the desire (nor my wife's blessing, to tell the truth) to build and install numerous servers and disk subsystems throughout the house, stringing cables between rooms to create an appropriate network or storage area network (SAN) infrastructure. Instead, I chose to go the simpler route that more and more of my customers are going when it comes to different kinds of testing (albeit not production-ready stress testing): I loaded a single "large" HP ProLiant server with VMware's GSX product, connecting it to a lone although very capable fiber-based RAID-protected (redundant array of inexpensive/independent disks) disk subsystem filled with 72GB drives, as shown in Figure 1–1. The tradeoff in raw horsepower was well worth the time, space, and general support savings I realized, compared with the requirements of a more traditional approach. Indeed, the whole setup proved to be quite manageable, and very compact as well.

I then tucked everything quickly away, performing my base operating system loads and SAP installations over the course of the next few weeks with my family none the wiser (nor appropriately excited, in my eyes), oblivious to the fact that so many genuinely cool mySAP demo systems were running quite innocuously under their noses. And to think my 9-year-old boy, Phillip, would rather play with his Game Cube!

1.3.   My SAP Customers and Their Boats

Now that you understand my goal in writing this book, the perceptions I'm up against, and, to some extent, how I wrote this book, I think it's necessary to set the stage in terms of where SAP AG's customers are today (AG is Germany's equivalent for "Inc.," by the way), and how they got there. To that end, I like to think of my own SAP customers as boat owners. Not in a bad way, as in "the two best days in their life were the day they bought their boat and the day they finally turned around and sold it," but in a good way. My SAP customers' "boat" comprises all of the IT resources used to run and maintain their SAP systems. It includes their data center infrastructure, "brick and mortar" and other fixed costs, servers and disk subsystems, OS and database products, mySAP Enterprise Resource Planning (ERP), R/3, and Business Suite components, and all of the costly IT and business staff necessary to keep everything moving along.

Because these SAP systems represent core-enabling enterprise solutions responsible in large part for servicing the fundamental business processes used by a company, and therefore of great importance in that they keep the company afloat, we're talking about some pretty nice boats here. Indeed, most of my customers are traveling quite comfortably, at minimum in something like a very expensive and very fast speedboat. True, there might be a couple of really big home-made rafts and maybe a sleek canoe here and there, but no one running an SAP solution is floating the river in a dinghy. On the contrary, more than a few of SAP AG's customers are cruising the waters in plush hundred-million-dollar yachts. And my SAP-enabled customers in the armed services are speeding full steam ahead in nothing less than destroyer-class battleships and nuclear-capable submarines.

I like these latter illustrations best as they also lend themselves to aptly describing the conditions in which my customers find their boats floating. Because these waters are by no means calm; truth be told, no one is really doing anything as serene as floating at all. Rapids abound, twists and turns are common, and the current is constantly against my customers; if their IT infrastructures run out of steam, they find themselves in effect standing still or, even worse, floating backwards. To complicate matters further, traps surround all of their boats. Ill-tempered sharks wish only to see them sink, and competitors steaming alongside them are doing what they can to poke holes in others' ships, by hiring away their top SAP IT and business-focused talent.

1.3.1.   The Waterfall

Most significantly, there lies an enormous waterfall behind each of these SAP boats—stay with me a bit longer and we'll get to the meat of performance tuning and stress testing in just a bit. This waterfall I speak of is massive and deep and final, and it will inevitably claim all of the boats in which my customers find themselves today. All of them. Littered at the bottom of the waterfall are the remnants of both old and relatively new boats—IT infrastructures—unable to steam ahead under their own power any longer. If you look closely enough, you can still see the remains of everything from old Intel Pentium Pro Dell and Compaq servers to the original Sun UE10000 and IBM AS/400 servers, to direct-attached SCSI-based disk subsystems and piles of old tape drives and cartridges. Long-retired and unsupported versions of Digital UNIX, Microsoft NT 3.51, SQL Server 6x, and Informix serve only to stink up the place; indeed, the air is rank with the aroma of long-dead technology. Even once-cutting-edge SAP R/3 2.2 and 3.0F systems rot in the sun, smashed among the rocks.

Mixed in with all of this old technology can even be found some of my customers' staffs—people!—who failed to keep up with the needs of their business or the business of supporting mission-critical IT infrastructures. SAP IT directors who failed to address their own supply chain deficiencies with products like SAP APO and BW and IT managers who could never quite figure out how to retain their talented Basis and Programming teams are sitting around at the bottom of the falls, picking their way through the rocks, mumbling something about figuring out those "New Dimension" products. SAP infrastructure teams unable to grasp the concept of high availability are falling in regularly, too, and turning around just as fast to scuttle off in search of new IT environments unfamiliar with the term "5 nines of availability." Lately, ABAPers (SAP's proprietary programming language) uncomfortable with or uninterested in Java and Microsoft's NET products have begun dropping in regularly as well. Indeed, whole company IT departments that invested in SAP-enabling technologies but failed to get their arms around cost or availability may be found at the bottom of the waterfall, having been replaced more often than not by well-oiled and massively efficient ocean liners that I like to refer to as "USS Outsourcers."

1.3.2.   Keeping Your Boat in Good Working Order

The giant waterfall behind each SAP shop is inevitable and inescapable; the core of the boat in which each SAP customer finds him- or herself today will one day succumb to that waterfall, plain and simple. It's going to happen to everything and everyone. It's only a question of when.

The goal of each SAP customer, and indeed my own goal as an SAP consultant, therefore, is to help keep these boats and their crews in good working order. Together, we must strive to maintain them, keep them performing well, and address the inevitable leaks and other issues in a timely manner—while the boat is steaming up the river, of course. Dry-docking is unfortunately not an option—when was the last time you heard a CIO talk about putting R/3 up a few months while some issues are worked out? And, as if that wasn't tricky enough, the bigger challenge each SAP customer site faces every few years is completely revamping and even replacing its boat, simultaneously retooling its crew, while maintaining a safe distance from the waterfall. SAP technology partners call these major transformation processes "SAP upgrades" or "SAP technology refreshes," and, without exception, these are big undertakings. Smaller changes in terms of scope are often implemented on a more regular basis, and typically labeled something like "quarterly SAP change waves" or "monthly change control releases."

The key to successfully making changes to an SAP boat is to keep from losing too much ground to the river's current—that is, to keep the business running. Crucial to this process is what brings us together here, the need to maintain a well-performing system while avoiding weighing down our boats with so much technology, staff, and cost that we can't help but sink from the weight of our own total cost of ownership (TCO). In other words, together I can help you achieve a delicate balance between performance, cost, availability, and scalability within the constraints of your unique business requirements or service level agreements (SLAs). And who knows, maybe I'll help you avoid falling victim to the swift current that might otherwise sweep you in. In short, as SAP resource managers, our collective goal is simply to take care of our boats proactively, all in order to avoid hanging out again with those one-foot-in-the-grave Data General SAP computer operators looking for something to power up at the bottom of the rocks. This is where performance tuning and stress testing come in, making it possible for us to steer clear of becoming IT boat anchors ourselves.

1.3.3.   Performance Tuning and Stress Testing

Nothing short of a cost-effective, sound, and comprehensive approach to maximizing the performance of the IT infrastructure that underpins your SAP systems is in order, and this approach represents the basic premise of this book. As I explained earlier, performance tuning and stress testing actually go hand in hand, and I will illustrate how they should be a critical and recurring function within the lifecycle of every SAP system. For without a repeatable and customer-representative load on your system, performance tuning is hit-and-miss at best, no better than theoretical studies or mindless iterations in arbitrary tweaking of your system.

From new implementations through change waves, through full-blown functional and technology upgrades, performance tuning driven by cost-effective stress testing represents nothing less than a fundamental pillar of an SAP solution's long-term success. As alluded to previously, the other pillars include low TCO and meeting availability and scalability goals. Combined, these four pillars uphold a solid SAP system, as illustrated in Figure 1–2. If they are unbalanced, however, these pillars succumb to the weight of business and end-user requirements; rather than riding high, our boat risks pitching onto the boulders just a few feet below the water's surface. Because of the importance of this balance, I will address each of these pillars in detail throughout the chapters that follow. Solid performance without good TCO, satisfactory availability, and adequate scalability misses the boat, so to speak, and takes us to the bottom of the waterfall much sooner than we'd expect.

1.3.4.   What Exactly Is Good Performance?

OK, enough of the boat analogy for now. What exactly does good performance mean? Performance is measured in many ways, but it usually boils down to two metrics: response time and system throughput, as illustrated in Figure 1–3.

In other words, how quickly a task is completed (response time) or how much work (e.g., orders created, materials moved) is performed in a fixed amount of time (throughput) pretty well covers how you measure performance. Determining whether a system's performance is "good" involves simply mapping one of these performance metrics back to a customer's unique needs or an SLA. Thus, what might be acceptable to one group of end users might represent unacceptable

Riding High in Your SAP Boat

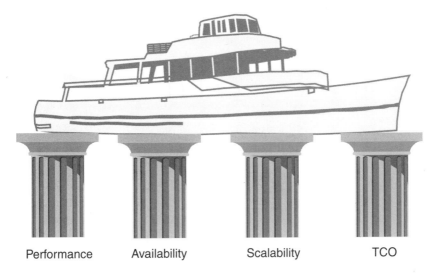

Performance   Availability   Scalability   TCO

Figure 1–2 The four fundamental pillars of a successful SAP system include performance, availability, scalability, and low TCO.

Throughput vs. Response-Time Performance

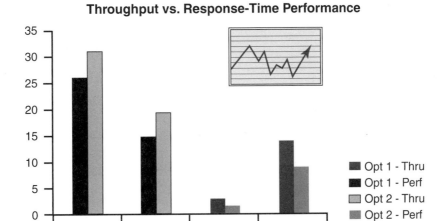

Figure 1–3 The response times or throughput that a particular system configuration or option enjoys describes its general performance.

performance to another group. Even within the same group, acceptable performance during "crunch time"—such as that observed at month-end close or during a seasonal peak—will vary as well.

Further, good performance might even be at odds with the company's financial analysts and budgeting personnel. A higher level of performance, along with availability and scalability, costs more, plain and simple. The key is therefore to determine what is both required by *and* minimally acceptable to all parties, from end users to the IT department, to the well-intentioned bean counters back in Finance. Accordingly, another one of my goals in this book is to help you find *and keep* the right balance in your own particular case as quickly and efficiently as possible.

1.4.   My Audience

Given that you've picked up this book, you're probably interested in either SAP or performance tuning and testing in general. As far as I'm concerned, if you fit either description, this book is for you. However, when I began writing, I envisioned four very different readers—perhaps one of the following descriptions fits you:

- The seasoned SAP Basis professional already engaged in maintaining well-performing enterprise SAP solutions, whether as an employee or long-term contractor of a company that has deployed SAP, or a consultant tasked with doing so on behalf of a company
- An experienced performance-tuning and -testing specialist recently introduced to the world of SAP, looking for a guide to get up to speed quickly
- An IT professional wishing to learn more about SAP, performance tuning, and stress testing, perhaps to make a career move into supporting SAP products and solutions
- A manager, director, or team leader of an IT organization charged with maximizing the performance and availability of an enterprise SAP deployment

Later, as I continued writing, I found myself thinking that quite a few other folks would benefit from this material, too. For example, given my focus on intelligently managing change through the judicious use of testing and tuning, any number of change management specialists would quickly realize their money's worth in picking up a copy of this text. As would IT specialists interested in learning of the various tools and approaches available for testing and tuning complex technology stacks that don't necessarily include an SAP application layer; that is, many of the principles and practices detailed in this book are as applicable to other mission-critical business applications (Web Server farms, e-mail systems, data warehouses, and so on) as they are to SAP. Finally, for those SAP Basis professionals ensnared in the world of systems administration and enterprise management, I'd like to think that this book holds the promise of helping you expand on your already valuable skills, making you either more indispensable in your current role or helping to make you a more viable candidate for a senior Basis or similar position. In all cases, as you strive to understand the bigger picture surrounding SAP stress testing and tuning, and in turn add knowledge to your repertoire, you'll only position yourself for bigger and better career opportunities down the road.

1.4.1. How to Make Use of This Book

As shown in Figure 1–4, I have written this book along the lines of a project plan: the sequence of chapters follows a logical progression, starting with understanding the basics of SAP and what you wish to accomplish in terms of goals and success criteria. Next, I work through the following key areas: staffing; piloting stress-test and performance analysis tools; preparing to execute a stress test; understanding your SAP system's unique workload; data mining; scripting, executing, and monitoring test runs; analyzing the results of these runs; and iteratively tuning your system based on your test-run findings.

Those of you familiar with one of my earlier works, *SAP Planning: Best Practices in Implementation* (Que Publishing/SAMS, May 2003), are no strangers to this approach. A project plan approach makes sense intuitively and lends itself to crafting both a cohesive book and durable standalone chapters, which in turn allows readers to work their way through the parts of the book they find most useful or compelling, without a lot of rereading.

Another holdover from *SAP Planning* is the use of "real world" sections within most of the chapters. It's in these sections that I share my actual experiences and some of the bizarre or unique testing and tuning engagements and events that helped give shape to this book. The names have been changed to protect the innocent, but rest assured that the stories are true. I'm sure you'll take comfort in the knowledge that many of your SAP colleagues out in the real world are not perfect either and have doubled back down some of the same goofy roads the rest of us have traveled in the course of implementing, upgrading, and tuning SAP systems.

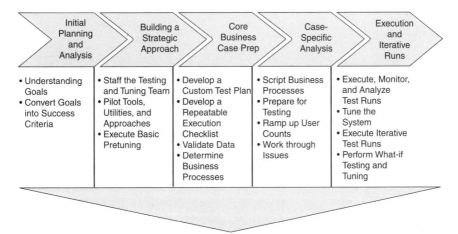

Overall Project Plan Tasks and Activities

Figure 1–4 The general organization and layout of this book follows a project plan, making it easy to read the various chapters out of sequence.

You'll also notice that an ftp site has been created that hosts many of the templates, scripts, pointers to freeware utilities, and other tools that are discussed throughout the book and high-lighted specifically in the "Tools and Approaches" section that concludes most chapters. Indeed, even a master stress-test project plan ready to be customized for your own use may be found here, among so many other just plain cool documents. Note that I prefer an ftp site rather than a CD to accompany this book for one reason—updates. As you uncover issues or seek clarification re-garding anything covered by the book, I can more easily share updated code, documents, scripts, tools, and so on, a feat simply not feasible otherwise. Trust me, it's a great way to go for a tech-nically detailed book, especially one trying to cover a moving target like SAP!

1.4.2.   What's a Toolbag?

When it comes to technology, no real technologist leaves home without his or her toolbag, espe-cially when a mission-critical SAP system hangs in the balance. Depending on your support role, however, the contents of the toolbag will vary: an SAP developer's toolbag, for example, will dif-fer greatly from that of an individual tasked with maintaining a well-performing and highly avail-able mySAP solution. Key materials in my own toolbag, a "performance-tuning/stress-testing" bag as shown in Figure 1–5, include the following items:

- My laptop and iPaq, containing tools, utilities, other customer-specific testing results, links to test tool vendor and other important Web sites, and much more.
- My CD "utilities" case, stuffed with testing tools and utilities, patches/service packs, technical whitepapers in electronic form, and so on—all to simply save space on my laptop or facilitate quickly moving these tools to a customer's system. I carry every-thing from hardware-focused utilities designed to measure server and disk subsystem throughput, to Microsoft and Unix-based OS performance-testing tools, to network and database load emulators, to full-fledged mySAP-sanctioned load-testing products from companies such as AutoTester, Compuware, and Mercury Interactive. I will discuss these and more at length in Chapters 6 and 7. These tools form the bulk of my personal toolbag.
- SAP installation and presentation CDs for many of the most common mySAP compo-nents and graphical user interface (GUI) releases, including R/3, BW, EBP/CRM, ITS, and others.
- Another set of utility CDs containing what I term "utilities," like screen capture utili-ties, compression programs, various file-format "readers," and ftp and Internet browser utilities, along with specialized SAP sizing and capacity planning tools.
- Various media-sharing devices, or tools that facilitate accessing another computer sys-tem, like a CD/DVD burner, blank CDs, Ethernet cross-over cable, USB disk, and yes, even a few floppy disks.
- Printed copies of new whitepapers or other technical documents related to new stress-testing or performance-tuning tools, or other materials that I feel I need to read just to

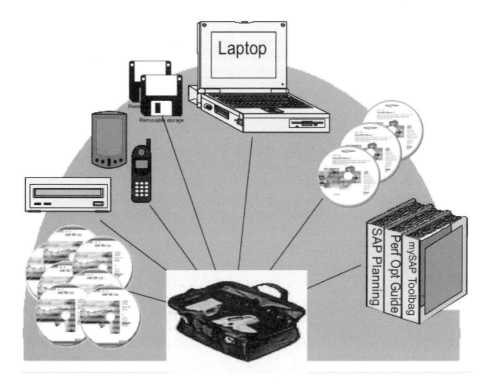

Figure 1–5 Although your own toolbag may vary, core contents like those pictured here are indispensable when it comes to testing and performance tuning.

"keep up." As you know, it's often much easier to curl up with the printed word than a laptop. Besides, paper doesn't tend to run out of batteries on a long flight.

• Other printed media, ranging from the latest *SAP Professional Journal* or *SAP Insider* to perhaps one of my colleagues' latest books. My current favorites are the third edition of Dr. Thomas Schneider's *SAP Performance Optimization Guide* (July 2003), an application-layer performance classic in its own right, and *SAP Hardware Solutions* (December 2000) by Michael Missbach and Uwe M. Hoffmann. In the recent past, I've also weighed down my bag with both of Jose Antonio's major works (if you've seen his books, the significance of *weigh* won't get by you), Dennis Prince's *Supporting SAP R/3* (September 1998), Naeem Hashmi's now-classic SAP BW book *Business Information Warehouse for SAP* (August 2000), and any number of Microsoft Press and Oracle Press books covering their respective database products.

A great technical book explains technical matters in a layperson's terms, using real-world examples to instill an understanding of the matter at hand. The best technical books also include the specifics necessary for you to actually perform hands-on what is covered in text, through the use of numbered checklists, detailed step-by-step instructions, and access to the same tools, code, scripts, and so on used by the author. In essence, a good technical book should become as indispensable as the other contents of your toolbag, helping you out of jams and pointing the way to additional tools and resources when you need them. When it comes to performance tuning and stress testing SAP systems, I am confident that this book will become a permanent component of your own personal toolbag.

So, again, welcome to *mySAP Toolbag for Performance Tuning and Stress Testing*. I'm certain you'll happily take away much of the knowledge I share in terms of tools, methods, and approaches, and apply it for your own gain as well as that of your SAP customers. In the process, you'll undoubtedly uncover new tools and approaches on your own, and your personal SAP toolbag will grow that much more valuable. I look forward to your feedback in this regard, as I seek not only to add to my own knowledge but to share it with your fellow readers and our colleagues as we all steam full-speed ahead in the sea we call SAP.

Performance Tuning and Stress Testing Reviewed

With millions of dollars and thousands of hours invested, the last thing you want after a major SAP implementation, upgrade, IT consolidation, or change control wave is a surprise on the big day of Go-Live or a cutover to a new or updated system. Yet, that is exactly what occurs time and time again in the real world. Why? Because even though a huge, carefully managed budget may have been set aside and painstakingly adhered to, many companies implementing, upgrading, or simply maintaining SAP AG's R/3 or a mySAP Business Suite component simply do not understand the value of or cost in performing a holistic stress test of both their critical enterprise business applications and the technology underpinning these applications. More often than not, a company focuses solely on functional testing—ensuring that the business can get its day-in and day-out job done using the new system to conduct company operations or business transactions—at the expense of stress or "load" testing. Because of this situation, instead of Go-Live representing a best-case nonevent, it more closely resembles a roll of the dice. And, chances are good that most companies will not hit the jackpot; indeed, the road of many SAP implementations and upgrades post Go-Live is littered with poor code, misconfigured hardware, and less than optimally tuned databases. In these cases, although it's true that the system can functionally perform what it was intended to do (e.g., create and track sales orders or facilitate inventory management), it does so either slower than is possible, or in a manner that hinders much of the value originally envisioned in deploying the new application—to the point of hurting the business's ability to service its end users and other customers in a timely manner. In the end, the business is forced to limp along for a period of time until the performance and tuning issues are finally worked out over time, if at all.

Fortunately, the great majority of performance-related unknowns surrounding Go-Live may be identified and mitigated, if not completely eliminated, before cutover, by giving proper attention to stress testing and follow-on performance tuning. This book's primary goal, therefore, is to help you understand exactly how stress testing and real-world performance tuning fit within the big picture of an SAP system's lifecycle. In the next several hundred pages, I will walk you through pretuning your entire SAP Technology Stack, planning for and executing an end-to-end application-layer SAP stress test, and leveraging your newfound knowledge to optimize your SAP system before a single one of your system's end users is ever asked to log on to your new or updated system. In doing so, I will address not only the critical nature of working with the business to identify success criteria and approaches useful in staffing your SAP "testing and tuning" project team but also the detailed steps necessary to successfully navigate through a maze of technology and business-process decisions. Of course, serious attention to your unique mySAP applications, timelines, budgets, and performance goals is provided along the way, too. And, to keep all of us grounded in the real world, I have shared in many of these chapters my own customer stories, findings, anecdotes, and lessons learned, along with best practices and approaches as identified by me, SAP AG, or SAP's many technology partners.

2.1.   Who Needs Testing and Tuning?

As I mentioned earlier, any company that has implemented an SAP solution will benefit from using stress testing to drive smart tuning. Specifically, when I think of who or what reaps the most value out of stress testing, I immediately think of companies that find themselves in the middle of one of the following five SAP system lifecycle phases:

1. Deployment: preparing for a new implementation of SAP R/3, mySAP ERP, or any mySAP Business Suite component or solution
2. Change control: preparing for major change control waves, or the quarterly changes made at many different levels in the technology stack throughout the life of the system—changes that don't fall into the category of full-blown upgrades
3. Upgrade: planning for a major SAP system change, either functional or technology-focused in nature (indeed, both types of upgrades are often performed concurrently)
4. Consolidation: working on consolidating IT resources within an SAP environment, typically to better control costs while maintaining good system performance, availability, and scalability
5. Analysis and reassessment: poring over performance metrics and other factors, and revisiting a system's solution vision and its requisite solution characteristics to re-examine its role, its contributions to the company's core business goals, and so on

As shown in Figure 2–1, because every one of these five lifecycle milestones describes every SAP system at a particular point in time, and every milestone is followed by a period of tuning, it only follows that, at a high level, stress testing and tuning is for everyone. But, because testing and tuning actually represent an insurance policy, the dollars—what it costs to test and tune versus the potential cost of *not* testing and tuning—play probably the key part in the to-test-or-not-to-test decision-making process. That is, if the dollars just don't make sense for a particular lifecycle phase or in a certain case, stress testing and related tuning should be ruled out. I recommend performing at least a cursory cost-vs-risk analysis, therefore pitting the "with testing" and "without testing" scenarios against one another before a decision is made either way.

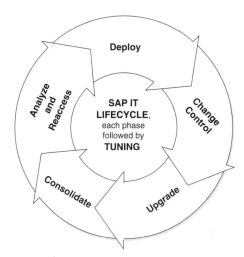

Figure 2–1   Each of the core five phases of an SAP system's lifecycle represents fundamental opportunities to leverage the advantages of stress testing and tuning.

2.1.1.   What Exactly Is Stress Testing?

What exactly is stress testing? What constitutes *stress* per se and makes such testing valuable? In a nutshell, I generally look at it as any kind of methodical and repeatable testing that emulates all or a portion of the *peak load*—online user, batch-initiated business transactions, or other—that is expected to be borne by a particular system. Granted, there are different types of stress testing, the core of which will be covered later in this chapter. Suffice it to say, though, that a well-executed stress test allows you to verify that your system's overall configuration meets your performance and scalability requirements or expectations beyond simple day-to-day needs. That is, it helps you verify the robustness of your specific SAP software application during month-end closing or in the midst of a seasonal peak. And, it does so typically in a multiuser scenario, letting you analyze not only the soundness of your development, customization, and coding efforts but all of the work and configuration effort put into the hardware, OS, and database layers. In this way, stress testing helps you understand the response-time performance and throughput capabilities of your unique implementation under a particular (or better yet, multiple and varying) peak workload and user-driven scenario. This, in turn, allows you to validate and quantify the performance metrics of the proposed system environment, helping you understand to what degree the following major subsystems or components function well, and at what point each might represent a blockade to greater performance (in other words, a *bottleneck* negating better performance). The major subsystems or components are as follows:

- Central processing unit (CPU) performance and utilization
- Memory utilization

- Network design and throughput
- Disk subsystem input/output (I/O) capabilities and overall effectiveness
- Database layout, configuration, and performance
- Application-layer configuration and performance

For SAP transactional systems, like R/3, Customer Relationship Management (CRM), and Enterprise Buyer Professional (EBP), much of the average load to be borne by a system is driven by hundreds if not thousands of end users connected to the system, each performing their 9-to-5 work of taking customer orders, managing warehouse inventory, planning new product launches and marketing campaigns, and so on. The rest of the load consists of reports and other business processes typically run in batch mode—processes that can weigh heavily even on very well-tuned systems. Thus, a good SAP application-layer R/3, CRM, or EBP stress test would seek to identify and execute the most popular transactions and batch processes (sometimes called *top transactions*) run by the business and see to it that they are driven by hundreds or thousands of representative "real world" users on a system set aside for stress testing. This system in the best of worlds would be identical to the production system (indeed, in new implementations, such testing is usually conducted on the system earmarked for eventual production use), so as to observe firsthand the impact that different tuning and tweaking approaches would have on response times and general system throughput.

Similarly, a good SAP BW stress test might involve creating InfoCubes identical to those found in production, and executing many of the same queries that the business intends to execute day-in and day-out against these cubes (again, housed on a system identical to production or earmarked for stress testing). An SAP APO stress test might seek to simulate the demand-planning activities of a particular set of plants on the busiest day of the year. An SAP Enterprise Portal stress test might require the ability to simulate thousands of end users, each reflecting different user roles and performing different functions, representing an expected real-world mix of user types. As should be apparent, no single approach to stress testing fits everyone's needs; these needs, and the success criteria surrounding them, vary as much as the underlying systems and business processes themselves. The key is usually to identify the most "stressful" or representative transactions and user-mix (e.g., the *load*) followed by developing success criteria that establish how to define and quantify that the load is borne well, and go from there.

It's not enough to generate a peak load and run through a few tests, though. Remember I said that a stress test must be methodical and repeatable, too: a well-conceived stress test must therefore embrace a sound testing methodology. This approach, in turn, consists of various project phases, from planning through configuration, preparation, and execution, to analysis and documentation. In later chapters, we'll cover each of these phases and the key milestones and activities to be accomplished within each phase. For without well-documented and repeatable testing and evaluation processes, the value of test results is suspect at best. I urge you to keep this fact uppermost in your mind as you work your way through the book.

2.1.2. Other Forms of Performance Testing in the Real World

Other labels have been applied to performance testing or confused with stress testing over the years. One of my favorites is *smoke testing*, which amounts to an exercise designed to completely saturate a system so as to identify at what loads particular system components become complete bottlenecks—boat anchors, if you will. Smoke testing is not about real-world testing, it's about identifying limits and thresholds of a particular hardware or software configuration. For example, I've performed smoke testing on many different customer disk subsystems over the years to see how many I/Os per second a particular configuration can sustain, regardless of the database and application layers of a solution. In other cases, I've performed low-level CPU and memory-centric testing using tools specifically designed for the purpose of benchmarking different configurations against each other—a great way to get a feel for how much incremental throughput one hardware platform provides over another.

The term *smoke testing* is widely used by the programming and development community as well—be careful not to confuse the two, though, when discussing your plans for testing! Development-based smoke testing is much different, because it speaks to the nonexhaustive software testing of the most basic functions of a program to ensure that they work, leaving the minutiae associated with testing a program's granular features and functions for later. The term originated from a basic form of hardware testing where a passing mark was awarded if the unit managed to avoid catching on fire during the initial "burn-in."

Beyond smoke and stress testing, I hear the general term *load testing* used (and misused) quite often. Load testing speaks to exercising a system by placing a typical or average load on it, like the load associated with an average day of processing invoices, customer requests, and so on by an SAP R/3 system. It represents the natural precursor or stepping stone to true stress testing and is valuable in and of itself, as we see later. I prefer the expanded term *average load testing* so as to differentiate it from plain old load testing and true stress testing, but I tend to use both terms interchangeably throughout this book.

The simplest stress-testing philosophy I've come across and endorse is what I call *single-unit* or *single-user* stress testing. As the names imply, this type of testing involves a single process, user, or unit of work. The idea is to execute a single transaction or process and then to extrapolate intelligently the impact that multiple transactions or processes would place on the same system. It's inherently useful in comparing two different configurations, too, and a cheap way to go overall. As I've shown in Figure 2–2, it's the least complicated and least "stressful" test that can be executed in the name of stress testing. But it's beneficial nonetheless, especially for cost-conscious IT organizations still tasked with mitigating at least *some* of the risk associated with the unknowns of not stress testing at all.

2.1.3. The Stress-Testing "Big Picture"

Although by definition all stress tests seek to represent some or all of the load borne by a system, how this is accomplished varies. Often the most favorable approach when it comes to compre-

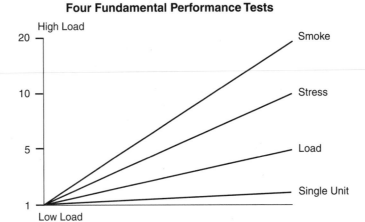

Figure 2–2 The four fundamental types of performance testing, and how the load placed on a given system changes based on the type of testing being conducted.

hensive real-world testing is to use a copy of a customer's mySAP database and script authentic customer-specific SAP business processes to drive a test executed by a suitable number of physical and/or "virtual" users. Other approaches include leveraging benchmark test data and processes provided by SAP or crafting hardware-specific tests that exercise certain subsystems underpinning your SAP system (the idea being to quantify the performance delta, or differences, between a baseline or current configuration versus a tweaked configuration). All of these approaches, and subtle variations, are discussed in more detail throughout the book.

Solid success criteria, well-prepared staff, a test plan, and the selection of the proper tools are all necessary for an effective stress test, regardless of the specific testing method. And it should go without saying that a stress test is only as good as the business processes and underlying data that drive it: the more realistic the business processes, and more abundant the data, the better. I will try to be careful about characterizing a stress test in terms of application, database, OS, or hardware layers, though, as each testing approach or situation is unique, often providing a certain amount of value unobtainable otherwise. In general, though, when I talk of stress testing, I will typically be referring to a peak load test that is executed at or via the SAP application layer; so unless otherwise stated, please assume this loose designation.

2.1.4. Alternatives to Multiuser Stress Testing

It would be unfair to omit a discussion of alternatives to multiuser stress testing. Why? Because not all SAP customers have the time, money, or bandwidth to conduct end-to-end stress testing, as mentioned earlier during the discussion of the four types of performance testing . Throughout this book I highlight areas where discrete single-unit "mini stress tests" or component-specific "delta performance load testing" can be conducted, both of which can represent good alternatives to multiuser testing. For the most time-sensitive and cost-constrained SAP shops, I recommend taking a closer look at the following forms of single-unit testing:

- Hardware component throughput testing, or smoke testing.
- Single-user database-specific performance testing, such as executing key queries natively (as opposed to driving them through the SAP application layer) against your test database, or using your database's inbuilt tools to execute similar test exercises. This method allows you to perform database-intensive testing without the need for the SAP application itself to be installed. The trade-off, of course, is that your testing is naturally limited.
- Single-user testing that inherently drives your ABAP or J2EE code (as applicable to your R/3 or mySAP environment) to help underscore misconfiguration issues.

Each of these alternatives is covered in more depth in later chapters. Suffice it to say, though, that single-user testing eliminates the need for lots of real or "physical" users (saving time and money) or the software necessary to generate and simulate lots of virtual users (usually saving quite a bit of money as well). Plus, single-user testing makes for excellent baselining, because differences in configurations can be quickly validated from a performance perspective: for example, did your R/3 VA01 transaction (a common "SD"—Sales and Distribution—transaction used for creating a new sales order) run faster after you tweaked your OS kernel parameters or SAP profiles? And, such testing can provide quite a bit of knowledge in terms of validating the basic design of your system from a sizing perspective, not to mention validating the fundamental viability of your tested business processes—that is, did your change to VA01 slow things down or speed things up? More to the point, as you inevitably run into issues, single unit testing allows you to quickly fall back to a known state and optimize or rewrite the offending programs, or reconfigure the poorly configured software or hardware layers. Later, even if you decide to perform multiuser stress testing to more completely test your solution and further minimize your risk, you have already completed a fair amount of tuning. And, you'll likely have minimized the number of test iterations a business process needs to go through as well, further speeding things up as you get closer to Go-Live.

There are a vast number of tool sets, utilities, and approaches that facilitate rapid scripting, load testing, stress testing, smoke testing, standard SAP benchmarking, and more. These test tools and utilities range from those that are commonly available and often inexpensive or free, to specialized monitoring tools, strategies, or approaches, to the various lab utilities and scripting tool sets that support virtual test environments, to other tools and utilities helpful in actually conducting test runs. I discuss these tool sets at length in Chapter 6, but only after working through costing, scoping, and staffing/planning in preceding chapters.

2.2. The Challenge—Getting "Real" Return on Information

SAP AG penned the term *return on information* (a play on the more traditional return on investment acronym, or ROI) years ago, and I like that phrase, because it holds true today as much as ever. ROI implies that a fundamental financial equation exists at the heart of each SAP implementation or upgrade, that the SAP solution more than pays for itself over time, and that the real value provided by SAP lies in how the system's data may be manipulated and accessed to create useful information. Thus, the characteristics that are useful in describing the system—its performance, availability, scalability, cost, and so on—play central roles in exactly how well the system provides "ROI." I'll be detailing each of these characteristics later in this chapter. Suffice it to say, though, that arguably if a system's performance is unacceptable, many of the other characteristics are immaterial: for example, a highly available but poorly performing system may essentially hurt the business more than it helps.

Over the last 7 years, I've been fortunate to play a part in fine-tuning and tweaking many an SAP customer's production system both prior to and post Go-Live. In cases where customers have already pulled the trigger and gone "live" on their SAP system without the benefit of sound testing and tuning, I might be found on the team that seeks to optimize things after the fact. This kind of work is reactive and usually extremely stressful, however, representing the flip side of my own goals: to assist a customer in going live and *not* being surprised by unforeseen performance issues. If these customers had truly load-tested their system first, and as a result understood exactly how well the system would perform under different end-user and batch-processing load conditions *before* Go-Live, my work would have been much easier, had it been needed at all. I call this the *proactive approach to performance tuning* and believe that sound stress testing is the most effective method to proactively and accurately performance tune your system.

2.2.1.   Investing in Stress Testing

If we consider the value that an enterprise application provides to its end users, and therefore to the business at large, an investment in stress testing that application before Go-Live, and then again after each major change or upgrade to the application, makes good business sense. Sure, the financial impact needs to be considered. As I indicated earlier, stress testing is much like an insurance policy. But at the heart of the matter is this: Your company has made the decision to implement or introduce change into your SAP system, with the understanding that there is a huge amount of business risk in the business implementation, in the organizational changes that accompany the implementation/upgrade, and in meeting the company's ROI goals in a timely fashion. The risk on the business side is so high, in fact, that there is virtually no room for risk in terms of the technical implementation. Thus, the gut-wrenching issue faced by your IT department is that it has to provide a sound and optimized processing platform before your custom business solution is ever tested on a large scale. All of the modeling, extrapolating, and promises made by systems integrators and hardware partners simply cannot get around the inevitable issue at hand: you require proof that your mySAP solution will perform as advertised, and you need this proof before the system is turned over to the business community.

Thus, the IT folks responsible for SAP need all of the help they can get from people who have made similar journeys and understand the pitfalls, issues, and resolutions. They need to work under the guidance of someone who has dealt successfully with these uncertainties and who can provide the processes, insights, and wisdom that will enable them to get their job done right, on time, the first time. This book is that guide.

2.2.2. Embracing Stress Testing

Not only do the best performing and most highly available SAP shops invest in stress testing but they embrace it in one form or another, plain and simple. Both the IT and business organizations responsible for their SAP systems understand that their system is simply not ready to be handed over to its end-user community until it has undergone an appropriate level of true-to-life load testing (the level of which depends on the nature of the changes made to the system). For every company running SAP that understands the value of stress testing their system after each and every major implementation, upgrade, or change wave, however, I can point to another 10 companies that would (unknowingly, I presume) rather risk huge losses in customer satisfaction and instead blindly turn their system over to their users. You might wonder why they don't stress test. In my experience, the answer usually boils down to the following two factors: they don't understand the value of testing, they misunderstand the costs, or a combination of both. Specifically, these companies

- Overlook stress testing because of high perceived costs, from IT and business people resources to software costs, because they are unable to simply set aside enough time to make a difference
- Mistakenly believe that it costs too much to develop and maintain a body of knowledge around the kind of stress testing that purposefully dovetails with their change management organization
- Might feel, similarly, that the investment in a stress-testing environment or related processes equates to poor ROI, preferring instead to throw hardware and consulting fees at performance problems
- Believe that stress testing only applies to new implementations
- Think their downtime or maintenance windows cannot handle the incremental time that would presumably be required to execute a stress test after each production change (and prior to turning the system back over to its end users)

2.3. Challenges Inherent to Performance Tuning mySAP Systems

Of course, if open performance tuning an SAP system were simple, the formal training courses, volumes of periodicals, and scads of SAP Notes, books, and so on would be unnecessary. But, with any business system that spans complex infrastructure, hardware, OS, database, and application-specific technology layers, not to mention elaborate interface, middleware, and front-end user interface options, it should be no surprise that performance tuning is nothing less than complex. Let's take a closer look at four core challenges inherent to SAP tuning.

2.3.1.   Fixed/Finite Systems versus Capacity on Demand (COD)

The fact that nearly all SAP systems deployed today run on a fixed set of hardware and software—a finite set of computing gear—makes tuning that much more important. That is, the number of processors and quantity or capacity of RAM, disk bandwidth, network bandwidth, and so on tend to be fixed in a production system, until the system undergoes a rather lengthy upgrade planning cycle followed by a physical hardware upgrade. The alternative to fixed or finite systems is called many things by different people, including COD, metered services, or pay-per-use, and involves turning finite processing power into just another enterprise computing variable. In my eyes, eventually much of the content of this book that addresses *how* to tune will become a thing of the past because of the broader adoption of COD. Why? Because I believe that a significant amount of the time and money spent on performance tuning today seeks to extract another few "performance percentage points" from fixed hardware and software solutions. With COD, though, the same or greater performance benefits will eventually be achievable at a lower overall cost or price point, plain and simple.

Thus, *how* the demand for an incremental 5% to 125% in response-time performance or throughput will be met—a challenge that most every company one day finds itself tackling—will change. Instead of paying an internal IT or external consulting team to dredge up another few percentage points of SAP throughput increases or response-time deceases, companies will turn instead to obtaining incremental SAP performance gains through cheap, well-executed COD offerings. COD options today include a variety of approaches and solutions, like the following, all of which will only become either more efficient and flexible, or simply extinct, over time:

- Application service providers (ASPs) and other SAP outsourcing providers offer the ability to pay as you go. This type of solution is often architected and paid with regard to complete SAP data-center offerings, and termed *utility computing* in many cases. Customers pay a monthly fee based on hardware resource usage rather than a monthly flat rate.
- The most flexible COD offerings allocate hardware and other resources to a particular system without requiring a restart of the system. Thus, not only does the hardware platform need to support such an approach but the individual SAP Technology Stack layers and components that sit atop the hardware stack must support dynamic reallocation as well. These types of solutions are labeled "hardware partitioning" and are typically predicated on less than commodity hardware platforms.
- Software partitioning is becoming more popular, too, as companies like Microsoft and VMware (recently swallowed up by EMC) promote virtualization software that allows a single physical server and its resources to be chopped up virtually into multiple servers, each capable of hosting applications in a "guest" OS instance. Combined with the ability to allocate shared resources based on demand, preemptively, or in a scheduled fashion, I expect software partitioning in the short term to completely change the

way that development, training, or other system environments are deployed, and in the long term, to reduce the overall hardware resources required of any SAP system.

- Simpler and less expensive COD arrangements exist, too, sacrificing availability (in that they require additional planned downtime because of system restart requirements) in exchange for lower cost. Hot, pluggable hardware devices (e.g., the ability to install or "add" incremental network cards and disk controllers) are good examples of simple COD practices.
- The most basic COD approach takes the form of rapidly deployed upgrades or updates. I've pioneered and deployed a number of methods in this regard, like in-place SAP cluster upgrades for SAP R/3, but timelines range from hours to perhaps a few days— not exactly the kind of timelines that meet everyone's service level agreements (SLAs) with their end-user community.

As COD offerings mature, becoming even less costly and more seamless, we'll see a fundamental change in how SAP computing resources are deployed and allocated "on the fly." But, the need for performance tuning will never simply disappear. Indeed, to keep costs as low as possible, and end-users' experiences as good as possible, the need to properly tune a system up and down the entire technology stack will always represent a fundamental starting point, or baseline deployment approach of sorts.

2.3.2. Quantifying Cross-Application Business Process Performance

One of the key challenges to performance tuning a complex SAP system lies in tracking and quantifying the performance of individual underlying SAP components, and then rolling up the results to determine holistically how a business process would benefit the most from further system tuning. This is because not all business processes execute on a single SAP system or mySAP component. Instead, you might find yourself working with business processes that commence on a CRM system that interfaces to a core R/3 system, which, in turn, updates a BW system to allow near-real-time status reporting of the underlying business transactions. As you can imagine, the challenges are many and generally include the following:

- Knowledge of the business processes themselves must be attained because it's impossible to optimize a process if you're unaware of the underlying systems that must in turn be analyzed and tweaked.
- Knowledge of the specific mySAP components or products is necessary: for example, performance tuning business processes that execute across SAP EBP or EP implementations vary in many respects from tuning R/3, which in turn varies from BW and APO, and so on.
- Beyond knowledge of the primary SAP systems, knowledge of the underlying hardware, OS, and database platforms upon which a business process executes is essential as well.

2.3.3.   Forever-Shifting Bottlenecks in the Real World

Another challenge inherent to performance tuning your SAP systems lies in the area of identifying, managing, and addressing shifting bottlenecks. As alluded to previously, a *bottleneck* is nothing more than the specific subsystem or component in your SAP solution that is holding you back from getting even better performance. If you take a close look at a task or a process, the most obvious bottleneck often tends to be the resource that consumes the most time during the execution of that process. If you have a CPU bottleneck, for example, adding more disk resources or RAM or something else besides CPU capacity will do nothing to change the performance of the system, or the speed in which a process completes. Only adding additional CPUs (assuming a multi-threaded process), or replacing the current CPUs with faster ones, will reduce the bottleneck.

If you add *enough* CPU horsepower, at one point you will finally eliminate the CPU from being the current bottleneck. But you'll never truly eliminate the bottleneck in a system; it will simply move to another subsystem or component. For instance, in my experience, resolving CPU bottlenecks usually equates to creating a disk subsystem bottleneck. Adding more disks, or faster disks or controllers, might further shift the bottleneck to the memory component in the system, or in some cases to the network infrastructure interconnecting two systems. Upgrading the RAM or network infrastructure might push the bottleneck back to the CPU or disk subsystem, and round and round it goes. The bottleneck in a system never disappears; it only finds a new home. It might come to rest anywhere within the technology stack, in fact—database layout/configuration issues or SAP application or profile misconfiguration are other examples. The good news is that every time a particular bottleneck is eliminated, even though a new bottleneck rears its head, overall throughput and/or response time of the system only continues to improve! Eventually, you'll find yourself arriving at one of two conclusions I've arrived at myself time and again, either that my system's overall performance is well within SLAs or my budget simply can't take the expense of finding and relocating any more bottlenecks!

2.3.4.   Quantifying Bottlenecks—Benchmarking

To quantify the performance gains realized through bottleneck reduction or elimination, a *benchmark* is used. A benchmark is simply a repeatable test designed to provide concrete evidence of how well a system performs. Benchmarks can be very component-specific, such as those designed to measure CPU throughput, or they can be very general and touch all technology layers in a solution, as in the case of SAP AG's collection of SAP application component benchmarks. Good benchmarking reflects all of the following:

*   Control variables are defined and maintained throughout a set of benchmark tests, or runs. This includes everything except for a *single* variable relevant to the testing.
*   Only a *single* variable is changed between benchmark runs, or prior to executing a new benchmark. In this way, it's apparent whether the variable in question truly impacted the performance observed in the test run.
*   The method used to test and then analyze the test results must remain consistent.

For example, suppose we want to test the impact that varying the OS blocksize (sometimes called *allocation unit*) exhibits on the performance of a particular disk subsystem. To obtain useful data from repeated benchmark runs, everything must remain unchanged in the system except for the variable being tested—in this case, the blocksize of a particular disk partition or partitions. Matters related to the amount of data residing on the partition, the make-up of these data, the layout of the physical disk drives underneath the partition, the configuration of the disk controller and other hardware, the version of OS-specific drivers, and so on all must remain unchanged throughout our testing. And, just as important, the process or method used to perform the testing must remain consistent as well: for example, if you are testing the performance of both reads and writes, it's important not to vary the length or nature of each test run; the timing between test runs; how a particular tool is used; how the raw performance data are collected, analyzed, and reported against; and so on. You must commence each test run from a consistent state, too, such as that obtained perhaps after a system restart or reboot. If you follow this example closely, you'll begin to understand exactly how many control variables there actually are in a test environment, and therefore how critical it is that each of these variables is preserved so as to create only a single variable throughout all of your test runs.

It's also important to understand that a low-level benchmark test cannot fully explain mySAP application-level performance; realizing the limits of your testing tools and methods is critical in keeping things as realistic as possible. The most basic tools, like those designed to benchmark server and disk subsystem performance, only provide insight (albeit powerful insight, when taken in context) into a small piece of a holistic solution's overall performance. Limiting yourself to a particular set of tools that focus only on a layer or two in the SAP Technology Stack, for example, makes it difficult to draw useful comparisons between totally different stacks.

2.3.5. Baselining a System

Although running a benchmark test allows "apples to apples" comparisons between different systems, what an SAP shop really needs is the ability to compare its current performance with that observed after something has changed. What the shop needs is a master baseline executed just before Go-Live, which represents a documented "starting point" against which all other system changes and updates are compared and measured. Before conducting any performance tuning, I start all of my performance consulting engagements by obtaining a baseline. Otherwise, I would be hard-pressed to prove to my clients that I sped up system throughput or decreased response times. A baseline gives me the concrete measurable data I need against which I can compare the results of my own tuning efforts.

Unfortunately, serious attention to baselining by many SAP IT shops is spotty at best. By the time one of my colleagues or I have been called into a reactive performance consulting engagement, countless changes already have been made to the system, minimizing the value of previously executed baseline tests. This situation exacerbates performance tuning, making it difficult to quantify exactly how much better or worse a system performs as different subsystems and components are optimized, changed, or otherwise touched over time. Perhaps the system underwent a number of functional upgrades or fixes (e.g., via SAP support packages or legal changes), or maybe the OS needed to be patched to plug up security holes or to generally stabilize a system. Regardless of the reason, these changes and many others become driving factors with regard to how well a system performs at both a holistic level and in terms of each discrete layer of the SAP Technology Stack, discussed in the next few sections.

2.4.   Performance-Tuning Overview

As we dig into performance tuning and stress testing, we need to step back for a moment and establish some fundamental groundwork. Different mySAP components and other SAP products may be deployed on any number of technology platforms, and optimized in response to various changing business needs or conditions. Thus, a closer look at these two broad areas of products and platforms is warranted.

2.4.1.   The SAP Technology Stack

What exactly is the SAP Technology Stack? Although it's been mentioned previously, before we move forward it is important to understand what the SAP Technology Stack, or stack, includes. As shown in Figure 2–3, the stack consists of the various layers of technology necessary to assemble a functioning SAP solution. The stack is therefore inherently quite complex because it consists of data-center utilities, network infrastructure, server and disk subsystem hardware platforms, OSs, database management systems, SAP application products and components, SAP-provided and third-party solution-enabling components, and various front-end client options. Further, each of these core layers may be further subdivided into more detailed layers; the overall hardware platform layer alone consists of server and disk subsystem layers, each in turn composed of low-level hardware subsystems, components, firmware revisions, and more.

2.4.2.   Four Essential Reasons to Stress Test

It is precisely because the SAP Technology Stack is so inherently complex that stress testing and tuning are paramount to a well-performing solution. Consider the time that goes into ensuring a particular solution performs at all, much less performs well. Add to this the caveats and other limitations that each technology vendor introduces to the mix in terms of what it will and will not support for a certain version or release of its products, and it's no wonder that crafting a solid SAP solution ranks as such a grand achievement. It's even less of a surprise when the team that assembled the SAP system balks at making changes to its carefully constructed solution; *every change will potentially impact every layer in the SAP Technology Stack*, potentially introducing interoperability issues, support issues, and other problems that only manifest themselves under load. This latter issue is the most problematic: How do you test a change to a system that will operate under load, without actually using the production system, complete with its real online users, batch processes, and so on? The answer lies partially in stress testing a system identical (or as similar as practical) to the production system, followed by the application of intelligent tuning, which may then be applied to an SAP system with regard to the following areas:

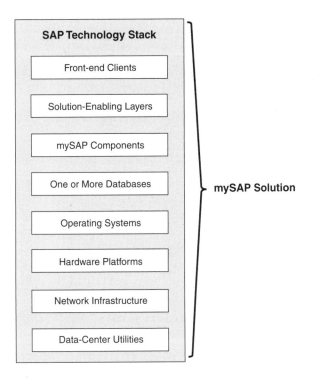

Figure 2–3 Every SAP system comprises the core layers of the SAP Technology Stack shown here, illustrating the complexity of even the most basic mySAP Solution.

- New implementations
- Upgrades
- IT consolidation approaches
- Major change control releases or waves

Stress testing helps to ensure that a production system continues to perform well or meets minimum requirements, even after changes are introduced; stress testing also proves useful in ensuring that availability metrics or service levels may be maintained in the wake of a fundamental or systemwide change to the system.

2.5. Real-World Factors Driving Changes in mySAP Solutions

When it comes to mySAP solutions and the business processes that execute within and across different mySAP components, a number of general factors drive changes. At a high level, these factors include

- New business requirements and the mySAP systems and components that enable these requirements

- The need to improve systemwide availability or stability (uptime)
- The need to reduce the costs inherent to a particular solution, through reducing or otherwise consolidating physical resources
- The desire to simplify or standardize on a particular set of platforms or system resources, or perform functional upgrades in support of new business-enabling features

Each of these general factors is touched on in the next few pages.

2.5.1.   New Business Requirements and mySAP Solutions

As a business tries to evolve to better service its customers, grow its customer base, or address new business requirements brought about by changes in strategic direction, mergers, or acquisitions, inevitably the SAP IT and business teams must introduce new or update existing business processes and even bring in entirely new mySAP components or similar competitive offerings from other enterprise vendors. All of these fundamental changes drive the need for comprehensive real-world load testing (after the requisite functional and regression testing takes place, of course). Unsurprisingly, the more "mission critical" or "business critical" the business process is, the more important load testing should become. Fortunately, most of these types of changes are straightforward in that they drive updates to existing code. For many SAP IT organizations, rolling up numerous functional changes into a quarterly change wave or change release represents the most common method of carefully testing and implementing change. This mirrors the approach that stress testing the impact of these changes should take as well—quarterly, unless the business risk versus reward equation dictates otherwise.

2.5.2.   Improving Availability and Stability

Behind functional updates, changes that are made with the goal of increasing an SAP system's stability—increasing availability and therefore decreasing downtime—represent the next most common reason for system changes. Although these changes may also represent functional updates, in my experience many availability-specific changes reflect new hardware/firmware updates, hardware drivers, OS patches and updated drivers, and database updates. In fact, most SAP system-related updates fall into this category, and necessarily require extensive testing up, down, and across all technology layers and components to ensure that the change indeed delivers greater uptime. More to the point, your testing should be focused on ensuring that the update does not break something else!

2.5.3.   Lowering TCO through IT Consolidation

One of the greatest trends in recent years is to revisit how expensive IT computing assets have been deployed and managed, and look for ways to reduce their TCO. In doing so, fundamental changes are introduced into existing mySAP implementations, driven by consolidation at all levels of the SAP Technology Stack. For example, adopting lower cost server and disk subsystem platforms, introducing streamlined NetWeaver and other Internet-based extended collaboration models, or collapsing multiple database or ITS instances onto one or very few servers all represent very real and compelling reasons to stress test.

Thus, the need to validate consolidation approaches new to your particular SAP environment will underscore the value of stress testing; this is paramount to ensuring that your new architecture, stack, or approach equates to a well-performing system both during normal day-to-day operations and under peak loads at quarter-end, for instance. Consider the relative unknowns related to using SAP's Multiple Components on One Database (MCOD) or adopting a new SAN and centralized tape backup/restore strategy within your own customized mySAP environment, and the obvious risks to performance and system availability should be clear.

2.5.4.   Other Factors Surrounding Consolidation

In addition to pure dollar-driven TCO arguments, other factors push SAP consolidation today. These include the desire to simplify, to migrate to easier-to-manage computing platforms, and to achieve a greater degree of standardization. Granted, all of these factors tend to lower cost as well, but oftentimes the driving factor is not the cost issue so much as the inherent ability to *simplify* the SAP system landscape. Once accomplished, though, the bonus at the end of the day lies in the fact that much of the key to reducing long-term costs is to simplify: one of my favorite pastors describes this process well when he tells those of us in the church band that "excellent musical arrangements are not defined by what we have added but rather by the fact that eventually nothing needs to be taken away." Granted, he's usually talking about my muted power chords or screaming "whah" pedal, but that's cool; he's neither a big fan of Christian Metal nor big-hair '80s bands. The same concept makes a whole lot of sense when it comes to IT consolidation for SAP: We can achieve excellence, albeit short-lived, only after we have weeded out what is unnecessary, and collapsed what must remain into a well-performing, highly available, and highly manageable enterprise solution.

Finally, SAP functional upgrades represent a huge driver of both change and consolidation. By their very nature, an SAP upgrade requires a resizing effort (as minimum hardware requirements differ—in some cases, remarkably—between different SAP functional releases). This in turn drives new hardware and supporting software procurement cycles, uncovering consolidation opportunities at all levels of the SAP solution stack, from technology to core infrastructure, organizational staffing, and more.

2.6.   Developing General Performance-Tuning Goals

Although stress testing is useful in characterizing the impact that a change has on an SAP system, the team responsible for maintaining the system must agree on exactly what is important, and to what degree, when it comes to quantifying performance. In the past, I have used the process of identifying a team's general solution vision, hammering out goals related to achieving this vision, and then ranking various solution characteristics and budget constraints to help identify precisely what is key to stress testing and tuning, versus what falls outside of these boundaries. I call the results "general performance-tuning goals," the purpose of which is to help keep a team focused on what's important to them when it comes to tuning and testing. This process is explained in more detail in the next section.

2.6.1.   Solution Vision

Because it is an iterative process, crafting a solution vision takes time. An organization's solution vision describes what the organization values in terms of the different characteristics of an SAP solution, especially when it comes to maintaining a well-performing SAP system, by focusing on the big picture. In the past, I have described this initially as an "eyes closed" process, where wishful thinking is unencumbered by head count, budget realities, and other constraints. Ultimately, the solution vision will meld with these realities, combining to bring to light your unique solution and performance goals. Goal statements such as the following are common:

- We need a system that allows us to as a company to focus on our core business, rather than consuming ever-growing head count and budget dollars.
- We need a system that is capable of meeting our unique service level, management, and accessibility requirements without impacting 7 a.m.–to–7 p.m. end-user performance.
- We require a system that boasts an average response time of less than 1 second for 90% of all core online transactions, and less than 5 seconds for 50% of all core reporting requirements.
- We need an approach to SAP system landscape management that *facilitates* stress testing, rather than forces us to constantly implement work-arounds or move testing to a back-burner.
- We need a cookie-cutter approach to managing and testing changes *before* the changes are introduced to our end-user communities, thus prodding us to follow through on our testing and tuning goals.
- We wish to adopt a "follower" strategy when it comes to introducing new SAP-related IT, leveraging the experiences of others at the potential expense of trailing new enabling technologies and the benefits that may be realized.
- Our SAP solution must be scalable to the tune of 50% growth in peak workloads without the need to purchase additional hardware or other resources, and we want the ability to double our peak workload without "fork-lifting" more than 25% of our current hardware investment.

I recommend soliciting the advice of SAP IT and functional experts familiar with your current environment and solution vision to assist you in identifying real-world product and technology constraints so as to further refine your vision. Afterwards, obtain buy-in from all IT and business stakeholders to finalize and ultimately ensure that your solution vision matches everyone else's.

2.6.2. Working Backwards—Mapping Goals Back to the Real World

With goals in place that describe your solution today, or soon-to-be-implemented solution, the next step is to then work backwards and map these goals back to the real world or your present situation. For example, if your goal is to achieve a 1-second average response time for 90% of all core online transactions, questions like the following must be answered:

Which transactions are "core" transactions?

How exactly will transaction-response times be measured?

How often and precisely *when* will measurements be taken?

How will the measurement process be made repeatable, such that it does not change over time and invariably affect transaction reporting?

How will this information be used in regard to completing a "feedback" loop back to the IT and other relevant SAP supporting organizations?

In short, the process of mapping goals back to the real world should fill in holes and resolve other questions left open during the solution vision stage. Goals may be uncovered, therefore, that are simply not achievable with the available budget, talent, and so on—this is an important benefit of the mapping process itself, feeding the iterative solution vision process along the way.

2.6.3. Ranking Solution Characteristics

The value an organization places on various system "descriptors"—solution characteristics—must be understood before it's possible to prioritize stress-testing goals and overall tuning success criteria. I often use something I call the "solution characteristics matrix" to help me understand how important certain characteristics are to an SAP IT group and the business organizations it services. The key solution characteristics for stress testing and tuning include identifying the value placed on the following areas:

- High availability or system stability
- Online user response times
- Batch processing (or similar processing) throughput
- Solution scalability
- TCO
- IT standardization
- Simplification; the value placed on managing fewer large components rather than many smaller ones
- IT system administration and basic manageability requirements
- IT and overall system security

- Mature technology offerings versus newer and potentially riskier technology
- System accessibility, or how easily the system may be accessed from both end-user and SAP IT perspectives

Once an organization agrees on the priorities of the solution characteristics outlined in the preceding list, it is ready for the next step, tackling constraints.

2.6.4.   Budgets and Other Constraints

If crafting a solution vision represents the eyes-closed phase of developing goals, then identifying constraints that bring a solution vision back in line with reality may be aptly described as the "eyes wide open for the next few years" phase. That is, constraints will temper stress-testing and performance-tuning goals for the remainder of a solution's lifecycle. Some constraints—those resulting from cost-cutting budget cycles or shrinking downtime windows—will rarely yield good news for the folks tasked with maintaining a high-performance SAP solution. Other constraints will come and go, though, as a system matures and evolves. For example, constraints surrounding standards, tool-sets, staffing, and more will ebb and flow throughout a system's life.

2.7.   Integrating People, Information, and Processes

Per SAP AG, beyond realizing a good "return on information," the success of any productive SAP installation also hinges on "maximizing return on relationships." This chapter concludes with a discussion of how the integration of people with your IT and business processes completes the review of performance tuning and stress testing.

2.7.1.   Selling the Value of Stress Testing

From the boardroom to the computer room, no one really questions performance tuning. It's pretty much a "given" for most SAP shops that some level of tuning and tweaking will occur throughout a system's useful life, driven as much in response to surprise performance issues as proactively planned for in support of major changes or system upgrades. The really hard sell, though, is to tie the value of performance testing—stress testing, specifically—with good performance tuning. This chapter is filled with information and facts that should help you do just that, sell the value inherent to stress testing. But to whom is it most effective to "sell" this information?

The answer is, it depends. If your system is managed and indeed carefully guarded by folks with titles like "Change Management Technical Liaison" or "Change Control Analyst" then the value of stress testing must be impressed on these folks sooner rather than later. Further, if the purse strings of your SAP IT organization are pulled primarily by a financial subteam within your IT organization, these folks need to be made aware of the favorable role stress testing plays in the risk-versus-reward equation. Next, given that most SAP systems are carefully and methodically managed simply to prove that they meet SLAs, the teams tasked with systems management, and especially high availability, need to understand how regular stress testing will keep them home after hours more than the alternative would. Finally, if upper management is made aware of all of these arguments *before* operational processes tend to evolve into de facto operational standards (normally before Go-Live or possibly prior to large-scale migrations or functional upgrades), selling the value of stress testing to all of the other IT and business-focused subteams will occur from the top down as well as the bottom up, and possibly become a much desired business-as-usual policy in the process.

2.7.2.   Quantifying Time, Resources, and Dollars

Any way you slice it, stress testing is not cheap. It takes time, and the testing resources—people, hardware, software/tools, and so on—cost money. But I believe that forgoing stress testing is even *more* expensive. Unfortunately, in this latter case, the dollars spent are easily hidden behind budgets earmarked for reactive tuning, upgrades, or new hardware and software procurement. The truth of the matter, and the core message that needs to be especially communicated to the people controlling the purse strings, is that stress testing will prove *cheaper in the long run*.

You'll want to quantify the cost delta to really get this message across and make an impact in your own organization, however. Thus, the following factors are key: acquiring the level of staffing needed to support all stress-testing phases and tasks; finding the time required to plan, prepare, and maintain a stress-testing approach; and obtaining the money required to procure and maintain a testing environment and test tools along with the money necessary to learn how to stress test and tune. Dump all of these data into a spreadsheet, and then begin collecting data that represent the dollars spent (or lost) by not testing or tuning, or doing so irregularly. I suggest first taking a close look at the money your organization has spent on reactive performance tuning. Don't forget to go through the entire SAP Technology Stack, paying attention to the costs of internal IT and external consultants tasked with fixing a broken system, or making a slow system perform well again. Then, review the downtime windows dedicated to managing changes, addressing performance tuning (e.g., applying patches or updates with the hopes of fixing performance-related issues), and so on. Next, take a look at your end-user productivity, especially time lost because of performance-related downtime. In fact, grab all of the availability data you can get your hands on. A completely "down" system is tremendously expensive per hour, and tends to grow exponentially more costly every hour. And even a painfully slow system (measured by response time or throughput) over the course of a few hours can add up to big bucks. Finally, don't forget to calculate the tenths of a second in average response time that users tend to wait when the system is merely "slower than usual"—a few tenths of a second per transaction per a thousand users every day can easily add up to a few hundred thousand dollars a year in lost productivity!

With your data in hand, it should become clear quickly whether or not the cost of stress testing is worthwhile. In my own experience, it's an easy sell when everyone understands the full financial picture. Drop your numbers into a presentation, do your pricing homework, read the rest of this book, and be prepared to get the "green flag" for proactive testing and tuning.

SAP Fundamentals and Testing Challenges

SAP AG has been in the business of developing and delivering enterprise solutions for quite some time now. But, particularly in the last few years, we have seen an explosion of new products out of Walldorf, Germany, ranging from updated core transactional systems, such as R/3 Enterprise, to updated analytical applications, supply chain and supplier relationship management offerings, e-commerce products, and more. SAP AG has evolved from strictly an ERP vendor a few years ago to become probably the most well-rounded provider of enterprise applications around. And, with the SAP XI, xApps, Mobile Business Solutions, Master Data Management (MDM), mySAP ERP, and other compelling enterprise integration or solution offerings recently released, SAP is pushing beyond applications per se and becoming something of a one-stop platform provider. Under the umbrella label of NetWeaver, this new enterprise-class integrated-processing platform is being touted by SAP as nothing less than the foundation technology on which all future applications will reside. NetWeaver promises greater connectivity and simpler integration than ever seen in an enterprise environment, nicely tying together everything in a company's computing environment in the same way a symphony brings together individual musical instruments.

I've been around long enough in the world of SAP to know that NetWeaver will be overwhelmingly successful: the folks at SAP AG are relentless in their consistency and drive to succeed, and they deliver. But what will all of these changes mean when it comes to testing and tuning? In my eyes, there will be more reason than ever to invest in stress testing: developing realistic SLAs for business processes that span multiple applications, leveraging different communications and integration vehicles, and traversing different systems will otherwise be too difficult to nail down. In other words, I am confident that the NetWeaver vision will deliver; at the same time, however, the newly extended systems and business processes will be subject to that many more points of failure, or points of suboptimal performance. Sizing and capacity planning are will only become that much more complex, for example, demanding that much more predeployment performance testing.

Besides the integration points, with all of this new and upgraded product activity come new individual SAP component technology stacks. The risk inherent to deploying the latest and greatest solutions and their underpinning technology stacks will rise exponentially as more and more technology stacks are combined to create massive company-wide (and beyond, to partners, vendors, suppliers, and so on) enterprise solutions. This is especially true with products that lack a fundamental degree of product maturity, and long-term success stories. That is, if you can't point to more than a handful of sites running a solution similar to one you plan to deploy or upgrade yourself, you inherently run a much greater risk of running into performance problems. Given this greater relative risk, it is therefore more important than ever to prove a system's real-world viability long before your end users log on. This is where stress testing and subsequent performance tuning will take their rightful place of honor in more and more SAP deployment and upgrade project plans.

Before we dive into staffing a stress-test team, piloting test tools, and executing a stress test, it's important that we step back and review where SAP AG is today in terms of solutions and products, architecture approaches and techniques, and testing challenges germane to all of this, and ultimately how the use of stress testing and tuning applies across the board.

3.1.   Reviewing the Core SAP Technology Layer

Once synonymous only with R/3, SAP now equates to a plethora of products both for the large enterprise and smaller businesses. In this section, we will look at the underlying SAP software technology on which most of these SAP products (often referred to as *components*) reside: the SAP Basis layer and its more comprehensive successor, the SAP Web Application Server (Web AS) platform. The goal in this section is simply to educate any readers not already familiar with SAP's core products. To gain a more detailed understanding of SAP Basis, Web AS, and so on, you'll want to take a closer look at SAP's primary support site, *service.sap.com*. If you run into any unfamiliar acronyms or products, you can refer to the book's ftp site as well.

3.1.1.   The Legacy—SAP Basis

As the name implies, SAP Basis is the term assigned by SAP AG that encompasses all of the software, tools, and utilities that establish the *basis* of an SAP solution, by effectively tying everything together. In a classic sense, then, SAP Basis refers to the client/server application architecture on which SAP systems are modeled, such as the front-end SAPGUI and other frontends, the back-end database management system, and everything necessary to bring it all together (e.g., the built-in monitoring and systems administration tools, the SAP development and change management environments, and data and interface management utilities). And that's only the beginning! Depending on whom you talk to or even from your own point of view, SAP Basis may also encompass any number of third-party management and configuration tools and utilities touching any layer of the SAP Technology Stack. For example, many SAP technology partners will lump their own proprietary hardware or software applets and tools into the category of SAP Basis if they happen to be used somewhere within the SAP Technology Stack.

The key, then, is that SAP Basis implies the "technical" layer of an SAP solution—the enabling layer—rather than the functional system itself. Basis makes the "life" of the system possible in the first place and is central in terms of systems management, performance monitoring, and general day-to-day maintenance.

When SAP Basis was initially conceived, however, the Internet was little more than a hard-to-access alternative to dial-up bulletin boards, "Java" was only a beverage pretty much confined to long nights cramming for college finals, and ABAP—SAP's proprietary programming and development language—was the only game in town for SAP systems. Over the last 2 years, though, SAP Basis has significantly evolved in response to a world that irreversibly changed almost overnight. The result was SAP's Web AS, initially targeted as a more effective alternate to SAP's ITS, but eventually broadened to include Basis and a whole lot more.

3.1.2.   Today—Web AS, the "New" Basis Layer

Because it is the underlying infrastructure for all new SAP solutions, and the enabling technology platform for SAP's newest and hottest products such as XI, MDM, and EP, proving the performance of the SAP Web AS within your own unique SAP environment is critical indeed. Web AS is a hybrid application server, able to satisfy development environments as diverse as J2EE (as of Web AS versions 6.30 and greater) and ABAP, along with providing enhanced support for XML (Extensible Markup Language, a much more powerful alternative to the Web's de facto mainstay Hypertext Markup Language, or HTML) and Web services technologies, including Simple Object Access Protocol (SOAP) and Web Services Definition Language (WSDL). Web AS also looks after many functions formerly handled by SAP's ITS, including load balancing, database connection pooling, serialization of update processing, and server-side data caching. With support for Unicode (see Note) as of version 6.20, Web AS is without a doubt a powerful application platform and worthy successor to traditional SAP Basis.

NOTE

Unicode refers to how characters are encoded and used by a computer. Unicode unifies all characters of all character sets (that is, languages like English, Mandarin, Portuguese, and so on) into a single encoding scheme. Thus, all letters, numbers, and other characters in a Unicode system are uniquely represented by the computer; each maintains its own unique numeric representation. Doing otherwise requires transforming among different encoding schemes running on different computers, and therefore invites the risk of data loss or corruption, not to mention the headaches associated with supporting multiple character encoding schemes. In SAP, non-Unicode systems use characters that are represented in binary with only 1 byte, whereas Unicode systems represent characters in binary with 2 or 4 bytes. Refer to SAP Note 79991 or *http://service.sap.com/unicode* for details.

Web AS also continues the traditions established by SAP Basis. In fact, I like to think of the SAP Web Application Server as a superset of Basis, as shown in Figure 3–1; it includes all of the legacy functions and interface abilities associated with Basis, plus all of the new capabilities outlined previously. All of this power is not without challenges though. For example, because Web AS can be distributed such that the SAP Web dispatcher process may reside on a server in your

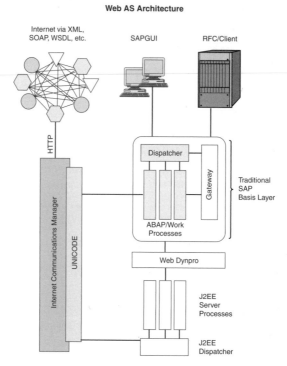

Web AS Architecture

Figure 3–1 Although SAP Basis seemed inclusive in its day, SAP's Web AS brings together much greater functionality and additional integration capabilities in a single powerful package.

company's DMZ, protected by front-end and back-end firewalls, while one or many other Web AS instances address core functionality requirements, opportunities for potential network and similar bandwidth-constraint issues exist. Thus, Web AS not only represents a complex technology stack in and of itself but, by extending the integration potential of mySAP solutions, it also dramatically underscores the importance of sound preproduction and postchange performance testing.

3.1.3.   Building for Tomorrow—SAP XI and MDM

Issues of data management are not new; indeed, corporate America has literally surrounded itself with islands of computing and information technology over the last 20 years, making enterprise integration and data management challenges a way of life for most IT organizations. SAP AG recognized the need for a simple, integrated, and modular approach to connect these islands of data together, and created SAP's XI and MDM products, allowing disparate systems from diverse vendors to be linked together to form a cohesive enterprise environment. XI and MDM are critical components of NetWeaver. In my eyes, within a few years, no level of enterprise-wide functional, regression, or load testing will be complete without taking XI and

MDM into account; business processes will be inextricably intertwined between the two, which in turn will be linked to an ever-expanding host of SAP-provided components, partner-provided xApps, and other entrenched enterprise applications. Given their young age at the present, though, both XI and MDM currently lack the level of maturity necessary for an organization thinking of skimping on performance testing to feel even marginally comfortable. True, the products make up for some of this lack of maturity in terms of ease of use and the comprehensive approach each applies to solving their respective business dilemmas. SAP XI in particular is a model of simplicity. It enables process-centric collaboration of SAP and/or non-SAP applications within and beyond enterprise boundaries based on the exchange of XML messages, nothing more—connectors are straightforward and included in more and more applications coming out of SAP AG. But it's still a very new approach to the old problem of enterprise application integration, and warrants attention to testing.

Though XI is at once exciting and compelling, I am especially intrigued by SAP's content MDM strategy: it solves a huge business dilemma that touches practically every company with more than perhaps a hundred employees and a few systems of record. Today, small business and enterprise customers alike have a need to enable data visibility between and within multiple applications. And they need a method for managing the uncontrolled proliferation of parts—descriptions, part numbers, and general inventory issues can wreak havoc on an otherwise solid supply chain. Finally, poor customer management and an inability to conduct cross-business-group reporting exacerbate an already tenuous link to customer retention. But, rather than enjoying a single master repository of data, most companies instead wind up managing copies and versions of these data across many different systems. Think about it: your core transactional systems, data warehouse, supply chain systems, customer relationship management products, e-commerce packages, and so on nearly all rely on "local" copies of what amounts to pretty much the same kinds of master data. This results in a huge duplication of effort. Even worse, it serves to introduce errors inherent to the longstanding challenges of synchronizing and managing different islands of data. And at the end of the day, all of this data simply and unnecessarily consumes IT resources.

The MDM team out of Walldorf has promised to rescue you from much of this effort and error-prone work. They have essentially signed up to take ownership of *all* of your enterprise data, from underlying databases up through middleware, applications, and even Internet tiers. In doing so, SAP AG is telling us that they want to be your one-stop shopping solution for all of your data management needs. As SAP has done in many other markets it has entered, I'm sure they'll pull this task off, too, and quickly become a de facto standard among competing standards and products.

3.1.4.   NetWeaver and mySAP Solutions Explained

Wrapping up Web AS, XI, MDM, and all of SAP's newest mySAP solutions is SAP's NetWeaver, which enables SAP's customers to lower their TCO with a comprehensive technology platform that integrates people, information, and business processes across disparate business and technology boundaries. SAP NetWeaver can help an organization integrate SAP and non-SAP applications alike, supporting complex business processes without the need for changing individual component technology stacks. I look at NetWeaver as the ultimate "IT umbrella," making it possible for a single entity to embrace and cover the bulk of your data center resources.

Some of my customers have described NetWeaver as simply the "extended successor" to SAP's mySAP.com offering—though a bit simplistic, I like this description well enough too. Be clear, though, that SAP NetWeaver is not a product per se, but rather a platform that expands on mySAP.com, much like the introduction of Web AS expanded on the original SAP Basis. NetWeaver consists of the following basic four-layer stack, also shown in Figure 3–2, that supports Web services along with more traditional methods of executing business processes:

1. SAP's EP: the "People Integration" layer
2. The "Information Integration" layer (consisting of SAP MDM along with SAP's Business Information Warehouse and Knowledge Management [KM] offerings)
3. SAP's XI: the "Process Integration" layer
4. Web AS: the "Application Platform" layer

Not all four layers must be implemented in every case, though; a modular approach is supported for most deployments (xApps is a notable exception). As SAP AG likes to say, SAP NetWeaver has "taken the high ground" in that it was designed, from nearly its inception, to be fully interoperable with both J2EE (specifically IBM WebSphere) and Microsoft's .Net environments. This allows IT organizations to leverage their existing systems, people, and business process investments. As a strategic platform, then, NetWeaver is both well positioned for the future and very capable in the near term. A growing subset of SAP's customer base has already deployed significant pieces or layers of the NetWeaver stack, whether they realize it or not: the latest versions of SAP's mySAP Business Suite are NetWeaver enabled. And, with every new SAP product release, more and more of the NetWeaver stack is introduced across the globe and ex-

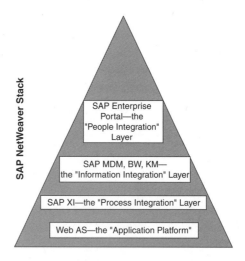

Figure 3–2   This four-layer technology stack provides a basic view of SAP NetWeaver.

posed to other systems every day. My suggestion is to learn and embrace it today, or risk a trip to the bottom of the waterfall discussed back in Chapter 1.

3.2. Stress-Testing Considerations for mySAP Solutions and Products

With the essentials behind us, we can now turn our attention to testing and tuning specific mySAP solutions, components, and products. My goal in the next few sections is to identify unique, critical, or differentiating factors that make stress testing so important in minimizing deployment risks. This includes identifying SAP systems that are probably central to your business, or identifying complex business requirements that must be understood from a performance perspective in multiuser environments prior to Go-Live. These products typically demand the most attention. In other cases, mySAP components are simply noted as technically challenging, warranting load testing perhaps for no other reason than to validate that the solution hardware design has been architected and tuned properly. Finally, unless I indicate otherwise, the specific SAP product or mySAP component version or release discussed is assumed to be the most current version supported as of this writing.

3.2.1. Testing Core Transactional Systems—SAP R/3 and R/3 Enterprise

When it comes to stress testing SAP systems, R/3 and its more recent successor R/3 Enterprise tend to command the most attention of all of SAP's products across the board. Reasons for this vary, but generally relate to the following factors:

- Core transactional systems, like SAP R/3, tend to host many end users, each utilizing the system in support of their primary day-to-day business-driven activities. Thus, a poorly performing system quickly equates to lost productivity on a large scale and across a large user population, which in turn becomes expensive quickly.
- Because of the business functions they support, highly utilized transactional systems become mission critical overnight; when R/3 is running slowly, expensive resources outside of end users are underutilized, too. For example, trucks that sit longer than necessary in a loading dock and materials that are not updated in terms of quantities, locations, and so on cost a small fortune (e.g., in lost end-user productivity, late fees, service level fines and penalties, reduced customer satisfaction, and lost business) over a short period of time.
- Transactional systems, like R/3, often represent the "system of origination" for business processes that span other systems, too. For instance, R/3 feeds data-warehousing systems (e.g., SAP BW), customer relationship systems (e.g., SAP CRM), supply chain and procurement systems (e.g., APO and SRM), respectively, and so on. Thus, testing key business processes that span multiple systems is critical not only to the success of the transaction in question but to every system that is touched, and therefore impacted from a performance perspective, by the transaction.
- Stress-testing baselines for transaction systems that tend to evolve over time are critical, too; if the system is ever updated to include additional functional areas or a slew of

new users, important basic data will be available to quantify response times and throughout *before* the changes, becoming useful afterwards to help troubleshoot performance issues.

• Finally, given the short average duration of each online transaction, it is important to fully understand and characterize both the active high-water user load and the peak transaction rate of a particular system. From these numbers, concurrent user numbers for peak loads can be calculated, and what-if analyses regarding scalability of a particular technology stack may be performed.

Although a large number of diverse functional areas are supported by SAP R/3 and R/3 Enterprise, when it comes to stress testing it's often the users associated with the "heavy" functional areas on which the testing is focused. Not to say that the value of modeling an exact load—comprising both heavy and light modules—is not useful. But the time spent in planning for, analyzing, executing, and monitoring stress tests that consist of light transaction loads like many of those associated with FI (the finance module) usually does little to identify or ultimately exercise the potential bottlenecks in many systems. In my experience, then, the core heavy functional areas that get the most attention in SAP R/3 stress tests, in order, include the following:

1. Sales and distribution (SD)
2. Production planning (PP)
3. Controlling (CO)
4. Plant maintenance (PM)
5. Materials management (MM)
6. Warehouse management (LE-WM)
7. Finance (FI; in particular, heavy or long-running reporting transactions)
8. Project system (PS)
9. Basis components (BC; especially in very large systems, where the work of monitoring a system can weigh heavily on a system during peak activity periods)

Other special areas like ATO, or Available to Promise, drive great loads on an R/3 system and therefore warrant special attention to testing. So, too, does any functional area that has been heavily customized for its end users, inherently introducing risk as to how well the customized code will perform under load.

Once the key functional areas are identified, it's necessary to obtain accurate *active* and *concurrent* online user counts and then to understand the mix of users within the various R/3 functional areas. For example, for a system hosting 1,000 logged-in active users, we might determine that about 600 of these users seem to be active during the busiest portions of the morning and afternoon: this is our concurrent user count. Next, of these 600 users, perhaps 25% represent SD users, 25% are MM users, 20% are PM users, and 10% are CO users. The remaining 20% of the users are distributed across numerous other modules. With these kinds of data in hand, it's fairly easy to use SAP's CCMS (Computing Center Management System, a long-time inbuilt SAP management tool) to determine the top five transactions for each core module, and therefore provide a solid base of transactions from which to start testing. I tend to ignore the 20% of transactions that are spread across a lot of functional areas, unless there's a particular transaction that is either critical to the business or especially CPU or disk intensive.

As your system evolves, you'll find that your top-five list for each functional area changes slightly, too. If additional transactions are determined to be part of the top five for a particular functional area, simply shift the list and insert the "new" transaction into it. Or, add the transaction to the list and make yourself a top-six list instead. Once we have an accurate list of the top five or so transactions for a particular period of time (say, a month or so), we can then fall back to the percentages of users distributed across each functional area to execute a stress test such that the percentages match what we see in the real production system. I also like to look at the number of dialog steps processed by each core transaction. This step helps me determine if it might make sense to maintain a top-three list for certain functional areas and maybe a top-seven list for others; I might use a dialog steps/functional area "cut-off" of sorts to make the decision regarding the use of short or long lists that much easier.

With user counts behind us, we need to turn our attention to batch processing. I know of very few R/3 systems that do not process a significant batch load, which often consists of scheduled or ad hoc report runs and other "background" processes that are not of an urgent real-time nature but need to be executed nonetheless. The key to accurate stress testing is to determine when this batch processing occurs and to identify typical batch processes that may then be used for testing purposes. For the first requirement, usually there is not a lot of overlap between an organization's peak online user window and its batch window, though if there is, this overlap must be understood and modeled—it likely represents the peak load handled by the R/3 system. Again, CCMS is useful in drilling down into the specific time periods and work rates that we need to get our hands on.

Other approaches also can be useful when it comes to load testing R/3. For example, some of my customers are less concerned with daily peak loads than they are with special month-end processing germane to their business. In these cases, it's important to characterize the performance of a limited number of infrequently executed but highly resource-intensive processes, whether executed by online users or in batch mode. Other customers might be more interested in whether a particular SAP Technology Stack, especially after upgrades and regular changes, can address a specific transaction load in a specific period of time. Payroll runs and other batch-intensive processes drive these kinds of stress tests: for example, perhaps 10,000 employee paychecks need to be processed in a 3-hour *execution window*. Or, a company might need to execute business-essential profitability analysis reports during a limited 60-minute period of time every morning in preparation for operational or even executive-level decision-making meetings.

Finally, lately the word of the day when it comes to R/3 seems to be *consolidation*. Because it is the most mature product supported by SAP today (outside of R/2, its mainframe-based forerunner), R/3 is also, by virtue of its popularity, positioned to benefit the most from IT consolida-

IT Connection for SAP Environments Can Impact Major SAP Technology Stack Layers

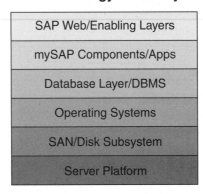

Figure 3–3 IT consolidation activity at many layers in the SAP Technology Stack is responsible for driving much of the increased need for stress testing, performance characterization, and subsequent tuning seen in today's R/3 environments.

tion. With more than 50,000 instances installed across thousands of companies around the globe, a huge number of R/3 systems are undergoing consolidation projects internally. As shown in Figure 3–3, application servers are being collapsed, database servers and their relational database management systems (DBMSs) are enjoying the benefits of instance consolidation and MCOD (discussed later in this chapter), multiple nonproduction instances are being squeezed together into smaller and more powerful server platforms (courtesy of both hardware- and software-led partitioning, the latter made possible by products from VMware, HP, and Microsoft), and Internet-enabling R/3 accessibility layers are undergoing server and instance consolidation efforts. Also, R/3 functional upgrades from 3.1I through 4.6C to R/3 Enterprise are driving consolidation activity as well. All of this SAP Technology Stack activity begs for performance characterization, baselining, and ongoing change-initiated risk-mitigating stress testing.

3.2.2.   SAP EP Load-Testing Challenges

Load testing EP can be quite a project in and of itself, because EP allows for access to many SAP and non-SAP resources, inherently touching and impacting so many mySAP components and other enterprise products. Unsurprisingly, though, the EP Server environment takes on most of the load and therefore represents the most critical component. But the Unification Server, which consists of a Web server and a database repository (allowing data to be shared and mapped between different SAP products) is also subject to quite a load: it is expected, in fact, that 20% of all EP hits will in turn impact the Unification Server. Typical SAP EP stress-testing scenarios include the following:

- Testing the impact that parallel logons place on the total solution; the total number of users logging into the portal during the peak hour of operation (typically 8:00 a.m. to 9:00 a.m., or perhaps 2:00 p.m. to 3:00 p.m.) drives significant, albeit short in duration, load.
- As with R/3, simulating the expected number of both logged-in and concurrent users that the portal is expected to support is common. It's important to note that the definition of think times, concurrent users, and other metrics differ a bit for EP than for other mySAP components. For example, the term *concurrent users* with regard to EP actually equates to the total number of users active in the system in a single hour, rather than the more precise and usual "at the same time" definition. Further, it is assumed that 60% of these concurrent users will exhibit an average think time (delay between keyboard-driven or other activity) of 600 seconds; 34% will think for 180 seconds, and 6% will think for 30 seconds. This range of think times, again quite different in terms of work rates than that defined for other mySAP components, takes into weightier account the impact that logged-in users have on the portal, in terms of connections, RAM, and other resource consumption properties.
- Finally, it may be beneficial to ensure that your expected or as-is measurable Content Management hits are handily addressed by your unique EP solution. Measured as a percentage (the number of hits per 100), this important metric seeks to quantify the number of documents stored in your portal that are actually "hit" by users. Such hits can drive significant network and disk subsystem activity, with incrementally higher CPU consumption, thereby adding significantly to a system's load.

The need to measure or quantify other performance metrics may drive stress testing, too. If your particular EP implementation consists of pages with significantly more than four iViews, or your users tend to perform a significant number of queries or access data that are managed by nonindexed tables, you'll want to characterize and track relative performance. Similarly, anything that deviates from EP "norms" might warrant the creation of specific testing criteria. Such criteria will help you play it safe as you introduce changes or perform test upgrades in preproduction environments, prior to promoting the changes into the real Production system.

3.2.3. Stress Testing mySAP Business Intelligence (BI)

From what I have observed, stress testing SAP's mySAP BI offering is not commonplace. Why? Because the primary mySAP BI offering, BW, is pretty much a reporting system, plain and simple, and *most* customers do not mind waiting for their reports to be generated as long as the overall turnaround on reports seems reasonable—a few hours, potentially. However, in environments where near-real-time data are made available to BW, and the requirement to rapidly access these data truly exists, the prompt execution of a BW query may become near mission-critical. In these cases, even systems like BW may benefit from repeatable stress-testing practices and the performance tuning that comes from follow-on system tweaking, not to mention the system validity checks made possible after major configuration changes, addition of data to the warehouse (as they tend to grow quickly), or infrastructure upgrades such as those related to disk subsystem and CPU upgrades.

Performance testing mySAP BI typically revolves around understanding how the SAP BW performs under what are (or are expected to be, in the case of new deployments) typical query loads and peak query loads, especially as the BW database grows in size. Unsurprisingly, you need to identify the top queries either way. In my experience, much of the day-to-day load of a BW consists of 20 to 50 to perhaps a few hundred queries. To simplify matters, while still seeking to identify a core set of daily queries or transactions, I recommend narrowing this list down to the top 10 queries. For month-end or quarter-end periods, though, it's much easier to identify the key performance culprits—those queries that tend to show up every month or quarter on a regular basis, usually seen running for hours at a time.

The classic BW stress test comes in two flavors. The first seeks to quantify the performance deltas observed when slicing and dicing cubes in different ways and is usually performed during the functional testing phase, in which the performance of single-user queries drives tuning. The second, and more common, test in my experience, pits different system configurations and perhaps even disparate architectures against one another. Barring rewriting or restaging the data and InfoCubes against which these queries operate—that is, assuming that a particular set of reports and queries are here to stay—I recommend scripting the top five or ten queries using the most popular data combinations (or at least most abundant data combinations) so that they may be re-executed in the following various test scenarios:

- Baseline BW stress testing may be performed months prior to Go-Live, often including a certain amount of validation of the proposed production system. For example, in the past, I've architected various two- or three-tiered BW hardware solutions and then executed simple customer-provided queries against standard BW cubes so as to prove the general performance capabilities of my custom solutions. My competitors usually did the same (or opted to bow out of the running), and the end result was a straightforward albeit limited apples-to-apples performance test.
- Shortly before Go-Live, long after hardware and software partners have been nailed down, a larger-scale stress test may be performed. Sometimes these tests are quite simplistic, consisting of three to five to perhaps ten top queries executed by something like 20 to 50 concurrent users. In other cases, I have assisted my customers in load testing the performance of their shared networks and shared SAN solutions, too: testing the nightly expected load time of the Persistent Staging Area (a transparent table for storing detailed requests in the original format of the transfer structure) or Operational Data Store (where raw operational data are combined and housed) to ensure the update window is adequate, or to ensure that queries execute well enough over slow links, may represent a critical success criterion.

- Stress testing may also be performed after Go-Live, especially if new cubes or an entirely new data warehouse is being deployed. For example, in the golden years of BW (before highly scalable commodity platforms were available), I found myself testing the performance of what was termed an "enterprise" data warehouse, fed in turn by numerous smaller "operational" or "independent" data warehouses. The smaller data warehouses allowed for a very granular departmentalization of popular functional data and queries, in turn supported by local IT teams—perhaps not the best TCO story in the world, but that's how it was back in 1999. In other cases, I found myself comparing the performance of a system with a certain number and type of preconfigured InfoCubes, but varying its attributes (e.g., dimensions, key figures, length) to determine how large and how quickly a particular database might grow.
- Also after Go-Live, verifying the impact that different BW releases have or, to a lesser extent, the impact that functional or technical support packages and other regular change waves have on the top "X" queries can put the time and money related to stress testing to good use. A sample screen shot from a productive SAP BW 3.0B system shown in Figure 3–4 reveals, in this case, that the most popular transactions were actually a mix of a few queries and Basis transactions. By using this information and com-

| Times | Database | Parts of response time | GUI times | All data |

| Task type | Aggregation | Single Records | | | | | | | |

Transaction: DB acc.: # No., T Total time (s), Ø Time/access (ms)

Report or Transaction name	# Sequential Reads	T Seq. Read Time	Ø Seq. Read Time	# Accesses	T Time	Ø Time	# Chang
SESSION_MANAGER	3,427	9	2.7	4,102	7	1.8	11
RSA1	15,363	74	4.8	12,094	8	0.6	8
RRMX	303	0	0.2	207	1	2.7	3
SM50	179	1	7.8	246	0	1.7	
ST03	218	1	6.8	494	2	3.6	
ST22	219	0	1.4	155	0	2.4	
SU01	49	1	11.8	63	0	5.3	
ST02	2,814	1	0.2	174	0	2.0	
ST07	76	1	11.3	133	0	2.9	
SM21	52	0	0.0	176	0	2.1	
Login_Pw	134	0	0.9	123	1	4.5	
<adm message>	0	0	0.0	0	0	0.0	
RSABAPPROGRAM	25	0	7.0	128	0	2.6	
Z_PPCO_INFOCUBE_MAINT	24	0	3.7	62	0	3.1	

Figure 3–4 Use the statistics displayed via SAP CCMS's ST03N to verify to what degree a change has impacted the performance of your key queries and transactions.

paring before and after database read times, it becomes clear to what degree a change impacted performance.

Factors that affect the database size and overall performance characteristics of the SAP BW system make excellent stress-testing scenarios, too. For example, simply testing different quantities of various types of users—each characterized by fewer think times and therefore greater work rates—can be useful. BW users are classified by the frequency of their activity and the average level or reporting that each user performs, the former of which is measured in navigation steps per hour (where 1 navigation step = 9 SD dialog steps): for example, determining the impact that fewer or greater information users (low/normal), executive users (also called *advanced*), or power users have on your system can provide you with valuable resizing data.

You may also want to test the impact that different mixes of users or types of queries have on a particular system. SAP AG leverages its three user classifications in this regard. For example, information users spend 80% of their time viewing reports and 20% performing online analytical processing (OLAP) analysis, whereas executive users split their time evenly between straight reporting and more complex OLAP activities. Power users, on the other hand, execute intensive data exploration activities 100% of the time. Testing different mixes of users (e.g., 120 information users + 70 executive users + 10 power users versus 150 information users + 30 executive users + 20 power users) makes stress testing a 200-user BW solution invaluable as companies change or evolve internally.

As you can see, if necessary, stress testing SAP BW can be quite challenging, though I believe that a useful chunk of knowledge can be gleaned pretty easily with a bit of planning and forethought. Much of the "big" work of stress testing BW seems to apply before Go-Live, too; I therefore recommend you work closely with your SAP hardware sizing and other technology partners to help mitigate mySAP BI deployment risks from the beginning.

3.2.4.   Tackling SEM Stress Testing

SAP's SEM solution consists primarily of a "cockpit function," the chief goals of which are to manage and report against key metrics and figures. The SAP BW serves as a foundation for this solution; thus, it is important to architect and implement a well-performing BW system before any real SEM stress testing can be performed. At that point, in addition to the potential BW load-testing scenarios just discussed, SEM brings a whole slew of additional challenges to the table given that its analytical application components rely on multidimensional system-intensive OLAP data structures. Stress-testing scenarios include the following:

- Modeling core business processes or activities that most impact your Balanced Scorecard—that is, anything that drives high CPU, memory, disk, or network bandwidth
- Comparing the three different SEM technical installation options against one another—standalone SEM versus SEM data mart versus SEM running on top of BW—in terms of the speed of business processes

- Focusing on SEM-BPS (Business Planning and Simulation), specifically the same types of "what if" scenarios executed by the business to support value-based decision making
- Testing how long it takes to gather and incorporate unstructured data across the Web and other external sources, to be used by SEM-BIC (Business Information Collection), and the impact this has on network and other infrastructure resources
- Adjusting Key Performance Indicators, or KPIs, to understand the impact that SEM-CPM (Corporate Performance Monitor) places on the system
- Testing "the usual"—that is, the concurrent number of maximum SEM users, broken down into high, medium, and low users
- Testing the impact that a particular closing has in terms of disk subsystem performance (data volumes can be great)

Throughout all of this, you should focus only on the key or most intensive SEM components you have deployed, much like the idea behind testing only core R/3 functional areas. Testing all deployed components makes for a more complete test but adds significantly to investment time and therefore cost. And, given the reporting role of SEM, your biggest enemy against stress testing SEM in the first place will be justifying the time and money spent versus the value gained.

When it comes to SEM, it's unusual to find yourself with a test or sandbox environment useful for stress testing. This is because SAP AG has never promoted the idea of maintaining a three-system landscape for SEM; when standard functionality is needed, only Development and Production SEM systems are necessary. Another one of your biggest challenges will therefore probably revolve around simply putting together a temporary sandbox of sorts from which to launch and execute a stress-testing project.

3.2.5.   Testing and Tuning mySAP CRM

Arguably the most difficult SAP solution to stress test (in terms of technical architecture and overall complexity) is mySAP CRM. Not that the testing process is any more difficult—it's just a far-reaching application, the unstructured testing of which can quickly grow quite time consuming. And, because so many special-function CRM servers, not to mention other products like SAP R/3 and APO, usually come into play to execute a single end-to-end CRM "business scenario," creating a full-blown production-like CRM stress-testing environment can also be prohibitively expensive. Specific challenges include the following:

- The ability to access a large cadre of hardware that truly emulates your real production environment is necessary. True, most of the mySAP CRM software components can be loaded on a single box. But there is no value in doing so if authentic load testing is your goal; a single-box approach supports functional and regression testing at best. Thus, acquiring, configuring, and tuning specialty servers like ITS, the InQMy Application Server, a TRex Server (Text Retrieval and Information Extraction, used for indexing and search capabilities), a Workgroup Server (small database server), a Communication Station, and a Multi-Channel Interface Server (maintains the relationship between the CRM server and any Computer Telephony Integration [CTI], e-mail, chat, and similar middleware/services), in addition to the core CRM database and application server or servers, is essential to performing real-world testing.

- Testing the performance of the Internet Pricing Configurator (IPC), a core software layer in the SAP CRM stack, is common. The IPC is a horizontally scalable Java application that provides pricing calculation and product configuration capabilities: testing the underlying configuration to determine whether it's capable of processing the peak number of orders expected to be received per hour, or creating the expected peak number of objects on the potentially heaviest day of CRM processing, makes sense.

- Simulating the expected number and types of CRM users, and in turn executing workloads typical to each user type, is common, too. CRM Internet Sales users, for example, are divided into either browsing users (the majority) or purchasing users. It's important to model the correct mix, because browsing users impact little more than the Web-server component of CRM, whereas users that actually take the browsing process through to completion and purchase something place a load across many other servers and systems. Other types include Mobile Sales and Customer Interaction Center (CIC) users. Regardless, you'll want to simulate the same kinds of activities that are performed on your own CRM system. Tasks such as creating customer orders, managing opportunities, managing sales orders, performing service-related transactions, and managing data related to customers, products, and even projects are all good candidates, because they represent core transactions that consume essential CPU, memory, disk, and network resources.

- In other cases, you might want to perform pure load testing, like that associated with simulating the actual number of incoming and outgoing CIC calls handled per hour or driving the expected peak volume of objects (e.g., sales orders) in a particular time period. Doing so will no doubt drive back-end ERP activity, too (necessitating a copy of your R/3 or other system within the test landscape). Even SAP APO may be impacted; availability requests are transferred between the CRM server and APO system via SAP's Remote Function Call (RFC) communication service. And finally, CRM's Mobile Sales users might use SAP BW for reporting and limited data mining; this impact may need to be modeled as well, if deemed time sensitive or otherwise critical.

On a final note, another stress-testing challenge might specifically involve testing your CRM front-end clients. If you maintain standard desktop and laptop configurations to be used by your SAP CRM sales force, for example, and you change the CRM configuration on the back end, it could impact what the client observes in terms of system performance. Thus, an important part of a holistic SAP CRM stress test should include testing each of your standard client configurations. And, if you use both the standard SAPGUI and one of the Internet-enabled interfaces—like the Java or HTML-based user interfaces—you'll need to include these in your testing plans as well.

3.2.6. Stress Testing mySAP Product Lifecycle Management (PLM)

One of SAP's newer mySAP component offerings is mySAP PLM, a comprehensive end-to-end solution that wraps up product innovation, engineering, new product introduction, production ramp-up, and ongoing engineering change management, most of which seamlessly communicate to Supply Chain Management (SCM). Once you understand the functionality you have implemented in mySAP PLM, stress testing becomes a simple matter of identifying a number of key scenarios. Your core PLM business processes probably revolve around managing product, asset, and process information at any point in a product's lifecycle, from selection and purchasing up through production ramp-up, installation, operation, engineering changes, maintenance/repair, retirement, and so on. I suggest modeling much of the lifecycle of a core product set, something germane to the business that is unlikely to disappear soon, from beginning to end. In this way, as you make changes to your technical or functional environment, it should become quickly apparent that a particular business function (e.g., the repair process) suffered in terms of throughput or response-time performance from a certain change.

PLM is tightly aligned with the mySAP SCM and CRM solutions, and is implemented as an EP solution. Like typical portal solutions, therefore, load is driven primarily by online users. You can review user-based testing discussed in earlier sections for more ideas on how to properly stress test based on different think times, concurrent user loads, and so on. And, I suggest you review the section on stress testing SAP EP, too.

3.2.7. mySAP SCM

SAP's SCM solution enables the complete modeling and optimization of a company's supply/logistics chain. When it comes to mySAP SCM, SAP's mature APO component is central, followed by the newer SAP Event Manager, or EM, product. APO consists of a number of different application components itself, most common of which include Demand Planning (DP), Supply Network Planning (SNP), Production Planning/Detailed Scheduling, Global Available to Promise, and Transport Planning/Vehicle Scheduling. So stress testing should naturally relate back to the basic components you're executing; for starters, model the key parts of your core business processes. Next, consider some of the following data- or architecture-specific matters:

- The number of DP versions and SNP versions you plan to execute—used in forecasting or simulating demand—directly affects the amount of disk space you need, which in turn impacts disk subsystem performance (until the models are loaded in the liveCache server). More important, though, if you need to execute a planning run within a certain execution window, CPU processing power will be impacted more than any other resource.
- How often you intend to execute your planning runs—daily, weekly, monthly, and so on—and how many you intend to execute concurrently or back-to-back also represent excellent stress-testing scenarios.
- If your environment is very *characteristics heavy* (where objects are described by many different properties or combinations or properties), you will want to test the impact of

system or functional changes in regard to CPU performance—the greater the number of characteristics, the greater the processor load.

- Similarly, if you maintain a lot of key figures in the APO liveCache server, the amount of memory required in the liveCache server is directly impacted.
- Though not nearly as important as transactional systems like R/3 and so on, the number of logged-on or concurrent APO users also impacts CPU sizing, and can be used for very basic APO system baseline testing.

3.2.8.   Load Testing mySAP Supplier Relationship Management (SRM)

Like CRM, mySAP SRM solutions can also be very complex in terms of both technical infrastructure and pertinent business scenarios. SRM encompasses e-procurement capabilities and the Supplier Collaboration Engine (which provides functionality in the areas of sourcing and supplier enablement). In regard to the former, the e-procurement piece of SRM alone consists of SAP EBP, Requisite BugsEye, Requisite eMerge, SAP BW, and SAP EP—plenty of technology to undergo stress test and tuning by any measure. And the SRM business scenarios that run atop the platform are themselves quite involved, and vary substantially between one another. Consider the following:

- Required processing horsepower varies between the different SRM business scenarios that might be implemented; baselining each of these scenarios gives you a considerable advantage in troubleshooting future performance problems and helps you understand the peak number of different transactions—like those related to procurement, for instance—your system is currently capable of.
- The catalog, whether internally or externally hosted, impacts network activity. Similarly, the links between the EBP database server and other components like BW or EP also need to be scrutinized; the average document size you pass back and forth between systems impacts the load borne by the network, too.
- Modeling your whole "shopping cart" experience is an excellent idea, as it provides valuable insight into the performance of various core EBP transactions: creating, displaying, transferring, and updating your end user's shopping cart.
- Traditional user-based stress testing, where you emulate the load placed on production by a similar number of users performing a similar mix of activities (like those related to the shopping-cart experience, while others simply browse through the catalog) is a mainstay of EBP stress testing.
- If you support the auctioning functionality, you might wish to model this business process as well: auction users (bidders) for very popular items can bring an otherwise well-constructed mySAP SRM solution to its knees.
- OS-specific capacity planning and tuning related to the Java Virtual Machine (JVM) executing in your mySAP SRM environment is common, especially with regard to the memory heap and generational Garbage Collector. JVM tuning speeds up a system in terms of both memory and CPU-specific utilization. (See SAP Note 552522 [Java Hotspot VM Memory Parameters] for information related to your particular operating

system; tuning JVM can get quite granular, to the point of changing and testing the number of threads and number of dbpool connections to find the best settings for your implementation.)

- Finally, the need for tight security encircling your EBP solution necessitates stress testing: the deployment of firewalls, encryption, secured network links, and the configuration of hardware- and software-based load-balancing solutions all impact throughput and response times, often significantly.

The workflow for EBP does not halt within the boundaries of mySAP SRM, though. A workflow that commences with browsing for and then selecting a particular item, followed by creating a shopping cart, eventually drives other activities like cutting a purchase order, confirming delivery, and eventually invoicing—tasks pertinent to R/3, for example—and needs to be load tested end-to-end.

3.3. Stress Testing Other SAP Enterprise–Enabling Solutions and Products

It's not just an organization's mySAP solutions and components that rate stress testing; other SAP products that play a role in either connecting different systems or enabling access to them can be responsible for performance problems. Failure of products that interconnect multiple SAP systems can easily lead to unscheduled downtime of your core applications, too. Think about it— even though your R/3 system may be "up," if key business processes cannot complete or end users cannot access systems that front-end R/3, then for all intents and purposes, R/3 is down! And, because the downtime clock starts running as soon as your SAP system becomes unavailable to its user community, the expense of not testing and tuning complex mySAP environments can add up fast. The downtime clock continues ticking away as the problem or issue is noted by a systems management tool or administrator and researched; end users potentially sit idle as the problem eventually escalates and is finally resolved or a work-around is established. Even then, only once the SAP administrator validates that the restored system is truly in shape to be opened up for use by its end users again does the downtime clock stop ticking.

Given the preceding timeline, it's not hard to imagine how one 4-hour downtime event easily exceeds the costs of even the most elaborate of enterprise stress tests, countless exercises I've planned, conducted, and managed for my own customers—and you're probably no different. So, in the interest of being comprehensive in my approach to stress testing, and helping to bring everything together under the banner of SAP NetWeaver, let's next take a look at challenges and reasons why load testing SAP's XI, ITS, xApps, and SAP systems that take advantage of MCOD is not only indispensable from a technology perspective, but makes good business sense as well.

3.3.1.   SAP XI

The SAP XI brings both SAP and select non-SAP enterprise products together, enabling integration unlike anything we've seen in the past from products out of SAP AG. This evolving integration technology can be used today, or in conjunction with the latest and all future mySAP solutions and components. In a nutshell, XI provides an Integration Repository (to manage interfaces and mappings to each product being integrated into XI), an Integration Directory (to manage routing rules and mappings across your mySAP system landscape), and the necessary enabling proxy and integration engine components. Thus, business processes that must span multiple systems—like sales-order processes, which might originate in CRM and then proceed to R/3 and APO—can now be easily managed through XI. And, with the use of synchronous and asynchronous messaging, XI supports deploying business processes across heterogeneous enterprise system landscapes, such as those I see every day in the real world. SAP solutions surrounded by third-party enterprise applications, including commonplace solutions from the likes of Baan, Broadvision, JDE World Software, Oracle, PeopleSoft, Siebel, and more, as depicted in Figure 3–5. Note the use of industry-standard file adapters JDBC (Java Database Connectivity) and JMS (Java Message Service, an asynchronous messaging standard that allows J2EE application components to create, send, receive, and read messages), making it easy to link XI with the rest of the non-SAP world.

With this wonderful business flexibility and technology freedom comes a requisite level of end-to-end stress testing. That is, what XI does for the business in terms of capabilities can create an equally dramatic performance nightmare over time, one that is both difficult to pinpoint and hard to characterize. With so many systems and underpinning network and other shared hardware resources, each representing a unique solution stack, the need for stress testing throughout XI's lifecycle should be unquestioned. Fortunately, once an organization's business processes are linked into XI, a certain amount of the burden related to testing can be reduced if you take into consideration the following factors:

XI and the Integration Server

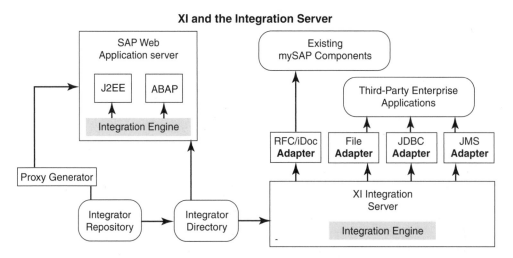

Figure 3–5 Because the SAP XI Integration Server can tie so many diverse applications and products together, it may represent a key stress-testing objective for your unique environment.

- The XI Integration Server is the embodiment of XI—it does the actual work of messaging. Thus, it's important that the number and size of the messages that your XI Integration Server needs to process are understood, and that a performance baseline is established. Not surprisingly, only messages from servers and systems that actually touch XI need to be considered. Through stress testing, you will also be in a position to establish a high-water mark, so that you understand your growth and peak processing limitations well before you unknowingly run into them.
- Given that the average size of a message is only about 31 kilobytes (the size of an iDoc with four line items), and all messages are held in a compressed format for only a day (and subsequently archived or deleted), you really do not need to concern yourself with database or disk subsystem–specific testing. Note, however, that data held in Unicode format consumes up to twice the amount of disk space as that maintained in a non-Unicode format.
- Network testing, on the other hand, should be a staple of XI stress testing. A number of back-end network segments will certainly be involved, as might a few public segments. Thus, characterizing the load during normal and peak periods will help you stay on top of the bandwidth curve, giving you the information you need to establish a network infrastructure capable of meeting current requirements, and later growing as your messaging needs dictate.
- Finally, like most of SAP's products, when it comes to average CPU utilization the general goal is not to exceed 65% under reasonable load; stress testing will make it clear what the message-to-CPU utilization ratio looks like in your own distinctive enterprise system landscape.

3.3.2.   SAP ITS

Even though one day soon it will be completely replaced by Web AS, SAP's ITS is as viable a platform today as ever, and makes itself useful in thousands of installations across the globe. Stress testing ITS is a simple matter of ensuring that the number of connected users per instance does not exceed the capabilities of the underpinning hardware. At a high level, ITS works by converting HTML to SAP RFC, and back again. In this way, Web clients appear like any other SAPGUI-connected user as far as the back-end R/3 or other SAP system is concerned. The performance question that needs to be answered is not solely the HTML-to-RFC conversion process but also the network bandwidth challenges behind it, connecting ITS to the back-end SAP systems, especially if a secure (and inherently more bandwidth-intensive) network protocol is employed. In addition, with the ability to install multiple SAP ITS instances on a single physical server and disk subsystem comes the challenges of ensuring that each instance meets its individual SLA levels and other performance metrics.

3.3.3.   SAP xApps

Given their custom nature and an inherent level of technical complexity because all four layers of the SAP NetWeaver stack are involved, the need to stress test SAP's xApps throughout each system's lifecycle is a no-brainer. SAP xApps are developed by SAP AG and a growing number of their select partners, combining people, information, and processes into a set of cohesive, collaborative, content-driven business processes that seamlessly span multiple systems. But it's not as though all of the risk inherent to such a seamless but still potentially complex solution ever disappears. Indeed, a custom solution, however much "canned," screams for regular and repeatable stress testing both before and after Go-Live.

3.3.4.   SAP MCOD

Although more of an approach rather than a solution per se, SAP AG's MCOD initiative absolutely demands a certain amount of at least initial stress testing (as does any IT consolidation approach, a number of which were discussed earlier in this chapter). MCOD allows multiple R/3 and mySAP databases to be collapsed into one or fewer physical databases, as seen in Figure 3–6, thereby simplifying the SAP system landscape and database management/backup administration in particular. Even more compelling, MCOD allows for a reduction in database licenses and reduction in the amount of physical disk space and tape resources necessary; combined with the benefits surrounding simplification, MCOD has the potential to significantly reduce the TCO of a select set of SAP AG's installed base.

Unsurprisingly, however, with all of these benefits come several tradeoffs, many of which represent a challenge handily addressed by load testing, as follows:

- As SAP AG touts, separate mySAP installations and even functional upgrades leveraging a single database are indeed achievable. However, from an infrastructure perspective, sizing and then verifying that the underlying disk subsystem performs well for all

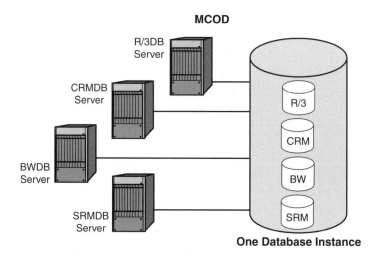

Figure 3–6   Minimize the risk of deploying and maintaining systems that leverage SAP's MCOD ability to share a common disk subsystem and database (DB) through the use of both upfront and regular stress testing/tuning.

components, during peak times (which may overlap, depending on your business needs), demand solid baselining and repeatable, regular stress testing.

- For production systems, high-availability solutions and the processes undertaken to perform a "failover" will impact more than one SAP component; how the disk subsystem performs during and after the failover needs to be characterized from a performance perspective.

- Backup and restoration of the database become more challenging, as the physical disks on which all of these data lie are still only capable of moving "X" MB per second (a throughput and overall sizing consideration), and the window of time to perform all SAP component database and other backups to tape may be limited as well (an execution window consideration).

- To actually host an SAP database, MCOD may leverage single or multiple servers running one or more operating systems. If the former approach is taken, and multiple components are collapsed at the server layer as well, a whole other reason for stress testing exists.

- When MCOD was first introduced, it was made clear that OLTP (online transaction processing) and OLAP systems should be housed on different databases; combining R/3 and BW, for example, was a no-no. Today, this restriction has been lifted. However, just because SAP supports lots of mySAP and other SAP products sharing the same physical database does not mean that your hardware solution is optimized for this use. Consider the fact that many disk subsystems operate best when certain parameters are set based on the nature of the I/O being supported. Even more fundamentally, consider that to achieve optimal throughput at a high level, disk subsystems are regularly tuned for high-read performance in the case of OLAP systems, or tweaked for maximum write performance in the case of OLTP systems, and you'll begin to understand the need for load testing your particular MCOD implementation.

In regard to this last point, note that SAP classifies only BW and SEM as OLAP solutions. All other SAP components—R/3, CRM, APO, SRM/EBP, Workplace, and so on—are looked on as transactional systems as far as MCOD is concerned.

3.4.   Testing, Tuning, and the SAP System Landscape

As you realize by now, implementing and supporting an SAP solution means more than simply running a production system; on the contrary, a single SAP production solution—like R/3 or SAP APO—typically requires, *at a minimum,* two or more other systems that support it in one way or another. Each of the supporting systems plays a role that simply cannot be played by production; indeed, maintaining the availability of production would be nearly impossible without its supporting cast.

Unfortunately, each incremental system requires its own server and disk subsystem hardware, OS and database software, mySAP component instance, and so on, adding significantly to the cost to deploy and maintain an SAP solution (or any enterprise solution, for that matter). But, as I said before, the tradeoff equates to sacrificing the availability of the production system: Would you really want to take the risk of developing, functionally testing, load testing, and training your end users and others on the same system used to host what is most likely a mission-critical application? I didn't think so!

Thus, a dedicated system useful for stress testing your environment is often added to the mix of other systems responsible for hosting development and other testing and training activities. The collection of all of this gear—all of the systems—is referred to as the SAP system landscape. A three-system landscape consists of three systems (e.g., Development, Test, and Production), and a four-system landscape consists of four systems (perhaps a Staging or Stress test system is added to the mix), and so on. Note that there is no real "standard" landscape, though most of the time a three-system landscape like that described previously is implemented.

In turn, each SAP product requires its own SAP system landscape, too. Thus, if you have deployed SAP R/3, you'll probably have a three- or four-system landscape (or larger) deployed to support it, and for every mySAP solution in your environment you'll need a similar setup. Obviously, if a Stress-Test system was deployed for each SAP product or component, the costs would quickly grow out of hand for most SAP shops. A dedicated stress-testing environment might be warranted in other shops, however, if the risk of *not* meeting performance metrics or SLAs outweighed the cost of a dedicated Stress-Test system. I suggest doing the math to determine the right answer for you, with the understanding that, in my experience, very few shops need more than a single shared Stress-Test system (and it's not uncommon to make due with a dual-purpose well-equipped SAP Technical Sandbox, too).

The key role of your dedicated Stress-Test system—also called a Staging or Pre-Prod system, and sometimes implemented as part of your Test or Technical Sandbox system—is to prove that your uniquely crafted SAP solution meets your response time and throughput needs. Thus, it's critical that the stress-test environment matches what you run in production; in a perfect world, the entire SAP Technology Stack, from the architecture up through the hardware configuration, OS, database, and version/patch levels of the mySAP component should be identical. In other words, if in production you run a 16-way database server with 8GB of RAM and five application servers, each with four processors and 3GB of RAM, you really need the same hardware setup in your stress-testing environment. Variations make it difficult if not impossible to do apples-to-apples comparisons between Production and your Stress Test systems. And variations simply invite risks, risks that might very well be acceptable, but must be understood and taken into account when conducting performance testing.

3.4.1.   Typical Landscapes for mySAP Solutions

As mentioned previously, the most usual method of deploying an SAP product or component is in the form of a three-system landscape, usually made up of a production system supported behind the scenes by a dedicated Development system and another separate Test or Quality Assurance system. Outside of your Stress Test system, these and other SAP system landscape "residents" are listed as follows:

- Development system
- Test system
- Technical Sandbox system
- Business Sandbox system
- Training system
- Staging system
- Production system
- Disaster Recovery (DR) system

The Development system supports initial and continued SAP configuration and/or customization, maintenance, and lifecycle-driven updates and patches. As the originator of business-process–related configuration and customization changes that will eventually be promoted into the production system, Development typically plays a very limited role in stress testing; even then, it's at most single-user testing designed to quantify performance surrounding ABAP or Java code, database throughput, locking, and so on. Rarely is a Development system used for full-blown stress testing—there's simply too much development work to warrant this.

The Test system (sometimes called the Consolidation, Quality Assurance, or Integration system) is commonly deployed, making business process integration and functional testing possible. Given this "QA" role, it's quite common to see the Test system used for stress testing. But, like the Development box, the level of activity supported by Test means that carving time out of its busy schedule, to be used for stress testing, will be difficult at best. It is precisely this enormous magnitude of testing activity, in fact, that drives the adoption of many other, more narrowly focused systems, discussed in the following paragraphs.

A Technical Sandbox system, if deployed and properly stocked, can meet the stress-testing needs of a suite of SAP system landscapes. Many of my customers refer to their Technical Sandbox as their "best kept secret"; it supports much more than stress testing, often playing a key training role in helping the SAP IT staff maintain a high level of competency in their particular SAP Technology Stack. Of course, the Technical Sandbox is only as good as the technology used within it; an environment incomplete in terms of architecture, topology, hardware components, and so on—compared with the production system it is attempting to emulate—is only partially capable of modeling a true production load.

The often-deployed Business Sandbox, used by the SAP development team (SAP ABAP, HTML, and Java programmers and other developers) in support of learning, testing, and practicing their trade, typically plays no role in stress testing, with a couple of exceptions. For example, the Business Sandbox can prove helpful in characterizing and quantifying the impact of updated business-process and other functional changes. The Business Sandbox is also a good place for conducting basic single-user testing, discussed previously regarding the Development system.

Similarly, a dedicated Training system is earmarked almost exclusively for the benefit of SAP end users, and in some cases a subset of a deployment team's technical resources. As such, it usually looks nothing like production, and therefore is not capable of anything more useful than a subset of the single-user testing typically performed on Development or the Business Sandbox.

On the other hand, a Staging system (if deployed) is practically by definition identical to production, and therefore ideal for end-to-end mySAP Business Suite stress testing. The Staging system is deployed by companies that need to mitigate most of the risk related to change control, upgrades, and any technology stack updates, no matter how small the changes might be perceived to be. Thus, it is one of the final stops in the "promote to production" process in the largest or most mission-critical SAP system landscapes, allowing for real-world performance testing and tuning on a system identical (or nearly so) to production.

The production system itself sometimes plays a role in stress testing prior to Go-Live, or in the case of a mass technology refresh where a completely new SAP production system is installed and configured prior to retiring an older production system. This obviously makes a lot of sense, if financially possible. Normally, though, the production system is relegated to the critical role of supporting its various end-user communities and associated business groups, making the business processes running on SAP available—the sole reason an SAP enterprise solution was implemented in the first place.

Finally, for customers who need the greatest levels of business continuity, a DR system is often deployed within the SAP system landscape. The DR system may or may not look anything like production. The mission of a DR system is first and foremost to host the users normally taken care of by the production system (which would by default be "down" or otherwise unavailable when the DR system is in use, outside of requisite annual disaster recovery and failover training). For a number of years, many of my customers built out and maintained DR systems that modeled production or at least a subset of it. These resources tended to sit idle for extended periods of time, and therefore made excellent stress-testing platforms. But they were expensive! Today, I tend to see a greater mix of gear imperfectly matched to production, but earmarked nonetheless to take over in case of a disaster. I recommend looking into your particular situation, if indeed you have deployed or intend to deploy a DR system, to determine what role the system might play with regard to stress testing or SAP Technology Stack–specific performance tuning. After all, you might have a perfect foundation for stress testing easily within reach, without the need to spend a whole lot of incremental budget.

3.4.2.   Leveraging Your Landscape for Testing and Tuning

As discussed previously, a number of systems may be deployed within a particular solution's SAP system landscape. There is no one right answer for everyone, but in my experience, a four-system landscape or larger tends to satisfy the needs of both the IT team supporting SAP and the business groups which in turn represent their customer base. The tricky part is to determine exactly what your four-system landscape should include! Development, Test (for core functional and integration testing), and Production should exist for starters, but what should the fourth system consist of, and how should it be configured? If you have the budget, I personally prefer a Staging system configured identically to Production, shared among a number of organizations to satisfy multiple roles like supporting both DR and end-user training needs in addition to comprehensive stress testing. If this solution seems risky to you, you're probably a candidate for an even larger SAP system landscape. On the other hand, if this seems like overkill, then perhaps a three-system landscape with a robustly configured Test system is the right answer.

In the end, however, you will also need to consider different landscape component deployment options, like the use of physical hardware partitioning, software partitioning, installing and managing multiple SAP instances in a single OS environment (stacking), and so on. How you will leverage shared resources needs to be taken into account early on, too. Network infrastructure, disk subsystems (especially those tied to SAN solutions), and tape backup/restore gear all represent opportunities to save money but potentially complicate resource access, utilization, performance baselining, and future SAP Technology Stack upgrades.

3.5   Tools and Approaches

As I mentioned earlier, if you've forgotten what a particular acronym stands for, or need a refresher on SAP's products and components, please refer to SAP's Web site, or to the book's ftp site.

CHAPTER 4

Turning Business and IT Goals into Success Criteria

An unknown person said many years ago, "Some people dream of success, while others wake up and work hard at it." I couldn't agree more! To gain the most benefit from your mySAP solutions in terms of increased performance and lowest TCO, the IT and Business teams must wake up and recognize that a certain amount of effort will be required both before and after Go-Live. This chapter works through the process of converting your solution vision into business and IT goals, followed by concrete methods of determining to what degree these goals have been met. Thus, we will first need to take a closer look at how to map the high-level "solution characteristics" ultimately desired of your SAP system (e.g., awesome performance, high availability, and low cost of ownership) into SAP system business and IT goals. In doing so, I will discuss what I consider to be the three primary stress-testing/performance-tuning methods, each focused on very different but equally valuable approaches to repeatable testing and tuning. In the same manner, I will then take a closer look at the various tool sets germane to each method. Likewise, I'll note why certain tools are better positioned than others for a particular testing type, especially in light of meeting a company's unique performance-related desires or goals. Finally, with goals and objectives nailed down, tempered by the realities of the most appropriate testing/tuning method and its requisite tool sets, I will wrap up the chapter by identifying and discussing quantifiable stress-testing *success criteria*—the criteria against which your testing results may be measured to verify you indeed have been successful in proving what you set out to prove. For example, concrete success criteria will prove to IT managers without a shadow of a doubt, and in a measurable way, that their new system is as truly "awesome" as they were told it would be, in terms of a defined set of performance metrics. Figure 4–1 illustrates a process flow for clarification.

4.1. A Closer Look at Goals, Business Processes, and Data

As discussed in Chapter 2, the solution characteristics you value, coupled with your business goals/objectives, help shape the type of system you initially employ. Later, these solution characteristics color the types of changes and upgrades you introduce over time. It's therefore critical that your established solution characteristics and business goals be captured, carefully docu-

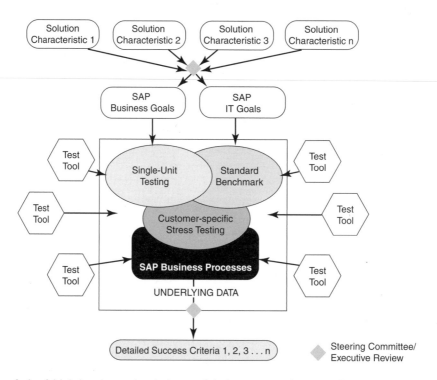

Figure 4–1   A high-level overview helps explain how to translate your "eyes closed" solution vision and specific solution characteristics into business and IT goals, followed in turn by stress-testing/performance-tuning success criteria.

mented, and regularly reviewed prior to making changes to your SAP Technology Stack. Just as important, the business drivers that drove each particular solution characteristic, or in some way supported your goals, must be documented! For example, if one of your business goals is to achieve an average response time of less than 1 second for 90% of your core SAP R/3 online transactions, you need to document from where that requirement came. Was it the result of a business stakeholders' meeting? Did your power users come together and agree on a set of service level and response-time metrics for each SAP functional area? Did your CIO simply toss out the number based on something he or she learned from an industry colleague or magazine article? No matter what the case, the details surrounding the goal—and the goal itself—need to be carefully recorded. If you think about the potential problems you could run into by *not* doing so (e.g., performance perception problems, incurring performance penalties, affecting end-user customer satisfaction, and even risking the loss of clientele to competitors), my reasoning should be self-evident. Review your goals prior to planning for any SAP system landscape system changes. Doing so will help ensure that your prechange test plans and postchange success criteria uphold or otherwise reinforce your goals. And, keep in mind that goals come in two flavors: business goals and what I call "IT goals." Although the former is obvious, the idea behind IT goals may not be. In short, IT goals tend to

- Reflect TCO and other budget-centric IT-internal matters that bound the scope and duration, and in other ways limit what IT may financially pursue
- Reflect current staffing skill-sets, again limiting the kinds of services and projects IT will be comfortable pursuing and delivering
- Focus on providing a competitive service to its user community—like a highly available SAP system—with or without the understanding that other entities are often just as capable of performing the service, too (e.g., outsourcers, in-sourced consulting parties, and application service providers)

Thus, IT goals at the end of the day should embody creating and maintaining a system that meets the business's high availability, scalability, and similar needs. Additionally, the goals themselves should be achievable, reflecting the organizations' core competencies and financial means. IT support organizations should never lose sight of one key fact—that they are there to service the business, not the other way around. Finally, I also recommend that you regularly review both your business and IT goals to ensure that they still reflect your business's needs *today,* as implied by your SAP system's SLAs and any other customer-driven requirements. That is, real-world goals rarely remain static too long—ever-changing SAP systems and fast-moving customer environments tend to make current goals obsolete. I encourage you to therefore review and potentially update your goals at least twice a year.

4.1.1.   Identifying Key Solution Characteristics

When it comes to stress testing and performance tuning, the key solution characteristics are, without a doubt, *response times* and *throughput metrics.* Examples include the following:

- Specifying the maximum time required to commit a change to an existing item, or insert a new item (e.g., a sales order) into your database. This is usually measured in terms of both SAP application server response time and DB server response time, though other measurements come into play (like SAPGUI build time, network time, the time spent waiting for an SAP work process, and so on).
- Similarly, you might quantify your response-time requirements to indicate the need to process all of the "screens" of a specific business transaction within a specific amount of time. Thus, the response times of each individual screen is important, but so is the throughput realized in a precise time period.
- In the same manner, it's common to monitor the response time of long-running batch or background jobs, often measured in start-to-finish "wall clock" time, as a batch process takes many minutes and even hours to execute.
- In other cases, you might wish to quantify the potential capacity or volume of transactions, reports, or queries that a particular SAP Technology Stack is capable of processing in a particular period of time (e.g., an execution window).

However, solution characteristics outside the realm of good performance are just as important to the community using the system, if not more so. Characteristics like an SAP solution's degree of availability, ease of manageability, potential to scale on demand or at least quickly, and so on often play critical secondary roles in the course of assembling measurable testing goals. Consider the following:

- Scalability: to prove that a custom SAP solution can scale to whatever level is necessary to meet not only the daily typical peak load expected but also the quarter-end and seasonal peaks that could otherwise bring a system to its knees, and frustrate its end-users. In one case, I worked with a branch of the military to prove that our proposed solution could scale in times of war to support 10 times the number of online users normally supported. More typically, though, the need to scale 2 times the number of online users in certain cases is fairly common in my experience.
- Availability: to prove that an SAP solution can indeed host a certain online user or batch load after a system *failover* (where the production instance moves or "fails over" to another node in a multinode cluster or offsite data-center facility, for instance, should the first node fail). In other cases, a system's *resiliency* might be more important to quantify, like how well a system performs after it suffers a failure of critical but redundancy-protected system components. Examples are abundant—failure of one or more disk drives in a RAID array, or one network card in a redundant pair of cards, or a fan in a server cooled by many fans all represent potential resiliency tests.
- Solution viability: in the case of new mySAP Business Suite components or the technology products on which an SAP solution resides, a particular solution stack might undergo testing just to verify that the stack itself—infrastructure, server and disk subsystem hardware, OS DBMS, and so on—is ready for the real world.
- Operational viability: in other instances, the performance or scalability of a solution might be unquestioned, but support in regard to enterprise management options, backup/restore software package capabilities, the ability to easily configure or change a technology component, and so on might be uncertain.

Many other solution characteristics exist as well. The key is to map your particular solution characteristics to your business and IT goals. Once this is accomplished, the next step—identifying actual business processes that represent a company's core processes, or represent processes that are expected to really exercise your SAP system—can then be addressed.

4.1.2.   Identifying Real-World Business Processes to Be Tested

Your goals will reflect more than a collection of solution characteristics. Why? Because no matter how important response times and throughput are, you must still quantify the "what" that is being measured—the discrete one-off business transactions, or more commonly, the multiple-transaction processes that make up an end-to-end *business process*. The time spent in identifying the best transactions or business processes to execute in support of your testing and tuning goals is time well spent indeed. In my experience, in fact, my production clients and I tend to spend many hours, sometimes days, poring over real-world performance statistics to identify not only the top X transactions in terms of popularity but also those transactions responsible for consuming the most CPU, disk, and other system resources (using ST03 workload data, for those of you who have forgotten already). As discussed in Chapter 3, it's a straightforward matter of pulling these data out of CCMS for your respective SAP systems, and paying attention to daily, weekly, and monthly peaks and averages to determine the usual system "hogs." The less frequently executed transactions, and processes that execute very few steps but consume great resources, are identified in this way as well.

Outside of strictly performance realms, though, it's important to identify the most appropriate transactions or business processes for other reasons, too. These transactions or business processes are as follows:

- Transactions that are essential to your business—for example, those that underpin the lion's share of your revenue (R/3 SD and whole CRM and APO scenarios) or impact the greatest number of end users (R/3 systems in general)—are natural candidates for stress testing.
- As mentioned earlier, transactions that drive your key "heavy" functional areas tend to be favored over those that drive your "light" functional areas when it comes to stress testing your end-to-end technology stack. Not to say that the light transactions aren't important, they're just not *as* important!
- Business processes that are particularly complex in terms of the number of underlying mySAP components and other applications on which they execute or depend can also make good testing candidates, if for nothing else than the fact that they are predisposed to eventually becoming resource hogs. Why? Because in my experience, their complexity tends to mask tiny initial performance concerns, making full-blown problems that arise later difficult to understand and time-consuming to rectify. Thus, the kind of performance baseline that can be realized through comprehensive stress testing of these complex processes is very important up front.
- Business processes that exercise your system in a specific manner may have value, too. Consider a business process that performs many database updates, such as write operations like inserts and appends. It would be an excellent candidate for a disk subsystem upgrade project, where the goal of the upgrade might be to dramatically increase write throughput and decrease average database update times. However, the same business process would not be a good candidate if your goal was simply to simulate your typical database load, which tends to be read intensive rather than write intensive (though, as I've stated before, these types of systems are actually often optimized for write access, despite the fact that many SAP OLTP systems like R/3 and CRM tend to run something closer to 94% read operations and 6% write operations).
- Other business processes may show up on a stress test's radar simply by virtue of the fact that they need to execute in a particular timeframe (e.g., 2 hours), or during an es-

tablished execution window already heavily loaded with other online or batch processes. Consider a company that pulls data from SAP BW into R/3 during the same 2-hour period in which they are attempting to complete heavy month-end processing, and it should be apparent that all processes executing within the execution window (and all systems on which these processes execute) are excellent candidates for optimization.

- Finally, various business processes or transactions may be limited in terms of when or how they're executed, which by their very nature therefore prohibits their use in a stress test. For example, not all R/3 transactions may be executed by the HTML browser when it comes to ITS-enabled systems—certain transactions simply do not exist natively in certain versions of ITS. Similarly, transactions that "roll up" results or otherwise perform a one-time operation (e.g., a "pick list" function performed at the end of a day of creating new sales orders) simply do not lend themselves to repetitive processing; other stress-test approaches need to be taken if the process is earmarked as critical.

Identifying the best business processes to serve as your testing and tuning foundation is very important. Equally important, though, is our next topic—identifying whether your preferred business processes encompass the data behind them to be truly testworthy.

4.1.3.   Identifying Stress-Test Data Requirements

Once your key business processes are identified, you must determine if you actually have the data to support a stress test. Without the proper data *mix,* in conjunction with a sufficient *quantity* of data, you risk executing business processes that fail to really exercise or "stress" your system at all. Consider the following scenarios:

- It almost goes without saying—your data mix must represent the data necessary to execute the business transactions you wish to test. If, for example, you wish to have 100 users execute R/3's VA01 to simulate the creation of many sales orders at once, it might not make for a valid stress test (in your particular case) to execute sales orders against a particular set of company codes, or plants, or storage locations; your need for data might be very specific in this regard. That is, you might wish only to execute sales orders that trigger your configure/build-to-order mechanism, or you might desire to test new underlying inventory check and fulfillment processes that are only applicable to a certain company code. The set of data that is valid, then, is therefore merely a subset of all of your sales order input data.
- Taking the idea of a proper data mix to the next level: if you don't have *enough* good data, you'll only wind up using the same data over and over again in your stress test— for example, picture your 100 users all executing the same sales order process, consisting of identical goods from a single plant for the same customer. By limiting the quantity and variety of these data, the SAP Technology Stack being tested will not be truly "stressed"—the load borne by the disk subsystem will taper off to nothing, as it quickly

caches the little bit of customer and master data necessary to execute the sales transaction. After the first few sales orders, subsequent sales orders will never even exercise the physical disk drives behind the cache! In the end, your system will therefore appear very capable, when in fact the whole stress test was contrived and artificial, and no performance tuning will be performed simply because it never seemed to be necessary in the first place.

- Lack of data can also result in *data locking*, where many users and the business processes they are executing are waiting for a piece of data—an object, a table, and so forth—to be released. Data locking has the reverse impact on a system as that already described: response times and throughput rates appear dreadfully slow, instead of artificially fast, though the system's resource utilization seems to be low by many measurements.

- In my experience, your data mix will rarely be too large. However, too many data can be a really bad thing, too: if you expect your database not to exceed 500GB over the next 2 years, for example, you would be doing your stress test a disservice to build out a large testing system housing a terabyte of data. The load borne by the disk subsystem would be unrealistic, just as it was in the case of having too few data, and the value of the entire test would therefore be suspect as well.

Given the previously described scenarios, if the data at your disposal are lacking in any way, and you simply cannot obtain more, the business process you wish to use in your stress testing should probably be tossed in favor of a more "data-friendly" process. On the other hand, if your goal is solely to test a particular business process, rather than the application or technology underneath it, understand that you will be limited to single-user testing at best—not a bad way to go in some instances, but certainly not the best answer for many situations.

4.2. Understanding Stress-Test Methods

All SAP computing environments benefit at one time or another from different approaches to performance testing and tuning, because of the simple fact that not all SAP system landscape changes dictate full-blown and relatively expensive stress testing. Instead, to test smaller-scope SAP Technology Stack changes or to evaluate new SAP business processes, platforms, and solutions, other methods tend to be both more appropriate and less taxing from a budget, people, and other resource perspective. I tend to assign these distinctive stress-testing approaches into three high-level "umbrella" methodologies or methods, discussed next.

4.2.1. Level One—Single-Unit Testing: Confirming Component Hardware Stack Performance

Sometimes called single-unit, single-user, or system-level stress testing, this most basic stress-testing method focuses on optimizing discrete technology subsystems, testing the impact of a particular process or load generated by a single source, or conducting other "single-unit" testing. Thus, rather than leveraging the load placed on a system by hundreds or even thousands of end users and/or batch processes, single-unit testing is accomplished through the use of a single "user," be it at the SAP front-end client level, the SAP application layer, or any other technology layer underneath. Single-unit and single-user testing was covered in some detail back in Chapter 2. For the sake of simplicity, I have rolled up all of this kind of fundamental performance testing into what I call "Level One" testing. Major reasons for Level One testing include the following:

- To learn the impact that new features, increased volumes, or alternate business decisions have on a particular technology stack. This is often referred to in the industry as *capacity characterization tests* and is a mainstay of testing, where a single factor or condition is changed, and then the overall performance of the system is measured through single-user testing. I also call this *delta testing*.
- To establish a baseline for each subsystem or component in the SAP Technology Stack, to be reanalyzed and measured again throughout the lifecycle of an SAP solution as changes are promoted through the system landscape.
- To better understand what the future holds—for example, where the greatest potential performance bottlenecks lie in the future, based on different load and growth scenarios.
- Ultimately, to drive intelligent budgeting for system upgrades and other changes—if a system's current performance and overall capacity are understood, it's easier to plan intelligently and proactively when it comes to SAP Technology Stack upgrades.

Overall, Level One stress testing directs the tuning of your current production or soon-to-be-deployed new system, in that it lets you intelligently tweak and tune the individual technology stack layers and discrete subsystems/components so that each operates well in a standalone manner. Such a precursor to full-blown testing and tuning, or *pretuning,* serves as an excellent foundation for broader end-to-end system or solution tuning, too—when each underlying component is optimized, it makes it easier to intelligently optimize the holistic technology stack. Throughout the book, therefore, I devote much attention to Level One testing—the testing and tuning of low-level components that make up a system in terms of its underlying network infrastructure, server hardware/OS, disk subsystem and database, mySAP Business Suite component, and front-end client. Level One testing makes Level Two and Level Three testing—described next—that much more valuable and in most cases that much easier to quickly conduct!

4.2.2.   Level Two Testing—Where SAP Standard Benchmarking Fits In

Beyond system-level and single-unit testing lies a unique stress-testing opportunity applicable to fewer scenarios or customers but valuable in its own right. This is called *SAP Standard Benchmarking,* and, in a nutshell, it allows an organization to test many different mySAP solutions and components and even key transactions or entire business processes. The downside? Neither the business processes nor the underlying data are "yours"—each benchmark kit ships with standard data and business processes to execute against these data, neither of which might be applicable in your own case. Rather, the configuration and contents of the entire system are fabricated for the sole purpose of allowing testing and general system characterization below the SAP application layer. Level Two testing is really just another way to conduct delta testing *between* different platforms, but from an application-layer perspective. The load placed on the system, by virtue of the fact that it's SAP related, is presumably more valuable in testing a system compared with low-level component testing.

SAP AG creates and publishes *Benchmark Kits* for most of its products, making these kits available to SAP technology partners for the primary purpose of executing benchmarks. The benchmarks are then published, providing comparative results; these in turn allow prospective SAP customers the opportunity to intelligently compare different vendors' hardware configurations. Beyond this primary use of benchmark kits by technology partners like HP, IBM, Fujitsu, Unisys, Dell, and so on, it may still make sense for a prospective SAP shop to execute its own custom SAP Standard Application Benchmark. This Level Two approach to stress testing is valuable in that it allows you to characterize your one-of-a-kind SAP Technology Stack, in effect benchmarking it against your older system at each stage in its own lifecycle evolution, as changes are introduced over time throughout the stack.

Before you run off and perform a huge technology refresh or begin planning for a major SAP release upgrade, the findings from executing a standard SAP benchmark can be worth a small mint. This repeatable, canned approach to technology stack testing can provide great savings when it comes to preparing for upgrading various hardware technology layers or investing in new OS and DB software licensing. True, such a "canned" approach does not leverage your own customer-specific data and business processes. But the ability to compare your current system against a newly architected system—and do so by driving the SAP application layer rather than simpler, less compelling hardware subsystems underneath the covers—makes for excellent apples-to-apples testing between different hardware and software vendors. It's a great way to "prove" the overall viability of a custom-architected SAP solution, too, hence the generic term *proof-of-concept* testing sometimes applied to this and other forms of stress or load testing.

From an SAP customer's perspective, this standard benchmarking approach pays great dividends, too: first and foremost, the SAP IT organization benefits from observing firsthand a specific SAP Technology Stack in action. Second, because the same benchmark kit is used by each hardware vendor, such an approach crosses the lines of disparate hardware technologies; the processes and data used in the execution and monitoring of an SAP benchmark are necessarily unswerving and consistent, as you would expect of a world-class enterprise benchmark. This consistency is the only reason you can truly compare a SAP Sun/Oracle solution to one built on Intel/SQL Server. Third, because a hardware purchase may lie in the balance, it's not uncommon for a hardware or other technology partner to foot at least part of the testing bill, making the project's budget more palatable. And finally, given the variety of standard benchmark kits available from SAP, it's an easy way out for companies still in development, or simply considering the likely deployment of a new mySAP Business Suite or ERP system. Here are the mySAP components and technology solutions for which a standard benchmark kit is available today:

- mySAP BI, which focuses on SAP BW
- mySAP CRM, addressing Internet sales and the CIC functions
- Several e-commerce solutions
- mySAP Financials, focused specifically on SAP R/3's FI functional area
- mySAP Human Resources (HR), specifically R/3 Cross-Application Time Sheets (CATS) and HR's payroll process
- mySAP Product Lifecycle Management
- mySAP SCM, which consists of SAP APO, ATO (Available to Promise) functionality, and R/3's core supply chain functional areas (MM, PP, SD, and WM)
- Various industry solutions, such as retail and banking utilities

In the end, then, Level Two testing such as that made possible by SAP's benchmark kits can prove especially useful in new implementations or major upgrades, where the new or refreshed hardware platform has not likely been nailed down. Level Two testing is also ideal for evaluation-focused testing once you're in production; different configurations and even technology approaches or options can be quickly compared to one another because the application layer remains consistent. Standard SAP benchmark kits provide another minor but useful benefit, too: for organizations or individuals unfamiliar with a particular SAP product or component, a benchmark kit provides a certain amount of insight into what are "typical" business processes or data constructs. This kind of fundamental application-specific knowledge also can prove especially useful in the next type of testing, Level Three testing.

4.2.3.   Level Three Testing—Custom Proof-of-Concept Testing

The most challenging type of stress testing, in large part because of the inherent complexity surrounding what it takes to build and load test an operational SAP system, goes by many different names. I sometimes refer to it as Level Three testing, but use many other labels as well. Terms like *application stress testing, customer-specific business process load testing,* and *proof-of-concept stress-test engagements* all boil down to essentially the same thing:

- An SAP Technology Stack must be built that closely emulates the actual production environment (unless, of course, the production environment is available "off hours" for testing—not very common but possible—or you're in a position to lease or otherwise borrow hardware).
- A customer's actual business processes and data must be dropped into the system's DB server, usually in the form of a database copy or restore (or even a database migration if different database releases or vendors are involved).
- Customer-specific business processes need to be analyzed and then scripted such that they can be executed over and over again in a repeatable, measurable, and realistic manner. This represents the most time-consuming portion of many performance tests, in my experience, ranging from a few days to perhaps 2 months.

- A test execution infrastructure needs to be designed and deployed, including a test's Benchmark Driver, which is nothing more than one or more servers configured with software to manage and host the "driver" of your business process scripts and any other load-generating programs—it is from this type of infrastructure that individual stress-test runs are executed, monitored, and analyzed.
- Both a test plan and execution checklist need to be developed that reflect all of the aforementioned points. The former lays out the high-level tasks relevant to the stress test, whereas the latter details the precise step-by-step process each individual stress-test run will follow as it is executed, monitored, and analyzed after the fact.
- Real or virtual "users" or batch processes must be "kicked off" such that the previously scripted business processes are executed concurrently, in effect performing transactions and other workflows that simulate the load of real-world users. This load may range widely, depending on what needs to be tested. In my experience, this load ranges from a subset of the average user load, to a number of hard-hitting batch processes, to a load identical (or nearly so) to the load expected to be borne by the real production system during peak processing periods.
- Finally, the results of each stress-test run need to be compiled and compared against a baseline, or other test runs, to drive intelligent tuning of the SAP Technology Stack.

The steps outlined in the preceding list are by no means comprehensive but seek instead to outline the general amount of work that needs to go into architecting and executing a Level Three stress test. Additional steps, including validation of the business processes, creation of the data necessary to perform test runs, starting from a "known" state prior to each stress-test run, and determination whether to use virtual users or real ones, may be necessary in your particular case, as might many other tasks and activities. Fear not, though; the bulk of this book beyond Chapter 5 discusses when those tasks are necessary, and how to execute those tasks, in great detail! Suffice it to say here, though, that a Level Three stress test only affords the kind of real-world value it provides *because* it seeks to model your equally complex production SAP system. This modeling takes time, careful planning, and an array of resources, as you'll see later.

4.3.   Developing Solid Real-World Success Criteria

With solution characteristics, goals, and stress-testing methods behind us, it is time to look at developing stress-test "success criteria"—the specific measurements and other decisive factors identified up front and then tracked to validate to what *degree* a particular testing and tuning effort has been successful. Chapter 6 discusses how this information will help us select and pilot what look to be the most appropriate test tools. But first, we must determine what the "measuring stick" looks like—the thing against which future measurements will be taken. In the world of testing, this is called a baseline.

Baselines come in two fundamental flavors, each of which maps back to how I defined "performance" early on in the book. In the first case, a baseline might be represented by the amount of work, or throughput, a particular SAP Technology Stack can process in something like 30 minutes. Such a measurement is recorded in transactions per hour, SAP dialog steps per hour, or some other such dimension, and the timeframe for executing the test (in this case, 30 minutes) remains constant. In the second case, though, *time* becomes the variable, and the workload is instead locked down. Thus, a workload-driven time-oriented baseline might refer to the average response time of 1,000 representative transactions, or how many minutes 1,000 transactions took to execute beginning to end. Tests that execute faster imply a faster underpinning technology solution, confirming that recent performance tuning you may have performed resulted in a positive increase in performance (versus what the baseline configuration was capable of pushing). In the end, all baselines, and indeed all performance measurements, can be captured and evaluated against one another using this "time versus throughput" method.

Some of you may wonder why a performance baseline needs to be established: your thinking may be along the lines of "you either meet a system's SLAs or you fail to meet them, period." Although such thinking is logical, it does not take into account the granularity necessary to measure performance. And, without measurement, there is little way to tell if you can simply tweak a system's performance to meet your SLA requirements, or if the current system is nowhere close to meeting your requirements and must instead be completely tossed out in favor of starting over. Other reasons for capturing a baseline include the following:

- To quantifiably prove that your SAP implementation delivers better online or batch performance than the system it replaced (assuming that "better" is indeed a goal; lower cost or improved availability might be the motivating factors in your particular case).
- To verify that a new mySAP solution performs as expected, promised, or advertised. That is, a baseline might simply represent the "minimally acceptable worst case" performance expected of each layer in the technology stack. Thus, a baseline helps determine whether future stress-test runs are indeed successful.
- To provide a useful measuring stick after every major change wave. My smartest or most risk-averse SAP clients execute a small core set of transactions and basic hardware utilities after any changes are made to the Production system, to ensure that it still performs at least as well as it did previously. In other cases, a baseline will also help prove that a solution component upgrade or replacement indeed resulted in a faster system; the proof lies in the performance delta between the baseline statistical data and the results of your updated testing performed shortly after the component upgrade.

As mentioned earlier, quite often stress-test success criteria relate to either the performance observed by the end users of the system or the amount of work completed in a specific time period. In many cases, both relative performance and hard throughput statistics are collected. Some of the most common success criteria in my experience include the following:

- The ability to track the specific number of users logged into the system, to ensure, for example, that 1,000 users are logged in. Use SAP CCMS transaction AL08 or ST07 to verify this value, along with output from the tool used to drive your testing.
- The ability to track the percentage of logged-in users who are actually "busy." Also called concurrent users, this is a subset of total logged-in users, and can be mapped back to what a real production system is expected to host. Use transaction ST07, specifically looking at the number of users actively using a work process.
- The ability to achieve an average response time for all online users or for users executing transactions in specific functional areas. You might want to prove that the typical SAP FI user enjoys a half-second average response time, and an SAP PM user has an average response time of less than 1 second. After executing a stress-test run, update CCMS numbers (using the "Build Totals" button in transaction ST03), and then rerun transaction ST03 to verify the average response time for a particular set of transactions or application servers.
- The ability to achieve a specific number of concurrent processes while monitoring the average SAP system utilization. This process indicates how much work a system is capable of processing. And, by tracking the specific number of SAP dialog, batch, and update work processes that are active simultaneously, along with user and batch job counts, the overall load on the system may be characterized quite well. For example, if you have configured your system with four online user application servers and two batch servers, where the former is configured for 24 dialog work processes and the latter for 8, a stress test might seek to utilize 65% of these work processes and then observe average response times or throughput values (using transactions like SM66 and SM51 to track work processes, ST07/AL08 to track users, and SM37 to track background jobs).

On the other hand, your success criteria might be geared around completing a specific amount of work (consisting of a specific mix of online users and batch processes) in a certain amount of time, say 30 minutes. For instance, a system might be required to process 18,000 one-line item sales orders and 6,000 five-line item sales orders in a 30-minute execution window (perhaps this represents the peak processing needs of the system). In another case, you may need to process 30 custom reports in less than 1 hour, or completely execute a certain "standard" suite of business transactions in an hour. It's especially easy to measure how well you meet your success criteria in this way: simply compare the number of completed transactions to your goal, such that you prove your system can process 93% of your load (thus failing your success criteria), for example, or 104% of your peak expected load (in this case, passing with room to spare).

Don't forget to quantify your throughput-based success criteria. As I mentioned earlier, you'll want to specify maximum average resource utilization parameters. Thus, your success factors might involve ensuring that you process a certain load but with the caveat that you truly meet your success criteria only if the average CPU utilization does not exceed 65%, or the average disk queue lengths never rise above two per physical disk, or memory utilization never drives greater than 2% of Pagefile or Swap consumption, for example. And, you'll want to set peak parameters in addition to the averages just noted, again to give you a set of "not to exceed" boundaries within which to quantify the performance of your system. More details regarding crafting various success criteria and metrics are presented in the following section.

4.3.1.   The Basic Measurement: Wall-Clock Time

Though I used to view this first method of measuring performance as a crude last resort of sorts, I have actually found it more and more useful to me over the years. In short, measuring wall-clock time can be as simple as kicking off or ending a stress-test run or a single-unit transaction run, and looking at a clock to note when you started and stopped the test run. As such, a wall-clock test is inherently easy to administer and apply to any test run involving any mySAP component or transaction *where a consistent workload is applied.* Wall-clock testing is especially useful when single-user testing makes the most sense (i.e., when a project team does not have the time nor budget to invest in scripting lots of discrete transactions executed by thousands of virtual users). The following points provide insight into what I have learned over the years, helping to make the data you acquire from wall-clock testing that much more valuable or precise:

- Wall-clock testing is normally all about measuring the amount of time that elapses in processing a known, consistent workload. The assumption is that the faster the workload is processed, the better tuned (or more capable) the SAP configuration is, as shown in Figure 4–2. Thus, it's of paramount importance first and foremost that the workload is indeed consistent. If you have modeled a particular business process from end to end and wish to really ensure that it is repeatable and consistent, you must script it. Doing otherwise—like manually watching for discrete transactions to end so that you can manually start the next transaction in a business process—introduces error and ultimately makes the test results less precise. You should be capturing the actual "wall clock" time via your scripts, too, so as to take this error-prone process out of the picture. If that's not possible, diligently use a precise timing tool (Barefoot Productions' eTimer preferably, or Microsoft's inbuilt clock, worst-case).
- Wall-clock time also depends on your business processes using consistent data. Therefore, do not try to invoke any special randomization techniques in your scripts or manual execution processes, period. True randomization has no place in this kind of testing. To create a business process that can truly be measured in an apples-to-apples context between disparate SAP Technology Stacks, the same customer numbers, materials, stock numbers, invoice numbers, and so on must be used between different test runs. Of particular stickiness might be date ranges—perhaps one of your transactions defaults to selecting a particular number of days or weeks when executing a search/query or sort. If so, this date range probably needs to be hard-coded so that subsequent test runs exe-

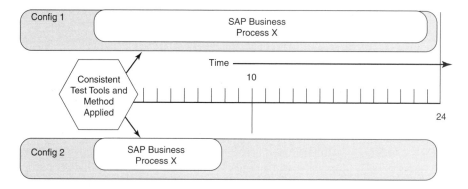

Figure 4–2 Note that Configuration 2 ("Config 2") can execute the displayed business process in less than half the wall-clock time of Configuration 1 ("Config 1"). This is a simple, yet effective method of comparing system performance between two configurations.

cute against *exactly* the same data and timeframe. Consider the differences a retail organization might run into running a 30-day search in January (after the busy holiday season, which results in a huge number of orders and subsequent downstream system activity, all captured within the database) versus running the same search in March; the speed of the search might be faster the second time simply because fewer rows of data resided in the tables being searched.

- If you allow your database to grow (as would be true in the previous case), however, test-run times will be impacted by this as well. More to the point, as the months roll by, executing a query against a database will tend to take longer and longer simply by virtue of the number of *new* rows of data added to the various tables in the database (assuming no data archiving is taking place). So, for true apples-to-apples wall-clock testing, the database must be in an identical state, which therefore implies a tape or file-system backup that is restored prior to executing new test runs on different technology stacks. In effect, the database behind the scenes must be consistent.

- It should be evident by now that wall-clock testing revolves around measuring the delta in elapsed time of a particular business process or transaction between two different technology stacks, or configurations, or as the result of other changes introduced between two systems. In my experience, though, you can also use wall-clock time to help you quantify test results from throughput-based stress testing, which is discussed in more detail later in this chapter. For instance, if you execute 10,000 SD dialog steps in 24 minutes on a particular hardware configuration, you might wish to benchmark how many dialog steps you can process on an alternate configuration in the same 24-minute time period.

- Walk-clock testing should embody fairly long-running scripts, as opposed to the kind of scripts normally associated with stress tests (transaction specific, relatively short in duration). I like to script business processes that consume at least 15 or 20 minutes of wall-clock time on the "baseline" system—this gives me plenty of room either way to prove or disprove that an alternate configuration is indeed faster or slower. Why? The deltas might be as small as 1 or 2 minutes; thus, creating scripts that quickly execute in 1 or 2 minutes would yield deltas of only a few seconds, making it much more involved to comfortably quantify the real performance differences between two systems.

- Finally, the process used for wall-clock testing must be carefully documented and followed. I recommend that a DB server be shut down and then brought up in a fresh state prior to executing a test run, not just the database, but the entire server—a reboot, if you will. In this way, all cache is cleared (verify this for your particular configuration!) at the hardware, OS, database, and application layers, and therefore the entire server is in a consistent and easily repeatable state. Doing otherwise leaves data in cache that may or may not be used by the transaction in question, resulting in an unpredictable load back on the disk subsystem. And, because the disk subsystem is generally the weakest solution component of an enterprise solution, as is commonly the case, test runs that benefit from excellent cache hit rates compared with other test runs will be artificially performance inflated—they will seem to execute faster, when in fact the real delta would remain unknown.

With regard to this last point, because so many variables can be potentially involved in an individual stress-test run—the DB server is but one of many system components, after all—I recommend crafting and using a custom and very detailed execution checklist as previously mentioned. This will help prevent your testing process from inherently straying test run to test run. Developing an execution checklist is discussed in depth in Chapter 8; using it is covered in Chapter 11.

4.3.2.   Transaction and Business Process Response Times

The most common mainstay of measuring a system's performance revolves around measuring response times—the faster a particular transaction executes, the better. This is usually measured in terms of the length of time an end user sees an "hourglass" on his or her computer screen after pressing the "Enter" key or a similar key that executes SAP screen logic. As such, response-time testing is also often called *application server response-time testing*. Like its wall-clock counterpart, response-time testing requires consistent workloads, data, and processes. However, because wall-clock times tend to be measured in many minutes or even hours, whereas response times tend to be measured in seconds or tenths of a second, response-time testing does not lend itself well to single-unit testing. Instead, it makes much more sense to drive hundreds or thousands of users such that an *average response time* is afforded at the end of a test run. In the end, regardless of whether many discrete disjointed transactions are executed in parallel, or a series of tightly connected transactions are united to create an end-to-end business process, response-time testing should seek to capture individual transaction response times. This approach is useful in that

- It allows for analysis at the lowest level—the individual transaction. For transactions with multiple screens, like VA01, where a sales order is initially started in one screen and then later populated with materials and quantities, I recommend capturing the response time for each screen, too.
- With the granularity afforded at the transaction level, it then becomes possible to "roll up" transaction response times in a number of handy ways, the most compelling of which is by functional area (assuming you scripted and executed discrete scripts driving different functional areas). The effects of changing logon load-balancing schemes, adding and removing various application servers, trying new front-end user interfaces, and so on may be effectively tested in this manner as well.
- Finally, the cumulative response-time data associated with an entire business process (again, assuming this is the approach you took when scripting) may be captured as well.

The biggest key to response-time testing is to maintain the same number of online users or batch processes. That is, the number of users driving the workload within the test run must be identical between runs. In this way, I can easily correlate actual performance gains and losses between different systems in otherwise complex scenarios like the following:

- I set up a stress-test run to execute 800 online users on two different SAP hardware platforms, running the same OS, DB, and SAP EBP releases.
- In the first case, using a very "dated" SAP Technology Stack (in terms of hardware technology), I observed that the average end-user response time was 900 milliseconds—just shy of a second.
- In the next test run, executed on a much newer and faster hardware platform, I observed that my average response time was indeed faster—but it was not nearly as fast as I would have predicted, averaging a little over 800 milliseconds.

Why the unforeseen "less than impressive" showing? As it turned out, much of the performance gains I had expected to see reflected in improved response times were instead reflected in tremendously increased throughput values—in fact, I had processed nearly twice as many sales orders! Thus, I had unintentionally configured a test that achieved a remarkable bump in throughput while keeping response times essentially flat—not my goal at the time, but the fact that I maintained a consistent number of users across both tests helped me uncover the truth pretty quickly. In the end, I changed the nature of the test to execute the same number of transactions in a finite period of time, staggered evenly one minute apart. In doing so, it became apparent that the second configuration was indeed much faster in terms of response times, reflecting an average less than half of the original configuration.

4.3.3. Measuring Performance and System Throughput Numbers

As stated earlier, one of the most intriguing methods of measuring performance involves computing the quantity of transactions executed, or more specifically, the number of work orders, invoices, financial statements, and so on generated from what usually amounts to a collection of ex-ecuted transactions. Instead of "output," throughput might be measured in raw SAP dialog steps executed per hour, too, the details of which are available via transaction ST03. Regardless of the vehicle used for measuring, this kind of testing is known as *throughput testing*. It is popular in certain scenarios (e.g., in those cases where a peak-processing SLA is tied to a particular through-put metric) and has been discussed a bit in previous sections of this chapter. Suffice it to say here, though, that consistency is still the word of the day, especially when it comes to the length of time that a stress-test run executes—be precise! More to the point:

- If you have assembled a collection of transactions to execute—to emulate a particular workload mix, for instance—that is fine. However, you must carefully control when each transaction or group of transactions is kicked off within the context of each stress-test run. Differences in how long each group of transactions remains dormant (e.g., un-til a staggered launch takes place and forces execution) need to be eliminated. That is, staggering is fine, but be sure to employ a consistent method for doing so.
- Login time—the time it takes to log in to the SAPGUI or other SAP user interface—must be consistent; otherwise, differences in the remaining amount of time left to a set of transactions to execute will skew the throughput observed in that particular run. My advice is to take the login subroutine out of the picture—don't actually commence your test run until all users have logged in and are "sitting" at the main screen, for example. If this is not possible in your particular case, take care to at least track some kind of metric that can be used to promote consistency in later test runs: for example, I might ensure that the number of users I already have executing in the system are essentially the same. Or even better, I might kick off each group of users at precisely the same time intervals for every test run, and in doing so "assume" that the login time will stay relatively consistent.
- Take care to ensure that nothing else within your scripting will act as a variable during test runs. For example, if you write a subroutine to collect data germane to what your scripted user just did (e.g., the wall-clock time he or she logged in, the transaction he or she executed, or the output created by the transaction), verify that the time this subrou-tine executes does not change—for the same reasons surrounding login times, to keep things consistent.

Next, let's take a closer look at how the number and types of users can be manipulated to fashion different kinds of stress-test success criteria or satisfy different performance measurement points of view.

4.3.4.   Number and Type of Users Supported

In many stress-test engagements, I've been asked to monitor response times and throughput rates. But nothing seems to get the attention of my clients like tracking the number of users who are con-nected, logged in, and executing business transactions. And, a significant amount of time usually goes into determining the precise makeup, from a functional perspective, of this stress-test "user community." In the past, in fact, I've invariably wound up working with countless functional experts to hear their opinions regarding the installed base mix of users. Of course, with real-time and historical data easily accessible via CCMS transactions like ST07, AL08, and SM04, I viewed giving my sole attention to these functional experts as more of a professional courtesy than a necessity. Still, I learned a lot when it came to understanding what was *valued* by a particular client.

Why the great interest in the number of users? It probably parallels the benchmark numbers published out of Walldorf and SAP hardware partners every few months, as new mySAP and R/3 solutions are benchmarked and the results published by SAP AG. Historically, these numbers represented some number and type of benchmark users, a number which was at once useful (in terms of apples-to-apples comparisons) and merely interesting (considering that, in the real world, end users tend to execute more than just a few core transactions over and over and over again). The bottom line is that the number of users a system can host within a proscribed set of response time boundaries is an easy metric to understand, and an easy one to use for comparison purposes.

But, the natural tendency for an SAP IT staff to want to communicate the hosting capabilities of their latest SAP CRM system with their business community, for example, yields success criteria like "our CRM system must host 1,000 logged-in 'Interaction Center' users, each boasting less than a 1-second average response time for 95% of all transactions, along with the ability to process 19,000 order line items per hour during quarter-end." The details surrounding user counts are wonderful, but in this particular case the line items per hour details are probably unnecessary. Instead, nail down the number of users you wish to see logged in, and the number of those that need to be concurrent, and move on from there.

4.3.5.   Specific Disk Performance Metrics

Given that the disk subsystem represents a common bottleneck in any enterprise system, it's not unusual to specify disk-focused performance metrics and success criteria designed to ensure that changes, or new subsystems entirely, provide increased performance. The disk subsystem metrics I have commonly found myself measuring in support of stress-test runs in the past include the following:

- Disk queue lengths, or the amount of work queued up and waiting to be processed by a disk subsystem, controller, or physical disk drive.
- Actual throughput, measured in MB per second that a particular OS-based disk partition (sometimes called a LUN), a group of partitions underneath a database, or an entire disk subsystem is processing.
- I/O requests per second, usually measured at the OS-based disk partition level, controller level, or even physical disk level. Through sizing calculations and data published by hardware vendors, it's always possible to determine what the ceiling of a particular configuration is in terms of I/Os; thus, a stress test should seek to quantify the *maximum* number of I/Os a particular configuration can push (versus what is *observed* in a

realistic load test), to ensure that plenty of additional headroom exists for future growth (assuming future growth or headroom is important).

- Mix of reads performed by a disk subsystem versus the number of writes committed to disk. As I shared previously, for many of my customers' established OLTP systems, a mix of 94% to 6% (reads to writes) is common. For newer systems, you'll observe more writes as a percentage; for OLAP systems like BW, you'll probably see close to 100% reads. Whatever the numbers, do your best to ensure that the stress-test run emulates real life for your end users.
- Mix of sequential versus direct (or random) reads or writes. In monitoring this mix, you can "prove" that a particular type of disk activity indeed emulates what a production system processes or is expected to process in the real world.
- Pagefile or Swap utilization. Monitoring this metric can prove quite useful, as greater utilization of these types of virtual memory resources implies the need for additional physical RAM, or simply poor buffer or database tuning.
- Cache hit rates, noted at the database level as well as through SAP CCMS. These rates help to explain or rationalize disk performance observed at lower levels in the technology stack, and overall high-level business process throughput at the application layer.
- Average size of I/Os. With regard to what's occurring at the lowest hardware levels in a disk subsystem, it may be necessary to validate the average size of I/Os taking place at this layer, too. Just because a database like Oracle is configured to move 8-kilobyte blocks by default does not imply that the best blocksize for the OS or underlying disk controllers is also 8kb, for example. The best number can be found through stress testing and tuning, and in regard to "reads" is usually closer to 32kb, 64kb, or something greater for the OS, and quite a bit larger for most disk controllers.

Normally, I find myself monitoring nearly all of the aforementioned elements when a new disk subsystem is introduced into one of my customer's SAP system landscapes. But smaller changes drive disk subsystem–specific stress testing, too. Changes as seemingly small as firmware updates to physical disk drives, other firmware and hardware driver updates related to the disk controllers, or entirely new disk layouts or configurations make stress testing necessary. Of course, similar types of performance metrics—stress-test success criteria—exist for other layers of the SAP Technology Stack, too, and are discussed in the next section.

4.3.6.   Other Technology Stack Performance Metrics

Not surprisingly, every layer in the SAP Technology Stack presents a tuning opportunity; however, the trick to rapidly planning for and executing a stress test is to not get bogged down in the minutiae of every layer. Instead, I recommend simply starting with the following "high value" points, adding to this list only if explicitly required to support a particular SLA or other specific requirement:

- Network infrastructure. Unless you are testing different types of network-centric performance options, like Gigabit Ethernet versus 100Mb, one network interface card

(NIC) card over another, or the advantages of NIC teaming or bonding (where the bandwidth of two or more network cards can be virtually fused together to create a higher performance or more highly available link), I suggest keeping the network layer "static," so to speak.

- Disk subsystem infrastructure. Although I have already covered the most popular disk metrics, you need to consider any "infrastructure" that ties your disk subsystem to your servers. In the case of SANs and older fibre-channel arbitrated loop networks, the infrastructure consists of switches or hubs, some type of cabling and interface adapters, and host bus adapters (HBAs) that reside in each server. A stress test may seek to quantify the impact that new HBA hardware drivers (or software settings!) or switch/hub firmware has with respect to disk subsystem throughput. Or, perhaps a new SAN fabric configuration needs to be evaluated. Outside of these areas, though, there is really little else to tune or tweak.

- Servers. Any changes that impact performance, from CPU to RAM to network, or changes to local disks housing the OS and Pagefile/Swap, give cause to stress test. This goes for firmware upgrades as well, but does not apply to hardware systems that have nothing, or typically very little, to do with performance (e.g., cooling subsystems, hardware-based systems management options, or power options).

- OS. Different OSs present inherently different testing and tuning challenges. I've pitted completely different OSs against each other (e.g., SuSe Linux versus Windows 2000 Advanced Server), while keeping everything else in the stack essentially the same, including the hardware platform, database release, and SAP application layer. Normally, though, you'll be more interested in pitting the latest drivers, service packs/patches, and the like against your mature in-place OS configuration. You may also compare the impact that different allocation units or blocksizes have on performance, or how configuring the manner in which a system's RAM is allocated and used by the OS impacts throughput and end-user response times.

- Database. Outside of different release levels by the same manufacturer (e.g., Oracle 8.1.6 versus 8.1.7, or 9i versus 10G), and different patch releases, most of the testing you'll likely look to as success criteria revolves around inherently different database configurations. For Microsoft SQL Server 2000 implementations, for example, I have tested the impact the multiple data files had versus a smaller number of files, how changing the sizing and placement of TempDB impacted query times, how hard-coding the amount of RAM used by the database increased typical throughput levels in mixed-load environments, and so on.

- SAP application layer. Kernel patch levels and the impact that new support packages and other updates (e.g., legal patches, plug-ins) have on a system scream for at least minimal load testing, no matter how matter-of-fact these changes appear to be. Changes to buffers, the number of configured work processes, and other profile parameters also demand basic stress testing. Similarly, the addition of application servers or redistribution of logon load balancing—and any other fundamental changes that impact the basic system architecture, like upgrading the CI or distributing batch processes across all servers previously dedicated to online users only—benefits from performance testing too.

- Internet and the client access layer or layers. Noteworthy changes to any servers or software components that enable access to your core mySAP systems (like Citrix MetaFrame) dictate stress testing. Changing the configuration of ITS or Web AS dictates testing as well. Thus, if you need to change your standard front-end client image, are curious as to how well the latest JavaGUI works with R/3, or need to measure the impact that multiple ITS instances have on a single server (versus dedicated ITS servers, each running a single ITS instance), you should execute an client-layer stress test.

Throughout all of this testing, you'll want to draft both "average" metrics and "not to exceed," or maximum, metrics, as discussed previously. For instance, for any stress-test run to be valid, you might make the decision that network or SAN traffic will not exceed 65% of capacity under peak load, or 40% capacity under typical day-to-day loads. Similarly, you might say that 80% of response times observed at the SAP application layer must fall within the boundaries established by a bell curve defined by a range of time, such as 300 to 1,100 milliseconds. And, for every layer in between, you'll want to quantify what constitutes a successful run and what does not. More on how to quantify and actually measure your success criteria will be completely hammered out in Chapters 11 and 12.

4.4.   Tools and Approaches

With each level of stress testing described previously comes a specific set of tools and approaches. Level One tools range in variety the most, from simple utilities that test the throughput of hardware devices, like network cards and disk controllers, to full-fledged testing suites that help you characterize individual subsystems across the hardware and software technology stacks. Most typically, though, Level One tools tend to be hardware or software specific. That is, nearly every SAP technology partner maintains a set of hardware-specific tools that assist in not only configuring a particular piece of gear but also measuring and testing performance.

On the other hand, Level Two testing is the simplest from a test-tool perspective in that only the standard SAP benchmark kit to be executed is required—all data, scripts, tools with which to manage and monitor the execution of the scripts, and even the method to be used during the testing are necessarily set in stone, as is the case with any industry-standard benchmark. After all, if benchmarks were subject to change or interpretation, the results observed from benchmark kits would be worthless. Thus, Level Two stress testing, while comprehensive in scope and time-consuming up front, tends to be fairly straightforward once everything is set up. The greatest challenge that Level Two testing introduces over its more basic counterpart is the SAP application layer, and therefore the potential to use SAP CCMS and the SAP Solution Manager (SSM or SolMan) to track performance metrics (which in and of themselves rate practically a chapter of their own. Suffice it to say here, though, that transaction SM51 will underpin much of your real-time monitoring. SM51 allows you to easily move around between different application servers within a particular instance found in your SAP system, noting and collecting relevant performance data, and much more; by double-clicking any active server, you then create a connection to it, which may in turn be leveraged to execute additional application server-specific transactions with which to collect SAP application server–specific data along with cross-application global data.

Level Three stress testing also inherently includes CCMS and potentially SSM. But it is by far the most complex of all stress testing, as it encompasses the end-to-end scope already discussed with regard to Level Two testing, but also brings into the picture customer-specific business processes and data, no set method of testing and tuning, and a plethora of different testing suites that not only represent learning curves in and of themselves, but can often be costly as well.

Each of these three types of stress-test methods, and the tools useful in executing and monitoring test runs, are discussed in greater detail in Chapter 6. The fact that on-demand computing and other types of pay-as-you-go arrangements are not an intrinsic component of 99% of all data-center environments, though, says to me that all three types of stress testing will continue to flourish for the near future. As much as I'd like to jump right into Chapter 6 and test-tool piloting, however, the next chapter necessarily steps back from the technology for a while and focuses our attention instead on building a "testing and tuning" team—the T3.

Staffing the Testing and Tuning Team (T3)

Although stress testing and performance tuning is very much focused on technical and business process matters, it is not replete without an appropriately organized and staffed team structure. That is, at a fundamental level, certain activities must first be addressed by a team leader or manager, just to support the actual work of stress testing and performance tuning. Some of these core activities are as follows:

- Identify project/team requirements and goals
- Based on goals, determine whether a project- or support-based structure is most appropriate, and then define the project/team structure
- Identify skill sets based on proposed tool sets necessary to achieve the testing/tuning work at hand, and as the SAP system matures
- Determine whether the requisite skill sets exist internally, or need to be obtained through third-party contracting/consulting firms
- Staff the testing and tuning organization, focused on minimizing head-count and other costs between active projects or regular testing iterations
- Determine ongoing training and similar "team maintenance" requirements, in part to maintain high employee job satisfaction and low turnover

With these basic staffing activities foremost in your mind, let's take a closer look at how to staff a team responsible for SAP performance testing and tuning, giving attention to what I perceive as best practices as well as visibility into real-world customer testing organizations. Remember, the key to creating or modifying your SAP-driven business processes rests in comprehensive testing. My goal here is to help you craft an organization capable of effectively testing your business processes; no implementation, upgrade, technical infrastructure refresh, or functional/technical change wave is complete in the absence of testing. Indeed, as I've said throughout the preceding chapters, without load testing no SAP system can truly ever be optimized from a performance perspective, nor can your system's peak capabilities be identified or truly understood, or system availability ensured.

5.1. SAP IT, Meet "The Business"

SAP AG touts its enterprise applications as business solutions configured by business consultants. Given this claim, it's safe to say that the developers who perform the functional configuration of an SAP system are experts in their particular business area and bring with them the added advantage of programming or systems development experience. This business knowledge is important to the team responsible for maintaining a well-performing system. But, building such a one-sided team to conduct performance testing—a team unfamiliar and largely uninterested in the system's underlying *technical foundation*—will result in failure. Conversely, building a team strong only in SAP Basis and test tools but ungrounded in the business at hand will fail as well. Instead, it is essential that your testing and tuning team represent the proper balance of both business-savvy "functional" folks and IT specialists. In this way, the business expertise as well as SAP Technology Stack experience and testing/tuning tool-set skills useful in testing, analyzing, and generally managing a system's performance can be brought together under one roof.

In general, your goal is to staff a lean testing and tuning organization, not just for the obvious cost benefits but in the name of "effectiveness." In my experience, bringing together a lot of people (relatively speaking, of course, depending on the breadth of your SAP enterprise) tends to be counterproductive, as it slows down decision making related not only to planning but also to execution, and clouds what should be a clear team vision. Other key aims include the following:

- Appoint a leader or manager with both the responsibility and empowerment necessary to drive the team while effectively working with sister IT and business-oriented groups. This leader will provide overall vision to the team, keeping individuals both focused and aware of their unique role within the organization. Not surprisingly, the sound team and project-based leadership provided by the person holding this role will go a long way in making the team successful—a team I loosely refer to as the *T3*—the "testing and tuning team," to be detailed later.
- Identify both IT and business process (functional area) leaders *outside of the team* to act as single points of contact back into the T3.
- Keeping minimal staffing in mind, do your best to bring in folks experienced in a number of cross-disciplines rather than a number of folks each of whom are highly focused experts on a single subject, or subject-matter experts (SMEs).
- Seek folks with a combination of both SAP IT and SAP business process experience—another way of killing two SAP birds with one SAP stone.

So, based on what you hope to achieve, you'll tweak your staffing plans in any number of ways; new implementations and major upgrades may be handled one way, whereas technical refreshes may be dealt with in another. And, stress testing your regular post–Go-Live quarterly updates will probably be handled in yet another way.

Regardless of your particular team structure, or whether its central focus is on maximizing performance, availability, or scalability, I find that the T3 is most successful when it is tightly aligned to the company's change management organization responsible for SAP. In the case of large SAP environments, I encourage my customers to deploy the T3 as a blended functional/technical department that works hand-in-hand with the core business groups that use the systems and the core IT organizations that support them. Within the context of smaller SAP environments, I find that the lines between the core business/IT organizations and the T3 are much more blurred, to the point of disappearing entirely in many cases. But, there are a few key interteam relationships that remain pivotal despite the size of your SAP implementation or IT department:

- The T3 leadership component must have a keen understanding of, and relationship with, the business organizations and IT groups with whom they form a liaison. This implies that, for credibility reasons (among more obvious reasons), the T3 itself must be staffed with both business process staff and IT-centric staff.
- With regard to the business side of the house, this experience is often quite specific to an individual's business area of focus, such as R/3 materials management or APO demand planning; relationships with each group helps ensure that its needs are brought to bear, promoting the T3's continuing value proposition in the process.
- Similarly, company internal IT relationships must be cemented at a number of levels— at the "colleague" level, where colleagues call on each other for assistance, as well as at the midlevel and senior management positions, where relationships are pushed "down" the organization by virtue of strategic vision.
- The specific experience each tester brings to the table in terms of his or her test tool and mySAP Business Suite or other SAP application experience is huge—for example, different SAP products lend themselves to different testing methods, tools, and so on. Thus, relationships with your technology partners represent the final relationship "ingredient" in a fully baked T3 staffing plan.

The effectiveness of the stress-testing work performed can be directly tied to the level of experience of the team, as should be evident in the preceding list. One reason for this situation is that there is very little formal education offered on stress-testing methods, building test cases, or even planning and executing load tests (hence, one of the key reasons for this book). Even the materials published by various test-tool vendors and SAP AG are light, subject to large gaps when it comes to end-to-end stress testing and tuning. The formal training that SAP programming and functional folks receive includes some level of necessary single-unit testing, often under the obligatory umbrella of Computer-Aided Test Tool (CATT-) or eCATT-driven functional testing, detailed in Chapter 6. Thus, on-the-job training (OJT) tends to prove most valuable in building a core testing competency within an organization—typically not the most cost-effective method of doing anything!

On the other hand, if the alternative to OJT is staffing your T3 with experienced though expensive contractors and consultants, OJT may look pretty good for satisfying long-term organizational needs while keeping your budget in check. We'll go over the trade-offs of staffing with third parties later. In the meantime, remember that very few functional or SAP Basis courses devote more than a few cursory minutes to load testing—so a flexible approach to learning is mandated, regardless. Begin thinking about how you can take advantage of nontraditional learning approaches within your own team.

5.2.   General Staffing Considerations and Best Practices

When it comes to staffing a team responsible for the performance of your mySAP solutions, a number of matters need to be addressed, ranging from how a team is strategically aligned within an organization's IT department to the role it plays in supporting ongoing change management, testing, and tuning. Beyond this, organizational decisions surrounding your discrete SAP IT and business projects will tend to make one organizational model more effective than another. This is especially true when it comes to organizing around a limited-term project versus staffing for long-term support, all of which are discussed next.

5.2.1.   Tactically Staffing Discrete Stress-Testing Projects

As an SME in testing and tuning SAP solutions, I'm often pulled into one-off consulting engagements with my customers. Nearly all of the time, the goal at hand is a discrete or otherwise short-term project, usually centered around the last few months of a new implementation or a major functional upgrade or technical refresh of an existing system. Of course, my definition of short term is pretty subjective—sometimes it means weeks onsite, sometimes months. Nevertheless the process of planning for, testing, and replacing a customer's SAP disk subsystem or standard server platform with newer, faster models, or introducing a new version of an OS or a database, all represent simple and quite common stress-testing projects. Along the same lines, server technology refreshes and certain IT consolidation projects are also commonplace reasons for stress testing. But, because these are short-term technology-specific projects, it may not make financial sense to staff the T3 internally and then augment it with in-house or formal training and OJT. Instead, hiring a third-party consultant or other SME might be a much better way to go.

5.2.2.   Staffing and Stress Testing in the Real World

While working with SAP customer teams, I'm frequently asked for input regarding the staffing of discrete stress-test projects. Questions like "Who else should we bring in," "When should we hire someone," or "Where do we find people adept at testing and tuning" are as common as the free consulting and knowledge dumps I'm asked to provide. What this has taught me over the years can be summed up in the following project-focused real-world practices:

- Companies seem to be inconsistent when it comes to stress testing; when times are good and budgets are bloated, money is spent—outside SMEs like myself are brought in, new automated testing suites are purchased, and so on.
- When budgets are tighter, full-blown stress testing tends to take a back seat to single-unit testing, or worse, there is no testing done at all. The risk-versus-reward equation seemingly fades away, when in fact it's probably more important than ever to ensure

that the system remains highly available in the wake of unavoidable functional and technical changes commonplace regardless of a company's financial situation.

- Regardless of budget conditions, more companies than you think consistently fail to understand the value of stress testing in support of regular change waves. Perhaps that's because "change" implies a process, whereas most stress tests and performance-tuning engagements tend to be viewed as discrete projects with a beginning and an end.
- Companies also tend to underestimate how much value a true SAP-savvy stress-testing expert can bring to the table, and therefore initially underplan his or her utilization. For example, "finding" a high quantity of high-quality data takes time, as does determining the best mix of business processes to test for a unique mySAP Business Suite implementation. An SAP-experienced tester can make great progress very quickly in these areas, though.
- Finally, in the past I have had to convince customers that there is great value in looking at the completion of a one-off stress-testing project as a discrete service, rather than a procurement and management exercise tasked with bringing together an assortment of tools, testing methodologies, data collection/reporting processes, and people. My favorite approach for short-term testing projects is to simply wrap all of the necessary ingredients together into a single service with a single price, a service replete with all of the necessary human resources, tools, and attention to knowledge transfer. Such an approach makes a lot of sense when it comes to leveraging outside consultants and the relationships they probably already have with test-tool vendors—I push my customers to let go of thoughts they have of using their own tools and approaches, when, for example, I can use my relationships with Mercury Interactive, AutoTester, Compuware, and so on to get the project done faster and cheaper than would otherwise be possible.

More to the last point, if a third-party consulting house can deliver a 3- to 4-week end-to-end solution (a comprehensive custom stress test), walk away, and then leave an invoice for something like a quarter of what it might have cost otherwise to build a local team and buy a full-blown testing suite, then why not consider that route? In other words, it might not make financial sense for every single SAP IT shop to purchase SAP load-testing tools that they will never use more than a few times a year; instead, let your third-party partners leverage their experiences and relationships to your benefit. And then, you can turn around and simply "lease" both the services and the software from your partner, which helps you to accomplish your stress-test goals while simultaneously leaving a lot of your own budget money still on the table.

But remember, this third-party partner approach doesn't always automatically make sense; you may find yourself in the position of needing to purchase an updated software testing suite to support biweekly testing anyway, or you might leverage an existing corporate-wide agreement already executed within your own company to effectively use a set of SAP stress-testing tools "for free" on your particular stress-testing product. My point is simple—do the math. Try to avoid a rigid mindset that says you absolutely *need to buy* something, even though it might be better handled through short-term leasing, or that says you *need to do it in-house* because that's how IT projects have always been done in your organization.

5.2.3. Staffing Long Term and Strategically

For large SAP system landscapes or enterprise environments that change monthly rather than quarterly—or simply to create a consistently staffed testing outfit—you may consider assembling a long-term core T3 rather than continually piecing one together as projects come up. Keeping a team together indefinitely to handle day-to-day change control questions, plus analyze the impact that future upgrades, consolidation projects, technology refreshes, and so on might have on the SAP Technology Stack, can be a smart move. By doing so, the stress-test learning curve is minimized, and the ability to better utilize and take advantage of expensive test software suites is increased, to the point where the savings over a project-based approach may pay a core percentage of the team to stay together even during slow periods (whereas a project team would be simply disbanded). Again, do the math to see which approach is more favorable.

The key to staffing long term lies in whether such an approach to stress testing and tuning really saves money or in some other way increases the organization's ability to meet key solution characteristics (e.g., availability SLAs), which in turn normally relate back to the complexity or critical nature of the SAP systems being supported. Think about the following benefits:

- A consistent T3 team lead or manager will help keep communication lines open to the business and IT organizations year-round.
- A consistent core team can serve as the heart of future projects, where team members are required for weeks or months at a time and then returned back to their business or IT homes. In doing so, the time necessary for new members to "ramp up" is considerably reduced—they will have colleagues immediately available to answer questions and generally help them get up to speed.
- As the team's experience and maturity in handling the company's mySAP change control-initiated testing, special projects, and so on grows, the cost of performing incremental testing and tuning shrinks. This is especially so when an easily accessible and easy-to-use repository of lessons learned is available.
- The performance testing and monitoring tools, software packages, and so on—including scripts, configuration files, and other byproducts of stress testing—lend themselves to reuse. On the other hand, when teams are abandoned, these kinds of byproducts tend to "disappear" and therefore need to be re-created the next time around, wasting time.
- The ability to quickly turn around a new stress-testing project, or help the company understand the impact of a proposed upgrade, is significant. That is, the time advantages, as compared to the time required to staff a special testing project, can give a company the edge it needs to make business-critical decisions fast—and intelligently. A strategic T3 can rapidly arm the company with the right information.
- The ability to leverage dollars spent in the name of training, whether formal or in the form of OJT, also aids in the full-time T3's ability to drive greater ROI than its project-based staffing counterpart.

In the end, the question of whether to go the project route or full-time T3 route should be grounded in financial analyses, potential benefits to the company overall, and study of the pitfalls that surround each approach in your specific case. Put together a matrix of sorts to compare the two approaches, and see for yourself how each stacks up.

5.2.4. How Your Tool Set Impacts Staffing

Staffing your test team depends in part on the tool sets being currently used, and perhaps more important, on the tools being considered for deployment (discussed in depth in Chapter 6). Some tools offer only limited testing capabilities, perhaps designed to stress test a particular layer of your SAP Technology Stack (e.g., Iometer or SQLIO, which are geared toward testing the throughput and load associated with hardware and OS variations). Other tools support full-featured SAP application programming interface (API) driven, single-user, application-layer business process scripting (e.g., AutoTester ONE, Compuware TestPartner), whereas still others support managed multiuser load testing as well (e.g., AutoTester AutoController and Compuware QALoad). Regardless of the tool set, though, a learning curve exists that must first be conquered and then maintained; the maintenance of skill sets takes time and money. And, because very few tools are similar in terms of their use, knowing how to effectively use a particular testing suite does not imply that using other testing suites significantly minimizes the learning curve. In many cases, the best you can hope for is that an *understanding* of a particular class of testing tools—like SAP virtual load-testing suites—will ground you in functionality. In this way, at least you'll understand what the tool is probably capable of, if not how to actually use it.

The selection of your test tool also impacts staffing in a more direct way. Many tools require that a physical user—a "real" person, if you will—drive the stress testing. For discrete technology-focused stress-testing projects driven solely by IT, that's probably not a big deal. But, in the case of multiuser application-specific load testing, it becomes quite cost prohibitive to begin staffing the team with a lot of testers who will execute and supervise business processes in the same manner as the real world—manually. Tools that support virtual users, on the other hand, help you "shrink" your staff back to a much more manageable number simply because these end users may be emulated—no need to pay overtime, plan for smoke breaks, or try to staff a team to work lots of weekends and nights. Of course, emulation is not exactly cheaper, either—check software pricing with your test-tool partners and be prepared to consider software license fees that might rival a number of your staffed full-time equivalents!

You also need to consider and seek tools that support reusable code—for example, repeatable scripts or reusable packages—because this impacts the T3 favorably. Why? Because scripted test cases are inherently easier to duplicate project to project, or to leverage for baseline purposes, and fewer test runs are ultimately required. Every test executes precisely the same steps, in precisely the same order, as every other test. Because such an approach is highly repeatable, problems like data omissions, errors, timing inconsistencies, and so on are virtually eliminated with automated testing. By reducing the number of test runs required, you also reduce planning, scripting, executing, monitoring, and postrun analysis time, all of which free up your T3 resources for other tasks, or reduce the number of team members or expensive consulting hours otherwise required.

Finally, a sound stress-testing approach should not be limited to the tools you currently have on hand. On the contrary, you will want to revisit and research new tools on the market that let you do more with less, especially as your SAP systems evolve and tie generally into NetWeaver- and specifically into XI-enabled business processes. Case in point, you may easily "extend" SAP's eCATT product to include third-party testing and scripting tools, including Compuware's TestPartner. In this way, fewer and simpler testing packages become necessary to support testing cross-platform business processes or simply to support multiuser load testing, which simplifies everything and in turn drives lower staffing requirements.

5.2.5.   Staffing and Your Particular mySAP Solutions

When it comes to staffing the T3, the makeup of a testing team is probably most impacted by the actual SAP solutions being supported or deployed. This is true across the board, from the front-end client technology you deploy (e.g., SAPGUI, WebGUI/HTML, JavaGUI, and other access devices used to communicate with your system) to the various SAP Technology Stack layers underneath R/3, APO, BW, CRM, and so on. A business person skilled in testing R/3 functional areas like SD and MM might know very little about demand planning in APO or BW's standard InfoCubes. And similarly, an IT resource familiar with the SAP Technology Stack that underpins the company's R/3 implementation might know very little about the completely different technology stack underneath SAP EP. The philosophy of "best practices" tells us to staff for mission-critical business processes first, then for systems that support the bulk of an organization's business processes. In small SAP shops, I find that the SAP Basis or technology team tasked with supporting each mySAP solution generally has a single qualified resource onsite who can take on the added responsibilities associated with the T3. In larger shops, though, it can be more difficult to pull out the most experienced or otherwise "best" resource; the trick becomes identifying the individual who not only appears to have a career in front of him or her, but the individual who enjoys conquering the inevitable learning curves associated with each mySAP Business Suite component and the requisite technology stacks.

5.2.6.   Training Your Internal Team

Bringing together a limited cadre of internal candidates to staff your fledgling T3 represents the most popular option taken by SAP IT teams when it comes to short-term stress-testing projects. It's rare that such a team is ready to hit the ground running, though, because each member almost certainly has "holes" in his or her knowledge of the SAP systems, business processes, test tools/methods, or the IT infrastructure making your SAP solution possible. Thus, the need for some kind of training presents itself, of either a formal or informal kind. The risks are many, though, as shown in the following:

- Spending perhaps thousands of dollars on all kinds of SAP-specific, technology-specific, and tool-/approach-specific formal training for many employees and long-term contractors adds up fast. If the training is related to something that quickly becomes obsolete, it may not represent good ROI; the employee must be retooled, only to return back to the team with his or her head full of new knowledge but still no practical application experience of that knowledge. In cases like this, a "throw-away" consultant easily replaced by a different consultant knowledgeable or experienced in the new tool, technology, or mySAP component might better serve the team.

- Similarly, training a team through OJT may not represent good ROI; unstructured or too much OJT wastes time and achieves little, in that the team members eventually wind up in the position of "not knowing what they don't know"—they make progress only to a point, finally giving up rather than beating their heads over and over against an unfamiliar wall of technology-specific ignorance. The smart ones will come up with clever "workarounds" (and I applaud these!), but rarely will these workarounds reflect the "right" answer, much less what experts in that particular field would consider best practices. In the end, then, I recommend OJT only when guided by an experienced team member, and then only in moderation.

- Beyond the fact that training of any type is costly, training simply does not yield experienced resources. That is, training gets you moving in the right direction, but it does not get you moving very fast. In the end, resources that are trained but not experienced will typically take much longer to accomplish the same task than their experienced colleagues, often reworking tasks more than a few times until they get them right. If time is abundant, this caveat might be acceptable. In most cases where timelines are pretty tight, though, the trade-off in time versus dollars might not make good business sense—as I always say, do the math.

- To make matters worse, employees or long-term contractors armed with recent training courses and a nice position in a team supporting SAP can suddenly update their resumes to look very appealing to your competitors, consulting firms, and so on. This is true of *any* investment made in people, of course. I suggest that you spend your training dollars wisely, on people with a proven track record of loyalty, and keep your fingers crossed for good measure.

So, even if time is on your side, you'll be in a sticky situation for the short term as you train your team. Fortunately, what you lose with respect to time you'll gain later when it comes to employee/contractor job satisfaction, increased loyalty to the team and company, and overall long-term return on investment. And the fact that you'll keep key technology and business knowledge inside the company represents perhaps the greatest benefit to training your internal team.

5.2.7.   Leveraging Peers, Partners, and Consultants

Even if I didn't fall into this category myself, I would still readily concede that SMEs outside of your own organization can and should play a critical role in your testing and tuning projects. I like to categorize these outsiders into three groups: (1) your in-house company-wide peers and colleagues who are not already a part of your T3, (2) third-party SAP Technology Stack partners, (3) and third-party pure consulting organizations.

Of the three groups of outsiders, leveraging experienced in-house colleagues from other company departments, IT groups, or business units can make the most sense overall in terms of the following:

- Cost. As a current company employee or long-term contractor, your peers cost substantially less than their third-party outsider equivalents, both from a salary/hourly rate perspective and in lower travel expenses (as it's generally assumed that consultants bring with them 10%–20% of their bill rate in incremental travel/expense fees).
- Company familiarity. Simply having core knowledge of the company can pay big dividends when it comes to hitting the ground running. Your peers in the next office building already know the various IT and business organizations; in addition, they are "communications-enabled" in that they have a phone, e-mail address, and so on, and can leverage existing relationships throughout the company to expedite project tasks and generally make things happen.
- Experience. General and specific knowledge relevant to stress testing and tuning will pay huge dividends across the board. For example, in the case of one very large customer of mine, we found a QA testing team that was already familiar with Mercury Interactive's QuickTest and LoadRunner products and another internal organization that was able to provide an excellent DBA/technology specialist. In each case, the value—a company resource with specific knowledge needed by the T3—was unquestionable, making it that much easier to meet our timelines and project objectives.

Of course, third-party SAP Technology Stack partner resources represent an excellent source of manpower as well, especially those associated with a particular difficult-to-find product or solution skill set needed within the overall scope of your T3 big picture. Some of my favorite partners to work with—partners that provide quite a bit of quality "free" presales support in addition to fee-based services—include Microsoft, Intel, and HP. In most cases, be prepared to pay something a bit less than traditional consulting rates. But, if you represent a strategic "win" for one of these partners, if you will eventually displace a competing vendor's products, or if you simply play your cards right, it's not uncommon to find some kind of partner-based funding to reduce the cost of these companies' consulting resources. I find that nearly all of my partners have access to a stash of their own internal "marketing money"—marketing organizations wishing to push their latest and most exciting (although perhaps not very mature) products. Sometimes you'll find "sales team funding" as well, because sales teams hoping to stuff a wedge into a new account (with the hopes of greater returns in the future) are sometimes in the position to partially or completely fund one of their company's consulting resources for strategic opportunities. I call this funding "buckets o' cash"—be sure to explore this option prior to plunking down your hard-earned budget money!

Trade-offs exist, though. The trade-off when it comes to funding is usually reflected in the availability of this "free" resource you have been provided—you may have to wait a few days or even weeks for the right person to become available. And, unless the partner's consulting bench is full of experienced bodies, you might wind up with a resource who is more available than experienced in the specifics of your particular testing project. Of course, if the funding is in support of a new product without the benefit of a "history" of success behind it, at the end of the day you might wind up with a longer project that expected, something true regardless of whether the partner was funded. The point is that even though you got a free consulting resource, you might still need to spend some incremental budget dollars to fill in technology/experience holes left in your project plan. I recommend simply managing this situation as you do any other risk or hole in your project plan, and enjoy the savings—investigate free presales or consulting opportunities, do your homework, and be prepared to negotiate and take advantage of what you can. You never know what kind of deal you might run across.

Finally, a pack of potentially expensive consultants can always be brought in! They're easy to find, and happy to help—if you have the money. All of the usual suspects should come to mind, like the recently relabeled "Big 3" consulting outfits in the market today, or the big consulting entity recently gobbled up by a large, faceless entity out of New York, and so on. If you find the right people with the right skill sets (they exist, but can still be hard to find), you could quickly be on your way to making great progress, or you might simply be well on your way to accruing enormous consulting fees. On the plus side, though, once you find the right consultants in terms of experience levels, and then proceed to manage and motivate them properly, a focused team of experienced consultants will lead you to a successful stress-testing and tuning project outcome faster than any other alternative—the "been there, done that" benefit has the potential to pay off fast. In terms of excessive costs, due diligence on the part of the hiring manager (who must refrain from simply turning over the keys to the project's consultants and walking away) makes all the difference.

Spending the time necessary to effectively manage these resources makes all the difference, too. Why? The former Assistant Secretary of Defense Lawrence J. Korb said it best when he stated, "You hire me a consulting firm, and I'll prove whatever you want." Like any statistical data, success criteria and actual test results can be massaged in any number of ways: averages can be weighted; timing and results can be skewed intentionally or otherwise; statistical outliers may or may not be factored in, depending on how they change the test results; and so on. It should go without saying that you want to closely manage the execution of each iterative test run. I suggest you maintain a high degree of control managing the collection and analysis of your test runs as well, simply to keep everything in the open and minimize surprises later on.

5.3. Staffing for New Implementations in the Real World

Brand-new implementations no longer represent the core activities many of us in the world of SAP consulting see day to day. Rather, although new SAP implementations continue to unfold, especially in the areas of SAP CRM, APO, and EP, most of the stress-testing work I've seen in the last 6 months was related to functional upgrades and technical refreshes of existing solutions. But those new implementations are around the corner! Just look at new licenses sold by SAP AG, or have a discussion with one of SAP's partner competency centers—you'll hear the same story over and over again, that companies with approved budgets and money ready to spend are preparing to implement or upgrade to a whole lot of new SAP solutions. At HP, we've seen a huge up-tick in SAP CRM and EP implementation planning, and to a lesser extent in SAP APO and BW, since the beginning of 2002. And, through 2003, new sizing/solution design activity soared, which means we should see a whole lot of implementation activity throughout 2004. Migrations to R/3 Enterprise are really starting to take off, too. I predict that as all of these NetWeaver-en-abled solutions gain traction, and companies begin to understand the value proposition of SAP's MDM and XI products, in terms of how to effectively tie together multiple systems and better in-tegrate complex business processes, we'll continue to see a healthy stream of implementation work through at least the end of 2005.

Thus, the question becomes "How do I best staff a T3 component within my current SAP implementation team, such that I give them the room and resources they need to not only com-plete their primary mission at hand—implementing current and probably new business processes on SAP—but also to effectively perform the load testing necessary to prove the new system's true peak capabilities?" This question is addressed in the next section.

5.3.1.   Closing the Gaps in Your SAP Technology Stack

From a staffing perspective, stress testing new mySAP implementations is unique because of the following factors:

- Staff and budgets tend to be earmarked early on for at least a minimal level of testing and tuning, as opposed to special projects or upgrades where the time between the budgeting process and the need for the funds is much smaller.
- Although they vary, timelines are often set in stone that don't effectively allow for *com-prehensive* load testing. Instead, new implementations tend to give stress testing less at-tention—and less time—than is truly required.
- Funding for load testing new implementations may be hard to come by simply because the company believes it's investing in the latest and greatest hardware solutions, solu-tions seemingly offering such tremendous "speeds and feeds" that the risk of poor per-formance is negligible.
- When a new SAP Technology Stack is being deployed in a new implementation, the new underlying technologies represent "unknowns" and therefore collectively beg for risk-mitigating load testing.

Thus, the challenge is to redirect existing efforts without slowing down the primary imple-mentation goals—to push the project full steam ahead while identifying and clarifying the need for stress testing and follow-on performance tuning. In my experience, this is accomplished most effectively through staffing the "gaps" in the new implementation.

Bear in mind that gaps are plentiful in new implementations—don't let anyone tell you dif-ferently! Gaps with regard to the technical and business/functional staff tasked with testing are no exception. Do your best to staff the various "testing" functions—integration, regression, and so on—with folks who are also experienced in some kind of load testing. Development folks familiar with the low end of stress testing, like those adept at single-unit load testing, are probably the most readily available and least expensive testing resources you'll find, too—use this to your advantage!

5.4.   Staffing to Support Operational Change Management

If new implementations represent one end of the performance-testing spectrum, the idea of supporting post–Go-Live functional and technical changes, also called *operational changes,* represents the other end. Certainly, you could lump any activity that represents a system change and occurs after Go-Live into this broad category. But I prefer to break out strategic changes—like those resulting from upgrades, consolidation efforts, and so on—from the tactical everyday or regularly scheduled operational updates to a system. Strategic changes are discussed in the final sections of this chapter; the management of tactical changes is covered next.

5.4.1.   Managing Real-World Tactical Change Post Go-Live

The term *post Go-Live* should be self-evident. It simply represents anything that occurs after a system is initially turned over to its end users, to be used in a productive day-to-day manner. You may be asking what exactly a tactical change is, though. The short answer is it's a small modification to the SAP system—if you add a new bit of functionality, apply an update or bug fix to avoid problems in the future, or tweak a few database or SAP profile or configuration parameters, you've introduced what I describe as a tactical change. They are short in timeframe and specific in purpose, potentially apply to every layer of the SAP Technology Stack, and are very much a normal part of doing business. The following represents real-world tactical changes I've introduced at client sites, organized by technology stack:

- Applying firmware updates to disk subsystem controllers, server system boards, SAN fabric switches, tape drives, and so on
- Replacing failed (though usually redundant, and therefore of little real consequence!) hardware components
- Making OS-specific changes or updates, like applying kernel patches, security updates, or service packs, resizing pagefiles or swap space, or reconfiguring OS settings to improve performance or availability
- Applying database updates or patches, creating new data files and then redistributing data across all of these files, dropping and recreating indexes, and so on
- Applying SAP kernel updates, making profile changes with regard to buffer sizing or the number/mix of configured work processes, updating specific tables to enable/disable caching (in the name of minimizing the impact of "expensive SQL," or SQL statements that place an inordinate load on the system), and making other SAP Basis-layer activities or technical configuration updates with the intent of improving availability or performance
- Applying SAP support packages and code modifications intended to improve system functionality or stability (bug fixes)

Given the preceding list, it might appear that an SAP customer site would forever be introducing and managing changes. That's certainly true in a broad way—there always seems to be a new patch or fix needed in the system to improve availability, reliability, or functionality. Most of my customers decided long ago to get a handle on these changes by testing and managing them in bundles or "waves," though, hence the term *change control wave*. Such an approach to managing change involves piecing together lots of little tactical changes into a large virtual package of sorts, followed by thorough testing and subsequent "promotion" throughout the SAP system landscape (e.g., from the Technical Sandbox to Development and then to Test/QA). Eventually, the change control wave is applied to the Production environment in what usually amounts to a quarterly (or monthly) regularly scheduled outage-based activity. Sure, emergency changes— things that severely impact customer satisfaction or are necessary from a legal or tax perspective—may be implemented outside the scope of these large and orderly change control waves. Regardless, it's important to remember that change control waves, bigger than emergency changes only by virtue of their "size," still represent one of the most effective methods of introducing tactical or operational changes to an SAP system.

5.5.   Staffing for Strategic Projects

As I said previously, staffing for projects that fall out of the realm of new implementation or operational changes tend to fall into the category of *strategic* changes. Three core types of strategic changes include the following: (1) discrete technology "refreshes," (2) larger scale SAP infrastructure projects or consolidation efforts, and finally (3) SAP functional upgrades, all of which are tackled next.

5.5.1.   Discrete Technology Migrations in the Real World

Perhaps my favorite general stress-testing projects stem from a planned discrete upgrade to a customer's SAP system. I like these projects because there are fewer dependencies to manage and an excellent baseline—the current system—is readily available. Further, discrete technology refreshes, by virtue of their, well, *discreteness,* are very *focused* projects. The staff necessary to pull off a technology-specific stress test fall comfortably into a particular layer of the SAP Technology Stack, and thus the needed skill sets are by default well understood and quantifiable. Consider the following projects I've worked on, and you'll understand what I mean by discrete:

- Given my background in SQL Server-based SAP implementations, I'm no stranger to SQL Server updates and upgrades. In moving from SQL Server 6.5 to 7.0, and then to 2000, a number of my long-time customers leveraged my Microsoft colleagues and me to help them plan for and execute SAP application layer or pure database-focused stress testing. The current move to 64-bit SQL already finds us engaged in simple "delta throughput" testing (32-bit versus 64-bit technology stacks) as well as full-blown stress testing. In terms of staffing, the key was and will continue to be identifying one or more resources skilled in both the "before" and "after" database releases (especially when it comes to deploying specific database releases within a specific SAP environment or release), along with the usual technology stack, business process, and test-tool players. I prefer to leverage the RDBMS vendor itself, like Microsoft, to provide the "best" resource, because this gives the project what I believe to be the best chance of succeeding. After all, who knows Microsoft's products better than Microsoft? Or for that matter, Oracle 9i or 10G better than Oracle? Who has more skin in the game—more to lose and more to gain—than the vendor? And who has better lines of support when things invariably go south once in a while in a stress test or similar performance-tuning project?

- I have helped my clients migrate between many different physical disk subsystems over the years. From various flavors of direct-attached Small Computer Systems Interface (SCSI) disk subsystems to fibre channel arbitrated loop (FCAL) solutions, to the first SANs, and more recently to network-attached storage (NAS) and virtual SANs, I've supported a large number of SAP-specific disk subsystem–based stress tests. Without such testing, I'm confident that the level of throughput enjoyed by my customers would never have been close to what they finally enjoyed in their production systems—these types of discrete hardware migrations really benefit from the iterative testing and tuning of which I'm so fond. Note that when it came to staffing, identifying the "before" and "after" technology specialists made all the difference.

- Stress testing various server and OS combinations has consumed much of my time as well, especially in the last 3 years, as commodity-based solutions pushed much bigger but more expensive iron out of the data center. Variety has made these projects nothing if not fascinating. Projects have included server migrations at the SAP database layer, the SAP application (online and batch) server layer, the supporting middleware/integration layer, and even the client access layer (in the form of ITS stress testing, to identify the maximum number of supported HTML-based WebGUI front-ends). In some cases, the technology stacks have been completely different (IBM AIX/Oracle versus HP/Intel/Microsoft, or pure Microsoft stacks versus Linux/Oracle). Most of the time, though, these stress tests are focused more on just the impact that a new server model has, or just a particular version of a new OS. Staffing varies based on what's being compared, but is still *focused*—in this case, on the server/OS (and to a lesser extent, database) combination.

- Official "SAP Migrations" sometimes fall into the realm of discrete technology migrations, too, though quite often such a migration is anything but discrete. For instance, I consider moving from Oracle to SQL Server a fairly discrete technology project. Yes, it's a significant change, as is any database migration between different RDBMSs, but it's a lot less significant that throwing a new hardware platform and OS into the mix!

5.5.2.   SAP Infrastructure Projects in the Real World

I have participated in a number of infrastructure load-testing projects as well, which are also arguably "discrete technology projects" in and of themselves. When I think of the term *infrastruc-*

ture as it pertains to SAP environments, I typically envision the physical data center hosting the SAP solutions. Thus, network infrastructure and server platforms come to mind first. Network infrastructure in particular can drive very interesting stress-test projects, requiring network-savvy personnel typically not found in the core SAP support organization; on separate occasions, I've been asked to

- Identify the network load that a T1 network link hosting 600 online and concurrent SAPGUI users can comfortably carry (before the days of EnjoySAP, 600 SAPGUI users would consume only 10%–15% or so of a T1; today, it's closer to 30%–40%, not including print and other traffic)
- Compare and quantify 100-Mb versus 1-Gb network architectures when it came to supporting both the database-to-application server backend network and the front-end client network
- Quantify the performance deltas between maintaining a single "shared" network for all SAP traffic—both back-end and front-end—versus the performance observed by clients when a tiered network architecture was put in place

Beyond the servers and network infrastructure tying everything together, however, there are other "shared resources" that may drive a stress test in your particular case. I was involved in a short-term keyboard/video/mouse (KVM) stress test once, for example, where I helped my client validate the server and user load that a remote KVM-over-IP (Internet Protocol) solution could support. Granted, it was not an SAP project per se, but the results were applicable to their entire enterprise environment. In a similar fashion, one of my colleagues and I helped quantify the thermal load a particular data center could handle comfortably before heat thresholds were exceeded; this aided my customer in sizing and building out their new data center and later served as a baseline when they migrated to new server and disk subsystem platforms, each generating different, though generally greater, thermal loads (in smaller and smaller packages!).

In the case of the KVM project, testing without benefit of direct access to the vendor would have made things much tougher. We didn't require an onsite resource, but the time we took to identify a phone-based support person prior to doing the testing paid off. As for the data-center thermal testing, though, we never engaged an "expert" from any outside vendors per se, other than myself. But without my data-center rack-and-stack knowledge, my knowledge of HP and Compaq server and disk subsystem platforms, my general knowledge gained from supporting and working in data centers for a number of years (I got my real start in IT as an IBM mainframe computer operator in the USMC), and access to online materials regarding Liebert cooling equipment, we would have spent much more time iteratively trying different rack/server combinations, power combinations, and so on.

5.5.3.   SAP Consolidation Efforts

Consolidation is hot everywhere in IT, from customer-facing Web-server farms to back-end data warehouses and core transactional systems. The world of SAP is no exception. In fact, given the "largeness" of most SAP system landscapes and their supporting environments, it's no wonder that IT consolidation for SAP is discussed in many different circles today—CIOs want to better understand the TCO ramifications of consolidation, IT managers want to get a handle on performance and manageability considerations, the business wants to better understand how "all your eggs in fewer baskets" might actually be a good thing, and so on. Indeed, the topic is broad enough and compelling enough to warrant its own book. For our purposes here, though, let's take a look at common consolidation scenarios and how each impacts staffing a T3.

First of all, consolidation for SAP impacts every single technology layer, including even the fundamental data-center/infrastructure layer (e.g., collapsing many data centers into fewer). But the most common form of SAP consolidation I've seen hinges on reducing the number of SAP application servers servicing a database server. The second most common consolidation scenario involves bringing together expensive storage and tape subsystems into a few well-architected SANs (as an aside, avoid collapsing everything into a *single* SAN—you still need a place to test changes to the SAN fabric that connects all servers, storage, and tape components, without the possibility of impacting your production environment). Consolidation is also becoming more common at the Web AS and ITS layers, especially in nonproduction environments where the need for a whole server dedicated to a particular mySAP component or product server simply wastes resources in most cases. Finally, consolidation of multiple database instances onto fewer Database Servers (and still maintaining the same number of instances—not MCOD, but something close) seems to be growing in popularity, too.

What does this all mean in regard to staffing? Simply put, you'll benefit from having both an SAP sizing expert and a true SAP performance-tuning expert on your team—and a person as comfortable with SAP Basis as he or she is with writing and executing business process scripts that touch multiple SAP systems. Outside of this, you'll also want an expert in the core technology stack layer undergoing the consolidation. That is, if you're collapsing many servers into fewer servers, you'll want to get the most performance and highest levels of availability out of those fewer servers and therefore should bring an expert in that particular server model into the T3.

For example, are you trying your hand at SAP's MCOD approach to consolidation by combining CRM, R/3, and EBP together on one database? If so, you'll certainly need not only an SAP technology expert in each of the core components (CRM, R/3, and EBP), you'll also need an SAP technical sponsor, someone with whom you can immediately work to help you understand or internally escalate your MCOD test results. And, when it comes to MCOD, the requirement to understand peak business loads within each component/business area cannot be underestimated— get your business representatives on board early to determine the true peak load that you might place on a single database configured for MCOD. That is, be sure to analyze the workdays for each component so as to identify the busiest combined peak (e.g., the third or sixth workday of the month). And then take care to size and test the solution, to ensure it can indeed support such a load.

Similarly, if you're collapsing Web AS or ITS servers, you could do with an expert in these areas as well, someone familiar with installing and managing multiple instances on a single-server platform. The same is true in the case of using "virtual partitioning software" to effectively slice and dice a single physical server into multiple logical servers, each running its own nonproduction SAP instance. I'm a big fan of VMware's various products, Microsoft's Windows System Resource Manager (WSRM), and HP's various partitioning products as well—if you choose to pursue one of these consolidation approaches and are already an expert in deploying them for SAP environments, I suggest giving the respective vendors a call and arranging for some customized or formal training and onsite support. It's safe to say that the time and money you spend in doing so will be far less than the time you waste underdeploying or underoptimizing these products. And, with SAP's support for particular portioning solutions varying across the board, you want to be sure you are deploying a software solution that is indeed supported, especially in production environments.

5.5.4.   SAP Functional Upgrades

Many of my customers have confirmed that their SAP functional upgrades were successful because they staffed them heavily with their own employees, augmented by consulting and contracting agencies to fill in niche or small-impact needs. Further, well-known SAP patrons have said over and over again that underestimating the tools and methods necessary to deploy and test SAP's products will only get you in trouble. Sure, the tools can be daunting at first blush, and the methods complex. But, with no supported alternatives, your choices are limited. With all of this said, then, it should be clear that SAP functional upgrades—where a core release or version of a particular SAP product is upgraded to a newer release—are major projects. Very major! Besides their inherent complexity, functional upgrades impact everyone, too, from your technology-focused IT staff to business process and other functional and development folks, to the end-user community tasked with using the system day to day. The last thing you therefore want in an upgrade scenario is to be ill prepared from a staffing perspective—just like an SAP implementation, a lot of people's jobs are at stake.

Staffing should therefore address every layer of the SAP Technology Stack, from developing contacts with the Data-Center's SAP Operations teams all the way up to working with core business-focused representatives tied to each SAP module or functional area. You don't need full-time resources, necessarily, but you do need full-time T3 representatives from each area. And, because the business is likely reinventing itself to some extent, in preparation (or as a result) of the functional upgrade, tight links into your change management organization are critical, too.

Challenges will be many, though. First and foremost, the business processes leveraged by your team for baselining may very well change as a result of a functional upgrade. The change could be minor, or very significant. Either way, the value initially realized through the baseline will diminish and must be factored in to subsequent testing/tuning engagements. In a similar manner, the underlying technical infrastructure and perhaps even the system's architecture may change, simply because SAP has never released a new version of its software that would support the same precise workload as its predecessors. Accordingly, it's not uncommon to add 10% to 30% more processing power, memory, disk, or network bandwidth just to host the same number of online users and batch processes previously hosted by an older SAP release. This complicates measuring performance against your baselines, and so must be factored in alongside the functional changes occurring at the SAP application layer.

SAP functional upgrades are by no means short-lived, too, often consuming 6 to 9 months as they ebb and flow between pure functional upgrade testing, migration strategies, risk analysis, functional testing and tuning, change management processes, technical platform refreshes, and so on. What does this all mean in regards to staffing? Bottom line, you'll need a very experienced, capable, and adaptable team to tackle load testing for SAP functional upgrades. To top it off, you'll need a team that is flexible in terms of locating the best resources for supporting a particular technology layer or functional area; the team will represent a diverse mix of internal employees, contractors, partners, and third-party consultants. Links into other organizations will need to be established and managed, from the database and network teams to the DR organization responsible for business continuity, to any other technical or functional team that integrates with or otherwise touches SAP. And finally, you'll need to establish and manage a solid "feedback loop," so that the value you receive from iterative testing/tuning may actually be captured, tracked, and maintained as testing progresses (a full-time task in itself!). My advice is to seek management's unequivocal sponsorship and then give yourself plenty of time to find the best people, engage with the functional teams early, and tie off with your internal IT teams.

5.6. Concluding Our Staffing Discussion

By now, it should be apparent that failing to staff your T3 or discrete testing project team with "A" players will prove a severe handicap in the long run, regardless of the scope of your T3's mission. Your T3 is tasked with a great deal of responsibility and must meet that responsibility head-on with an attitude that says "bring the learning curve on!" In addition, the team needs to have a lot of real-world experience to boot, spanning both business process issues and technology alike. I recently read an article on staffing published by the folks at SearchSAP.com. Granted, the article was focused on new SAP implementations, but the advice befits us here as well. In a "Letterman"-style format, the author of the article, Eric Berkman, ranked *staffing* as a "top 10." In fact, it made number 8, ahead of other core success factors like establishing a vision and addressing continuous improvement. The need to *avoid the temptation* to use your SAP project as a dumping ground for folks no one knows what else to do with was declared, which makes perfect sense to me. After all, you don't want the team responsible for ensuring the performance, scalability, and availability of your mySAP solutions to be anything less than the "best and the brightest from all segments of the business." The article goes on to state that, on the contrary, your SAP staff should represent the folks that no other department wants to see go!

It is this last statement that really puts staffing in perspective for me—if you want to succeed, you're going to need to fight to get the best people you can on board, both internally and from third parties. Once you have the right people plugged into your testing and tuning organization, equipped with the appropriate vision, training, and empowerment, you'll see the extraordinary benefits of testing and tuning in action, in the form of predictable response times and consistently met SLAs. Happy staffing!

CHAPTER 6

Selecting Your Testing Tools

With so many tools, utilities, and comprehensive application testing suites on the market today, it can be a pretty daunting task to sift through everything out there just to identify the handful of core tool sets you'll use in the name of SAP performance management. It's the goal of this chapter, therefore, to identify many of the alternatives, and then help you narrow down your list of options. I share the experiences my colleagues and I have gained over the last few years, and detail what I consider to be best-of-breed products for many of the core SAP Technology Stack layers. So sit back and enjoy—now that we have the fundamentals behind us, along with the hard work of nailing down requirements and staffing the T3, we can finally begin the fun of piloting and ultimately selecting the best suite of products useful in stress testing and performance tuning your SAP environment.

It's been said that end users are the final measure of success when it comes to testing and tuning. Although I agree with this statement in principle, waiting for an up-down nod of the head from your users after every implemented change is neither cost effective nor practical. Instead, I like to think of meeting my success criteria as the affirmative nod, and my test tools as my users— the tools will confirm how successful the testing is. The key is to use the right tools, though. Thus, throughout this chapter we will work our way up the SAP Technology Stack, identifying the pros and cons of various tool sets, utilities, test suite applications, and so on. And, for consistency, I'll note whether a tool falls into the three categories previously described:

- Level One: tools that tend to be hardware- or software-specific, making it possible to characterize individual subsystems within the technology stack
- Level Two: the standard SAP benchmark kit for a particular SAP product or component
- Level Three: testing end-to-end customer-specific business processes and data, leveraging a somewhat customized method and any number of different SAP-aware testing suites

Finally, I'll identify whether a particular tool best facilitates delta testing (measuring the *difference* in performance between two alternatives), load testing (testing an expected daily load), stress or volume testing (reflecting peaks beyond the expected daily load, like those associated with quarter-end), and/or smoke testing (testing a system to the point at which a subsystem is saturated, thereby identifying the bottleneck that holds back greater throughput or better response times).

The term *test tool* implies a tool used in the active testing of a particular solution or solution component. As such, true test tools are not necessarily the same tools useful in verifying your solution's configuration or collecting performance data—these latter tools are what I call "monitoring tools" and will be discussed in Chapter 7. Instead, test tools do the work of stressing your system. They are the software utilities that emulate users, place a particular load on a hardware component, or in some other way push the system. In either case, though, how can you possibly know which tools to use? Outside of making a decision based on the various claims of test-tool vendors, or enlisting the assistance of a third-party expert (whether an internal IT colleague or external consultant), you'll be forced to make your choice based on some kind of research. In the name of due diligence, I actually prefer this latter method. But to do so intelligently, you will need a good test-tool evaluation process that goes beyond simple Internet-based research or installing a demonstration and evaluation version of the tool: you need a real test-tool piloting process. In the next section, I'll share the process I've used time and again, ideal when it comes to proving that a particular tool is up to the testing/tuning task at hand.

6.1.   Test-Tool Piloting Overview

As I said previously, instead of blindly selecting a few tools and going to town with them, or taking someone's word for it and jumping in head first, I recommend a simple *pilot* (a methodical and discrete test performed in a controlled environment) of each prospective tool you are considering adding to your toolbag. In this way, you can prove in a methodical manner that a particular tool not only meets your test criteria, but works well within the confines of your unique technology stack while supporting your custom testing and tuning goals to boot.

6.1.1.   Selecting the Right Tools for the Job—Reviewing and Piloting

At this point in your project, you must choose the best tools, utilities, and software testing suites to be included in your team's toolbag. However, going out and buying or downloading demonstration or evaluation software makes little sense without first rationalizing your long-term "pool" of tool sets and approaches against your SAP testing approaches and performance-management goals. In other words, as long as you're going to the trouble of proactively testing and tuning, you may as well invest in the tools—and in the time necessary to learn, load, and configure them—that offer excellent long-term ROI across your SAP system landscape first, and then perhaps across your larger computing infrastructure or enterprise. The tools should make sense in your environment as it stands today and as it might look in a few years. Thus, your first priority encompasses understanding your test project's or entire SAP team's testing requirements, making it possible to narrow down the list of utilities and applications that need to be looked at even more closely. This first close look or high-level review helps you map various tools back to your unique needs, which in turn helps ensure the following:

- The company that developed the tool has a good track record or reputation in the market.
- The tool appears to "do" what you think it does.
- The tool works in a manner consistent with documentation or other materials you have reviewed.
- The tool seems to meet your initial expectations, or at least creates testing gaps that appear (subjectively, of course) manageable.
- The tool supports your specific SAP environment—for example, hardware (especially if you have a mix of 32-bit and 64-bit platforms), OS, database release, mySAP components, and user interfaces.
- The tool will support your 3- to 5-year plan with regard to how your own technology stack might potentially evolve.

Note that most of the aforementioned bulleted items may be addressed without actually procuring the tool in question—it's all about performing initial research, working with available Internet-based and other resources, confirming the tool's company is viable long term, and so on. This initial research is the first step in a good test-tool piloting process.

6.1.2.   Obtaining Software for Piloting

Once it has been determined that a tool meets your basic criteria, step two involves making the decision to immediately purchase or otherwise procure a particular tool. I like to download an evaluation copy of a tool, if it's available. Many tools are not available for download, though. Should you just go ahead and spend the money, then? Maybe, if the dollars are small. But, for what would otherwise represent an expensive purchase, you might instead prefer to work with a software vendor to put together a structured demonstration of its software. These vendor-provided demonstrations will go a long way toward showing a tool's capabilities, but they rarely *prove* that a tool perfectly fits your needs. To help sway a quick decision in their favor, some vendors may conduct these demonstrations in your own unique environment *prior to purchasing anything,* but such arrangements are rare. In other cases, you'll be asked to visit one of their sites and walk through a "canned" presentation and demonstration. More often than not, though, a sales representative will run through a demonstration on his or her own laptop or other gear, typically at your own site during a sales visit. Regardless, when it comes to acquiring many of the essential tools and utilities that will eventually become a part of your toolbag, there are several methods, including the following:

- Nothing is faster than doing a quick search on the Internet and downloading a demonstration or evaluation copy of a particular tool. Many vendors of Level One tools provide evaluation copies. Pay attention to trial license restrictions, though, as you may only have 7 or 15 days to use the tool before your "license" expires. Note also that demo copies may not be full featured. Finally, be aware of the risk you run in piloting a tool in this manner—you're a prime candidate for "not knowing what you don't know"—and may therefore not do the pilot justice. That is, your lack of experience with the tool, and the need to make assumptions with regard to installation, configuration, and just plain usage may result in an otherwise acceptable tool not meeting your success criteria. You may even find yourself not using the best version of the tool! These are risks that simply need to be evaluated. Note that Level One tools are least risky, whereas Level Three tools represent the greatest risk.

- Given the shortcomings just mentioned, it might be better to actually pick up a phone and contact the vendor's sales organization. Much of the contact information you need is available from the vendor's Web site. Once you make the connection, explain your circumstances—you represent one of the best qualified leads to a test-tool vendor, after all, and will have their undivided attention. You'll likely get an offer of at least phone-based assistance to help you pilot their tool, and you may obtain a better demonstration version of the software in the process. You'll also have the inside track if you need support or have a few questions that need answering later on, a big help in mitigating some of the "don't know what you don't know" risks.

- Regarding a vendor's sales organization, if the tool is not available for download (or its feature-set is very restrictive) or the sales representative hesitates to provide you with a demo copy via overnight delivery, be quick to mention how easy it was to obtain an evaluation copy of a competitor's products—this is often what the vendor needs to hear to expedite matters. Discuss the size of the opportunity, too, as a large SAP implementation or other enterprise environment represents a nice potential regular revenue stream to software vendors. If none of this gets their attention, and other tools are on your evaluation list, I recommend moving on.

- Further, if direct avenues fail, consider working with your SAP technology partner to obtain the tool you'd like to investigate. Companies like HP, IBM, Sun, and a few others have longstanding relationships with test-tool vendors that allow prospects—people like you who haven't made the financial commitment (yet, at least!)—to test or demo a tool. Technology partners can also "lease" you the tool for a period of time, a cost-effective way to go for one-off stress-testing projects. And, given the partner's controlled presales "lab" or demonstration environment, and its experience in using and supporting the tool, this can be an excellent way to go, regardless. Your partner's sales or services team can usually get the ball rolling.

- Finally, if you've developed a good relationship with your partner's SAP Competency Center, you might leverage *that* relationship to gain access to test gear, equipment, tools, and so on. HP's SAP reference accounts, for example, do this as a matter of course.

The bottom line is that if you represent a potential sale for anyone, be it a test-tool vendor, a hardware/services partner, or even a third-party consulting organization, your chances of getting free access to a suite of SAP stress-testing tools and resources is quite possible. Work the system! Sell yourself, sell the revenue opportunity to anyone that stands to make a few dollars on the deal—and reap the benefits that come your way in terms of gratis support, better financial terms, and more.

6.1.3.   Piloting and Evaluating Test Results

Regardless of how you procure a tool, even if you get a free onsite demonstration of it, you'll need to *use* it in some fashion to prove it's worthwhile. The goal of piloting is to familiarize you with the product as well as to remove any doubt that the product will work for you. And, it represents the initial learning curve that your testing team will conquer in regard to the tool. Thus, it is important to look at the pilot for what it is—a critical first step in ultimately meeting your end users' performance goals. In my experience, the following holds true:

- To obtain the most value, a pilot must be executed on a technology stack as similar as possible to what you run (or intend to run) in Production. A disk subsystem load tool may only work for a specific vendor's hardware, or in a specific Unix environment, for example. Processor or memory test tools might be similarly constrained from an OS perspective. Use the right version for your particular situation, lest you incur the risks.
- A pilot should be focused on ensuring that the test tool delivers the core value you seek from the tool. If you're working with a SAP CRM load-testing tool, for example, you need to ensure that it indeed supports the version of CRM you have deployed, or the SAPGUI or other user interface being used. In addition, the pilot should be able to create and manage virtual CRM users executing transactions or business processes identical to those in production, including any user exits or third-party applications that host a portion of those business processes.
- To the best of your ability at this early stage in the game, test runs executed during this piloting stage must be conducted in the same repeatable manner as the test runs you'll eventually execute during your production testing. The idea is to ensure that iterative testing is easy to perform and the ability to manage and track test results is not hampered by the tool itself. For example, if a tool is incapable of capturing the kind of results you seek in some type of output file, you may need to develop your own data-capturing process. This might include the need to map your test results back to performance metrics observed at hardware, OS, DB, or SAP application levels, too, all of which adds substantially to the work of executing stress-test runs—and ultimately colors whether or not a particular tool is worth your time and effort.

The key to a good pilot, and step three in my test-tool piloting process, is to have a good plan. I generically refer to this as a *test plan* and it is not unlike the test plan you will ultimately leverage in your real-world performance tuning and stress testing. The only real difference here is that your pilot test plan will tend to be short in duration, consist of fewer goals/success criteria, and be geared toward demonstrating the specific capabilities of the tool set in question related to how well it fits your particular needs.

The number one evaluation criterion you must ask yourself as you work through and conclude your pilot should simply be "Does it meet our needs?" I call this the *fitness criterion,* and I recommend ranking your answer from 1 to 10, where 1 equals "no" and 10 is a resounding "yes." And, don't forget to capture your "yes, but . . ." comments and other observations as well. Doing so makes it easier to compare similar test-tool offerings and therefore quantify which tool indeed is best for your needs. Other questions that need to be evaluated and quantified in this manner, assuming the tool meets your fitness criterion, include factors like these:

- How well does the tool meet the organization's financial constraints or restrictions?
- Are there issues with the current version of the tool that represent unpalatable trade-offs or compromises?
- Are there timing or future support issues in terms of procurement, release strategies, and so on that will make the overall ownership experience less than satisfying?
- What about references? What other SAP shops are using the tool, and what are their experiences? These SAP-specific references can make all the difference.
- What kind of presales and postsales support is actually available (both fee-based and included), what does it cost, and what do the other reference accounts say about their own support experiences?
- Outside of the test-tool vendor's support organization, is support available from other sources? That is, does your hardware vendor's SAP Competency Center or your favorite consulting organizations have expertise in the tool set? What about your internal IT or business colleagues?

Insert your own questions and criteria into the previous list, and add up the results for each tool under consideration. You may wish to set a threshold below which no tool would meet your success criteria (to avoid selecting a tool simply because it was the "best of the worst"). All things being equal, select the tool from the company with the best reputation for staying on top of new technology and taking care of its customers. In this way, you're presumably covered both today and in the future. And I recommend paying particular attention to reference accounts—talk to the people who actually use the tool day in and day out, if possible, rather than a manager or senior technical representative responsible overall for an organization that might be using a particular vendor's tool. This is especially important if you're looking at spending significant time and money on a tool.

So, the overall piloting process is pretty straightforward! Once you work your way through piloting the tools that merit this attention, you can start actually conducting some testing. Let's take a closer look at many of the specific tools, utilities, and load-testing suites used in the real world of testing and tuning mission-critical SAP solutions, starting at the bottom of the SAP Technology Stack.

6.2.   Essential Infrastructure, Server, and OS-Specific Tools

Before you commence a full-blown stress test, it is important to verify that each server in your system and the network infrastructure that connects these servers are optimized. Testing that begins at such a fundamental component level and then continues through systems integration to deployment will serve you well going forward. Delta testing will prove useful over and over again, too, allowing you to quantify how much faster one system's configuration is relative to another.

What kind of stress testing does this boil down to, though? For SAP Application and Web Servers, processor and memory performance are key. For the latter, memory configuration at an OS level is just as important as hardware configuration, too. Windows-based SAP systems must be set to maximize data throughput for network applications, for example, rather than allowing their memory to be used for file caching purposes. In addition, memory swapping or paging needs to be monitored and minimized, and the impact that different configurations have in terms of network throughput needs to be understood early in the game. Thus, with these kinds of needs in mind, I have found a number of utilities over the years that provide for excellent hardware-, network-, and OS-level testing, the best of which are discussed in the following sections.

6.2.1. Smith Micro Software CheckIt Utilities

One of the basic utilities in my toolbag for years has been Smith Micro's CheckIt. It is inexpensive and effective, and offers an easy way to quickly benchmark different processors as well as altogether different servers. CheckIt is granular in its reporting, identifying metrics as diverse as processor/system, video graphics, memory, network, and disk performance. Specifically, I find the most value in the following:

- The ability to run all or a portion of what is defined as a standard benchmark; CheckIt rapidly executes a benchmark and captures data, such as CPU Dhrystone and Whetstone metrics, memory read and write performance measured in MB/second throughput, fixed disk transfer speeds and average access times, and video speeds measured in millions of pixels displayed per second
- The inclusion of an overall CheckIt proprietary Benchmark score, which allows for easily comparing at a high level the performance of otherwise seemingly similar systems
- The ability to generate simple bar charts between user-defined or predefined "reference systems" versus your recently tested system allows the creation of easy-to-read reports
- The ability to perform more comprehensive testing on each server subsystem or component, from modems to CD-ROMs and sound cards—not necessarily of interest in an SAP stress test, of course, but excellent from the perspective of an IT director interested in maintaining fewer test tools across an IT organization
- The ability to run multiple tests concurrently in what is custom-defined as a stress test, which allows for flexible baselining and system-to-system comparisons

CheckIt only supports Windows-based systems, and does not yet support 64-bit platforms. I also had problems using older releases in Intel systems with processors that supported hyperthreading. But for less than $70 for a new purchase, staying up-to-date is cheap. I find this tool indispensable for fundamental technology stack testing. And given the fact that the tool also supports easily capturing current-state configuration information (discussed in Chapter 7), I highly recommend it for your own toolbag.

6.2.2.   Server Hardware Partner–Specific Tools

Just as CheckIt allows system-to-system delta testing, proprietary server load tools developed and supported by each hardware vendor provide similar value. The difference is that they are typically free, and usually much more specific to the vendor's platform. In other words, they're not as portable between systems as CheckIt tends to be. They also might be a bit more difficult to obtain: if they are not available via download or on a supporting software CD, you may have trouble getting them at all. Unlike some organizations, HP, Compaq, and Digital Equipment Corporation have developed and shared to varying degrees a number of server load tools over the years, including the following:

- MeatGrinder, developed by Compaq for internal hardware-engineering testing and shared externally only in rare cases, and then only with signed test-tool–specific nondisclosure agreements (NDA) in place
- Thrasher, a simpler GUI-based follow-on to MeatGrinder that supports script management, improved logging capabilities, various configuration options (e.g., control over the number of threads and how they are utilized, ability to disable drivers), real-time script execution control and test-run monitoring, and other improvements as shown in Figure 6–1 (NDA also required)
- Performance Stress-Test Utility (PerfStress), which exercises the memory, disk, and network resources of your system
- System Stress Test (SysStress), which exercises memory, caching, and paging capabilities of Windows-based platforms (though limited in terms of RAM that can be addressed)

I recommend checking with each of your SAP Technology Stack hardware partners to obtain testing tools specific to their computing platforms. Everyone makes them—HP, IBM, EMC, even Dell. Look first to each partner's respective SAP Competency Centers; their insight and know-how regarding a particular set of tools will position you to obtain the best tools for testing SAP solutions. Then, turn to your partner's account teams so they can point you to their respective back-end engineering and testing organizations.

6.2.3. Microsoft Web Application Stress Tool

A number of years ago, Microsoft created an excellent load-testing tool designed to prove the viability and scalability of the Internet Information Server in the Web-enabled enterprise. Microsoft's Web Application Stress Tool (WAST) continues to be ideal for baselining and stress testing IIS servers that support SAP's ITS (specifically, the ITS WGate server, or Web-server

component). I find WAST of great value in that it allows you to stress your Web site and determine overall site throughput—it realistically simulates multiple browsers requesting pages from
your SAP Web-enabled system. In addition, WAST offers the following:

- It supports systems running Windows NT 4/SP4 and Windows 2000.
- It requires very little CPU overhead to create a nice load—in fact, it is considered "best
  in class" from this perspective in many cases, requiring less CPU than any other Web-
  testing tool I'm aware of, save for the simplest command-line utilities.
- It can be used to manually create new scripts.
- It can record a business process in real time (though not in virtual or "behind the
  scenes" mode) and save the results as a script.
- It can drive scripts that access multiple URLs, making it possible to stress test business
  processes that touch many systems.
- It's free!

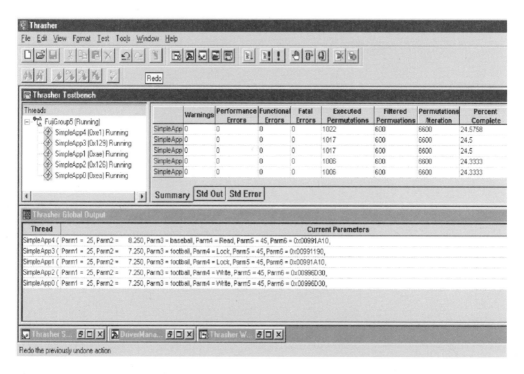

Figure 6–1   Thrasher, a popular load-testing tool supporting the backroom performance
engineers at HP, allows for script development, output management, and real-time test-run
execution through an easy-to-use GUI.

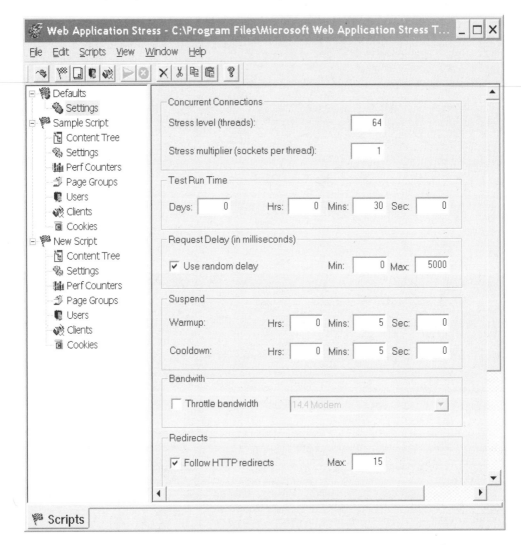

Figure 6–2   Creating a new script, or managing input files, is made easy with WAST.

If you're interested in obtaining additional information, or wish to download WAST, refer to the following Web site for detailed WAST best practices and more: *www.microsoft.com/tech-net/treeview/default.asp?url=/technet/itsolutions/intranet/downloads/webstres.asp*. It's one of the most straightforward Web-testing tools available, too, in terms of intuitively using the tool's GUI, developing new scripts, and so on, as shown in Figure 6–2. With limited platform choices and development on WAST at a standstill since 2000, you may need to consider including additional tools in your toolbag, though, like those described in the next section.

6.2.4.   Other Web-Server Load-Test Tools

For environments outside of the pure Microsoft environment, or to take advantage of new Web functionality generally available since 2001, you need to add additional Web server–based testing tools to your bag. Java-based stress-test tools may need to be considered in particular. The two top ones—Empirix's (formerly RSW) e-Load and RadView's WebLOAD—are quite robust in terms of feature sets, and are certainly leaders in the test tool industry. The e-Load tool may be downloaded as part of the e-Test suite, which includes e-Manager Enterprise for test management and e-Tester for functional testing. However, this 77MB download cannot be used without a license key, which is obtained only after an Empirix sales rep calls you to talk about your load-testing needs (for details: *http://rswsoftware.com/Empirix/Corporate/Download+Center.html*). From a sales perspective, I applaud the process they have put together—it tends to push casual "explorers" to the side, allowing Empirix's sales team to follow up with potential buyers willing to one day write them a check. But, it makes getting the e-Load test tool running in the middle of the night a bit difficult!

This minor inconvenience is easily forgiven, in my eyes, because e-Load is a remarkably thorough and well-thought-out load-testing tool. It supports both Unix- and Windows-based load clients, virtual users, and SSL, and can be extended through a built-in Visual Basic for Applications (VBA) development environment as well as VBScript, JavaScript, C++, J++, and more. And with its powerful Scenario Manager you can define and reuse custom load-test scenarios (e.g., defining one or more scripts to be executed, the number of users to execute each script, the browser type to emulate, or how quickly users ramp up), similar to much more expensive SAP-aware options discussed later in this chapter.

Which brings me to my next point: regrettably, e-Load does not provide native support for SAP's Web AS, supporting instead many other application platforms including BroadVision, Cold Fusion, Microsoft ASP, WebLogic, WebSphere, and more. But, given Empirix's philosophy of "test early, test often," the tools that underpin that philosophy, their excellent support staff, and a customer-focused attitude rarely seen in action today, your decision to go with e-Load as a platform-generic stress-testing tool is a safe bet.

RadView Software's WebLOAD follows a procurement process similar to that of Empirix, though you must go through a sales rep up front, period. There's no opportunity to even download the tool and set it up beforehand, but the entire process is easily initiated through their Web site: *www.radview.com/download/index.asp*. And the power that WebLOAD brings to the table is compelling indeed, in that it supports client-side JavaScript. Thus, business process scripts that are recorded with WebLOAD actually capture all of the triggers and events that take place behind the scenes of your Java-enabled solution in the manner of client-side JavaScript routines. In this way, when these business processes are executed again under the guise of a load test, they are played back in exactly the same manner, resulting in truly accurate Web-site load testing. This feature also allows such testing to be executed against any Java platform, opening itself up unlike most competing products. Finally, I like the fact that WebLOAD's scripting language is the same as the company's regression/functional testing product, WebFT—the end result is there's less work involved in testing your system across the board.

Of course, other tools exist as well—StressTool, Jmeter, and OpenLoad are examples of tools that may fit the bill for you simply because they're free. Many of the tools in this genre are not as flexible as their previously discussed counterparts, though, and tend to be quite simplistic as well. For instance, OpenLoad is a basic command-line utility where only one setting—the number of threads—is configurable. Similarly, StressTool only allows the hits-per-second parameter to be configured. But the price is right for these utilities, so if their tightly focused capabilities meet your needs, any one of these could very well prove a valuable addition to your toolbag.

6.2.5.   Ziff-Davis Media NetBench

NetBench is one of a small set of very capable though relatively inexpensive load-testing platforms that consists of a dedicated test controller and one or more client drivers. It has evolved over time since the days of NT Servers and Windows 95 clients, and is as useful and effective today as ever. NetBench is available for download at *www.eTestingLabs.com* and more directly via *www.netbench.com*. Thankfully, full-featured demonstration copies are available as well.

NetBench's user documentation is available in both compressed HTML (CHM) help-file format as well as HTML, and accessible over both the Web and directly from the NetBench Controller once you have it running. There's also a "docs" directory on the installation CD-ROM, a nice bonus if you happen to procure software in the traditional manner rather than by downloading it. The installation is so intuitive that you'll rarely need help—even the communication between the controller and client components of NetBench are uncharacteristically simple, relying solely on Transmission Control Protocol/Internet Protocol (TCP/IP), the defacto network protocol in use the world over, and the use of local HOSTS files, which allow you to define or map computer names to IP addresses (e.g., "computer1" to "192.168.13.109") on each client and controller. This makes unncessary special network services like DNS (Domain Name Service), a special utility or service that essentially does what HOSTS files do, though in an automated behind-the-scenes fashion.

What exactly is NetBench, though? In short, it's a file-server load-testing tool, designed to push network file I/O requests—not exactly comparable to SAP systems but certainly valuable when it comes to comparing the potential throughput a particular system configuration is capable of hosting. For instance, I've used NetBench to compare the delta in performance inherent to the following:

- File-server throughput of a two-processor system versus upgrading it to four or eight processors, so as to chart the system's scalability. In a similar manner, I've benchmarked different processor speeds as well (e.g., Intel Pentium Xeon 550MHz versus 700MHz and 900MHz upgrades, and likewise these results against the results obtained in testing a 2.8GHz Xeon MP system).
- Throughput of a system where only the network stack was changed—comparing various NICs, network drivers, NIC firmware, switch topologies, and the impact that spe-

cial high-availability NIC configurations (e.g., teaming two NICs to create a single virtual NIC capable of suffering a physical NIC failure) had from a performance perspective.

- Different OSs and patch levels. Though NetBench is limited to Windows-based systems, there's a lot of inherent power in comparing the throughput gains enjoyed by Windows 2000 Advanced Server over NT 4.0 Enterprise Edition. Similarly, we more recently determined that Windows Server 2003 was 84% faster than its Windows 2000 Advanced Server counterpart when it came to eight processor systems, a huge delta by any measure. Executing such easy-to-conduct apples-to-apples comparisons helps make the decision of whether to adopt one platform over another significantly less painful when all other factors are substantially the same.

Along these same lines, Ziff-Davis created a number of other standard benchmark utilities, arguably the most popular such collection of tools of late. These utilities are discussed next.

6.2.6.   Ziff-Davis Media WebBench

Like its counterpart NetBench, WebBench is also available for download from *www.eTestingLabs.com*, and similarly easy to set up and configure. WebBench allows for testing static and dynamic Web-based workloads, and is valuable for the same reasons discussed for NetBench; it makes comparing different systems or system configurations straightforward. For example, my colleagues and I found some amazing performance deltas between Windows 2000 Advanced Server and Windows Server 2003 using the WebBench tool set (377% for static loads in the case of otherwise identical eight CPU machines!). Again, these are not the kinds of numbers that can be directly correlated to a particular SAP solution or configuration. But they speak volumes when it comes time to conduct delta testing prior to a planned change to production, or when a new server platform is under consideration.

6.2.7.   Quest Benchmark Factory

One of the few books available on the market that covers industry standard benchmarking and stress testing, the *Benchmark Handbook* (2nd edition, published by Morgan Kaufmann Publishers, Inc.,. in 1998) speaks very highly of Quest's Benchmark Factory product. And for many reasons, as it takes stress testing to the next level compared with its less capable and equally less expensive counterparts (and it was directly involved with the book). The fact of the matter is that Benchmark Factory is powerful. It can execute file, database, and Internet server-based load testing (along with other forms of testing) and can do so by driving industry standard benchmarks or even custom stress-test benchmarking activities developed in-house. Because of these capabilities, the folks at Quest unabashedly describe themselves as the "highly scalable, load-testing, capacity-planning, and performance-tuning tool capable of simulating thousands of users accessing your database, file, Internet and messaging servers." Consider the following:

- Benchmark Factory is easy to obtain: a straightforward evaluation copy is readily available over the Web.

- During installation, you can specify a host-based installation (requiring only a single server for both software components) or a distributed installation. In the latter case, the agent and console components, called the "Visual Control Center," reside on separate servers.
- The Visual Control Center console is simple to use and complete in its approach to stress testing, as shown in Figure 6–3.
- A large number of standard benchmarks may be managed and driven by this single tool, including WebStone, WebBench, NetBench, AS3AP, Scaleable Hardware, Set Query, TPC-B, TPC-C, TPC-D, and more.
- A runtime version of Sybase Adaptive Server is installed, which allows for saving the results of stress-test runs in a true database, minus the hassles of licensing and paying for a "real" database.

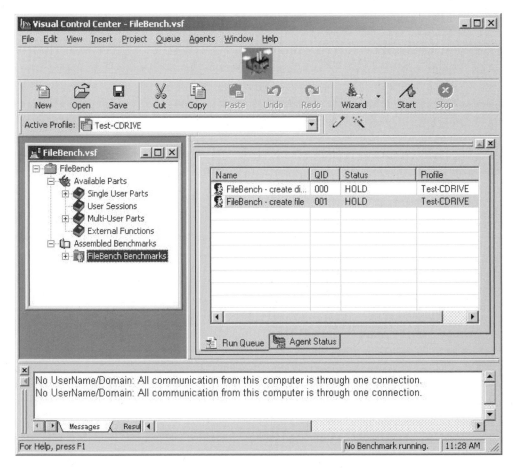

Figure 6–3 Benchmark Factory's console component Visual Control Center makes managing the development and execution of discrete benchmark tests easy.

- It supports SSL (Secure Sockets Layer) encryption, which still represents the de facto communication security standard of Web sites everywhere.
- It also supports Object Linking and Embedding Custom Control (OCX) controls, popular in SAP's user interfaces beginning with the EnjoySAP initiative and version 4.6C of the SAPGUI. As the precursor to ActiveX, OCX makes it possible to provide rich multimedia effects within a Web browser, and it supports mechanisms enabling interactive content and sophisticated user interaction as well.

I applaud the well-publicized goal of Benchmark Factory: to identify the "weak link" in a solution. Such a goal appeals to folks seeking to identify potential bottlenecks in systems prior to deployment. But, Benchmark Factory provides much more value than that. It also allows you to work through capacity planning issues, and in doing so isolate components in your end-to-end solution that are not robust enough to hold up under the weight of truly stressful business scenarios. Benchmark Factory also helps you identify other stress-related problems in your distributed computing environment.

Likewise, Benchmark Factory provides features not seen in similarly priced tools, like the ability to support testing standalone servers as well as clustered solutions. And, because it's a server-focused tool set, Benchmark Factory eliminates "client-side variables"—things like the amount of time a GUI screen takes to be constructed, the time between keystrokes in a client-side GUI-driven scenario, and so on—and therefore supports exacting stress-, load-, and even smoke-testing capabilities in the truest sense. In other words, because the GUI is taken out of the picture (replaced instead with a simple but highly effective client program optimized for low overhead), it no longer needs to be taken into consideration. This is perfect for conducting screaming high-water benchmarks! By focusing on server-side activities only, this tool gives you an excellent method of comparing the relative price/performance deltas between different system configurations. So, finally, if you need to completely stress a sole but critical server-based component of your SAP system, rather than perform a full-blown custom end-to-end test, Quest's Benchmark Factory may be the best tool in your toolbag.

6.2.8. OpenSTA

Another excellent load-testing and scripting tool used by a number of my colleagues at SAP AG and elsewhere is OpenSTA, open-source software licensed under the GNU (a recursive and rather goofy acronym which stands for "GNU's Not Unix!") General Public License. The source code for OpenSTA is available, free, at *http://opensta.sourceforge.net/*. Refer to *http://opensta.org/ docs/* for the OpenSTA user's guide and other valuable documentation. OpenSTA leverages a Common Object Request Broker Architecture (CORBA)-based distributed software-testing architecture and support of Web-based virtual users to generate stress-test loads. As such, it bills itself as a tool "to be used by Performance Testing Consultants or other technically proficient individuals."

OpenSTA can be used to neatly bring together resource utilization information and virtual-user response times in easy-to-analyze graphs, reflecting loads borne from all Web servers, application servers, DB servers, and operating platforms being tested. All of these reporting and analysis capabilities are made possible through the "Commander," which is OpenSTA's graphical user interface (GUI) that doubles as the tool's front-end driver as well. In this way, precise performance measurements can be taken across an enterprise system and collapsed into a central repository for later analysis.

Commander's interface is as intuitive as it is inclusive, allowing you to create, manage, execute, and organize test scripts. It is divided into three areas: a set of toolbars and function bars, a Repository window, and a Main window. The Repository window displays the contents of the construct used to store everything you bring together to define a "test" (e.g., scripts, input, data collectors, and other test objects), whereas the Main window consists of the Test Pane and associated properties of the object with which you are currently working. As such, and considering the power this tool brings to the table, the learning curve is quite reasonable.

Given its HTML focus, OpenSTA is perfect for driving SAP transactions through the WebGUI. And, with its support for SSL, a Simple Network Management Protocol (SNMP) module to facilitate systems monitoring, and other modules focused on collecting performance metrics, OpenSTA is a robust testing application that few toolbags can do without.

6.2.9.   Microsoft Windows Media Load Simulator

OK, don't laugh. I'll admit that this one seems like a stretch for load testing mission-critical SAP systems. After all, what's Microsoft's Media Player got to do with SAP? Well, nothing really. But the value that this tool can bring to the table is unquestionable, as you'll soon realize. For those of you unfamiliar with Media Player, it's a Microsoft utility that allows you to play CDs, digitally recorded music, participate in "Webinars" and other real-time online training/education, and so on. If you ignore the data types, though, it becomes apparent that Media Player is essentially a powerful load-testing tool in disguise, capable of moving lots and lots of data from a source to a destination, across a network—much of these data in large blocks, no less. The application of such a load simulation tool within an SAP application environment should look pretty interesting if you think about its capabilities in this light:

- Media Load Simulator allows you to stress your network infrastructure by simulating large SAP backup or restore operations (i.e., those which might surround a BW data load or SAP Database DR plan), without the need to actually install a database, install and configure SAP, set up a backup solution, and so on.
- Similarly, this tool facilitates testing the impact of a proposed back-end change to your network infrastructure (e.g., migrating from 100Mb to Gb Ethernet), in terms of measuring throughput deltas made possible by the network upgrade.
- Once network bottlenecks are worked out, the tool can be used to prove that a particular hardware configuration is capable of processing a quantifiable load of data in a rea-

sonable amount of time. Knowledge gained with regard to CPU and memory utilization can be translated to data warehousing and other large-block reporting systems, and measured against company-specific SLAs.

- Finally, it supports analyzing the throughput performance a disk subsystem is capable of achieving when it comes to moving large blocks of data, especially in terms of sequential read performance (a mainstay of large R/3 systems used for heavy reporting, not to mention core BW and SEM activities).

For these last two bulleted points, the metrics you capture during testing can be extrapolated back to real SAP systems, too. In other words, a particular configuration capable of "X" Media Player connections and downloads during a particular time period can be compared from a throughput perspective with the performance observed by your SAP BW system running "X" concurrent reports under "X" user load, for example. Even easier than this, proposed changes to your SAP Technology Stack's lowest layers can be evenly compared to quantify the performance results of a planned change.

Interested in using the Windows Media Load Simulator? If so, be sure to obtain the latest Microsoft Media Server/Service, which is free but must be obtained from your OS CD or downloaded, and then installed on top of the OS. And, pay close attention to configuration options like the following, taking care to create a consistent baseline environment from which to execute test runs:

- Note that the tool simulates a specific though configurable number of user connections and loads.
- Identify whether sequential or random activity is called for.
- Select a protocol (e.g., http or others from an available list).
- Note all user interface settings—although the Windows Media Load Simulator's GUI is very powerful, it's still extremely easy to use.
- Specify client profiles and authentication data.
- Specify the duration of testing.
- Finally, select what to log, whether to capture PerfMon data, and how often to capture these data, all of which facilitates later analysis of each test run.

6.2.10. Thoughts on Network Infrastructure Testing

Although the Media Player Load Simulator can be used for stress testing your SAP networks, it's inherently limited in that it naturally favors large-block activities. This is great for back-end SAP traffic (network activity between your database and application servers). But much of the traffic supported on your SAP system is between your SAP front-end clients and SAP's application servers, and it consists instead of very small data packets—not a good fit for Media Player.

At one time, prior to the EnjoySAP GUI initiative that arrived with the later R/3 4.6x releases, client traffic actually averaged somewhere between 40B and 1.5kB per transaction—small by any measure! Today, the 1kB to 15kB size of an average transaction is still well within "small" dimensions. But, even though the typical network bandwidth enjoyed by most organizations has grown over the last few years, it's still as important as ever to test the network infrastructure underpinning your SAP system landscape before making changes to the following areas:

- The network infrastructure itself, like cabling, switches, hubs, and so on
- The network cards in your database, application, and other SAP servers
- The OS-specific driver software stack that rides on top of each network card
- The release of the SAPGUI used by your organization

From the onset, the EnjoySAP initiative was all about improving the end user's experience; newer updates found in Web AS 6.20 and R/3 Enterprise GUIs continue this trend. The downside is that the SAPGUI typically continues to gain a bit of weight, so to speak, with each new edition. Not that it can't be trimmed down on the fly—the SAPGUI boasts controls that allow its innovative features to be throttled back, thus returning it to fighting condition when it comes time to run over slow network links. But this evolution of the SAPGUI represents another compelling reason for network-based stress testing. Coupled with the evolution of the HTML-based WebGUI and its JavaGUI counterpart, network testing should represent a fundamental proof point for all SAP testing/tuning organizations.

Beyond simplistic file-copy processes (moving data back and forth), or monitoring the network performance of a full-blown business process–based testing scenario, how can you effectively test the performance of your network? The bottom line is that any test tool that transfers data—disk subsystem test tools included—can create effective network test beds when executed from a network-attached client against a server. For example, Ziff-Davis brings excellent software benchmark utilities to the table, as discussed previously in the sections on NetBench and WebBench. And, a number of disk subsystem–focused testing tools like SQLIOStress and Iometer (discussed later in this chapter) are ideal network test tools when executed over a network share rather than in a "local" manner—in this way, repeatable and consistent testing of data block-sizes that vary from 2kB to 64kB and more is made possible. Finally, hardware alternatives exist, too, like PacketStorm's IP Network Emulator, which ships with a wonderful GUI, powerful scripting language, and the ability to emulate the most basic 10/100 network interfaces up to and including huge OC-3 (and T1, DS3, and other) data pipes. Together, PacketStorm's capabilities can be melded together and leveraged to perform a variety of network load testing, what-if testing, and so much more (see *www.packetstorm.com* for details).

6.2.11.   NetIQ Chariot and QCheck for Network Testing

NetIQ's very popular fee-based Chariot and its free though less capable brother, QCheck, are both excellent network throughput testing products. Chariot is script-based, can simulate many different load patterns or application mixes, and supports virtual load testing when used in conjunction with *setaddr* to create hundreds of virtual IP addresses. In this way, you can truly stress a single network card, monitoring not only raw performance and throughput but also the hit that your server's CPUs take when servicing hundreds of thousands of network cycles and interrupts. Even better, there are plenty of ready-made scripts available from NetIQ's Web site (and others), shrinking the time between setup and actually conducting performance tests, which in and of themselves range from fairly uncomplicated to quite complex. Note that, in all cases, at least two servers (which are called "endpoints" because of the one or more endpoint services that must be installed and started on each node) are required. To obtain true maximum throughput numbers, though, a third machine should be introduced, one that is dedicated to running the Chariot Manager (the test controller). And multiple endpoints need to be established for true load testing—try 10 or more on each node to put a really good load on most systems.

If you're short on cash and need a simpler though less flexible testing solution than Chariot, check out QCheck instead. It's easy to obtain (it's a 7MB download from the NetIQ Web site) and easy to use. For delta testing between different network cards or network topologies, or simply to validate the performance of a particular network connection (including complex long-distance routes encompassing multiple routers or "hops"), I find QCheck's simple test output an easy way to quickly measure throughput without going to too much trouble. Combined with basic CPU and network-centric PerfMon statistics, QCheck will probably take care of all but your most hardcore network performance-testing needs.

6.2.12. Another OS Consideration—Antivirus Server Stress Testing

My SAP colleagues who have traditionally supported Unix-based environments might not find this section as compelling as my Microsoft-centric colleagues; however, antivirus software has recently played an important role in SAP implementations riding on top of Microsoft's Windows NT and Windows 2000 OSs, given their "hacker magnet" status. Even Windows Server 2003, despite being more "locked down" by default than its predecessors, is as much a target as ever. To a lesser extent, the same can be said of the different versions of SQL Server available since it was supported by SAP. True, I know of many SAP shops that have placed their faith in firewalls and dedicated/nonroutable isolated network segments (a best practice, after all) and have left their core SAP server assets unprotected—in fact, at one time, I wholeheartedly recommended this practice. Granted, this was back when Intel processors strained to keep up with 50 concurrent SAP R/3 users on a single application server, leaving little CPU horsepower available for real-time virus scanning (shame on me, though!).

The world has changed considerably over the last few years, however, and in the last year or so in particular. Today I vigorously recommend that every server in an SAP environment—whether protected behind multiple firewalls, dedicated network segments, or other Open Systems Interconnect (OSI) layer filters—be protected from the temperamental 14-year-olds that toss their English homework aside in favor of flooding mom and dad's Microsoft-enabled businesses with viruses. Thus, characterizing the load that different systems can withstand comfortably while running virus-scanning software is no longer optional. Load-testing tools are relatively uncommon in this genre, though, save for one long-time exception—Symantec's Norton NAV LoadSim (short for Load Simulator, by the way, for my late-night readers who didn't already snap to that realization). LoadSim addresses challenges related to the following:

- The impact that virus definition file updates have on the network at large, either in push or pull configurations
- The impact that real-time or on-demand scanning has on individual servers
- The impact that scanning and subsequently finding a high percentage of infected files have on individual servers
- How any of the above are impacted when other components in the SAP Technology Stack are updated (e.g., OS updates, server firmware, network drivers)

At one time, real-time file scanning was not recommended by SAP AG, in favor of performing scheduled weekly scans (preferably during a downtime window). For the folks actually concerned with virus scanning back then, this was never a sound alternative, though. In those cases, I would typically recommend that virus scanning be performed at the core network router/switch layer, leveraging Cisco-supplied technologies. In other cases in which hardware solutions were out of the picture (because of budget constraints or a lack of understanding as to how these technologies enabled a more secured infrastructure), I recommended software alternatives. Stress testing proved difficult, though, for SAP shops that used antivirus products outside of NAV. In these cases, more traditional approaches to stress testing became necessary. Some of this testing drove the creation of nontraditional virus scanning architecture solutions, too. For example, in the past I've executed tests that simply moved data between a "client source" and an SAP application or DB server "target" by passing them through a dedicated virus-scanning (VS) server. Such an approach was promising in that it was close to being truly virus-software agnostic—any package that scanned on the fly could be configured in this manner. But, by the same token, the approach also had a number of key shortcomings, which are detailed as follows:

- I am unaware of any virus-scanning utilities that are capable of scanning SAP RFC traffic (if you know of one, please let me know!). A number of products can scan http and other Web protocols in this manner, however. This implies that systems enabled by ITS and Web AS would benefit the most; the VS server would presumably sit in the middle of ITS or Web AS and the end users.
- Thus, virus utilities incapable of scanning on the fly must dump each network packet of data to disk, reassemble the packets into a file, and scan it—time-consuming at best.
- Creating and using a RAM disk can be effective in this regard, as the data are simply moved and reconstructed in memory. But RAM disk size limitations tend to negate the benefits.
- Surprisingly, even RAM disks are relatively slow in practice, too. Combined with the load inherent to virus scanning, the approach still doesn't make practical sense.

- Finally, a VS server represents a single point of failure unless protected by clustered hardware, OS, network, power, and other resources; this limitation is by no means a show stopper but must be addressed nonetheless.

The primary tool I have tested and used in this manner includes Trend Micro's Interscan virus checker, which, back in 2001, was capable of scanning a mixed load of 404 MB of files in 9 minutes and 45 seconds (585 seconds), compared to a non–virus-scanned throughput rate of 8 minutes and 35 seconds (515 seconds). The 70-second delta equated to a 13.6% degree of virus scanning "overhead," most of which was traced back to CPU requirements. With today's much faster CPUs, this might actually be an interesting solution approach to revisit soon.

6.3.   Disk Subsystem and Database Testing

Quite a few tools are available that focus on characterizing the performance of databases or the disk subsystems on which they reside. Each disk subsystem vendor, in fact, has developed tools for load testing and performance monitoring, which is unsurprising given that disk subsystem vendors are no strangers to having to "prove" the performance of their systems; most long-term enterprise system throughput bottlenecks tend to be disk related, after all. Many of these tools are widely available through the hardware or software vendor's respective service and support organizations; others are maintained "internally" and treated like confidential data. SAP AG even provides a limited set of disk-specific stress-testing utilities (some of the SQL Server CDs include very basic "tools" like Windows Script, and still other tools may be downloaded from SAP's Service and Support site). Of course, there are plenty of third-party Web sites boasting tools that have been developed and published by vendors anxious to promote their own objectives. Many of these third-party tools are not only publicly available for download, but they are free (or nearly so). I encourage you to check out *www.acnc.com/benchmarks.html* for descriptions and downloads of a variety of I/O performance utilities, covering most hardware platforms and OS releases. There are some amazing tools available on this site! What I believe to be the best (or most interesting) of these are covered next, alongside other mainstays in the arena of test tools.

6.3.1.   Microsoft SQLIO Utility

Microsoft developed the original release of SQLIO long ago to help their SQL Server technical team characterize different computing platforms. Back then, it was described as "a disk workload generator that is designed to simulate some aspects of the I/O workload of Microsoft SQL Server." The key here was "some," of course, as simulating a production database is much more complex than simply executing a command-line utility with a couple of switches enabled. But, as every single one of my stress-test customers know, Microsoft's SQLIO utility has long been a mainstay tool in my personal SAP toolbag for performance tuning and stress testing. I continue to use the classic version of this product for three reasons:

- It's simple to set up, small (the executable and all configuration files fit on a floppy), and eminently portable across all Windows platforms (even old Alpha systems still running the Windows OS).
- It's highly configurable, easily allowing for testing the impact that different sizes of reads or writes, sequential and direct, have on a particular configuration.
- It provides the core information I seek when it comes to disk subsystem testing: MB per second throughput and the number of I/Os processed per second. Further, it also reports CPU utilization per processor, making it easy to correlate the relationship between disk loads and processor utilization.

Other capabilities include the ability to execute stress tests against multiple files (e.g., three or six "data files," similar to many SAP database configurations) to test the impact of multiple threads and to define CPU affinity and masks (round-robin or "ideal"). And, because the output is not only perfectly suited for disk subsystem stress testing, but also space delimited as shown in Figure 6–4, it's a simple matter to dump stress-test results into an Excel spreadsheet for subsequent analysis.

SQLIO allows you to define the time duration your particular test will execute, too—much better than hard-coded defaults of 4 hours, 1 hour, or 30 minutes, which are common to many other tools. SQLIO also allows you to control queue depth per thread. Thus, you can easily exe-

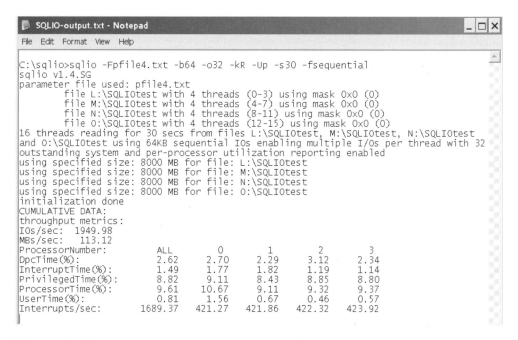

Figure 6–4 The space-delimited output generated by SQLIO makes it a breeze to import into Microsoft Excel for detailed comparative analysis against previous test results.

cute a smoke test where a disk subsystem is truly saturated (with a queue depth of 128 per disk volume, in fact!) or emulate a typical load test where the queue might be between 1 and 8 total (keep in mind that "typical" will vary depending on your circumstances, but usually is 2 or less for every physical disk drive in an array).

For simple delta testing between two disk subsystem configurations, for example, I like to execute one of eight discrete SQLIO tests for 60 seconds at a time. To do this, I create a batch file that executes SQLIO with the appropriate switches to run through sequential read, random read, sequential write, and random write 8kb blocksize operations. I then repeat the same set of four tests for 64kb blocksizes, for eight tests total, only consuming 8 minutes for the end-to-end suite of tests. Why test with different blocksizes? The SQLIO developers realized from the beginning that different databases, and indeed even different I/O patterns executed during the course of a day against a particular database, tend to transfer data in different blocksizes. SQL Server 6.5 moved data 2kb at a time, whereas Oracle has favored 8kb blocks in the recent past. And, with respect to data transfer sizes, OLTP systems have always differed fundamentally from their OLAP counterparts. Thus, the flexibility afforded by supporting different I/O blocksizes made the SQLIO tool that much more useful from its inception. And, all of this flexibility continues to pay off today as well. To obtain the classic version of SQLIO, it is necessary to work with your SAP technology partner or Microsoft technical account team directly—it has been typically shared only in this manner, not as a public domain utility.

6.3.2.   Microsoft SQLIOStress Utility

More recently, a newer version of SQLIO, called SQLIOStress, has been made available. This version can be downloaded from Microsoft's Web site by anyone (see Microsoft's Knowledge Base Article 231619 or *support.microsoft.com/default.aspx?scid=kb;en-us;Q231619* for additional information). Like its predecessor, SQLIOStress simulates the read and write patterns of a heavily loaded server running SQL Server. But it does so in a more "SQL realistic" manner, even to the point of using a Write Ahead Logging (WAL) protocol similar to that used by the actual RDBMS. This makes SQLIOStress much more SQL Server–specific, unlike the original and more generic SQLIO, which was more suited at a high level to simulate generic database activity. Likewise, it simulates page inserts and splits, updates, sorts and hashes, read-ahead activity, checkpoints, and activities associated with backups (e.g., "large and varied scatter and gather I/O requests," as described in Knowledge Base Article 231619). A very cool random generator is also available, making it possible to test random reads or writes ranging in size from 8KB to 1MB to help you understand how well your technology stack handles different I/O sizes and loads.

Perhaps the most compelling reason to use SQLIOStress, though, is that it creates a load so similar to a real SQL Server database that it actually drives a transaction log load, too. This is because during its utilization, both data and log file locations must be specified (just as you specify the location of mdf and ldf files for a real SQL Server implementation during installation). Take care not to use real SQL Server data and log files, as the data contained within them will be destroyed once you begin using SQLIOStress. Instead, let the utility create files for you, and enjoy the benefits of performance testing and tuning your SAP/SQL DB server before you ever even perform a real SAP Basis installation!

Using SQLIOStress is quite easy. Microsoft ships a "test.cmd" file configured with defaults of 3GB for a single data file and 400 kb for the log file. By default, these files are placed in the same x:\temp\simulator directory on a drive letter you specify. For example, to execute SQLIOStress against a 3GB data file residing on the G: drive, at a command prompt enter "test.cmd G"—it's that simple. A very basic GUI interface will provide real-time feedback as SQLIOStress creates the data and log files (if they don't already exist) and then proceeds with its testing (32 iterations by default, using five workers to conduct the I/O tests). To end a test cycle prematurely, terminate the test with the ubiquitous Control+C key combination. Otherwise, once the test has completed, you may review the output logs created in the default execution directory.

6.3.3.   Adaptec ThreadMark

Developed and supported by Adaptec, ThreadMark is a simple GUI-based disk subsystem testing tool. *Really* simple, actually. Further, ThreadMark only runs on older Microsoft OS releases, consumes something close to an hour per test run, and requires gobs of disk space to house the test files against which it runs. But, it can be easily leveraged to provide information on your disk subsystem's performance, measuring MB-per-second data transfer rates as well as the CPU utilization necessary to execute the data transfers. And because it takes the average value of data transfer measurements executed in a variety of blocksizes to create a summary report, ThreadMark is simple in its approach and perfect for high-level delta tests against a known baseline. The folks at Adaptec realized that its technical audience might also like to see the detailed results behind its summary report, too, and so they have provided this capability as well. Bottom line, there are better utilities out there, but given its free price tag and wide availability, it might be exactly what you're looking for.

6.3.4.   Symbios NTIOGEN

Another excellent command-line disk benchmarking utility that competes against the classic SQLIO product is Symbios's NTIOGEN, a Unix port of the long-time Unix benchmark favorite IOgen. NTIOGEN acts as a controller of sorts, spawning one or more processes that perform I/Os based on the particular switches you set. The usual things, such as blocksize, the mix of reads to writes, and the mix of sequential to direct operations, are easily configurable, as shown in Figure 6–5. Be forewarned, though, that NTIOGEN cares little if it is reading or writing into your OS partition, boot device, or anywhere else—it's a destructive test when writes are configured for a partition-level test, so be careful! Because it is file-system unaware, a nice byproduct is that NTIOGEN can run against raw devices, like those required with Oracle's Parallel Server and the first iterations of Oracle's 9i Real Application Clusters (9iRAC) for Windows. Other features that set NTIOGEN apart from the pack, and make it one of my all-time favorite test tools, are as follows:

- It supports a simplistic though effective random number seed—the seed used is actually the process ID of NTIOGEN.

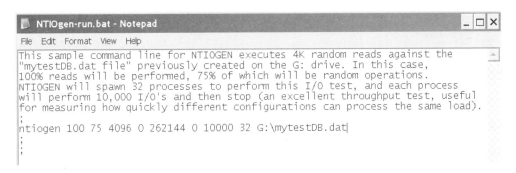

Figure 6–5 NTIOGEN is best used in conjunction with simple batch files, to capture otherwise complex switch and configuration settings.

- The NTIOGEN-spawned processes are configurable.
- You can specify the number of iterations a process will perform, thereby controlling with precision the number of I/O operations conducted in a test run.
- It can be configured to execute not only against formatted or raw disk partitions but also against a particular file created on top of a partition. In this way, the dangers inherent to writing over your important disk partitions that I alluded to earlier disappear.

In addition to these great feature sets, perhaps the best news is that NTIOGEN is free! For my SAP colleagues responsible for managing the performance of Windows-based mySAP solutions, add NTIOGEN to your toolbag by downloading it (and quite a few other utilities, as I mentioned before) from *www.acnc.com/benchmarks.html*. And, for my Unix colleagues, a version of the original Unix-based utility IOgen is available from *www.seeksystems.com/old/public/SeekIOGen.tar.gz*.

6.3.5.   Iometer

Originally developed by Intel, Iometer (rhymes with thermometer) is now a part of the open source community and is available at *http://sourceforge.net/projects/iometer/*. Many of my colleagues and customers alike who seek a fully featured disk/network load-testing package tend to lean toward using Iometer. It's perfect for testing disk subsystem and disk controller performance, as well as network throughput. Iometer is described as both a workload generator and a measurement tool, which essentially means that it not only generates an I/O load but can also monitor and measure its performance and impact against the system being tested. To be fair, though, Iometer itself is actually the controlling program—the program that provides the GUI, is used to define a workload, start and stop test runs, and so on. But, the real work is done by a program executed behind the scenes called Dynamo. Dynamo is the actual workload generator responsible for performing the I/O operations relevant to a test run, during and after which it monitors and collects performance data. Multiple copies of Dynamo can be executed concurrently, allowing for a very detailed and realistic set of database tests to be developed and conducted.

The open source community latched on to Iometer a while back and created its own Linux-specific version called PenguinoMeter. Like Iometer, it measures file-system data transfer rates.

And, the current version of PenguinoMeter can even read configuration files produced by Iometer, making it ideal for heterogeneous Windows/Linux systems (if there is such a thing).

I especially like Iometer for its granular level of test control; it may be used to test both individual drive letters and individual network cards. And, like SQLIO, it supports random and sequential accesses, allowing you to specify not only the average size of each data transfer but also the percentage mix of reads to writes. Finally, with the ability to assign CPUs to a particular worker class and then display test results real-time and in graphed formats, Iometer supports very granular performance testing and is a great long-term addition to your stress-testing toolbag.

6.3.6.   Open Source Nbench

Another interesting tool set you should consider for your heterogeneous SAP toolbag is Nbench, which can be used to support processor, memory, and disk I/O benchmarking. It's this latter capability that is most exciting in my opinion (though the memory test is a close second, given its unique ability to test different memory footprint sizes). Compelling features include the following:

- Nbench is available for every major Unix variant as well as Windows.
- It is easy to use; it can be executed from most shells or by double-clicking the nbench.exe executable via the Windows Explorer GUI.
- It incorporates a very basic though effective GUI interface.
- The three core testing options are clearly labeled and available under a simple "run" drop-down menu box.
- Under its "Setup" menu option, the level of precision for each test may be defined.
- The disk file's test file size (default of 10MB) against which your disk subsystem testing will take place can be made as large as you'd like, and you can select your *execution thread count* as well, useful in divvying up the workload among your processors.
- Finally, real-time data as to the progress of your test runs are made available, the results of which may be saved via the GUI-based window in a file format recognizable by Nbench ("*.rep," which is also readable by Notepad). And, even before a test run is finished, a "percent completed" indicator is displayed for each thread.

Other tools that compete with Nbench are described in the following section—many are quite good, some are getting on in years, and a few unfortunately require a fee-based installation key. Many of them are also GUI-based (at least to some extent) as well.

6.3.7.   Additional Basic Disk Load-Testing Tools

As I said earlier, given the tendency of a computing system's bottleneck to manifest itself in the disk subsystem, it's no wonder that so many tools exist for this kind of load testing. Some, like HD Tach and Bench32 are quite capable utilities but require a license key or registration with the parent company. Others, like IOzone, are command-line-driven (very similar to the classic SQLIO) but powerful in terms of their ability to test large blocksizes and to test both local drives and network shares. IOzone can run from a DOS shell or a Linux cygwin shell (enabling this Windows utility to execute in a Linux environment). And still others, like QBench and RAIDmark, look very much like the graphics associated with a NetWare Loadable Module (NLM) utility you might find executing in an old Novell NetWare 3.11 system; despite their ancient quasi-GUI interfaces, they still manage to provide good data transfer and response-time performance data, though.

Another decent tool that hails from the PC testing world is Ziff-Davis's WinBench, which includes a number of WinMark variants. WinBench is described as "a subsystem-level benchmark that measures the performance of a PC's graphics, disk, and video subsystems in a Windows environment." It supports most of Microsoft's OSs as of Windows 95, and still proves to be of value today.

HP has also put forth a number of excellent disk subsystem analysis tools over the years. The Performance Assessment Tool (PAT) allows you to test file system and raw disk read performance to help identify and plan tape backup times. This tool supports a quick analysis option in addition to long-running comprehensive analysis options too, making it handy in a pinch if you need to estimate how long a dump to tape for a particular disk partition might take, for example. Output from PAT includes the actual transfer rate observed during the test, an estimate of the total time it will take to dump the complete contents of the disk partition to tape, and details relevant to the performance of varying data sizes. PAT is limited in that it's only available for NT, Windows 2000, and HP-UX. However, another variation of PAT called HPReadData is available on NT, Windows 2000, Linux, Solaris, and HP-UX. HPReadData adds support for multipathing, meaning it allows you to factor in the performance gain enjoyed by a tape solution that can read from multiple data streams (whether based on multiple data partitions or simply due to the fact that multiple host bus adapters may be configured to interface with the disk subsystem housing the data being read).

Finally, tools like Disk to Disk (DD) and the much more capable LMDD (the Linux version of DD) provide the ability to measure raw disk performance between Unix file systems. I like to use LMDD to assess the true maximum read performance of a disk subsystem because it does so without OS file system overhead. That is, a true raw-disk performance ceiling can be identified for particular disk configurations, as can the speed in which a "serverless" backup might run (where the overhead of a server and its typically unavoidable file system serve to slow down overall I/O throughput).

6.3.8.   Microsoft SQL Profiler in the Real World

Long ago in the days of SQL Server 6.5, this tool was referred to as SQL Trace. Later, it was renamed SQL Profiler, and today it ships with SQL Server 2000 and is easily accessible via the SQL Server Enterprise Manager console (or by selecting its own icon from the "All Programs" Start Menu). The core value provided by SQL Profiler revolves around its ability to trace step-by-step the activities surrounding a database transaction. As such, events associated with cursors, locks, objects, table and index scans, stored procedures, T-SQL statements, user sessions, and so on are carefully tracked and safeguarded in an output file for later analysis. Thus, correlating the load placed on a system with back-end SQL Server activity is facilitated—all well and good for tracking and monitoring stress-test runs.

But its real value in regard to stress testing, and the reason I therefore discuss this tool here rather than from the perspective of a monitoring tool, is SQL Profiler's ability to record database activity and then play it back. Just like that, you have the makings of a repeatable benchmark, perfect for testing how the same exact database load is handled by different hardware platforms, for example. Simply record a nice load, and then play it back on a different system, noting the delta in CPU performance, disk I/O throughput, and so on. I've used SQL Profiler to quantify the difference in performance a new disk subsystem made for one of my customers prior to their actually signing a purchase order, and, in another case, my colleagues and I benchmarked different server configurations to give our client an idea as to how well a typical load would be handled.

Even more compelling, though, I assisted one of my SAP accounts in proving without a doubt that their in-place SQL DB server platform had the headroom available to support a 2x spike in database load. How? It was pretty easy, actually—as an added bonus, SQL Profiler also supports "playing back" a set of recorded transactions at different speeds. All we did for this particular client was to play back the load at twice the speed, making a few key assumptions in the process:

- The load the client would see during peak times would exactly model its more typical daily load in terms of the mix of online user versus batch job percentages.
- Only the *number* of end users and batch processes would then effectively double.
- The type of work being performed would also stay consistent (e.g., the mix of R/3 FI to SD to MM users was assumed to stay consistent).
- The application server layer was deemed out-of-scope. In other words, since we could take advantage of SAP's well-known ability to scale horizontally by simply deploying additional SAP application servers as required, we were not concerned with scalability at this layer. Rather, only the database layer was in question.

The value of this testing approach was unquestionable; it allowed us to quickly complete a stress test that would otherwise have required expensive virtual-user SAP API–aware software, a bigger investment in testing infrastructure, and custom business process scripting.

6.4.   Non–SAP API-Aware Scripting Tools

As you probably noticed, the tools just covered in the previous sections are classic Level One tools in that they are somewhat "packaged"—by and large, they focus on testing specific back-end components or subsystems, and therefore represent what I also term *discrete testing tools*. The tools discussed in this section, however, are wide open—which is good news and bad news. The good news is that they are infinitely flexible. For example, tools like AutoIT can drive most any Windows-based user interface.

The bad news is that these tools are, well, infinitely flexible. You'll need to create scripts that work for you, customized for your particular circumstances. And you'll need to maintain those scripts as your system changes—a script that drives a financial business transaction, for example, may no longer work at all once an SAP support package, legal change, or bug fix is applied to your system. For example, any system change that modifies the screen names associated with the SAPGUI has the potential to "break" your scripts (unless you're a master at using wildcards, and lucky to boot). There is the learning curve to consider as well—different scripting tools differ from one another in syntax, approach, online help, and so on. Therefore, if low maintenance is your goal, or if you need to get a jump on systems-level stress testing, scripting may not be the best answer for your immediate needs. Keep in mind, though, as you read through this next section, that the value of scripting tools only increases as a pool of useful scripts are developed and grown over time. Note also that for true business process testing outside of standard SAP benchmarking, there's simply no getting around the scripting process. That is, if you want to test how your business processes perform under load in your environment, you will eventually need to select and learn how to use a scripting tool, period—even the tools that purport to be GUI-based and user-friendly are purposely limited (hence their user-friendliness) until you tap the potential of the scripts generated behind the scenes.

The set of scripting tools discussed next are generic, however, in the sense that they "know" nothing about the application being tested. That is, they are not SAP API–aware; they work by simply driving the Windows GUI. In other words, the underlying application might be an SAP system, it might be a Web site, or it might even be an e-mail package. It doesn't matter to these tools—they work their way through executing a transaction or business process by "clicking" here and pressing "Enter" there using the same Windows-based interface a physical user would use.

As you well imagine, there are plenty of scripting tools available. For the sake of brevity, though, I only cover the few I have direct knowledge of—share your favorites with me so that I can check them out as well! And remember, what these tools lack in SAP-specific capabilities and general capabilities is made up in price, as you'll see next.

6.4.1. HiddenSoft AutoIT

Let me preface this section by saying that AutoIT is one of my absolute favorite "basic" scripting tools. AutoIT originated out of the need to automatically install software that was difficult to automate otherwise. It has been around for quite a while. However, I was first exposed to it via SAP's benchmarking kits, where AutoIT is still used today to work through the various WinGUI screens to ultimately generate a Perl script used by the actual SAP benchmarking program. AutoIT is perfect for this kind of work, and perfect for automating many otherwise repetitive or tedious tasks—anything that is performed by mouse-clicking/moving or keyboarding can be recorded and captured. And, AutoIT can be obtained in a pure version of the Dynamic Linked Library (DLL), a common type of configuration file associated with Microsoft operating systems). and even an ActiveX version, too, opening up scripting possibilities beyond simple clicking and keyboarding. Finally, there's a utility available to convert scripts into their own executable files ("*.exe"), excellent for creating standalone procedures that can be scheduled and loaded on a variety of platforms without the need for AutoIT's "script development" environment. And there's even a utility included with the full download that allows compiled scripts to be "decompiled," assuming you know the password used to compile the script in the first place. As shown in Figure 6–6, this easy-to-use GUI allows you to update your code after it's been compiled, without having to fall back to the original AutoIT scripts—perfect when you misplace or accidentally overwrite your source code! See *www.hiddensoft.com/AutoIt/* for complete documentation and excellent downloads. It's a great site for working sample scripts: for instance, illustrating the syntax necessary to execute window commands (e.g., maximize, minimize, wait for, hiding, and activating), describing how to use simple string and variable functions, illustrating how to take advantage of text clipboard functions, and more. There are even sample scripts that show you how to edit your window's registry, rename files, and automate the use of network troubleshooting mainstays like *ping* and *tracert.*

If you download the full AutoIT installation, you get the following:

- AutoIT program files, documentation, and examples
- Aut2Exe, the "script to executable" converter that allows you to create executables

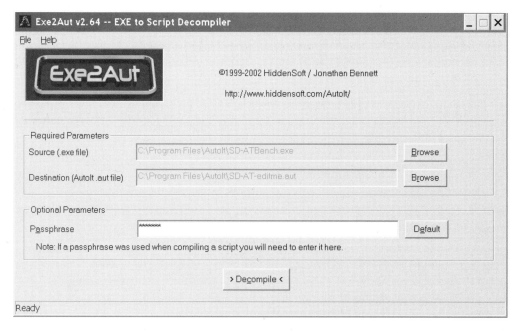

Figure 6–6 AutoIT "Script to EXE Converter" utility makes running scripts outside of AutoIT script development environments possible; in addition, it has the ability to password-protect sensitive scripts such that they cannot be decompiled without the password.

- AutoItDLL, a pure DLL version of AutoIT
- AutoItX, an ActiveX control version of AutoIT that self-registers as part of the installation process

Note that there is no AutoIT "scripting environment utility" per se, because AutoIT scripts are created and edited using Notepad (or any text editor for that matter). But AutoIT's installation process builds hooks into the OS such that it becomes aware of ".aut" scripts, and right-clicking an AutoIT script presents the user with the options to run, edit, or compile that script. If you absolutely must have a scripting tool that ships with a full-blown script editor, look elsewhere (e.g., Sapien's PrimalScript, covered next). Keep in mind, too, that AutoIT does not support virtual users, either—only physical clients. For excellent virtual-user scripting capabilities combined with low price and the ability to drive stress tests, review the section on SourceForge's OpenSTA, covered earlier in this chapter.

6.4.2. Sapien PrimalScript

Among the many scripting products available on the market today, PrimalScript is another of my favorite fee-based tools, delivering a versatile script editor that supports a variety of scripting languages (e.g., VBScript, JavaScript, Perl, HTML, SQL, DOS batch files, and XML), as well as full-blown programming languages like C++, VB.NET, and C#. And there's more! PrimalScript also offers Windows Scripting Host (WSH) support, server-side Web development, a built-in HTML browser, and the ability to customize its interface. The Workspace Nexus lets you create and manage projects and manipulate scripts and other files and includes an integrated debugging environment. Even more impressive, a spellchecker is built into the product, which has personally served me well in the recent past.

PrimalScript is a much better script editor than most, too, in that it leverages color-coded syntax to aid in developing straightforward code. There's also a number of useful pull-down menus that allow you to customize your font options, control the use of line number and column rulers, and more. And, with the ability to e-mail a script or launch an ftp front-end, sharing your scripts is easy. All in all, Sapien has done a wonderful job—grab a copy today by visiting *www.sapien.com/PrimalSCRIPT.htm*. The list price is less than $200, a bargain in my opinion, even if it only supported SAP. With all of the extra platform support, though, this is one of the best IT test-tool buys (and monitoring tools, for that matter) on the market.

6.4.3. TxShuttle

Voted by SAP FAQ as one of 2003's best products (alongside all three of Mercury's testing products discussed in this chapter, and quite a few handy tools like Snagit, Citrix MetaFrame, LiveReorg, and more), TxShuttle is special in a number of ways. First of all, it lets you record, map, and playback transactions in three easy steps without having to actually write a line of code. Data can be uploaded via Microsoft Excel, making it perfect for executing occasional data loads as well. In fact, TxShuttle is easy to use for both mass data corrections and general stress-test simulation. And, because all of this is possible without requiring SAP transports, you can quickly move from working out bugs in a test environment to executing a stress test in your Production system in a matter of days. I recommend that you check this out—TxShuttle is conveniently available off the Web in a demonstration version.

6.4.4.   Perl, Visual Test, and Other Legacy Scripting Tools

There's a huge number of scripting tools out in the marketplace; some have been available for years, whereas others are relative newcomers. As I've said before, it's my philosophy that if your company has standardized on a particular scripting tool, and that tool is capable of driving the Windows interface, you should consider leveraging it before looking elsewhere. The competencies, experiences, and existing scripts that may be found in-house can get you over most of the learning curve, especially compared with buying and learning the latest scripting tool. However, there are a few things to keep in mind:

- Certain older scripting languages are inherently more complex than necessary today; carefully evaluate the time that might be wasted in terms of coding and script maintenance should you choose to go with a legacy tool like Visual Test, for instance.
- Certain scripting languages support only a very narrow pool of hardware platforms and OSs; ensure you're covered in this regard, too.
- Most legacy tools will not support the latest OCX controls and other features found in the newest versions of the SAPGUI; this rules out most versions of Perl in use today, for example.
- Similarly, most legacy tools will have problems with Internet browser–based front-ends, including the SAP JavaGUI and HTML GUI.

Thus, a bit of fundamental "piloting" is called for even in the case of otherwise tried and proven legacy scripting tool sets. If their capabilities are lacking, or your SAP system will be undergoing, in the very near future, significant changes that put the tool's viability in question, I suggest cutting your losses and evaluating some of the scripting alternatives covered previously, or step up to the next class of scripting products—SAP API–aware tools.

6.5.   SAP API–Aware Application Layer Scripting Tools

Unlike their non–SAP-aware scripting counterparts, the Level Three tools and utilities covered in this next section offer huge and compelling advantages despite their proportionally larger price tags. Why use these relatively expensive "SAP-aware" tools when so many free or inexpensive test-tool options exist? The argument for testing tools that boast an SAP Business API– (BAPI-) certified interface, and those that do not, comes down to capabilities versus price. Tools that leverage SAP's BAPI make a testing tool SAP-aware, in that they can then communicate with an SAP system through a standard API rather than by relying on driving a front-end GUI screen. Because of this, SAP-aware tools boast the following capabilities unavailable from the load-testing and scripting tools already covered:

- They can "screen-scrape," which means that the German field names within the SAPGUI are exposed; thus, they pull information out of the SAPGUI, such as the phrase "transaction completed successfully" or "order 06011998 posted for customer 20030608," and use these data to populate a variable (which may then be used by another transaction, in effect linking multiple transactions into a single business process).
- Similarly, SAP-aware tools can read the contents of a field displayed by the SAPGUI even if the field displayed in a particular output screen is not actually "visible" on the screen (i.e., you need to page down to visually see the field). Thus, whether the SAPGUI is visible or not becomes immaterial, a key characteristic when it comes to driving many SAP virtual users.
- These tools can often take this capability one step further and execute SAP transactions without even displaying the SAPGUI; the transaction actually runs "behind the scenes" but does so in a virtual manner—input is processed, output is created, and so on.
- Finally, SAP-aware tools therefore inherently support SAP virtual users (with some exceptions based on the version of SAP being tested more than the tool itself), who, as I've said before, bring a wealth of cost-based benefits to bear.

On this last point, the ability to use virtual users saves money and time, both of which would be liberally consumed had real end users (or even hundreds of physical desktops) been required to drive a load test. Instead, tools that support SAP virtual users rely on high-powered controllers and one or more "client drivers," like those discussed previously, to set hundreds or even thousands of virtual SAP users in motion.

Capabilities like this don't come cheap, however. The most popular SAP-aware test-tool vendors charge upwards of $200K for the privilege of being able to host 1,000 virtual SAP users. Prices vary, of course—AutoTester's products tend to be most competitively priced—and individual vendor flexibility in pricing varies as well. I recommend looking at all three of the primary vendors before making a decision. Each product tends to leapfrog the others over time, as is typical in the IT industry, such that one of these products might be better positioned to meet your immediate needs than the others.

Even factoring in the significant cost of licensing these products, the overall savings are significant; the cost of paying real users to give up perhaps 1 or 2 weeks of productivity every year in the name of stress testing would be quite a bit more. And as I said before, the test infrastructure alone required to support hundreds of physical desktop clients would pay for the licenses a number of times over. But, only when we begin to think outside of the strictly "financial" box and start looking at the functional benefits an SAP-aware tool provides, do things really get exciting! For instance, an SAP API–aware tool can pull data like customer numbers, materials, and so on from a text or spreadsheet input file and populate the input needed to execute VA01, the R/3 sales order transaction discussed earlier. The output—a sales order number and any warning or error messages—can also be captured, to feed additional transactions, one after the other, that might be required to complete an end-to-end "assemble to order" or "order to cash" business process, for example. Previously discussed scripting utilities, on the other hand, like Perl and AutoIT, are simply not capable of screen-scraping or operating in a virtual manner and therefore cannot provide this level of value.

Much of this book is dedicated to covering how to use these specialized SAP-aware or SAP-enabled tool sets to perform custom load testing. In alphabetical order, highlighting first each company's respective script development/single-unit load-testing tools, followed by virtual load-testing tools that support thousands of both physical and virtual users, we will look at the key players in this important "SAP performance validation" market.

6.5.1.   AutoTester ONE (AT1) Special Edition for SAP

A long-time SAP-aware testing-tool favorite of mine, AT1 supports Windows 95, 98, NT 4.0, 2000, and XP development environments. AT1 is the company's flagship product, a fact that shines through in its capabilities, ease of use, and company commitment to product development in the name of continuous improvement. Most recently, the latest version of AT1 incorporated SAP Web AS 6.20 support, which in turn followed the addition of the Test Organizer module, an integrated package that makes storing and organizing individual test cases that much easier. The Test Organizer provides reporting information as well. Earlier last year, the folks at AutoTester also added a Scheduler module to allow for unattended testing of single or multiple test cases.

AT1's development interface is worth a closer look, too, having evolved over the years in response to customer and partner feedback. Today, I consider it one of the best in the business—it's intuitive, organized, and capable. Support for Web stress testing was built in long ago, setting the stage for testing what would become SAP's Web AS. And, with support of ActiveX controls in Internet Explorer, AutoTester jumped on the EnjoySAP GUI bandwagon early on. Finally, the fact that multiple instances of the AT1 interface may be used concurrently, leveraging a single instance of the AT execution engine, makes developing and testing complex business processes spanning multiple mySAP Business Suite components quite easy: for example, I've opened multiple SAPGUI virtual sessions into R/3 and CRM, sharing status information via simple text-based status files to drive the execution of a sales order from SAP CRM through posting in R/3. Tools that support only a single development instance must instead virtually log off and log on each system as the business process's underlying transactions require, slowing down overall execution and inviting timing variables (the time required to log in) into what should really be a consistently executed process.

The folks at AutoTester recommend adhering to the following best practices when recording and managing scripts in an automated testing environment; most of these tenets apply across the board to competing products as well:

- Use standard mouse cursors and the hour glass (rather than "animated" versions).
- Set the Windows Taskbar properties to "Always on Top" rather than "AutoHide."
- Disable all screen savers, power-down settings, and hibernation settings (basically anything that can cause a change to the focus of a particular screen).
- Turn off Personal Information Manager (PIM) alarms.

- Turn off all pop-ups (e.g., network or e-mail messaging).
- Turn off or disable all Terminate and Stay Resident (TSR) programs.
- Disable virus scanners after their initial start-up and subsequent file system scan.
- Close all application desktop toolbars, like the Microsoft Office Toolbar.
- Remove any accessory clocks on the Windows desktop.
- If Internet Explorer 4.0 or above is installed, turn off Active Desktop and disable the *loadwc* service, if present.

And, although not absolutely required, best practices dictates that all unnecessary programs and services are set to "manual" or "disabled." AutoTester's ideal recording and playback development environment only requires the following:

- Explorer
- AutoTester
- W32MKDE
- SAP services, if you're testing from an SAP Application Server or similar SAP system (which is neither likely nor recommended in anything other than a crash-and-burn technical sandbox environment)
- Systray (optional, but handy)

I realize that the aforementioned list is short—quite a challenge and pretty unrealistic in most cases; check with your desktop administration team to ensure that any required company-internal services or processes remain enabled.

6.5.2. Compuware TestPartner

Like AT1, TestPartner is an automated functional testing tool that has been specially designed for testing complex applications based on Microsoft, Java, and Web-based technologies. Because it is one of very few certified test platforms for SAP, TestPartner allows both testers and developers to create repeatable tests through visual scripting and automatic wizards. Script developers have access to the full capabilities of Microsoft's VBA, allowing tests to be as high level or detailed as needed. And, because TestPartner has the added distinction of being the first tool on the market to be certified by SAP for eCATT integration atop the Web AS 6.20 platform, it offers some unique capabilities not found elsewhere. For example, TestPartner allows for testing SAP applications that leverage the SAPGUI for HTML, or WebGUI.

And, given the tight eCATT/TestPartner integration, in that eCATT can effectively "wrap" TestPartner scripts within eCATT scripts, a single centralized test asset repository is created. This simplifies test case management in a big way, as you can imagine. The integration between TestPartner and eCATT also provides the SAP tester with a single interface for creating, editing, storing, and executing both TestPartner and eCATT scripts and other "test assets" like input data, processes, necessary test objects, and so on. Note that during TestPartner/eCATT script creation, TestPartner works at the object level of the SAPGUI for HTML—ultimately, Compuware's support for the mySAP Business Suite, especially the WebGUI interface, helps testers create repeatable test assets quickly, easily, and early in the development phase. And, with traditional Windows-based SAPGUI support forthcoming, business processes that have not been WebGUI-enabled in your unique environment will also be supported by TestPartner soon.

Another key characteristic of Compuware TestPartner is the automatic test execution function and how it is handled between the eCATT Workbench and TestPartner. That is, eCATT will automatically pass test execution to TestPartner when a test case requires either the WebGUI or access to a non-SAP application. This greatly simplifies the scripting and testing process. Further, data are easily shared and integrated across the board in a real-time manner. During script execution, runtime test data are seamlessly passed between eCATT and TestPartner via the eCATT Argument Container. This allows the tester to run repeatable tests by passing variable data between applications, thus allowing validation of all SAPGUI and non-SAP applications in a single script execution. Plus, the TestPartner product supports common Web technology (e.g., HTML, Java, DHTML), ActiveX controls, Common Object Model (COM) objects, and more, effectively extending the tool's reach across an SAP enterprise.

I especially appreciate TestPartner's script development process, what is described as a "tiered" approach. Novice testers without a programming background can use the TestPartner Visual Navigator to quickly create tests and execute them. However, for developers and more technical testers, the full power of the Microsoft VBA language is available. The net result is that Compuware's tiered approach to learning and using TestPartner provides both a shallow learning curve to fast-track new testing projects and a more traditional fully featured development environment once the newbies get up to speed. It's a great approach, and one I wish others would adopt—too often, the pure complexity of an enterprise testing tool stands in the way of using it, which works directly against achieving an organization's performance-tuning goals.

TestPartner provides additional tools for novices and advanced testers alike. For instance, one of the many powerful wizards included with TestPartner allows you to create scripts behind the scenes and then begin executing test cases immediately. Another wizard, ActiveData, allows testers to create a single script for data load and data validation purposes, which eliminates the need to modify otherwise complex data load scripts directly, making it a breeze to construct complex test cases. In the end, using wizards results in fewer scripts that must be maintained over time, and a less daunting approach to scripting in general.

6.5.3. Mercury Interactive WinRunner for R/3 and QuickTest Professional

Mercury Interactive has been a leader in automated SAP functional testing for years; it is no stranger to helping companies design and execute complex test cases used to satisfy equally complex predeployment functional and single-unit load-testing requirements. SAP AG, SAP Labs out of Palo Alto, and SAP Australia all use Mercury Interactive's WinRunner and QuickTest Professional to test the reliability of Web client interfaces to R/3. WinRunner for R/3 is touted by Mercury as "offering the fastest and easiest way to test an R/3 business process." Like competing products, it captures and replays script content automatically. But WinRunner for R/3 recognizes business objects in that it leverages SAP's "open client" architecture, and it supports other applications integrated with your SAP environment as well. WinRunner for R/3 has for many years also featured QuickTest, which supports the WebGUI as well as the standard SAPGUI. The real differentiator is that QuickTest does not rely on testers manipulating test scripts. Instead, real SAP screen captures and icon-based data allow testers (and even nontechnical business analysts) to control and test their SAP applications "graphically" in the same manner transactions are developed. In this way, the scripts are maintained "behind the scenes," available for use in both functional/regression testing as well as load testing.

Designed from the ground up, QuickTest Professional represents a fresh approach to automated testing. Like Compuware's TestPartner offering, the combined Mercury offerings provide a tiered solution approach to testing, too. Similar advantages apply: more than simply offering a reduction in the time necessary to create and manage test cases, the Mercury product set supports nearly 40 different enterprise applications, databases, and front-end clients. And QuickTest Professional in particular not only supports multiple SAP products but also integrates seamlessly with Mercury's LoadRunner load-testing product, discussed in the next section.

6.6.   SAP API–Aware Application Layer Load-Testing Tools

The three companies previously discussed with regard to their functional and single-unit load-testing products offer the three most robust load-testing applications for SAP as well. Note that because these products do not simply "emulate" an SAP client connection, there's great value that can be obtained from using them for load testing. You can, for instance, prove that your network infrastructure is up to snuff, that a particular desktop or laptop configuration meets a company's needs, or observe how well a proposed back-end system change handles a known baseline workload. Of course, realistic testing implies not only that an appropriate test infrastructure is in place, but that it is nearly identical or in some measurable way equivalent to the Production environment being tested. Each of the SAP API–aware core load-test offerings, from AutoTester, Compuware, and Mercury Interactive, is discussed next.

6.6.1   AutoTester AutoController

AutoController is designed to allow the processing and control of many tests running concurrently from a central console—a single console guides the activities of remote virtual clients executing atop client-driver satellite workstations. These satellites execute AT1 scripts in virtual or real mode; the software stack may ride on top of anything from marginally powered PCs capable of hosting only a few concurrent SAP users/connections to large enterprise-class servers executing a Microsoft Windows server OS like Windows 2000. Note that AutoController is limited in that it does not support Unix test infrastructure—this only impacts the test infrastructure necessary to run AutoController, however, not the system being tested. That is, the system being stress tested may be a Unix-based solution, IBM mainframe, Intel-based hardware platform running Windows or Linux, or whatever. As long as AutoController's virtual clients can connect to the system via TCP/IP, just like any other SAPGUI or WebGUI connection, you're in good shape.

Once the AutoController components are installed in your test infrastructure environment, the AutoController satellite workstations process the tests scheduled by the AutoController console component using a local, unshared installation of AT1. For SAP-specific testing, of course, the "Special Edition for SAP" version of AT1 in either full or runtime versions is obviously required.

AutoController allows you to create multiple test groups or packages, each with a unique configuration, timing/execution criteria, scripts to be executed, and so on. Test runs can be scheduled for immediate playback (the usual setting), set to run at a specific time in the future, or controlled by a countdown timer. Then, during testing, AutoController's user interface clearly identifies each virtual client in terms of status, activities, which tests are being executed and their execution sequence, and the workstations on which the tests are running. If you like, you can even drill down into the line-by-line AT1 code that is being executed (assuming this communication option is enabled), thus giving you a real-time view into running tests. Finally, during test execution, you may stop or restart tests, abort one or all tests, or abort individual virtual clients, giving you flexibility and complete control over your load testing.

And, once stress testing is complete, AutoController makes the test results available in a number of ways. I usually collect most of my data through the AT1 scripts themselves, capturing most of the response-time and throughput data I need to prove that I've met my success criteria. But other information regarding test times, script failures, virtual client drop-out rates, and so on is also readily available via a "results" output file. Combined with historical baseline data, Auto-Controller makes it easy to compare one test run to another, measure individual system performance, and track how the changes to your test infrastructure over time impact system performance.

6.6.2.   Compuware QALoad

QALoad is part of Compuware's QACenter suite for automated load and performance testing, covering a mix of ERP, client/server, and other enterprise applications. QALoad therefore supports a variety of databases, middleware, protocols, and applications, such as the following:

- Oracle, SQL Server, DB2 UDB, Sybase, and Open Database Connectivity (ODBC)
- Tuxedo, Distributed Common Object Model (DCOM), CORBA , and more
- http, SSL, digital certificates, Internet InterORB Protocol (IIOP), and ftp
- SAP R/3, PeopleSoft, and Oracle eBusiness Suite

QALoad emulates the load generated by hundreds or thousands of users on your application. Simply set up the load-testing scenario and relevant conditions for your test run, create the virtual users you need to simulate the load, and then kick-off and monitor the test run using QALoad's Conductor module. During the execution of each QALoad test case, performance statistics can be viewed online in a variety of report, graph, and chart formats. The output data from each test case run can also be automatically imported into Excel and other tools for more detailed analysis.

How is the load generated, though? Competing products leverage an interpreted language, which in itself creates a front-end client load. QALoad is a bit different, however. It uses a complied ANSI C script to create an ultra-light front-end load. Of course, if your goal is to test the front-end load, other approaches are readily available. But the beauty of QALoad's Script Development Workbench is that you can develop lightweight custom testing scripts that need only a fraction of the footprint required, for example, by products like AutoTester AutoController and AT1. This in turn allows a test infrastructure to support more load with less gear—in other words, physically less hardware is required to run a test case. The test cases themselves, labeled "EasyScripts," are nothing different than a recording of the traffic an application generates—the resulting scripts directly reflect the actual traffic generated by SAP and measure the time taken to perform these transactions to ensure that the system under test can be mapped back to a specific client-driven workload. Note the following real-world benefits and trade-offs:

- Flexibility, in that QALoad supports not only traditional Web applications, but SAP R/3 as well. And different virtual-user types are not required either; instead, Compuware's EasyScripts plug into QALoad and benefit from a single set of virtual users.
- Scalability, in that, as I mentioned earlier, QALoad's compiled ANSI C scripts are fast! In fact, the footprint per virtual user is somewhere around 100kb to 200kb per virtual user, instead of the more typical 3MB to 6MB per virtual user. This can represent a huge savings in test infrastructure once you start working through the math!
- Accuracy, in that QALoad does not create unnecessary and intrusive front-end overhead. Instead, it captures and plays back various application layer and middleware calls, giving the application server the workload it needs without working over your client's infrastructure.
- Data management tools, which, as we discussed earlier, are key to a successful and representative stress test.
- Information without great overhead, in that QALoad's agents are nonintrusive and sit in promiscuous mode on the server infrastructure being tested, requiring as little as 2% overhead compared to the more traditional 30%-plus!
- Gratis support, in that QALoad comes with 5 days of consulting services. In this way, the learning curve is remarkably flattened and you're granted access to experts in the field.

For more information of how to obtain and use Compuware's QALoad tool and the entire QACenter umbrella suite, look to *www.compuware.com/products/qacenter/performance*.

6.6.3.   Mercury Interactive LoadRunner

LoadRunner for mySAP solutions and R/3 emulates thousands of users and uses real-time performance monitors to identify and isolate problems. By using LoadRunner, according to the folks at Mercury, organizations can minimize test cycles, optimize performance, and accelerate the deployment of SAP applications. SAP AG agrees it's valuable—SAP Labs in Palo Alto uses Load-

Runner to benchmark and stress test the SAP Employee Self-Service (ESS) application, for instance. Some of LoadRunner's most valuable features are as follows:

- It supports multiple OSs—Windows, HP-UX, Linux, and others are covered—which gives you more flexibility in setting up an infrastructure for stress testing that best meets your unique technical skill sets, allows you to use hardware otherwise sitting around, and so on.
- A new tuning-module add-in, the LoadRunner Tuning Module, allows you to isolate and resolve system performance bottlenecks. Once an SAP application has been stress tested using LoadRunner, the Tuning Module provides component test libraries and a knowledge base useful in isolating and resolving performance bottlenecks.
- Wide area network (WAN) emulation support enables LoadRunner to quickly characterize how well your system operates over a wide area network, or to point out the effect that the WAN has on application reliability, performance, and response time. WAN emulation capabilities include the ability to test for bandwidth limits, validate network latency, track network errors, and more.
- Sun ONE, Enterprise Java Beans, JBuilder for Java IDE, and XML add-ins are included or supported as well, opening up application testing support outside of traditional SAP boundaries.
- Native Independent Computing Architecture (ICA) support for Citrix MetaFrame supports Citrix's ICA for the testing of applications being deployed with Citrix MetaFrame.
- A data wizard enables you to quickly create data-driven tests and eliminate manual data manipulation. It connects directly to back-end DB servers and imports desired data into test scripts.
- The LoadRunner Controller can control at a granular level the execution of a test. For instance, native load balancing is supported, allowing you to evenly distribute a load generated by virtual users across a pool of Load Generator (test infrastructure) machines. And, to ensure an accurate load test, you can also use the LoadRunner Controller to dynamically start, initialize, and stop virtual users during a running scenario, thereby fine-tuning the requested load on a system under test. The LoadRunner Controller can also be configured to gradually allow running virtual users to logoff (e.g., after they have completed running a test iteration or action). And an enhanced scheduler lets you ramp-down and manipulate a test case start time—for example, you might schedule a test run for tomorrow morning at 6 a.m. Enhanced rendezvous features even provide additional rendezvous policies based on the percentage of total virtual users. In the end, the capabilities provided by the LoadRunner Controller support consistent stress testing.
- Similar to AutoTester's AutoController package, you can install a component within your firewall to allow the Controller to support virtual-user access to resources through a firewall.

- An enhanced output window provides an intuitive way to view and manipulate the output messages, including message icons, multiple views, drill-down capabilities, freeze view, message export to file, and indicator of new messages.

The default virtual-user runtime settings automatically change to accommodate a load-testing scenario when you add a script to a Controller scenario, too. Ultimately, then, as you see from the previous list of features, LoadRunner is one of the most powerful load-testing tools on the market for SAP systems testing. The folks at Mercury are well aware of this fact, too, which is reflected to some degree in the product's cost. I therefore recommend that you look into leveraging your SAP technology partners if your need for LoadRunner is occasional at best—HP and others can offer limited-time use of LoadRunner and other Mercury Interactive products at a much more attractive price point in one-off cases.

6.7.   SAP AG Testing Tools and Approaches

SAP AG is no stranger to providing testing tools, utilities, approaches, and methods when it comes to stress testing and performance tuning. Much of SAP AG's "tool" capabilities are built directly into its Computing Center Management System (CCMS) and focus on performance monitoring, which is discussed in the next chapter. But other tools and approaches can prove quite useful when it comes to testing various mySAP Business Suite components, as we see next.

6.7.1.   Using CATT and eCATT for Stress Testing

A long-time tool provided by SAP is CATT, which is useful for single-unit and limited concurrent user stress testing despite the fact that it was originally written for functional testing purposes. Stress testing—the systematic verification and analysis of real-world business process—is made possible in that CATT testing can be automated through the development of scripted business process test cases. More recently, with the advent of SAP's Web AS version 6.20, CATT has been extended and improved, and relabeled eCATT for "extended Computer-Aided Test Tool." The newer eCATT picks up where CATT could simply not go, taking advantage of its mySAP hooks to drive complicated back-end–enabled business processes. In this way, eCATT has the ability to test how well business processes perform, even when those business processes span multiple mySAP solutions and components. This is made possible by leveraging the functionality of the R/3 Test Workbench to create a set of test cases that can be executed serially or even simultaneously, in either case creating a load that can be repeated, quantified, measured, and then used to drive performance tuning. The bottom line is that eCATT lets you confirm that your SAP system adheres to technical performance criteria as set forth by your user-driven SLAs.

Neither CATT nor eCATT natively supports virtual users, however, relying instead on SAP's testing partners like Compuware to provide true multiuser load-testing capabilities. But it's worth taking a closer look at eCATT prior to investing in third-party API-aware stress-testing tools. SAP's eCATT ships free with Web AS 6.20, after all, and, as I mentioned previously, it can be useful even beyond single-unit stress testing. That is, several eCATT test cases may be executed simultaneously by a number of users, making the production of a significant load possible (it all depends on what's scripted, of course). I find this feature particularly useful when it comes to real-world delta performance testing for before-and-after changes to a system configuration, especially with regard to general disk subsystem performance. Running a number of hard-hitting reports and batch processes concurrently is both simple to do and easy to monitor in terms of the system load being borne. And, in the end, this simple method of creating a repeatable load on your back-end SAP DB server allows you to characterize expected-versus-actual performance without the need to spend more money on tools.

6.7.2.   Leveraging SAP CCMS Transactions to Create Load

Of course, anyone remotely familiar with SAP from a technical perspective understands that SAP's CCMS is used for monitoring your SAP systems. In that light, it's covered in depth (along with CEN, Solution Manager, and more SAP-provided utilities/tools) in Chapter 7. But the fact that CCMS is installed and ready to be "used," even in an unconfigured out-of-the-box SAP system, presents some very interesting alternatives for SAP application layer testing where customer-specific configuration is not yet completed. In short, there's great value to be had in delta testing different hardware, OS, and database configurations by harnessing the load that executing CCMS transactions places on a system.

How so? Many CCMS transactions are quite system-intensive, both at a hardware component level and in terms of holistic SAP layer stress testing. CCMS allows you to execute real-time performance-monitoring transactions or drill down into historical statistics specific to an individual application server, for example, or across all application servers within a particular SAP system. And, because CCMS transactions are pretty much the same between different mySAP releases or versions, unlike business processes which vary considerably, they nicely lend themselves to being scripted and therefore automated. In the past, for instance, I have easily scripted transactions that automatically collect systemwide performance and availability metrics, like ST03, ST04, ST06, ST07, DB02, SM04, and so on, tweaking them only slightly to stress test completely different systems. Again, not only the data provided by CCMS are important in these cases. Rather, the load generated by simply *executing* these transactions is the key. Automating this load through scripting simply enables the creation of a very consistent, very repeatable load-testing utility. My suite of portable single-unit load-testing scripts makes it a breeze to compare the performance of one configuration to that observed by another—and at an SAP application layer no less.

6.7.3.   Driving Cross-Application Stress Testing via SE38

In addition to eCATT test cases and single-unit CCMS test scripts, especially in light of the potential complexities associated with testing business processes that span your enterprise, I also find transaction SE38 useful. SE38 can easily be scripted to run a variety of reports and other jobs, both online and in a background manner, the latter running as batch processes. Selecting jobs that not only represent your typical workload but also make calls to other mySAP components is one of the most straightforward methods of driving an enterprise stress test. And there's nothing really special that needs to occur outside of creating a suite of scripted SE38 transactions that represent your business or that help you otherwise prove your unique success criteria.

The results of this kind of testing can guide you as to where and how you run your batch jobs, the impact on other workloads, how you configure your update, batch, and other work processes, and more. And, with a bit of analysis, such an approach can help you quantify the amount of parallelism realized in your specific batch processes, and therefore which processes can execute together as opposed to which ones can execute faster sequentially.

But using SE38 to drive stress testing is not the final solution to all of your load-testing needs, of course. On the contrary, it's pretty limited in the real world of complex business processes. For example:

- It's doubtful that many of your key business processes can be neatly executed in this manner; you'll be lucky to identify a few at most.
- In the same way, you'll be hard pressed to identify more than a few transactions in your environment that not only can be executed via SE38 but also touch multiple mySAP systems—assuming your goal is a cross-application stress test in the first place.
- Finally, by its very nature, SE38 drives heavy continuous loads. Thus, if your goal is to emulate more of an online user environment—lots of small reads and writes separated by plenty of think time—SE38 is not the right answer.

As I've told my customers in the past, most of the time SE38 is only a piece of a much larger puzzle. But it's a wonderful tool for discrete application layer delta testing and should definitely have *some* kind of home in your SAP toolbag.

6.7.4. Seven Simple Ways to Load Test BW and SEM

Scripting end-to-end BW queries for use in load testing has been a challenge since BW's inception. Even though a number of stress-testing utilities support communications through the SAPGUI or WebGUI, there are problems inherent to starting a virtual-user session in one interface and then passing control of that script to another interface. Specifically, if you start a BW transaction or query through a virtual SAPGUI session, and a Web interface or Microsoft Excel screen is subsequently invoked, you are hard pressed to actually "talk" to this new active window. Conversely, if you script your business process to establish a virtual link via the Internet Explorer API, you can only "talk" to the initial WebGUI screen—subsequent WebGUI screens used to enter variant data or to view the results of a query are not accessible via the virtual interface. But there are ways around these issues, if you're willing to make trade-offs. Specifically, I have found seven simple ways to stress test SAP BW or SEM, each of varying application or value:

- First, leverage SAP BW's inherent capabilities to "trace" its own activity and then to replay it (see SAP's "accelerator" whitepaper on how to accomplish this task). Specifically, this involves RSRTRACE, which is used to record BW user-driven activities, and RSRCATTTRACE, which replays those activities.

- Use one of the SAP API–aware scripting tools available from AutoTester, Compuware, or Mercury Interactive, but do not waste time trying to take advantage of virtual-user capabilities (e.g., which would then be driven via AutoController). Instead, script everything to execute in single-unit fashion but leverage an appropriate number of physical front-end desktops, laptops, and so on. This is a much more palatable stress-testing approach for BW and SEM, as opposed to R/3, given that it's rare to require more than 20 to 50 physical desktops to simulate an active business warehouse. And, if you simply don't have the resources yourself, consider contracting with your hardware vendor, most of which maintain equipment specifically for this kind of use, for a short-term engagement.

- Forgo the physical front-end requirements and instead leverage AT1 and AutoController (or a competitor's) virtual capabilities, but script simple "administrative" tasks, like those associated with managing SAP or the database (typical Basis and DBA scripted transactions), rather than true BW queries or other business processes. This is a good approach if you only need to prove that your hardware platform or a particular layer in the technology stack still performs well even after a change is made—execute a delta test as described earlier in this chapter in the section on leveraging CCMS for stress testing.

- Use the Internet Explorer API rather than leveraging an SAP API–aware approach, and script only WebGUI or Web-based activities; the same limitations apply, as described previously.

- Script BW or SEM queries as you normally would, but leverage external status files to control when a particular script executes and when it waits for another one to finish; in this way, SAPGUI- and WebGUI-driven scripts can be executed sequentially to complete a query. The only real requirement is the ability to open and read from or write to a file (e.g., a simple text file); scripts can be coded to check the contents of a control file periodically (e.g., every 15 seconds), and only when the contents finally read "startWEBGUI" or "startSAPGUI" or something programmatically similar will the associated script continue executing.

- Use SE38 in conjunction with a virtual tool for solid delta testing, as described earlier.

- Finally, use transaction RSRT in SAP BW to drive your queries. This transaction can execute any user-based query, but the difference compared with other queries is that the output (the query results) are kept "inside" or "within" the SAPGUI session rather than piped out to Excel or an Internet Explorer session. For stress-testing and regression purposes, this is perfect, because you can script your complex BW queries in a virtual and repeatable manner without losing focus between the SAPGUI and the Internet Explorer or Excel interfaces.

These last two bulleted items are my two favorite approaches for scripting hard-hitting BW queries. In particular, by executing RSRT, you can perform all of your stress testing via the SAPGUI, and still continue to use virtual users. This avoids the need to gather and manage a bunch of physical assets (outside of the testing infrastructure, of course) or the need to try to co-ordinate a complex process involving both SAPGUI and WebGUI scripts.

6.7.5. EP and SRM/EBP Stress Testing

When it comes to stress testing HTML-based and Java-based mySAP components like EP and SRM, these products should be driven by the same Web-based interfaces as they will be in the real world. Fortunately, all of the big players in the SAP stress-testing market today have this capability, as discussed previously, both in physical- and virtual-user modes. But many other browser-based scripting and stress-testing tools are available to drive EP and SRM business processes, too. The key to making your life simpler is to obtain a product that supports the various controls and other constructs used by SAP. Beyond this, ensure that your tool of choice supports the version of the Web browser on which you have standardized, as not all testing tools support all browsers.

6.7.6. Other mySAP Components and Considerations

Generally, if an SAP component can be accessed via the SAPGUI or WebGUI, you can script a business process using a tool like AT1, TestPartner, or WinRunner/QuickTest. Of course, complications exist as we saw in the case of SAP BW and its use of different interfaces to complete a single query. By and large, though, if the mySAP component or other SAP application in question supports a standard SAP interface, you're well positioned for stress testing.

On the other hand, if you find yourself in the position of introducing a new mySAP component to your organization and are unsure of exactly what to script, and therefore perhaps can't leverage functional specialists, I recommend obtaining the mySAP component's completed sizing questionnaire that was shared with your SAP technology partner. Here, the number of users and transactions, and more important, the functional areas and even the types of transactions to be eventually executed are normally identified. All of this information can then become a foundation for developing a list of potential stress-test transactions and general business processes to execute. For example, if a completed SAP sizing questionnaire tells me that 400 users will execute MM (materials management) functions, and another 50 users will execute in a few other functional areas, it would be safe to assume that MM01, MM02, MM03, MMBE, MD04, ME57, MB1B, and MB1C should be considered first for scripting, as these represent typical MM business transactions and reflect the bulk of activity conducted by many of the future system's online users, regardless of company-specific customization.

Another tool that has helped point me in the right direction when it comes to scripting business processes that ride on top of mySAP components with which I am not very experienced is the component's SAP benchmarking kit. Think about it—by its very nature, each benchmark kit must provide a sequence of transactions that can be executed in support of the benchmarked business processes. If you take a look at what constitutes the CRM IC benchmark, for example, it will quickly become apparent that after logging in to a CRM system, you execute core transaction CICO to walk through various screens relevant to managing a "call," a typical CRM business process. With regard to R/3, on the other hand, creating a new sales order via VA01 is followed by running VL01 to create the order's delivery, which in turn is often followed by VA03, VL02, VA05, and VF01 (to display the order, change the delivery, post goods issue, list the order, and invoice it, respectively). As you can imagine, this kind of direction and fundamental SAP education are invaluable if you are asked to stress test a system before all of the business activities that might surround such an effort are fully realized, too.

Finally, SAP AG should be applauded for including basic scripting as an option that can be enabled or disabled for any user. Called SAPGUI Scripting, it's not portable between releases or versions of different SAP products. Another restriction includes an inability to script any business process not authorized to be executed by the logged-in end user. Still, SAP GUI Scripting is useful nonetheless—many complex controls are supported, including tree, grid, Textedit, and so on.

6.8.   Tools and Approaches

Throughout this chapter, a great number of tools—from free and very simple test utilities to very expensive and full-featured SAP application test suites—have been discussed. Many of these tools are probably new to you or your testing team, though, so I decided it would be helpful to put together Table 6-1, a matrix of sorts that might help you compare and contrast them. I've grouped the tools by SAP Technology Stack layer, left a few blank lines for you to add your own utilities, and included a couple of fields that, while subjective, should still prove valuable. For example, my personal rating system (where an A+ is best-of-breed and a D– is only marginally acceptable) should be viewed as just that—my subjective take on a particular tool. In the end, I hope this information helps you make better *piloting* decisions. The final decision on the selection of a particular tool for inclusion in your toolbag, though, should instead be based on your own hands-on experience whenever possible.

After reviewing the matrix and working through piloting and test-tool selection, you can finally turn your attention to the other end of stress testing: monitoring and evaluating stress-test runs. Chapter 7 will address the various monitoring tools and approaches available across the SAP Technology Stack. Enjoy!

Table 6-1   Tools Matrix

Technology Stack Layer	Tool	Interface (CL/ command line or GUI)	Physical and/or Virtual Users (single/multi)	Pros, Cons, and/or Limitations	Rating
Network	Batch files	CL/script	Physical/single	Creates file-copy processes to test network throughput.	C–
	Chariot	GUI	All	From NetIQ, excellent for smoke testing everything from a particular network card to an entire infrastructure. Investment in at least two server "endpoints" required in the latter.	A
	Media LoadSim	GUI	All	Good for large-block network or disk subsystem delta testing; limited otherwise. Executes on Windows platform only.	C–
	NetBench	GUI	All	Limited to Windows, but relatively inexpensive given its capabilities. Full-featured demo copy available.	B
	QCheck	GUI	Physical	Free but capable offering from NetIQ.	B+
	Any disk stress tool	Varies	All	Utilizes any disk subsystem stress-test tool over a network connection to provide network load.	C–
	IP Network Emulator	Hardware solution w/GUI and scripting	All	Excellent GUI, powerful scripting language, and the ability to emulate basic 10/100 network connections to T1, DS3, and even huge OC-3 data pipes. Comparatively expensive.	B+
Disk/DB	Bench32	CL	Physical	Extremely basic.	D
	Benchmark Factory	GUI	All	Supports standard benchmarks focused on database, file-server, and Webserver testing. Very capable, relatively easy to learn and use. Highly regarded in the industry.	A
	DD	CL	Physical	Extremely basic, Unix only.	C
	HD Tach	GUI	Physical	Extremely basic.	D
	HPReadData	GUI for Windows, CL	Physical	Simple but powerful, supports 8 paths to disk and multiple Operating Systems, perfect for testing proposed backup solutions, network-based for Unixbackups, etc.	B+
	IOgen	CL	All	Unix only, "an old-timer" though capable utility.	C
	Iometer	GUI	All	Free, excellent disk subsystem and network throughput test tool.	B
	IOzone	CL	All	Free, similar to SQLIO but can run in a Windows DOS shell or a Linux cygwin shell.	B+
	LMDD	CL	Physical	Basic, but more powerful than DD. Reports MB/second transfer rate between source and destination.	C+

Table 6-1   **Tools Matrix (Continued)**

Technology Stack Layer	Tool	Interface (CL/command line or GUI)	Physical and/or Virtual Users (single/multi)	Pros, Cons, and/or Limitations	Rating
	NTIOGEN	CL	All	Windows only (port of the Unix IOgen). Can run against raw devices, making it good for testing Oracle 9iRAC or OPS solutions leveraging raw disk devices. Also supports file systems and testing against specific files.	B
	PAT	GUI	Physical	Supports disk and network testing as well. Basic but effective GUI.	C+
	Penguinometer	CL/scripting	All	Free, Linux port of Iometer that actually supports both Linux and Windows environments.	B+
	QBench	Old GUI	Physical	Free but antiquated.	D–
	RAIDmark	Old GUI	Physical	Free but antiquated.	D–
	SQL Profiler	GUI	All	Included with SQL7 and SQL2000, can record and playback SQL statements. Windows environments only.	A
	SQL Trace	GUI	All	Included with SQL 6.5, can record and playback SQL statements. Windows environments only.	C
	SQLIO	CL/scripting	All	Free, classic disk load-testing tool, for Microsoft platforms only. More difficult to obtain than others, but easy to use.	B
	SQLIOStress	Basic GUI	All	Free, SQL7 and SQL2000 emulator. Extremely capable, though only available for Windows environments.	A
	SQL Profiler	GUI	All	Included with SQL7 and SQL2000, can record and playback SQL statements. Windows environments only.	A
	SQL Trace	GUI	All	Included with SQL 6.5, can record and playback SQL statements. Windows environments only.	C
	ThreadMark	Basic GUI	All	Free, though given its lack of support on newer Windows releases, it's very limited in scope. Fairly detailed output.	D–
	WinBench	GUI	All	Designed for testing disk, graphics, and video subsystems, the latter of which are fairly useless in SAP server environments.	C
	Server	CheckIT	GUIPhysical/single	Inexpensive, supports testing all major server subsystems.	A
	Interscan	GUI	All	Trend Micro's real-time virus checker, interesting possibilities.	C–
	MeatGrinder	CL	Physical/single	Dated and limited, difficult to obtain, but powerful.	D+

Category	Tool	Interface	Scope	Description	Grade
	NAV LoadSim	GUI	All	Norton Antivirus load simulator, best-in-class. Highly focused on NAV testing, however.	B
	PerfStress	GUI	—	Exercises memory, disk, and network resources of Windows systems. Old Compaq Resource Kit CD resource.	C+
	SysStress	Basic GUI	—	Tests memory, caching, and paging subsystems of Windows systems.	C+
	Thrasher	GUI	Physical/single	Capable and configurable, builds on MeatGrinder's capabilities.	B–
Web Server	e-Load	GUI	All	Java-based, supports Unix and Windows. Download available, but requires a license key only available from an Empirix representative.	B
	Grinder	—	—	Free, Unix open source.	C
	JBlitz	GUI	All	Free, supports ASP and JSP, very flexible, up to 500 threads. Better than average GUI supports graphing and real-time statistics.	C
	Jmeter	GUI	—	Free, very flexible, but more CPU-intensive than others and weak reporting capabilities.	C
	OpenLoad	CL	—	Free, limited to configuring the number of threads. Supports Windows and Linux, but only runs from CL. High load on CPU as well.	D
	OpenSTA	GUI	All	Powerful open source, used by many of SAP's technology partners plus SAP's own consulting organization. Supports SSL, and features awesome reporting/analysis capabilities along with excellent virtual capabilities.	A
	StressTool	CL	Virtual	Free, limited to hits-per-second. Good for testing your servlets/JSP pages. Comma-delimited output (limited to time of request and response time).	C
	WAST	GUI/scripting	All	Free, easy to use and very flexible, but no updates since year 2000. Only supports Windows environment.	C+
	WebBench	GUI/scripting	All	Inexpensive and very capable.	C
	WebLOAD	GUI/scripting	All	Supports client-side JavaScript.	C
	WebFT	—	Physical	Functional and regression testing only (single-user load testing at best).	D
Non-SAP API–aware	AutoIT	MicroSoft Notepad	Physical/single	Free, and best-in-class in terms of ease of use and overall capabilities. Different versions available (DLL and ActiveX along with classic Windows). Decompiler and public sample scripts available as well.	A
	Perl	UI	All	Classic programming constructs, support for virtual users, but limited capabilities regarding new technologies.	B–
	PrimalScript	GUI	Physical/single	Outstanding script-building environment.	B

Table 6-1   Tools Matrix (Continued)

Technology Stack Layer	Tool	Interface (CL/command line or GUI)	Physical and/or Virtual Users (single/multi)	Pros, Cons, and/or Limitations	Rating
	TxShuttle	GUI	Physical/single	Voted one of top 25 best products in 2003 by SAP FAQ, useful in both stress testing and performing data loads.	A–
	Visual Test	GUI	Physical/single	Dated, no longer viable in most environments.	D–
SAP API–aware	AutoTester ONE	GUI	Physical/single	Mature SAP-aware scripting test tool, used for single-user testing or as the underlying scripts used by AutoController for multiuser virtual testing. Supports Web and SAPGUI-based testing.	A
	AutoController	GUI	All	Best product available for value-conscious SAP environments that need virtual-user support. Limited to Windows infrastructure (can test any SAP solution on any hardware platform, however). AutoTester product, a long-time SAP partner.	A
	CATT	SAPGUI	All	SAP's integrated testing tool; supports single-unit and limited concurrent-user stress testing in SAP Basis releases prior to 6.20.	C
	eCATT	SAPGUI	All	Ships with Web AS 6.20 and supports OCX controls and other newest SAP features.	B+
	LoadRunner	GUI	All	Most capable SAP virtual test tool available, supporting diverse front-end (e.g., Citrix) and back-end components (e.g., WAN emulation). Mercury product; among the most robust and expensive.	B
	QALoad	GUI	All	Midpriced virtual load-test tool by Compuware, capable of supporting complex multivendor enterprise environments. Requires different core scripts than those provided by TestPartner, however.	B
	QuickTest	GUI	Physical/single	Mercury's easy-to-use nonscripting tool. Supports WebGUI and SAPGUI.	B
	SAP GUI Scripting	SAPGUI	Physical/single	SAP's scripting tool, tied to the SAP physical user currently logged in (and the transactions that the user may execute). Allows client-side applications to collaborate; scripts saved in VBS format.	C
	TestPartner	GUI	Physical/single	Compuware's scripting tool's tiered approach to scripting appeals to novices and experts alike. Ties into eCATT to drive multiuser virtual testing in an extended environment.	A
	WinRunner	GUI	Physical/single	Mercury's long-time scripting tool. Supports R/3 and the extended enterprise.	B

Monitoring Tools and Approaches

With our SAP toolbag full of a variety of testing tools, from component-level testing utilities to all-encompassing SAP-aware test application suites, let's turn our attention to selecting and piloting tools that allow us to monitor and subsequently quantify our stress test results—because without closing our testing loop in this manner, there's little hope for methodical tuning. And, for consistency and completeness, let's first review the plethora of monitoring tools and approaches in terms of how they apply to the SAP Technology Stack.

In my experience, monitoring tools tend to fall into five very broad categories. Specific or discrete monitoring tools that carry out a single purpose, tools that measure and monitor general system or systemwide performance, and SAP-aware tools that provide information extracted from the bowels of an active SAP system are the most common of these tools and represent the first three categories. Sometimes, the best monitoring tool for the job at hand is the one that actually drives the testing, such as the tools discussed in the previous chapter. This type of tool represents the fourth category of monitoring tool. More often than not, though, a combination of third-party tools that help you analyze the performance of your end-to-end technology stack is more appropriate. A fifth type of tool, one that captures current-state configuration data, is also key when it comes to performance tuning. Regardless of the labels I assign to these monitoring tools, the overarching goal in this chapter is to understand when one monitoring tool or approach is favored over another and to select the most appropriate monitoring solution.

7.1.   The Role of Monitoring Tools

Given all of the monitoring tools, utilities, and full-blown systems-management applications available today, it's important to keep in mind the scope of this chapter. That is, in a perfect world, there would be significant overlap within an SAP technical support organization in terms of the monitoring tools deployed for day-to-day management as well as performance tuning. Advantages of overlap include the following:

- Skills learned in using the tool in the name of performance tuning/stress testing can be transferred to the other technical teams responsible for day-to-day systems management.
- In the same manner, skills picked up by the SAP Operations, Basis, and other teams can be transferred to the Performance team, too.
- Favorable bulk licensing arrangements are possible.
- Fewer tools equates to lower TCO, regardless of licensing discounts; the time necessary to learn and use the tool is reduced proportionate to the experience of the overall team.

In a nutshell, though, our scope here is limited to reviewing tools useful to the team responsible solely for performance tuning, not the larger subset of tools used by other SAP technical support teams (e.g., SAP operations, enterprise management, and teams tasked with development or functional testing). Because we already looked at many testing tools in Chapter 6, it's assumed that you'll leverage the built-in capabilities that ship with each of these products to support your system-monitoring requirements. This leaves us with four types of tools that we'll cover in depth here, including

- Current-state data collection utilities, which are used for documenting the state of various configurations (i.e., the technology stack baseline and any number of as-is configurations that evolve from the baseline)
- Discrete utilities useful in managing, monitoring, or otherwise supporting the preparation of stress testing and actual test-run execution
- General systemwide tools that measure overall performance of a system without the benefit of being SAP-aware
- SAP-aware systems-management applications, geared toward end-to-end monitoring, reporting, and detailed analysis of SAP applications

Similar to the approach I discussed in regard to selecting the best testing tools, it's important to pilot your monitoring tools as well. Review Chapter 6 for piloting details, but suffice it to say here that you'll probably want to consider a "broad-based" SAP-aware systems-management application first, relying on additional niche, specialized, or best-of-breed utilities as necessary to fill in any holes left in your monitoring solution not already covered by your selected testing tools. Your choices will be driven primarily by budget constraints, the time necessary to conquer learning curves, and the level of effort necessary to actually deploy a monitoring tool. In my experience, however, at least from a timeline perspective, you'll want to identify the best current-state tools first, which are covered next.

7.2.   Current-State Configuration Documentation Tools

Configuration documentation tools are not often thought of as "monitoring" tools per se; however, it's essential that you capture the configuration details of the system being tested, so you can track how future tests (executed perhaps months later) vary and how the system's performance changes over time. For only a select few of my customers, changes to their systems are rare; they remain largely static month after month. The best that most of my customers can hope for, though, is a production system that changes or otherwise evolves slightly on a monthly or quarterly basis. Tracking these inevitable real-world changes, however minor in scope, is critical, because it allows an SAP shop the ability to track and evaluate changes against the original baseline. This in turn provides insight into how future changes might impact performance because it makes extrapolating performance gains and losses based on specific delta testing and experience possible. Most important, though, maintaining before and after snapshots lets you quantify real-world performance deltas realized through configuration tuning, updates, upgrades, and so on. And doing so lets you "prove" to your end users and other stakeholders that no changes outside of those that have been formally tested and approved have made their way into your SAP Technology Stack.

An effective set of tools is required to pull this off, of course. No one tool can do it all. Some are better than others, of course, depending on the following factors:

- The environment in which they are deployed
- How easy they are to learn
- How easy they are to use
- Which layers in the technology stack they pertain to
- How well they meet your particular monitoring needs at each layer

Tools that allow you to quickly and easily capture the salient details as to how your system is configured end to end are key. For example, most of my customers define a good monitoring tool as one whose use does not require that a system be taken "down" or otherwise offline. A good tool does not significantly impact end-user response times either (or at least allows for granular manipulation and scheduling, so that the impact of the tool is felt during off-peak times). The best tools do not make changes to the system being tested either. That is, truly innocuous tools do not create or update registry entries or environment variables simply by virtue of being loaded on a system (though usually the best you can hope for is that the installation of the tool itself may be easily "backed out" once the tool has served its purpose). Finally, the output from a tool should be presented in an easy-to-read, easy-to-search format, preferably broken down into technology stack layers or in some other well-organized manner.

A number of current-state tools focus exclusively on recording only server and disk subsystem configuration details, whereas others capture holistic OS-specific data. Still others are adept at both hardware and OS monitoring, adding the ability to track the versions of firmware layered on top of each hardware component, or the OS version and patch levels. And a special set of monitoring utilities specifically facilitates database and SAP application layer monitoring. The tools I find the most valuable across the board are discussed in the following sections. Some of these are free, some are extraordinarily easy to use, and some are just plain cool in the way they work or in the information that may be gleaned across an entire SAP enterprise. In all cases, they complement the built-in capabilities of your OS or hardware platform. These tools include the following:

- Microsoft WinMSD (also called Microsoft System Information) is a utility that can be executed at any time to take a real-time configuration snapshot of a server running a Microsoft OS. WinMSD is detailed, and these details can be exported to an output text-based file for archival purposes. Further, it allows you to capture configuration data of both the "local" machine and any remote machines—simply click View and provide the host name.
- HP Systems Insight Manager is a free add-on that not only collects current-state data but also proactively monitors a system. It's available for a number of OSs and covers servers and desktops/laptops alike, from the lowest levels of each machine's technology stack (e.g., firmware and hardware details) to a certain amount of application-specific data. To a limited degree, Insight Manager also supports non-HP/Compaq servers. And with its ability to "snap in" to full-featured enterprise management products like HP Openview, Computer Associates (CA) Unicenter, IBM Tivoli, and more, Insight Manager makes a wonderful addition to SAP and non-SAP monitoring tool bags alike.

HP GetConfig, HP/Compaq Survey, and many other vendor-specific utilities exist as well, some of which are described in more detail later in this chapter. The demand is so great for good current-state "inventory" tool sets, though, that third-party software companies got in on the act years ago. Many of these tools are useful for disaster recovery purposes, and marketed to companies as a way to identify and "fill in the gaps" in the company's disaster recovery plans. Ecora, Troux Technologies, and quite a few other software companies tend to focus a great deal of energy targeting this niche. Other software vendors focus more on the financial due-diligence that may be realized by a good inventory package, like SofoTex and Compulsion Software, whereas still others (e.g., TeamQuest) tout their tools' ability to support proactive capacity planning. Regardless of the marketing slant, the value across the board is pretty much the same—very high. Many of these tools are discussed next.

7.2.1.   SmithMicro CheckIt Utilities

Although covered previously in Chapter 6, it's worth repeating that CheckIt does a great job of collecting and monitoring current-state data of a single Windows-based server or other computer (e.g., those you might use to drive scripted client activities). Thus, it is excellent for organizations that have deployed SAP on Windows and that leverage a Windows-based testing environment as well. Basic data collected by CheckIt include an individual's computer name, the version of the Microsoft OS installed, total RAM, amount of pagefile configured and actually being used, number of CPUs, and more. Once you get through your various benchmark and stress-test exercises (which can be fine-tuned to drive only specific hardware subsystems), CheckIt also allows you to easily view your test results against a baseline system that you specify by simply "pointing" the tool to use the output file of one of your previous test runs as the "new" baseline run. Thus, you might create a baseline for your DB server configured with four CPUs and 6 GB of RAM, and then use this feature to easily compare subsequent test runs where you added or upgraded CPUs or RAM.

Bottom line, CheckIt is an inexpensive and effective tool for small enterprise testing environments, lending itself to simple Windows GUI scripting to make up for basic limitations. One limitation in particular is that CheckIt is limited to executing on a one-at-a-time basis on every server or desktop that needs to be inventoried. Further, it does not include any database or SAP-specific features, nor can it capture technology stack details like OS patch levels or hardware firmware levels. But, for something like $60 per computer, it's a cheap and simple way to go for basic current-state analysis and monitoring.

7.2.2. Breakout Software MonitorIT

Breakout Software's MonitorIT tracks current-state hardware, software, and OS configuration data, as well as OS performance. A relatively new ServerWatch feature monitors all network and Web services on any computer in your test environment, regardless of the OS installed. ServerWatch can also monitor Internet-based and database-specific services for proper operation and performance, making it ideal for SAP ITS and database monitoring alike. You can also poll any computer in the enterprise to confirm basic availability (using a built-in *ping* command) and to capture response times for http, ftp, Simple Mail Transfer Protocol (SMTP), Domain Name Service (DNS), and Post Office Protocol (POP) services. Services that are unavailable to ServerWatch generate alert notifications through e-mail, or trigger the execution of a program (as defined by you) to take corrective action.

MonitorIT can run on Windows 2000, Windows NT, and Windows 9x systems and supports Microsoft SQL Server for use as a back-end database to store the operational data it collects. Thus, there's a lot of flexibility afforded in terms of searchability, and you can put your organization's experience in working with SQL databases to good use. Pricing starts at less than $300 for a MonitorIT Server and a three-agent license. Check out *www.breakoutsoft.com* for details.

7.2.3. Ecora Configuration Auditor

No stranger to meeting the documentation needs of businesses around the globe, Ecora's Configuration Auditor eliminates the need for hours of manual data collection to document your current state. And, its agent-free approach is less intrusive than others, letting you quickly pull configuration details on your entire infrastructure, including servers, Cisco and other network devices, and database configuration. Even better, once a baseline is established, Configuration Auditor can rapidly identify deltas in your environment, helping you to manage and track change across your lab environment. All of these data can be brought together into meaningful reports presented in a number of formats, too—HTML, Word, Excel, and even Visio. Check out their free download trial version at Ecora's site *www.ecora.com/baseline*.

7.2.4. Ecora PatchMeister

Another product from Ecora fits into the category of current-state analysis products. If you're looking for a free tool to not only document the current-state of your SQL Server databases or IIS Servers but also help protect them from security vulnerabilities, you need to consider Patch-

Meister. PatchMeister is a breeze to install, easy to use, and allows for creating reports quickly. Its GUI interface also lets you control a huge number of SQL Server installations from a single console. And it can be used not only to automatically discover and analyze the patches you've installed on your SQL Server hosts but also to identify any patches that are missing—very nice! Other benefits include the following:

- There is no need for agents.
- It operates from one administrative desktop.
- It scans multiple systems quickly.
- It lets you group output/reports into an easy-to-navigate tree format.
- It provides sortable views for easy patch analysis—you can sort by host, product, patch levels, or simply by whether patches are installed or not installed.
- It uses both registry and file integrity checks to validate if patches are indeed installed.

You can download this tool for free from *www.ecora.com/ecora/patch1/*. I recommend it highly to my own SAP/SQL Server customers and anyone using IIS (which underpins the bulk of ITS WGate installations out there today). PatchMeister is adding new OSs and vertical software solutions to its support list all of the time, so be sure to check with their Web site often—they've got a slew of products, ranging from freeware to free trials of highly capable enterprise packages. Look to Ecora's Web site, *www.ecora.com,* for more information on all of this company's offerings.

7.2.5.   HP Survey

A mainstay of Compaq (and now HP) for years, the Windows-based Survey utility is the perfect way of capturing your server's hardware, firmware, and software configurations. By default, Survey typically runs as a Windows service on each of your supported servers, taking weekly "snapshots" every Wednesday. It may also be executed ad hoc by simply running survey.exe from a command prompt. My favorite feature, besides the fact that it displays before-and-after versions of anything that changes in the system (wonderful for proving a client did indeed make a change to his or her system after emphatically denying "nothing has changed" during a troubleshooting session!) is that it is so thorough, to the point of even tracking changes to a system as it evolves over time. Almost nothing at the hardware and OS levels escapes Survey—I count it as one of my quintessential tool-bag utilities for quickly capturing and later sifting through my customer's server configurations. The output file—a simple text-based file—is clearly organized, easy to understand and search through, and, by virtue of its file type, small in size.

7.2.6.   HP GetConfig

What Survey is to Compaq and newer HP Proliant servers, GetConfig is to the classic HP NetServer and other lines of servers. Like Survey and similar utilities on the market, GetConfig can actually run on most any server or desktop/laptop executing a 32-bit Windows OS—I've used it on NT 4.0, Windows 2000 Server and Professional, Windows XP, and Windows Server 2003 systems. A simple 1-minute installation gets you ready to use the tool, which, on executing, presents you with a list of HP NetServer models from which to choose. Unless you're running the tool on one of these NetServer models, select the option labeled "Other" instead, and then enter a serial number like FR12345678 (if the area for entering a serial number is "grayed-out," simply click on one of the NetServer models, like LH4, and then click Other again). After a serial number is entered, click Next and GetConfig will begin the process of collecting data, as shown in Figure 7–1. This data collection process places a significant CPU load on the system for perhaps 2 minutes or so, after which GetConfig allows you to save the results of its work in either a Web Report format (default) or, if you choose "Save As," in a ZIP file.

The output is very good—technology-layer–focused, well organized, and amazingly complete even for non-HP products. A partial list of configuration data gleaned from GetConfig is provided here:

- Network information, like IP addresses, binding order, routing information, snapshots of the hosts, lmhosts and services files, DNS info, Dynamic Host Configuration Protocol (DHCP) info, SNMP configuration data, and more
- Hardware error logs, Dr. Watson, and other "crash" information available through the registry
- System uptime details—this information alone is worth deploying GetConfig
- Installed hot fixes and other software patches
- MSI-installed software
- Boot information (from boot.ini)

Figure 7–1 With HP GetConfig, real-time current-state configuration data are easily collected at the expense of a few minutes of impact on a server's CPU.

- Specifics related to how pcAnywhere and Citrix may be configured on your system
- Local user and group information
- Array controller and other storage data (the depth of which is severely limited on non-HP machines)
- Cluster configuration, if clustered using Microsoft's Cluster Service (MSCS)
- SAP and Oracle registry entries
- Printer configuration and details

Overall, the output is divided into six classes—Hardware, Software, Drivers, Accounts, Printers, and Network—which makes drilling down into details quite intuitive. I recommend that you at least test drive this software, especially because it is free and is, in a basic sense, SAP-aware and Oracle-aware.

7.2.7.   Compulsion Software AssetDB

Another current-state favorite of mine is AssetDB, a tool that lets you scan Windows XP/2000/NT servers and desktops remotely, providing information about services, disk space, and memory utilization. It also lets you track the history of all software and hardware changes, similar to HP Survey. The scan is necessarily both hardware and software focused, therefore making it possible to determine things like the specific OS version installed on a machine, the patch level of the OS, whether a particular PC is low in disk space, and much more. AssetDB costs about $200; more information is available at *www.compulsionsoftware.com*.

7.2.8.   Windows Management Instrumentation (WMI) Scripting Tools

If you've already invested time and money into learning how to use and script WMI, Microsoft's implementation of the Web-based Enterprise Management industry initiative, enabling network devices and systems to be managed and controlled, you'll be pleased to know it's got yet another use—collecting current-state configuration and performance data to support your stress-testing and tuning projects. I covered PrimalScript back in Chapter 6, probably the premier WMI scripting tool available today. Another excellent WMI-enabled tool set is Microsoft's Scriptomatic (sometimes called Script-o-Matic). Like PrimalScript, Scriptomatic takes advantage of WMI to make your life as a tester and tuner that much easier. WMI scripts will let you automate many of the tedious and repetitive tasks that otherwise consume a significant amount of your time up front, collecting system configuration details, or afterwards between executing test runs as you make upgrades and other changes. Check out *www.microsoft.com/downloads/details.aspx?display-lang=en&familyid=9ef05cbd-c1c5-41e7-9da8-212c414a7ab0* for more details, including the Scriptomatic utility itself, which runs on Windows 2000, Windows XP, and Windows Server 2003.

7.3.   Discrete Monitoring Utilities and OS Applets

Although actually monitoring the execution of your load test is covered in detail in Chapters 12, it's important at this stage to select the tools that best meet your monitoring needs. There is nothing more frustrating than spending weeks planning for and executing a series of stress tests only to discover that you never collected the data necessary to prove or show anything of value, or that you missed key baseline metrics! I encourage you to go through the next few pages with the idea that important data can be collected at every layer in the SAP Technology Stack; indeed, looking at your own test plans from this perspective will help ensure you don't miss a key performance metric or throughput statistic. Key selection criteria include

- Support for your specific SAP Technology Stack; your hardware, OS, database, mySAP component, and any additional middleware or accessibility hardware or software (e.g., load balancers or front-end client solutions like Citrix MetaFrame) need to be taken into consideration
- The ability to quantify network lag time, or the time consumed by the network when it comes to breaking down transaction response time into its component areas
- The ability to measure, verify, and report end-user response time or batch job throughput performance for discrete end-user transactions, or for a component of this response time/throughput

As you probably suspect, there is unfortunately no single tool that can do all of this perfectly in most SAP environments. But there are some good ones that come pretty close, and others that offer excellent capabilities or value. SAP AG's hardware partners offer hardware-specific utilities, as do every OS vendor, database vendor, and so on. The key here is to find tools that support not only point-in-time performance snapshots but also fundamental historical performance analysis. Similarly, there are plenty of infrastructure systems-management applications on the market today that leverage common protocols, such as SNMP, Desktop Management Interface (DMI), and Web Based Enterprise Management (WBEM), to help you manage much of your technology stack. Most of these applications have matured to the point where they even offer "snap-in" modules capable of monitoring specific mySAP components, specific databases, and more. We will take a look at many of these broad-based management applications shortly, after we first address the various utilities available for managing discrete pieces of the technology stack, followed by a closer look at systemwide testing tools.

7.3.1. Disk Subsystem Utilities

In short, you'll need to work directly with your disk subsystem storage vendor to obtain the low-level utilities necessary to monitor disk performance at the controller, HBA, and underlying I/O levels. And even within the same storage vendor's offerings, monitoring tools will differ. For example, HP's tool sets vary between the original direct-attached storage offerings, FCAL offerings, original SAN products, and the newer virtual SAN products. Many of the legacy tools were command-line oriented, requiring serial or other physical cable connections to a disk controller to allow you to monitor their performance. Even some of the newer SAN offerings still leverage this type of utility. HP's DSview and Virtual Terminal Display (VTDPY) are good examples of these low-level utilities, the former of which is a GUI-enabled version of the latter.

Newer disk subsystems tend to boast Web-based access, however, often leveraging dedicated single-function servers to act as storage managers for complex SANs. Termed *SAN Management Appliances,* such black boxes mask much of the underlying complexity, making it as easy as driving a few clicks deep into a Web application to monitor an entire SAN's performance. Details relevant to the load hosted by a particular SAN switch are as easily accessible as physical and logical disk performance metrics, or identifying the peak load of a pair of redundant disk controllers. Combined with the ability to create and publish Web-based reports, it's clear we've quickly come a long way from basic command-line utilities.

7.3.2.   Built-in Unix OS Utilities

A host of Unix command-line utilities can be used in support of monitoring and performance tuning. One of the most common utilities is *vmstat,* used to monitor the run queue, swap file page-in count, paging daemon scan rate, CPU status, and more. And ps lists all active processes. Another common utility is accessed by executing the single letter "w," which shows process usage by monitoring load averages and generating an abbreviated Top Sessions report with load averages over 1, 5, and 15 minutes. For a full CPU activity report, *top* may be executed. And for swap file performance measured as a percentage of swap space utilized, *swapinfo* is valuable. I also like to use *sar,* the System Activity Reporter, to report against buffer, swapping, or disk I/O activity, or *iostat,* which shows elapsed I/O on each physical disk (a nice real-time utility, in that the display may be updated automatically every 10 seconds, for example, by executing *iostat 10*). Finally, *lsdev* with all of its switch-driven variations can be used to view devices like CPUs and so on.

The following tools ship with their respective Unix OSs or, in some cases, are added as part of a core update or "resource pack":

- HP-UX MeasureWare and Perfview analyze a system's performance and allow you to create graphs.
- HP-UX and other OSs also support *glance* or *gpm,* useful in viewing memory details.
- IBM AIX's *nmon* is an online performance monitor and capture utility.
- IBM AIX also supports the Performance Toolbox and a Performance Diagnostic Tool, both useful for system capacity planning and performance analysis.

And monitoring tools like HP's Cluster Consistency Monitor (CCMon; for HP-UX clusters only) help an SAP shop manage the inherent complexity of an SAP cluster. Even an SAP Cluster specialist can miss defects and inconsistencies easily identified by CCMon, such as the following:

- Different versions of SAP Start/Stop scripts between cluster nodes. In the best case, inconsistencies at start-up are observed, and other support problems are likely. Worst case, though, SAP will be unable to start after a failover to a different node.
- A file or login group exists on the primary node, but not the secondary node. In this case, TCP/IP-based communications may not work after a failover.

- Important R/3 Kernel parameters are at different values. This could lead to system-monitoring thresholds never being reached in the best of cases. On the other hand, if a failover is caused by this situation, and the node that SAP fails over to maintains even lower thresholds, the system may continually start and immediately crash and fail over again in a continuous loop.
- Software products installed on the primary node, but not the secondary node. This could simply indicate an extra application not necessarily needed at all, but it might also reflect a critical missing application such that failover would simply not work because of an unsatisfied application-dependent prerequisite.
- Patches installed on only one node, or a difference in patch release versions between nodes. This might never manifest itself if the differences in patch levels are small and the reason for developing the patch in the first place never manifests itself. However, if the patch fixes a critical error, a failover to the node running the older patch release would appear to exhibit an old "resolved" problem, and possibly complicate troubleshooting the issue again.
- Swap size significantly smaller than another cluster node. Performance degradation will therefore occur after a failover. Worst case, if the swap file is too small, SAP might actually crash again under what appears to be a normal load of online users and batch processes.
- Crash dump area not present, differs in size between nodes, or is occupied. In this case, it would be possible to suffer from a crash and execute a failover, but obtain no dump data to analyze later.
- An SAP-specific group missing. In the best case, some functionality is sacrificed; worst case, SAP cannot even be started again on a particular cluster node.

As should be clear, the value provided by a good cluster-management utility is clearly worthwhile and should have a home in the toolbag of any clustered SAP enterprise.

7.3.3. Built-in Microsoft Windows OS Utilities

Since the days of Microsoft NT Advanced Server 3.1, Microsoft has included a number of utilities that assist in monitoring server performance. The list has grown over the last few OS releases, and today includes core utilities like the following:

- Window's Performance Monitor (PerfMon) should be used for any Microsoft-based solution component both to create a baseline and then to monitor system performance proactively on a regular basis. I typically take system "snapshots" or capture PerfMon statistics every 10 to 30 seconds or so; longer intervals are less valuable when it comes to performance tuning, especially if your test runs are short. Although the actual PerfMon objects you collect statistics against will vary based on your particular test cases, basic parameters surrounding disk queue lengths, mix of reads to writes, CPU statistics,

RAM utilization, pagefile utilization, and network I/O should play fundamental roles in your use of PerfMon as a monitoring tool.

- Windows Microsoft Management Console (MMC), which is Microsoft's inbuilt OS management tool. Combined with SAP's MMC snap-in, the MMC becomes a full-featured SAP solutions management tool—it supports managing the OS, database, and mySAP components all from the same console. During an SAP installation, the MMC and SAP snap-ins are loaded on the central instance, DB server, and any installed application servers. Thus, it's quite easy to manage these individual servers from a local perspective. And SAP AG also put together a set of instructions that allows the SAP MMC snap-in to be installed on a central management station and configured to manage and monitor multiple SAP instances. In this way, even machines without any installed SAP instances, for example, can be used to monitor any number of SAP instances remotely. And, for Windows 2000 environments, no prerequisite software need be obtained or loaded (as opposed to NT 4.0 environments, where minimum versions of Microsoft Internet Explorer 4.0, Microsoft Active Directory Services Interface (ADSI), and the core MMC version 1.1 must to be installed). For more details, see SAP Note 373963 "Setting up SAP MMC Snap-Ins on Non-R/3 NT Computers."
- Microsoft Cluster Administrator, which allows you to monitor the status of your Microsoft clusters during a test run. There is typically not a whole lot to look at, however—I typically use Cluster Administrator only when I'm working through a test case that includes measuring the impact that a failover has on a test run. Cluster Administrator helps me verify that a set of services indeed failed on one node and was subsequently brought up successfully on the failover node.
- Microsoft's *chkdsk* utility, which is an excellent current-state tool useful in validating the blocksize (allocation unit) in which an OS disk partition has been formatted. It may be executed from a command prompt for any locally attached drive letter. I use chkdsk to verify that my SQL Server data files are formatted for 64kb, which has been recommended by Microsoft's SAP Competency Center since the advent of SQL Server 2000. That is, when I walk into a new account that is suffering from disk performance issues, I can never be 100% sure that a system's data drives were indeed formatted for 64kb via either the Windows Disk Administrator or the format command-line utility; chkdsk quickly removes any mystery. And, because I execute this utility without any switches, there's no risk of inadvertently writing to the partition—without switches like "/F," this utility safely works in read-only mode. As a final note, keep in mind that you must execute this command directly from each drive letter on which a database data file resides; mapping a drive via a network share does not give you the ability to execute chkdsk.

7.3.4.   Oracle and SQL Enterprise Manager Utilities and More

All database vendors include management utilities with their products. Oracle and Microsoft incorporate an "Enterprise Manager" for Oracle and SQL Server databases, respectively. Although in the strictest sense these are not monitoring tools, they provide most everything you need in terms of identifying current-state configuration data. There's often a diagnostics component or similar tool that provides additional value as well, like the ability to identify SQL bottlenecks, inefficient indexing, or space usage problems. These tools nicely complement SAP's own database-centric monitoring capabilities found in various STxx and DBxx CCMS transactions.

Other tools also aid you in monitoring. Oracle's Statspack utility, and Unix-based *bstat* and *estat* command-line utilities are classic examples, for example, as are various SQL trace tools like SQL Profiler. And *iostat* can be used to display real-time disk subsystem performance, along with *sar*, which reports disk I/O and buffer activity, both discussed previously.

7.3.5.   IBM Insight for SAP and Oracle

IBM publishes a number of tools that assist in analyzing workloads and characterizing general performance. The IBM Insight for Oracle Database collection utility lets you drill down into an Oracle database's configuration while the database is up and running, pulling out detailed and high-level data and presenting it in a nice report format. The IBM Insight for SAP R/3 workload performance analysis tool is executed in a similar manner, and according to IBM, lets you predict system bottlenecks before they occur. For IBM shops that have standardized on Oracle environments rather than DB2 or another DBMS, IBM Insight is worth pursuing.

7.3.6.   Other Discrete Monitoring Tools

Additional hardware management and discrete monitoring tools enable you to monitor specific pieces of your technology stack. Examples include the following:

- Uninterruptible Power Supply (UPS) utilities ship standard with nearly all UPSs today, and are useful in managing and tracking battery consumption and status. In some cases, third-party enterprise management applications can perform some of the same general features as well.
- Tools that measure or monitor the configuration and availability of a specific disk subsystem are common, too, especially those related to managing the availability of redundant storage paths. Examples include OpenPath and SecurePath.
- Tape drive and tape library management tools and utilities, like those offered by leading tape backup and restore vendors.
- Utilities specifically designed to manage network infrastructure that interconnects SAP solution components, or special software applications that facilitate managing a server's network cards, represent common network management tools.
- Utilities that manage hardware-based IP load-balancing devices (e.g., those found front-ending SAP eProcurement or Employee Self-Service solutions). Java applets and other Web-based utilities are quite common in this regard, too.

Of course, other utilities prove themselves useful to a technical support staff responsible for maintaining well-performing systems day in and day out, like PKWare's ubiquitous compression tools, any number of virus protection programs, PrintKey (useful for taking screen shots to be used later for documentation purposes), and so on.

7.4.   Systemwide Lab Utilities and Applications

A number of free and fee-based systemwide monitoring tools and other utilities are available from a variety of places. For example, each of the major SAP hardware partners, like HP, IBM, Sun, and Dell, offer system-management utilities that typically come bundled with their respective hardware platforms. These include products like HP's Insight Manager and Toptools offerings, Sun's Sun Net Manager, and Dell's OpenManage. Utilities like these provide a foundation for enterprise-wide systems management, often working seamlessly with all-purpose management applications I'll discuss later, like HP OpenView and CA Unicenter, to provide deeper insight into a technology stack's performance.

7.4.1.   Lab Utilities

Other tools, many of these free or nearly so, can play a pivotal role in your monitoring efforts. I call these "lab utilities" and they include useful little tools designed to make your life a little easier. The following list is by no means comprehensive but illustrates the value these utilities bring to the table:

- TxShuttle and TablePro, both from WinShuttle, may be used to help you set up a test run, in addition to their more obvious role in actually driving a test run. For example, TxShuttle's support of multiple sessions and its ability to leverage Microsoft Excel-based data to drive transactions lets you "stock" a database in a consistent way. Even cooler, TablePro's ability to download data from your SAP tables and dump them into Microsoft Excel or Access with the click of a button makes it easier to work through detailed post–test-run validation in an automated fashion.
- Utilities like the ubiquitous Ghost and Winternals' Recovery Manager represent time-saving ways to restore your test infrastructure or other servers to a point in time, making it easier and faster to engage in repeatable testing that inherently makes changes to a layer in the SAP Technology Stack (e.g., testing the amount of time necessary to introduce a bundle of updated OS and database binaries or security patches).
- AutoShutdown Pro lets you schedule system shutdowns or reboots, or perform these activities based on a time (e.g., in 1 hour). It is not network-aware, meaning that you'll need a third-party scripting tool capable of establishing network connections to drive shutdown/restart processes for your entire test-lab infrastructure. But the possibilities are compelling. For instance, you could automate shutting down your test front-end clients first, followed by ITS/Web servers, then your SAP application servers, then the SAP Central Instance, and finally the back-end DB server (reverse the process to bring everything back up in the correct order). There's even a "force if hung" option, which is perfect for stress tests gone awry. Finally, AutoShutdown Pro allows you to schedule a

particular time to reboot, such as every morning prior to the start of the day's testing activities. And, because this product supports hot keys, I believe it will prove useful in your day-to-day activities as well.

- Another great tool, eTimer, is perfect for counting down (or, if you prefer, counting up) a test run. I suggest you run out and download a free 15-day trial from the folks at *www.barefootinc.com*—there's much more value to this product than meets the eye. One of the best uses I've found is that I can copy the current counter time, which is accurate to the thousandths of a second, into the clipboard and then dump it directly to my execution checklist or even a test run's output file. Also, eTimer lets you save a point-in-time snapshot of the current counter without stopping it, if, for instance, you want to record when a certain event occurred (e.g., when all of your SAPGUI virtual users finally logged in to the system you are testing). Thus, I keep the timer running to time the entire test run and maintain important checkpoint data as well. Finally, eTimer provides another function as well—it flashes wildly and makes a lot of noise once the countdown is complete, helping to ensure you don't forget to do something (e.g., end a test run!). Given that I am rather forgetful at times, especially when my testing takes me late into the evening hours, I like having one less thing to worry about.
- Print-screen utilities like Snagit and Printkey will save you countless hours during and after your stress-test runs. Snagit is probably the industry standard if such a thing exists, making it a breeze to easily capture screenshots and save them to a Word document whereas Printkey is nearly as capable and free. Check them out—their inclusion in your toolbag is another no-brainer.

Many other useful tools abound as well, from ftp and other network utilities to various "readers" that allow you to view a particular type of file without the need to install the requisite application itself. The aforementioned list should simply give you an idea as to what's out there and get you started in the right direction.

7.4.2.   Sysinternals PsTools

An excellent suite of products for managing as well as monitoring Microsoft-based stress tests is available in a set of free utilities from Sysinternals. Among other things, Sysinternals' PsTools can list and then kill processes matching a certain name, a function that the Windows NT and Windows 2000 Resource Kits were unable to provide back when I first went hunting for better tools. In my own experience, this capability has been useful in killing stress tests that have gone awry, preferable to rebooting every client driver or other machines. But PsTools offers so much more, too, like the ability to manage remote as well as local systems. And this great set of utilities may be downloaded individually or as a package. The following tools may be obtained from *www.sysinternals.com/files/Pstools.zip*:

- PsExec, which lets you execute processes remotely without having to manually install client software (in this way, command prompts can be opened on remote systems and

utilities like *ipconfig* that otherwise are not capable of displaying remote system information)
- PsFile, which displays files opened remotely
- PsGetSid, which is used to display the system ID or SID of a computer or a user
- PsKill, which can kill processes by name or by process ID
- PsInfo, which lists information about a system
- PsList, which lists detailed information about processes
- PsLoggedOn, which is used to identify who is logged on locally or via resource sharing
- PsLogList, which is used to display event log records
- PsPasswd, which is useful for changing account passwords
- PsService, which is used to view and control services
- PsShutdown, which is used to shut down and optionally reboot a system
- PsSuspend, which suspends processes
- PsUptime, which shows you how long a system has been running since its last reboot (this functionality has also been incorporated into PsInfo)

All of the utilities in the PsTools suite work on Windows NT, Windows 2000, and Windows XP. None of the tools requires any special installation either, nor do you need to install any client software on the remote computers being managed. And given that the PsTools download package includes an HTML Help file with complete usage information for all the tools, plus support for the command-line option "-?" to show how to use a particular command, the far-reaching benefits of adding PsTools to your toolbag make their inclusion essential.

7.4.3. EventComb for Microsoft OSs

If you're an SAP shop betting your business on Microsoft OSs, pay attention to EventComb's capabilities. This product will save you a huge amount of time and frustration when it comes to monitoring and auditing security events that are captured in each server's Security event log, for example. EventComb actually supports concurrently searching through all event logs—system., application, and security—as well as the File Replication Service (FRS), DNS, and Active Directory (AD) logs. If you begin to think about the number of servers and client drivers you might maintain in a large testing environment, the benefits should be clear—searching for a specific security event ID would otherwise consume countless minutes, if not hours. Of course, you could go out and purchase MOM (Microsoft Operations Manager). But EventComb is free, provided by Microsoft in support of its *Security Operations Guide for Windows 2000 Server*. Simply navigate to *www.microsoft.com/downloads/release.asp?releaseid=36834* and download the file secops.exe. Once you execute secops.exe, it'll create a folder called SecurityOps and another folder underneath it called EventComb, which contains the EventComb program, an excellent compiled HTML Help file, and a simple "readme" pointing to further documentation available from Microsoft.

EventComb supports complex searches and is easy to use, though the user interface is a bit simplistic as shown in Figure 7–2. Simply right-click inside the box on the left side of the user in-

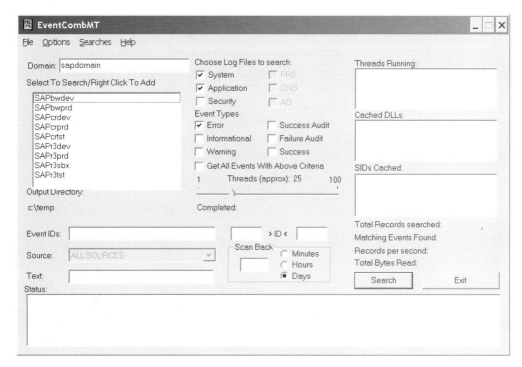

Figure 7–2   EventComb's user interface lends itself to easily searching multiple servers' event logs.

terface (labeled "Select to Search/Right Click to Add") and then type in the name of the computer. Each computer you enter will be searched using the search criteria that you specify, which can involve event types (e.g., failure, warning, failure audit) or specific event IDs. You can specify how far back to search in the various logs, too, making it easy to check the results of only a specific stress-test run or other period of time. After making your selections, click the Search button and step away from the keyboard. Once EventComb finishes searching through the specified computers, the search results will be displayed in individual files maintained in a user-defined output directory, sorted by machine name. You can even specify that the results be saved in comma-separated value (CSV) file format, to make for easy searching via Excel. For testing that is security specific (i.e., where your goals include some level of security auditing or leveraging Single Sign-On), using EventComb is invaluable. But even for standard performance-related stress tests, where a combination of real and physical users might be involved, EventComb can come in handy—the need to validate that your hardware did not succumb to "atapi" disk failures or network retries during a test run, for example, makes for plenty of applications of this monitoring tool.

7.4.4.   Leveraging Winternals' Administrator's Pak

Another tool that can come in handy when it comes to managing or monitoring a stress test or performance-tuning exercise is Winternals' Administrator's Pak 4.0, a suite of utilities that are more diagnostic in nature than anything else. The Administrator's Pak lets you repair damaged or unbootable systems, diagnose Windows OS and file-system problems, and restore lost data, among other functions. It consists of ERD Commander 2003, Disk Commander NTFSDOS Professional, Remote Recover, Monitoring Tools, and TCPView Pro. Look to *www.winternals.com* for more details or pricing information.

7.5.   Enterprise Management Applications

Although the expense and complexity of full-blown enterprise management applications like OpenView, Tivoli, and Unicenter generally put them out of the running when it comes to validating and monitoring stress-test runs (collecting basic configuration data relevant to tracking baselines and the iterative changes that impact the baseline), they are still worth a bit of discussion. Why? Because many of these tools are used in some capacity by your company already, and therefore you may have access to leverage the licensing and experience already in place. Before we get started, though, you may wish to evaluate whether the complexity of these applications is worth your time by evaluating the following factors:

- The time necessary to install, configure, and use the management console.
- The agents that may be required to manage your environment, and then purchasing, installing, and configuring these agents, which can encompass OS-specific, database-specific, and even mySAP-specific components.
- The incremental costs of any necessary server, high-end desktop, and related OS licenses that may need to be purchased to support the systems-management console or a specialized software distribution server—perhaps a dedicated machine is required.
- The cost to acquire and leverage training, documentation, and so forth necessary to put the enterprise systems-management solution into use.
- The cost and time spent in designing or architecting a systems-management approach that makes sense for your testing environment, which includes "production" as well as "crash and burn" resources, including any time that needs to be spent reassessing requirements.
- The cost of integrating and maintaining your smaller discrete tools underneath the bigger systems-management umbrella.
- The investments that must be made to perform ongoing configuration of the management solution as it and your testing environment evolves over time. This is especially true when it comes to fine-tuning alerts and thresholds to configure, monitoring specific events, setting up any kind of external alerts, creating reports, and so on.

Of course, *who* actually performs all of the tasks outlined previously makes a big difference, too. Will you need to enlist the aid of the systems-management vendor? Third-party consultants? Pull your own internal folks off of existing projects to help get the performance-tuning lab set up? In the end, costs vary significantly depending on your approach, and need to be factored in to a cost-versus-benefit analysis. So let's take a closer look at some of the most common

SAP systems-management applications on the market today, and how they might help you achieve your testing and tuning goals.

7.5.1.   BMC Patrol

One of the best-known tools for managing SAP systems out there today is BMC Software's Patrol, a very capable tool that allows for great flexibility when it comes to developing reports, creating custom events, and so on. However, Patrol is steeped in ABAP rather than relying on database-external agents, which means you'll need to be comfortable in loading ABAP code and using BMC's custom scripting language called Patrol Script Language (PSL)—this may be a bit too much to expect for simple testing environments. And it's not the cheapest answer to SAP monitoring by a long shot. But, with BMC's support for SAP APO, BW, CRM, R/3, SRM, ITS, and more (see their "Patrol for SAP Solutions Suite" Web site at *www.bmc.com/products/prod-docview/0,2832,19052_19426_23176_7206,00.html* to review all currently supported mySAP Business Suite components), they're well-positioned to monitor your entire SAP system landscape.

7.5.2.   CA Unicenter Application Management for R/3

CA Unicenter Application Management for R/3, a bit less popular than most of the other products I discuss in this section, is nonetheless capable of monitoring conditions that range from the creation of ABAP "short" dumps to the status of long-running or otherwise active processes, enqueue locks, users, print spools, and more. It's adept at what I call "central monitoring," because it allows for multiple servers across your SAP system landscape to be monitored simultaneously from a central Event Console. It can also determine whether your system is optimally configured for a particular workload, making it a good fit for load testing, and track both historical and real-time end-user response-time performance. Even more compelling, with Unicenter's cross-application capabilities (included with the core product, rather than obtained as an expensive bolt-on), insight into both SAP and non-SAP computing resources can be brought together to provide a powerful monitoring and analysis platform. That is, you can use Unicenter to schedule test cases (jobs) with dependencies across applications, such that the successful completion of a non-SAP job might automatically trigger an SAP R/3 job to start, and vice versa. This allows you to automate testing, making for repeatable results while eliminating human errors.

7.5.3.   HP OpenView VantagePoint Operations

HP's systems-management architecture for mySAP is one of the best approaches I've seen in that it's extremely modular—HP uses "SMART Plug-Ins" for various applications and products, such as SAP R/3, SQL Server, Oracle, Informix, IIS, and many different OSs, letting you custom-build a management solution based on your enterprise environment and checkbook. And, through building "maps," only the pieces of the technology stack that you want to monitor are displayed on your management console. This lets you create specialized views that are application-specific or even business process–specific, perfect for monitoring load tests that exercise complex business systems. Given its breadth of coverage and the potential complexity of your environment's individual solution stacks, HP OpenView may not be the fastest enterprise systems-management product you can implement for a testing environment; giving due attention to the various alerts, events, and corresponding thresholds at a number of different technology stack layers takes time, after all.

OpenView VantagePoint Operations (OVO) is nothing if not comprehensive. Its tight integration into SAP CCMS makes it a breeze to manage multiple SAP systems running different release versions while ensuring that end-to-end response-time service levels are met. You'll be paying for "extras" not necessarily needed in a testing and tuning environment, though, like the ability to trigger corrective action from system faults or other events, a feature that's designed to increase uptime and system availability. OpenView allows you to construct or define relationships between technology and business services, too, giving you insight into how technical issues impact the business processes riding atop the technology.

HP's relationship with SAP is also noteworthy. As SAP's number one global technology partner, and given that fully half of all SAP systems deployed in the world today are on an HP hardware platform, going with HP makes strategic sense at a number of different levels. Initial HP OVO acquisition pricing is middle-of-the-pack, but it incorporates annual software maintenance so your overall cost down the road is actually much less than the price of most competing products. Coupled with support for R/3, BW, ESS, SRM, ITS, and more, and its strength in managing both Windows- and Unix-based SAP systems (including HP-UX and Tru64 as well as Sun Solaris), OpenView is indeed well positioned to help you manage a complex heterogeneous SAP testing environment.

7.5.4.   IBM Tivoli

Although my personal experience is limited, my colleagues at IBM tell me that the following benefits help IBM Tivoli Monitoring for Applications stand out from other enterprise management packages when it comes to SAP applications:

- Its Web-based interface/console, which front-ends and unifies other Tivoli management packages
- Its ability to monitor not only R/3 and the newer R/3 Enterprise but also SAP BW, APO, and, to a limited extent, CRM
- Its ability to automatically discover SAP infrastructure components, ranging from SAP application servers to ITS servers and more
- Its integration with the Tivoli Business Systems Manager, which lets you visualize your system in real time
- Its similarly tight integration with Siebel applications, which until recently held the top position for CRM applications in terms of market share

As is evident from this list, integration seems to be the key to Tivoli's moderate success in the marketplace. With products ranging from the Tivoli Storage Manager for ERP to fundamental network infrastructure-centric offerings, Tivoli provides the breadth of coverage necessary to monitor your SAP systems end to end. If you have already standardized on Tivoli across your enterprise, it can make a lot of sense to use it in support of performance testing and tuning as well.

7.5.5.   NetIQ AppManager for R/3

NetIQ's AppManager suite has matured into quite a nice systems-management package over the last few years. Once a Windows-only management tool, today it offers capabilities typically seen in only the most robust packages, for something like half the price of many of its more mature competitors. For example, AppManager for SAP R/3 offers central monitoring and management capabilities for SAP, and interlocks well with other AppManager components responsible for managing Oracle and SQL Server databases, with the added plus of being able to do this from a single master console. And NetIQ's approach to systems management will certainly appeal to the purists at heart. AppManager relies on a unique proxy solution for managing servers and resources, rather than an agent-driven approach, keeping your SAP servers in pristine shape—no agents equates to no risk of technology stack conflicts, memory leaks, or other conflicts/issues that can arise with approaches based on fundamentally changing a system to enable monitoring. On the other hand, such an infrastructure approach costs money in and of itself, in that the proxy component must be procured, installed, and managed. Your testing and tuning budget may be stretched the same as other agent-based approaches, then, at the end of the day.

There are other limitations as well. A key Unix flavor, SuSe Linux (one of SAP's key Linux partners) is still not supported. Further, as of this writing, only SAP R/3 is supported. And AppManager's proxy approach can only support monitoring between roughly five and eight SAP instances. Finally, there is no support for archiving or even purging old performance and availability data; instead, each customer must custom-develop its own (admittedly easy) solution to this shortcoming. All of this probably helps explain NetIQ's weaker penetration of the SAP enterprise management market relative to the previously discussed enterprise applications. But, with NetIQ's historically tight partnership with Microsoft, going with AppManager could still prove quite beneficial to SAP customers already betting their business on Microsoft's OS and database products, too.

7.5.6.   Enterprise Management Applications' Rules of Thumb

Given the inherent complexity and cost of building a powerful, full-featured enterprise management solution for your testing environment, I assembled the following rules of thumb to help you start off on the right foot and stay focused on the task at hand—to build an effective monitoring solution big enough to do the job but small enough to keep everyone still employed:

- Keep things simple; embrace a "good enough" strategy, and deploy the core systems-management package before attempting to implement additional hardware vendor–specific snap-ins, specialized agents, and so forth.
- Utilize "out-of-the-box" SAP monitoring capabilities. In other words, refrain from changing the default management parameters associated with deploying the basic package.

- Turn off monitoring of parameters that are not of immediate or critical need, and focus instead on the most critical performance and availability statistics first.
- Pilot your tool before getting in too deep—deploy a "systems-management test-bed" and utilize this sequestered environment to validate the vendor's claims in an offline manner.
- Once the piloting is complete and a particular solution has been selected, adjust SAP and other technology stack performance, availability, and system thresholds based on input from consulting or in-house SMEs. Leverage experience in this regard—it'll save you significant time and money. Otherwise, I suggest sticking with the defaults until you have a better grasp of the tool.
- Develop a fall-back plan in parallel to deploying your testing and tuning systems-management solution—I recommend something as simple as a paper-based checklist replete with the various performance metrics and measurements that can be obtained manually through CCMS your discrete tool sets, and various OS and Database utilities. In this way, you avoid placing all of your eggs in one basket should the broader systems-management solution ultimately prove too cumbersome, complex, or costly.
- Treat your systems-management solution like a "production" system, and practice good change management techniques when it comes time to introduce configuration changes, upgrade software components, and so on.

With the various third-party monitoring tools and applications behind us, let's turn our attention to monitoring solutions provided directly by SAP AG.

7.6.   Monitoring Tools Provided by SAP AG

One of the things I've always appreciated about SAP's systems is how manageable they are even without the benefit of third-party tools. SAP AG put a lot of thought into making their applications manageable out of the box, incorporating key technology stack coverage like OS and DB support alongside application layer support. In the next few pages, we'll go through some of these monitoring utilities and solutions you should evaluate with an eye toward deploying them in your own testing environment.

7.6.1.   SAP CCMS

Someone ultimately needs to be responsible for monitoring not only the infrastructure that drives your stress testing but also the SAP systems themselves. The key tool provided by SAP AG to accomplish the latter task is SAP's CCMS. CCMS allows you to monitor application performance in real time as well as from a historical perspective. It underpins the full-blown enterprise management applications discussed previously, because it consists of the data collection engine leveraged by HP OpenView, Patrol, and so on—CCMS gathers these data through a service or daemon called the SAP OS Collector. The HP OpenView–like products of the world simply present these data in unique or more valuable ways than CCMS is capable of—hence their value.

A SAP OS Collector service or daemon runs for each installed SAP instance, collecting data related to the performance and configuration of the particular server's OS, database, and mySAP component. Most of these data are unfortunately focused on the details of that particular SAP instance, however; cross-system performance, or the performance of an entire SAP system made up of multiple servers and instances, is usually much more difficult to rationalize using only CCMS.

Using CCMS is simple, however. SAP conveniently created hundreds of shortcut transaction codes (T-codes) that exist solely to pull performance and availability data out of CCMS. For example, T-codes like ST06 and DB02 provide us with OS- and database-specific data, respectively. ST03 and ST04 give us information related to system-level performance. ST07, SM04, and AL08 provide us with end-user–focused data, such as the number of users logged into a particular functional area or executing specific functional transactions. And ST30 gives us the ability to drill down into an SAP Performance Analysis. A couple of observations regarding SAP T-codes are in order before we continue:

- T-codes that end in "01" (e.g., SU01) are often used to create something.
- Similarly, "02" transactions are typically used to change or update something, and transactions that end in "03" are used to display something.
- The first two characters in a T-code reflect the functional area or technical area in which a T-code operates. "ST" provides system-related data, "DB" provides database-related data, "RZ" addresses system profile and monitoring data, "OS" reflects operating system–related statistics, and so on.
- Most T-codes are four characters long, like ST07 or AL08. The majority of other T-codes have five characters, like ST03N (though some have only three characters, and even fewer transactions have T-codes greater than five characters in length).
- Many times, you cannot execute a transaction from the current screen. One solution is to "back out" of the current screen by pressing F3 (back). Another, more convenient solution is to precede the T-code with a "/n" (pronounced "slash n") Thus, ST03 would instead be typed in as /nST03.
- Rather than a "/n" you might use a "/o" instead. The difference is that the "/o" opens up a new session of the SAPGUI.
- Transactions like SM51 and OS07 can be used to connect to a different application server within your SAP system landscape, without the need to log out and log back in to the system. In this way, for example, it becomes easier to more quickly collect statistics for multiple application servers within a particular system (especially if you ever have to do so manually!).

You can also access CCMS through SAP's basic menu system, navigating through countless umbrella transactions until you find the one that suits your purpose. Of course, this can be time-consuming, but, in the same manner, it can prove quite educational to new CCMS users. Take care, though, when randomly navigating and executing transactions! A number of CCMS

Workload			
CPU time	240,340.2 s	Database calls	148,904,700
Time elapsed	2,678,370.0 s	Database requests	487,591,395
		Direct reads	298,612,729
Dialog steps	125,018	Sequential reads	176,899,262
		Changes	12,079,404
Av. CPU time	1,922.4 ms		
Av. RFC+CPIC time	138.9 ms	Time per DB request	0.6 ms
		Direct reads	0.1 ms
Av. response time	6,933.3 ms	Sequential reads	1.2 ms
Av. wait time	32.3 ms	Changes and commits	2.9 ms
Av. load time	208.3 ms		
Av. Roll i+w time	2.2 ms	Roll in time	275.5 s
Av. DB req. time	2,373.0 ms	Roll-out time	1,360.0 s
Av. enqueue time	13.3 ms	Roll wait time	0.0 s
		Roll-ins	175,166
Av. bytes req.	783.6 kB	Roll-outs	220,493

Figure 7–3 Scripting ST03 and similar CCMS transactions makes it a breeze to collect post–test-run performance statistics in a standard and repeatable manner.

T-codes are quite system-intensive, whereas others can be unwittingly used to make unwanted changes to the configuration of a system. I therefore suggest taking your time when it comes to learning how to use CCMS, and more important, to use your SAP Technical Sandbox for these kinds of initial educational activities, rather than a system used by developers, functional testers, or production end users!

Because of SAP CCMS's hooks into your system's OS, database, and SAP application layers, it will naturally play a big role in how you monitor your testing and performance-tuning efforts. In fact, you'll find yourself executing many of the core performance-related CCMS transactions over and over again. In the past, to save time and avoid errors, I've scripted many of the most popular performance-monitoring transactions for particular systems (e.g., ST03, ST07, ST04, AL08, and more for SAP R/3 4.6C or BW 3.1). In effect, this scripting automates much of the data collection processes necessary to analyze the impact that a particular change to a system has in terms of performance. And, because scripting implies consistency, I never needed to worry about changing the outcome of a test by introducing monitoring variables. Things like my data collection windows, the data I collected, and the steps I went through to obtain those data were preserved by virtue of the scripts.

I therefore highly recommend that you consider scripting these core-monitoring transactions yourself, too. Of course, you'll need an SAP API–aware scripting tool like AutoTester's AT1 or Compuware's TestPartner to pull the data out of the SAPGUI ("scrape the screen") and dump what you collect into an Excel spreadsheet or text file. The few thousand dollars spent on one or a few licenses is money well spent, though, because these API-aware tools provide you the kind of value you simply cannot get from traditional scripting utilities like AutoIT and PrimalScript (discussed in Chapter 6). For example, scripting with AT1 allows you to track key response time and throughput-centric success criteria like the following: average wait times, roll times, database request times, number of dialog steps processed in a particular time period, and so on for dialog, background, update, and other work processes. This and more can be pulled from ST03 as seen in Figure 7–3.

7.6.2.   Transactional Monitors and CEN

Although CCMS is an excellent tool all around, a number of holes or gaps still exist when it comes to monitoring SAP systems "holistically." Consider the following:

- Before Basis release 4.6C, CCMS did not let you consolidate performance and other data across multiple instances within a single SAP system. For example, to monitor a system with 12 application servers required executing the same transaction 12 different times, after "connecting" to each application server via SM51 (or logging into each one, which was even more time consuming).
- In the same way, CCMS prior to 4.6C was not the most adept tool when it came to re- porting performance, availability, and other metrics across more than one server (al- though some exceptions existed). Instead, reports had to be run separately and then combined manually or through a scripted process afterwards. More often, expensive enterprise systems-management tools came into play.
- Even today, CCMS graphics for the most part are still quite limited; communicating trends and changes in the performance of a system over time is better left to other tools.
- Not surprisingly, a lack of intuitive T-codes combined with the need to drill down into SAP's CCMS menu system has never made for a system that is easily monitored.

SAP AG remedied a number of these shortcomings with Basis release 4.6C in the form of transactional monitors, which are a group of transaction-specific dialog monitors accessible via the "SAP CCMS Monitors for Optional Components" monitor collection. It also finally became possible to set up a transactional monitor for each instance, even entire system landscapes. This was good for monitoring the performance of a particular set of business transactions, like your "top 10" online end-user transactions or background jobs. In doing so, you could easily monitor overall response time, queue time, load+gen time, DB Request time, front-end response time, and so on across a complex R/3 solution, for instance. But this approach was still limited in terms of holistic performance-monitoring capabilities; outside of the core transactions monitored by a specifically configured transactional monitor, little incremental value was provided over older CCMS releases, a fact that to this day still drives much of the success of third-party SAP enter- prise monitoring applications like BMC Patrol, HP OpenView, and others.

SAP AG continued to improve on its own native SAP tool sets and more recently gave us a new management alternative in the form of the Central Monitoring System (CMS, or more commonly CEN). Accessible and configurable via transaction RZ20, CEN can monitor the following conditions or factors:

- Overall availability of the system, including general status, cluster heartbeat, status of sessions and threads used, and more
- Detailed server and disk subsystem "hardware" properties, like disk space, RAM, and CPU utilization, status of system parameters, and so on
- Detailed system information, such as the OS or Java version running on each server, the server's host name, and similar current-state configuration data
- Performance, measured in business or functional terms, like how many documents are processed per hour or the average size of these documents
- Performance, measured in technical terms similar to classic CCMS capabilities, including factors like buffer quality, other memory conditions, disk-hit ratios, swap/pagefile utilization, and so on
- Error logs and similar system-generated messages and events

CEN is quite capable today, allowing you to develop custom monitors in addition to leveraging SAP-provided ones. CEN leverages a typical software "agent" approach to monitoring servers; agents are loaded on SAP systems, thus enabling them to be monitored. The actual agent deployed in each environment differs, depending on the release of the system being managed. For example, SAP AG publishes agents for systems running SAP Basis release 3x (SAPCM3X), release 4x/6x (SAPCCM4X), and even non-Basis systems (e.g., SAPCCMSR; be sure to review SAP Note 420213 as well). As good as CEN is, though, monitoring holes still exist for companies that have deployed business processes spanning multiple mySAP Business Suite components, R/3, and non-SAP systems. SAP AG has sought to further plug these holes via the SAP Solution Manager, discussed next.

7.6.3.   SAP Solution Manager (SSM) and the New CCMS Monitoring Infrastructure

Available since Basis release 4.6x, the SSM (also called SolMan) is much better known and more readily associated with Web AS (releases 6.10, 6.20, and 6.30, for SSM 2.1, 2.2, and 3.1, respectively). Even in its limited life, SSM has improved significantly. Although the very broad SSM addresses much more than performance monitoring and systems management, for monitoring you'll only need to concern yourself with SSM for Operations, as seen in Figure 7–4. Note the following fundamental benefits it provides beyond CCMS and CEN:

- SSM (Operations) can monitor multiple mySAP components from a single centralized management console.
- SSM ties directly into support and service functions, through both online and "packaged" best-practices documentation.

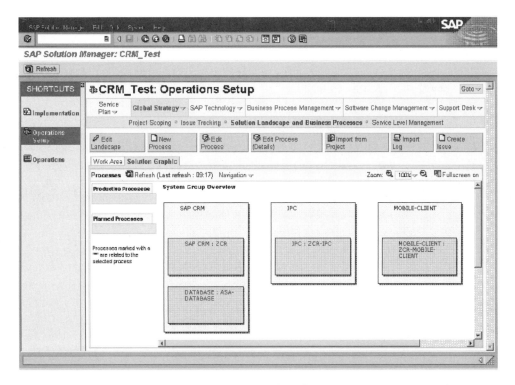

Figure 7–4   SSM for Operations provides an intuitive and extremely powerful user interface.

- SSM also extends monitoring beyond mere systems management; it enables real-time business process monitoring, taking transactional monitors to the next level.
- SSM supports Service Level Management (SLM) .

The SSM is more than a bolt-on to CCMS, though. A dedicated server installation for SSM alone is the preferred way to go, to avoid dependency conflicts with other Web AS–enabled mySAP solutions. Of course, for pure performance-testing environments, I still suggest going with the simplest configuration possible to save money. The installation process is quite uncomplicated, fortunately, and commences by executing transaction SAINT and selecting the option to install an "add-on." Both the "Implementation" and "Operations" components of SSM are installed in this way, incidentally, either of which is available to be used afterwards.

The newest versions of SSM use the CCMS Monitoring Infrastructure provided in the latest Basis releases (6.20 and later), allowing for truly systemwide monitoring, like that associated with the following: interfaces; complex components like EBP and CRM, XI, and APO; and the status of other SAP products like ITS, SAPRouter, Business Connector, and more. RFC connectivity between SAP systems can be checked, too, along with the status of XML, Java, and ABAP technology components within Web AS. In this way, large and complex SAP system landscapes can be monitored through a single central console. And, to make reporting simpler, SAP now supports exporting the pool of collected performance data out to an OS-based file format. Long-time T-codes have been updated or augmented as well, providing data never available before. For example, although ST03N and STAD are still available, the new ST03G and STATTRACE provide for a more global (though still extremely detailed) view into your SAP system landscape.

7.7.   Tools and Approaches

We have covered quite a bit of material in this chapter. It's my hope that by identifying some of the most popular monitoring tools useful in quantifying SAP systems performance, I have helped you narrow down the list of tools you ultimately will need to pilot and use. Certainly, many other excellent monitoring tools exist as well, but space precluded discussing them here—tools like Microsoft's Network Monitor and the Microsoft Product Support reporting tool (the latter of which makes no registry changes or other modifications to your OS, and supports gathering data relevant to Microsoft clusters), for example, are both simple to use and quite powerful. Go ahead and get started now, though—by doing additional research, talking with the third-party software vendors, and downloading and installing some of the more promising tools in your test environment. In parallel with piloting these tools, feel free to read ahead to Chapter 8; there's still much to be done in terms of the preparation surrounding the deployment of your toolbag's contents and the infrastructure underpinning everything.

Starting on the Right Foot: Preparation

Without a doubt, your testing and tuning efforts will only pay big dividends if you pay due attention to preparation and planning tasks often overlooked in the kind of "seat-of-your-pants" performance tuning that way too many companies force themselves into. Compared to this common backdrop, where "Ready? Fire! Aim!" might represent business-as-usual, structured stress testing and tuning saves time, money, and jobs; indeed, given the potential costs of down-time, business and technology constraints, limited resources, and ever-shrinking ROI-derived project timelines, a project-plan-derived approach to testing and tuning is simply a necessity. The focus of this chapter is to apply or leverage everything covered thus far, mixing in core tasks and processes like those described next, to commence such a structured approach and thus start our testing on the right foot. The core tasks and processes are as follows:

- Address team leadership and other organizational issues.
- Develop your "strawman project plan" template.
- Create a sound and repeatable testing method.
- Identify "testable units" (TUs).
- Customize the strawman project plan and repeatable methods to reflect the needs of a specific TU.
- Engage your SAP Competency Center for technical buy-in.
- Identify where your testing and tuning efforts shall take place, including how "test assets" will be procured and configured.
- Determine how to capture your test baseline.
- Document the SAP system landscape and each technology stack.
- Conquer test-tool and monitoring-tool learning curves.
- "Pretune" the SAP Technology Stack, from hardware up to each stack's application layer.
- Finally, address "next steps" surrounding input, processing, and output requirements.

Each one of these areas is examined next. Failure to address the tasks listed previously increases risks, clear and simple—risks associated primarily with missing scheduled milestones, which equates to lost time and budget overruns. In short, I believe there is too much that can be "missed" when preparation for testing/tuning is shortchanged.

8.1.   Team Leadership and Organization

Many of my SAP customers organize their testing and performance-tuning teams around special projects—functional upgrades, technical infrastructure upgrade projects, infrequent scheduled change-driven updates to the system, and so on. In some cases, the members of the subteam responsible for performance tuning SAP R/3 are different than the team responsible for other SAP applications, especially the newer products like EP or XI. For the most part, these teams come and go as projects are conceived and put to rest.

In other cases, companies employ a "core" T3 to help establish continuity among various other specialized teams tasked with tuning specific components or specific layers of an organization's SAP Technology Stack. I personally prefer this latter approach to the project-oriented approach and other approaches not discussed here, because it tends to

- Maximize ROI by making the most of expensive human resources, expensive software packages, and expensive technology infrastructure investments.
- Encourage cross-team training. The overlap created by this approach naturally helps to push performance-tuning practices, ideas, processes, and approaches borne by one subteam into being considered and often adopted by another team. In this way, a long-term "body of knowledge" regarding SAP stress testing and performance tuning is established throughout the entire virtual SAP support team.
- Create an entity responsible for internally promoting the team's value; typically, a senior person on the core team becomes the "point person" and provides representation of the performance tuning/testing team in other venues, meetings, and so forth.
- Promote knowledge of a particular application across an organization beyond pure performance tuning; a set of subteams organized around a core T3 helps you avoid the problems inherent to creating vertical stovepipes of expertise that become indispensable over time simply because no one else knows how to do what they do.

Such an approach provides not only essential leadership to the subteams created around the core team, as shown in Figure 8–1, but also facilitates continuity between different testing/tuning projects. And it helps ensure that tools, processes, and the testing environment in general are maintained over time, that licenses are kept current, and so on—administration activities that could otherwise fall through the cracks and essentially slow down new testing projects at their inception.

Regardless of the organizational approach you use, ensure that your structure addresses leadership, continuity, knowledge sharing, and administrative processes. Then turn your attention

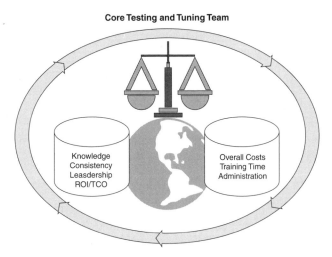

Core Testing and Tuning Team

Knowledge
Consistency
Leasdership
ROI/TCO

Overall Costs
Training Time
Administration

Figure 8–1 Organizing the performance-tuning team around a core team provides leadership, facilitates continuity and knowledge sharing between projects, and encourages attention to general administrative activities.

to how the team members will leverage project planning and repeatable testing methods to prove their worth to the SAP organization as a whole, over and over again. This concept is worth a closer look and is discussed next.

8.2. Developing a Strawman Project Plan for the Real World

Anyone familiar with project planning understands the value a plan provides in terms of helping to ensure that a project stays on course and that it has a better shot at meeting its objectives. With regard to testing and tuning, I like to leverage a high-level project plan that is both reusable (in that it's not tied to a particular type of testing, goal, or set of success criteria) and customized enough to act as a template for most foreseeable testing projects. Such a project plan therefore represents a balancing act between the need to stay general enough to be applicable across many projects versus detailed enough to actually be useful. I call this type of project plan a *strawman project plan*—it's not completely fleshed out, so to speak, but nonetheless accomplishes most of the goals of a more comprehensive project plan.

In the past, I've used strawman project plans between different testing efforts at the same company, and even between different testing projects (sometimes called *testable units* or TUs in testing circles). Such a project plan can prove its versatility if it meets the following key avoidance criteria:

- It avoids details surrounding *how* a stress test is conducted—testing tools used, mention of specific infrastructure necessary for particular tools to be useful, and so on are not applicable in a strawman project plan. Save these details for later, as you seek to customize the plan to meet the needs of a specific TU.

- It avoids mention of specific monitoring or current-state data collection tools necessary for the stress test to be conducted.
- It avoids details regarding the SAP Technology Stack to be tested—for example, keep the plan generic enough such that you do not need to spell out the particular version and release of the database technology or mySAP application component to be tested.
- It avoids organization-specific details, much of which change on an annual or even quarterly basis in so many IT and business organizations. Things like the unique name of an IT department, business/functional group, Basis subteam, and so on might prove useful for a few months but then become just details to be changed in your templates.

And, if you're a consultant or other third-party contractor subject to working with multiple companies (as I am), I also suggest you avoid company-specific references, like identifying the names of specific IT organizations, project teams, and so on. Instead, use references to general roles or teams (as opposed to customer-specific names), and refrain from identifying any other names or labels that companies assign to their internal organizations. By following the afore-mentioned "things to avoid," you'll put yourself in a position to reuse your strawman project plan in the manner it was intended, as a highly useful template upon which you can base your project-specific or TU-specific project plan.

8.2.1.   TUs and Your Test Plan

Armed with a strawman project plan, you should be able to make quick work of a more compre-hensive project plan, albeit "draft" at this point. It is your goal to turn your high-level plan into something that is now detailed enough to drive day-to-day project management activities sur-rounding the execution of a very precisely defined TU. For example, you may create a TU with the goal of characterizing the performance impact that applying a particular set of support pack-ages has on an existing SAP R/3 Enterprise system. The before and after states are very clear in this case, as is the change to be implemented and tested. Your test plan should reflect the activi-ties necessary to make the change in a controlled manner, followed by a rigorous and repeatable load-testing process that identifies a specific set of users, business processes, data, and so on. Next, you'll need to indicate in your test plan which particular test tools are leveraged, in what manner they are configured, and the precise steps in which a test is executed. All of this should be documented in a step-by-step fashion, like that of a standard hierarchical checklist.

The fact is, a good strawman project plan will leave no general stone unturned—you'll be forced to consider all of the broad areas outlined previously. This will help you effectively fill in your plan's holes or replace unknowns with specific product releases, organization names, test-tool minutiae, and so on. Your knowledge of things to be avoided in creating a strawman project plan will help highlight areas that need to be fleshed out, too. In the end, your strawman project plan will give way to a customized TU-specific *test plan*, and you'll be well on your way to iden-tifying and managing all of the resources necessary to pull off a successful performance-oriented stress test. Just as important, you'll preserve the value of your template while building a repository of more detailed plans that in and of themselves will probably prove useful over and over again, too.

8.2.2. Engaging Your SAP Competency Center

Although not everyone agrees, as a former member of an SAP technology partner's SAP Competency Center I believe there is great value in enlisting the assistance of your own hardware or software partner's SAP Competency Center. This assistance comes in many forms, too, and while their inclusion in your testing/tuning process (often in the form of a quality-control or sanity check) may slow down your project's timelines a bit, consider the benefits as shown in Figure 8–2 and detailed in the following list:

- Most of these SAP-centric partner organizations are anxious to gain visibility into their accounts—by including them in your test plans, you not only gain access to a second pair of eyes (from a QA perspective, so to speak) but also benefit *them* directly. That is, they gain exposure to what companies are doing in the real world, keeping them better plugged in all the way around.
- Your SAP Competency Center may very well be aware of "known issues" that are unknown to you. After all, they work with and are exposed to many hardware, OS, database, and SAP-specific problems across many different accounts. This level of exposure provides insight directly beneficial to you and your project in terms of the viability of your planned change.
- Having the SAP Competency Center review and sign off on your planned changes implies a certain amount of buy-in (typically of an informal nature, unless explicitly requested), the same kind of value you seek from any of your SAP colleagues when you ask them to review your plans.

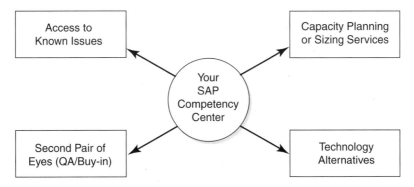

Figure 8–2 The value your SAP Competency Center can provide in terms of free services is compelling from a number of different perspectives.

- The SAP Competency Center may offer technology alternatives, or provide you information that completely halts or significantly changes your plans, resulting from their relationship with SAP and their own back-end SAP-focused product engineering organizations. In this way, their visibility into new products, feature sets, or support details coming down the pipeline can again be invaluable to the success of your own project.
- Finally, if the planned change warrants it, the SAP Competency Center may also perform a resizing of your system or in some other way work through capacity-planning exercises, all of which provides another proof point for you as you work on and revise your test plans.

I can't say enough about this last bulleted item—resizings based on increased workloads, increased user counts, changes to functional areas, planned technical or functional upgrades, and so on provide tremendous value. After all, each SAP Competency Center not only has an intimate understanding of its particular technology platforms but also possesses the tools, experience, and relationships useful in quantifying a planned change before it's ever implemented. So when it comes time to introduce changes that will significantly impact how well your system performs, don't automatically fall back on your own testing and tuning processes—leverage the experts.

And perhaps the best news is that access to these SAP experts is almost always free. Your SAP Competency Center is not just a presales or postsupport organization. It also typically provides resizing, testing, and other services as just another normal part of doing business. Many of these experts are tied into their particular company's benchmarking, marketing, and other SAP-centric technical organizations, all of which should prove useful to you over time. I encourage you to develop a relationship with your SAP Competency Center. Worst case, you'll rarely call on it, but still operate with the peace of mind of knowing that you have a knowledgeable partner waiting in the wings should you have the need.

8.3.   Creating Repeatable Testing Methods

T3s live and die based on the processes they use in their testing endeavors. A team unconcerned with creating repeatable processes that quantify or essentially "prove" the impact of a proposed change or upgrade will not survive long term, as their value will immediately (and rightly) be questioned at the onset of performance problems. So once your organizational decisions have been made, it's important to begin putting together the step-by-step processes you will eventually use when testing, borne from your project-specific test plan. That is, a detailed, well-crafted, and customized test plan should naturally lend itself to evolving into a project-specific execution checklist, which basically reflects the minutiae inherent to executing your stress test in a repeatable manner. I encourage you to cover things beyond the actual steps necessary to execute a certain test case or stress-test run, too, such as the following:

- How to capture current-state or baseline configuration details, including the tools or processes used to do so
- Monitoring tools that need to be installed, configured, and "turned on" prior to a test run
- The actual configuration of a test run—what it includes in terms of hardware, test tools, users/batch processes, input data, and so on
- How long the test run must execute to be valid
- How to actually monitor the test run—for example, detailed real-time performance metrics to be observed, data to be collected
- Where output generated from the test will be held prior to analysis, including creation of a directory structure that helps to organize the various test runs by date/time executed, environment tested, and so on

Other details that should be covered include documenting the steps necessary to analyze your particular test's results, what to do in case the test run goes awry, how to gracefully stop the test at its conclusion, and how to clean up after the test run. We'll take a closer look at these kinds of repeatable methods embodied within customized execution checklists in the chapters that follow.

8.4. Where Should You Test and Tune in the Real World?

Precisely *where* the T3 does its work is up for discussion at this point. Most of my customers tend to take advantage of investments they made, in the form of an SAP Technical Sandbox or other Test system, to perform much of their basic delta testing and simple tuning exercises. A good sandbox or other test environment should, after all, look something like an organization's production environment. In the real world, though, sandbox environments typically fall short in terms of the following factors:

- Actual relevance to the SAP Production system. Many technical sandbox environments only look *something* like production, instead of truly representing a copy of it. Thus, it's common to find a single server in your sandbox rather than multiple ones like those found in Production. In the same way, I often uncover underconfigured disk subsystems instead of robustly configured production-like disk subsystems, and sometimes uncover completely different server hardware components between the two environments. In other cases, the actual OS or RDBMS release may vary, too, which is the result of anything from short-sighted spending freezes or budget necessities to an oversight, to just plain ignorance.
- Horsepower. In a nutshell, underpowered servers and disk subsystems do little to prove how well a production environment can host a particular load. Extrapolation becomes

necessary, a process that's useful to some extent but invites risk nonetheless. This is particularly true when RAM or CPUs differ between production and sandbox environments, or when a company seeks to save money otherwise tied up in replicating a production disk subsystem with fewer drives (spindles) or different approaches to RAID technology.

- Version control. In terms of hardware firmware and OS revisions, even the best of SAP Technical Sandboxes often either lag way behind production, or more often, embrace the latest and greatest technology stack update without the benefit of going through good change control procedures. The result is that the inconsistencies between the two platforms negate much of the value associated with testing proposed production changes in these sandbox environments. They're simply too mercurial, too subject to the whims of many different SAP technical support organizations tasked with other types of support activities.

In an ideal world, what you really want is a system within your SAP System Landscape that is managed exclusively for the benefit of production-driven change control testing. Such an environment typically stays one methodical step ahead of production and is managed like production in terms of making and testing changes. Many of my larger customers embrace precisely this type of mind-set and refer to this collection of systems as their Staging or Test/QA system. They use this system to test the impact a change has, and benefit from the fact that actual production loads can be simulated as well. This is the preferred way to go if your checkbook can handle it.

Other customers take even greater advantage of the value such an arrangement provides and dual-purpose this environment for Disaster Recovery. In this way, they not only protect themselves from business continuity issues but also give themselves the ultimate technical sandbox, where every proposed change can be clearly tested and the impact noted across the end-to-end technology stack. Unfortunately, because DR sites inherently exist outside of the production datacenter's boundaries, using DR resources for load testing implies traveling or, in the best case, working through remote access. And such access often complicates what is usually uncomplicated in production—things like SAPGUI or other user-interface access issues, third-party bolt-on interface issues, complicated access to the various technology stack layers, network latencies atypical of production, and so on represent deltas between DR and production, and therefore result in systems that look less like their production counterparts at the end of the day.

Still other customers do not believe they can "afford" to deploy a production-like DR site and instead enlist the aid or assistance of third-party DR hosting facilities and other partners/vendors on a part-time basis. In this way, they can sometimes leverage a pay-as-you-go model when they need it (e.g., quarterly or annually), at the risk of sacrificing flexibility in times of critical testing needs. This isn't a bad DR approach in principle, actually, but by the same token it isn't the best way to go for many T3 organizations.

Beyond *where* your test environment resides, and the role it might play in your unique situation, additional test assets come into play. For example, infrastructure capable of emulating physical or virtual users, or of controlling these users, is required in addition to the SAP testing environment itself. A reserved network segment or two, dedicated management/monitoring tools, and even a static set of server and other infrastructure resources (e.g., DNS, Active Directory, Internet Transaction Servers, firewalls, load-balancing gear) set aside for testing purposes may be required, too, as we see next.

8.4.1.   Leveraging Tier One Test Infrastructure

When I speak of "Tier One" test infrastructure, I mean infrastructure that's already deployed in your SAP system landscape, whether it represents production assets or some kind of other test or development asset. Most often, these assets are truly production-oriented, though. Examples outside of the obvious SAP system landscape components (e.g., application servers, the central instance, or the DB Server) include steady-state or production resources like your DNS servers, your directory services infrastructure, shared production network resources, file and print servers, and so on. Most of the time, these resources work just fine when it comes to load testing or stress testing the incremental burden placed on them. Other times, though, these Tier One infrastructure resources may need to be augmented with test-only per-project assets. The important thing is to take these kinds of resources into consideration during your preparation phase, so you (or others) are not surprised later on.

8.4.2.   Tier Two Test Infrastructure

Unlike Tier One test resources, Tier Two resources are not production-oriented. However, they tend to remain in a static role serving a long-time purpose once they are introduced in your testing environment. The classic example would be servers that act as virtual client drivers. When virtual users are required of a specific TU or test run, you should have a set of gear expressly set aside for this purpose. The idea is to learn from the past, so that you understand the load a particular client driver can emulate, for example. This kind of knowledge makes it easier to plan for and execute subsequent stress tests—if you know that a particular model of a four-way 2GHz server with 2GB of RAM running Windows Server 2003 can comfortably simulate 500 active R/3 users, for example, it becomes a simple exercise to plan for and execute a 1,000-user stress test.

And, because Tier Two resources are not true production resources, you have more freedom when it comes to blowing them away and reloading them to meet specific conditions or criteria. For example, if you need to test a particular mySAP component that only supports a particular test tool, which in turn is only certified to run on a particular OS, you should ideally have few internal processes to go through to wipe and reload your Tier Two resources. Thus, the beauty of this infrastructure tier is in its ability to meet your general needs over and over again, 90% of the time, while still retaining the flexibility necessary to meet your specific needs the remaining 10% of the time.

Other core Tier Two resources include the following: server infrastructure earmarked for controlling test runs (i.e., the server where the "controller" component of a particular test tool resides), machines set aside for monitoring particular components or layers of the SAP Technology

Stack (e.g., BMC Patrol or HP Insight Manager consoles, or perhaps a console dedicated to collecting and analyzing disk controller I/Os and related throughput statistics), and similar quasi-production resources.

Like Tier One resources, I recommend maintaining a standard server "build" as much as possible—refrain from tweaking your Tier One and Tier Two resources by adding or removing RAM, CPUs, disks, network cards, and so on. In this way, it becomes quite a bit easier to capture the test system's current state, an otherwise time-consuming process detailed later in this chapter.

8.4.3.   Test "Crash-and-Burn" (C&B) Resources in the Real World

As you would imagine, C&B resources are temporary at best. They are by no means production/Tier One or near-production/Tier Two resources. Your C&B servers, disk subsystems, network segments, and other highly fluid resources are used to build out a temporary system to be tested. But their role in fulfilling the infrastructure needs necessary to conduct testing makes them nearly as critical as Tier One and Tier Two resources.

I suggest that you organize your C&B assets into multiple groups—those that reside internal to your test environment, which tend to represent long-term C&B resources, and those that are pulled in from other areas as required, to be used typically once (e.g., a special server platform pulled from your internal evaluation team) or "wiped and reloaded" as necessary. For instance, if you have deployed an SAP Technical Sandbox, you might consider breaking its resources down into these two C&B groups: your sandbox application servers might represent wipe and reload resources, whereas the DB Server and requisite disk subsystem might serve more permanent roles along the lines of long-term C&B resources or even Tier Two resources.

C&B resources imply exactly what their label suggests—these assets are not subject to change control processes, but instead are made available between different projects or TUs based on need and scheduling requirements. Thus, if you have a need to load a new testing tool, or try out a new monitoring solution, you'll use C&B resources rather than meddle with Tier One and Tier Two technology and solution stacks that already work. And, unlike its Tier One and Tier Two counterparts, it's expected that you will configure C&B resources to meet your needs—adding or removing CPUs or RAM, upgrading firmware to support newer disk drives, and so on are common activities when preparing these kinds of resources.

8.4.4.   Assembling Your TU Test Systems

Once you understand and document the requirements of a particular TU or stress-test project, you're in a position to begin identifying and assembling the various technology components necessary to make a stress-test attempt. For example, you might require three client drivers, two different systems for monitoring different technology stack components, and a single controller. You might also determine that you can leverage the network infrastructure found within your technical sandbox but need to have a separate "back-end" network put into place to simulate your production environment. In a similar way, you might also determine that you can leverage the Citrix server and network infrastructure deployed for production today, rather than require a complex load on a new set of server platforms.

These kinds of decisions are based on requirements derived from the business units or IT organizations driving the need for testing in the first place. For example, if the business has indicated that it would be satisfied with a test based on 100 users executing a concise suite of queries against their SAP BW system before and after a proposed upgrade, then you might make the decision to use existing resources in some cases, and acquire incremental resources in other cases. More to the point, you might decide that your existing Tier Two resources are adequate except for a shortcoming in virtual client drivers, choosing to additionally deploy a number of C&B resources to make up the difference. Of course, you'll also need a copy of your current BW system that you can then upgrade and test, not to mention the disk space necessary to house your BW's database. Such needs will naturally drive the requirement to acquire even more C&B or other resources, all the while driving and illuminating people- and time-related needs and constraints as well.

8.5. Capturing Your Current State and Baseline

With test assets identified and then assembled into a collection of resources capable of meeting your testing needs, the next big step in preparing for a series of test runs is to completely document the environment. This is much more involved than simply documenting a simple SAP Technology Stack—you need to take into consideration the Tier One, Tier Two, and C&B resources you are using, the roles they will play, and how they will be configured. All of this data collection could conceivably take longer to perform than performing the actual stress tests if it were not for the fact that you by now have a number of excellent current-state configuration tools at your disposal (discussed in Chapter 7). Remember, current-state data collection utilities are used for documenting the state or "baseline" of various configurations and changes to these configurations as they evolve from the baseline.

Also keep in mind that tracking these inevitable real-world changes, however minor in scope, is critical in that it allows an SAP shop the ability to manage changes within the test environment as well as against a production baseline. These before and after snapshots make it a breeze to quantify real-world performance deltas realized through configuration tuning, updates, upgrades, and so on, ultimately making it easy to prove that a proposed change truly resulted in better response times, for instance.

Not all tools are equally effective in capturing these types of comprehensive data—some are naturally better than others when it comes to particular operating environments, mySAP components, and other technology stack specifics. And some are easier to learn and use than others, whereas other tools come up short in key areas but make up for their lack of "coverage" in terms of price. Some tools require that a system be taken "down" to do their job effectively, and by virtue of their installation routine many of these tools also inherently change the SAP Technology Stack being monitored (in terms of environment variables or registry entries, for example). Finally, each tool differs in how it presents and manages the current-state data previously collected.

8.5.1. Documenting the SAP System Landscape and Individual Technology Stacks

As discussed in Chapter 7, a number of current-state tools focus exclusively on recording only specific layers of the SAP Technology Stack. Some focus on collecting server and disk subsystem configuration details, whereas others capture holistic OS-specific data. Others gather fundamental hardware and OS configuration data, perhaps even tracking the versions of firmware layered on top of each hardware component, or the OS version and patch levels inherent to a particular OS. Still other tools help you document the database and application layers of your solution.

The problem is that there's no single tool that can do it all! My long-time free favorites—HP GetConfig and HP Survey—do a fine job of covering the bottom of the solution stack for HP/Windows-based SAP solutions, from hardware and firmware up through disk configuration, OS configuration, and basic OS overlays like database and SAP services details. HP GetConfig even goes so far as to collect data relevant to SAP profiles, Oracle configuration files, and more. But these tools are far from being SAP Technology Stack inclusive; even in the best of cases, they are unable to collect the really comprehensive database and SAP application-specific parameters you might need to document. Worst case, they are nearly or completely useless (like in the case of a SAP system residing on HP-UX and Informix). And, as I've mentioned before, many of these tools are single-server–centric in that they execute on a single server and only collect data relevant to that particular server—they cannot automatically review and pull together data that reflect an entire SAP system landscape.

Regardless of the shortcomings of these tools, my suggestion for the most price-conscious of you is to get comfortable with tools like these—in the case of Windows-based mySAP Solutions, especially GetConfig—and schedule their execution across your test system landscape. Alternatively, you can use a relatively inexpensive tool like AssetDB or Enterprise Auditor, which make it possible to define servers to be reviewed without the need to schedule anything through any number of OS-based or otherwise readily available scheduling utilities. You may even consider leveraging Windows-GUI-based scripting freeware like AutoIT to automatically map drives to various servers, execute your data collection utility of choice, and copy/rename the results file back to a common holding area.

But you'll still need to augment this core technology stack data with database-specific, mySAP component–specific, and other SAP-specific data, much of which varies between products and platforms. I often seek out application-specific configuration files like SAP's three core profiles, or make a copy of Oracle's control files (init<SID>.ora), and so on, or execute a simple command like *sp_configure* from Microsoft's SQL Enterprise Manager to capture key SQL Server configuration settings. If this is not enough, or to make it very clear how a particular system is configured, I might augment these data with screenshots taken from HP OpenView (leveraging Smart Plug-Ins, or SPIs, to drill down into numerous SAP Technology Stack layers), SAP CCMS, Enterprise Manager, or Microsoft OS specifics as gleaned through Control Panel—what-

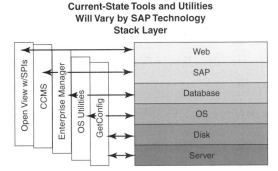

Figure 8–3 Capturing your test environment's baseline configuration is only made possible by leveraging a number of utilities and approaches.

ever utility I must execute to display the needed configuration data. The specifics vary by solution stack, of course, but if you think of it from a technology stack perspective, you'll be more inclined to assemble a complete picture of your current state, as shown in Figure 8–3.

8.5.2. Capturing and Freezing the Baseline

Although it would be nice to dump all of the configuration data associated with a particular test environment or stress-test run into a database of sorts, which could later be sorted and sifted through, the bottom line is that you really don't need this kind of capability. Sure, if a single tool could gather all of your SAP-wide configuration data and drop them into an SQL database, I wouldn't complain. But because the real world requires me to use multiple tools and even manual processes and screen shots to capture a system's current state, I stay away from forcing myself to do additional work that has little long-term value, like manually entering configuration data into a database simply because *some* of the data are easily captured by a particular tool. Instead, I rely exclusively on the ability to collect as much electronic-based data as I can—output files captured in text format, configuration files readable through Notepad, and so on—and do my best to steer clear of collecting paper-based data. When it comes to screen shots, I annotate each figure with a short sentence that describes what the picture tells me. In this way, I at least can create a repository of sorts that is still electronically "searchable" using plain old Windows Explorer.

And I avoid filling up a bunch of file cabinets in the process. For example, rather than printing out and archiving a 35-page HP Survey output report for each server used in a particular test run, I instead rename the output file to something that describes the system's role in my test, the date, and a version number of sorts, and then electronically file this document away in an appropriate directory structure created on a long-term file server (or my own laptop, if I'm at a customer site). Such an approach serves as the foundation for creating custom documentation at a later date, too. You might want to capture salient test points in a PowerPoint presentation to be given to your change control team at the end of each month, for instance—capturing and saving screen shots and other configuration data can make for compelling slideware!

Once you have captured your baseline, it's equally important to avoid making changes to it. This seems to be a no-brainer, of course, but there's more involved in freezing a current state than meets the eye. Consider the following: if your current state *changes* based on the execution of a stress-test run, you must put together a process that lets you quickly "restore" your system to the original current state before executing another test run.

What kinds of things change after the execution of a test run? Plenty! The most obvious to you should be the database associated with a particular application being tested (I'll cover exceptions to this general rule later, but suffice it to say here that the database will nearly always be updated in the course of a test run). Thus, you need to look into the best way of capturing and "freezing in time" the state of the database, and more important, look at the fastest and cheapest way to restore the database back to your known state. I've used traditional tape backup/restore systems to do this, of course, but other methods are faster. A disk-based file-system copy of a database to a safe "holding" place makes a lot of sense in most cases. For customers with disk subsystems capable of supporting snapshots, clones, or business continuity volumes, "breaking off" an image of your database and then resyncing the updated image back to the baseline or current state is an even better way to go, and it's fast! Other changes brought about by the execution of a test run and which therefore require your attention up front include the following:

- Output files are generated from business transactions or the test tools that executed them. Requiring new test runs to append to a single log sounds like a convenient solution to managing output, but such files may take longer to open, read through, and write, which will slow down the test itself and impact its viability.
- Log files generated from the OS or database can also grow lengthy very quickly, and while their impact tends to be low, you want to ensure you avoid unusual events (e.g., log files filling up and "stopping" or being dumped to an "archive" during the middle of your test run).
- Printed output, or other pending SAP output produced from executing a business transaction, will queue up over time, again representing potential for slowdowns.
- User connections to the SAP instance being tested may continue to exist even after you've stopped or aborted a test run. These may need to be cleared manually via transaction SM04 afterwards.
- Other SAP-specific areas that may need attention include clearing the system log, deleting ABAP dumps or other "short dumps" (SAP's terminology for verbiage relevant to an aborted program), cleaning up the SAP BW Operational Data Store (ODS) or Persistent Staging Area (PSA), resetting database-specific counters maintained by ST04, and so on.
- Any special control files you leverage to stop or start your test runs, or handle error routines, must be restored back to their original state prior to executing another test run.

In the end, managing a baseline equates to managing change—ensure you address how you will manage change prior to stepping into a stress-test project, and you'll be better positioned for success.

8.6.   Real-World Methods of Conquering the Learning Curve

There's plenty to learn when it comes to testing and tuning, no doubt about it. The technology stacks themselves take time to master, not to mention the testing and monitoring tools necessary for effective stress testing. And then the real fun begins—iteratively tweaking, configuring, and tuning your technology stack to wring the most performance possible within the constraints of your high availability mechanisms, budget, and so on. In the best of worlds, you would walk into your testing scenarios armed with all of the requisite knowledge and experience to hit the ground running. In the real world, though, you'll probably fall short in a number of areas, as I've shown in Figure 8–4. The following points can help you get smoothly up to speed a bit faster:

- Take advantage of any installation, configuration, or support documents published by the vendor via read-me files, sizing/configuration guidelines, tuning resources, or similar product documentation offerings. The Web is a great place to find this kind of information, typically for free, as is the vendor's installation CDs.
- Leverage the skills and experience already on the team. Your colleagues in different SAP support organizations, from Basis to Operations to smaller organizations that might hold pockets of testing and tuning expertise can be invaluable. Perhaps they already support the stack you're working with, or are long-time users of a particular monitoring or testing tool. Maybe they're OS or database experts or have expertise in another layer of the SAP Technology Stack.
- Look to partners and vendors for presales expertise. As I mentioned in Chapter 5, you can find this type of expertise for "free" quite often, if you look in the right places! Such assistance is usually available either soon before or soon after you make a particular technology purchase. I recommend building in this kind of support up front, by making access to solid presales support a condition of purchase. Don't forget to vali-

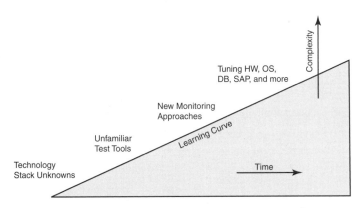

Figure 8–4   Here, the learning curve facing an SAP T3 reveals itself as both broad and potentially very time-consuming.

date experience and expertise levels through onsite or telephone-based "interviews," too, not to mention old-fashioned reference checks.

- Leverage your SAP Competency Center, as I discussed at length earlier. It embodies a certain amount of breadth and depth in a variety of technology areas, and can prove quite useful beyond simple SAP hardware and OS support. And its help is typically free.
- Leverage your SAP Technical Sandbox or other dedicated training systems. These types of hands-on resources are key to getting up to speed, assuming you have the time and resources necessary to do so.
- Attend formal training courses. Most SAP technology partners offer formal classes or other courseware designed to teach you their products. Sometimes, you can make inclusion of this training a prerequisite for purchase. Other times, you'll be able to take advantage of steep one-time discounts—of course, the value associated with your purchase is directly related to the "free" training you can conceivably get; inexpensive purchases give you little leverage in this regard, naturally.
- Leverage Internet-based and other "public" knowledge banks or discussion groups. These documents are published by sources outside of the vendor and often represent real-world challenges or issues overcome by the product's "installed-base" user community. Newsgroups are an excellent source of this kind of education, for example.
- Take advantage of technical conferences, user groups, and seminars. The major technology providers share best practices and other configuration/tuning data in technical venues like these. Not only can you find current materials in this way, but you'll benefit from the ability to develop technology-focused relationship "bridges" between you and the technology provider, and you and other customers.
- If necessary, bring in a hired gun to get you up to speed quickly. Such a postsales consultant strategy is common for projects in which the incremental expense represents only a fraction of the project's budget. In other words, consultants tend to be associated with fairly large projects simply because of the dollars involved. On the other hand, if the risk of missing project deadlines represents a great cost to the organization, you should consider bringing in a consultant in this case, too. And if the project is important enough to pursue, but you simply have no bandwidth available on the T3 to make it happen, again consider a short-term consulting arrangement.

Finally, don't forget to leverage the knowledge and experience of a technology partner's reference accounts. Like some of the bulleted items identified previously, such a resource acts as a somewhat biased though normally high-quality communications liaison, typically giving you the straight scoop on product shortcomings, tips and tricks to testing a particular application or technology stack, and so on.

8.7.   Pretuning the Stack

Once the right people are involved, and a baseline is established, you can move into another important preparation area: pretuning. Going through your technology stack to ensure that you're at least 90% of the way there in terms of core system configuration makes a lot of sense. In the past, I've created custom checklists for my clients that identified configuration tweaks and tuning relevant to a particular solution stack. This kind of approach saved everyone time and money, because it provided a solid foundation on which the rest of the performance tuning team could base their work. I suggest you take a similar approach, and outline the various layers of your solution stack annotated with configuration notes, "gotchas," and tips/tricks. To be effective, I recommend that you first assign a person to be responsible for tuning each specific layer, and then follow up by asking each member to assemble a checklist that reflects configuration tasks specific to his or her responsible layer. Combine all of the individual checklists into a master checklist, QA it for accuracy and completeness, and then use it as your initial configuration checklist or template. For example, if you are tasked with stress testing and performance tuning a SAN-attached R/3-on-SQL three-tiered solution stack accessible by WebGUI users, you might consider the following checklist as a rough starting point:

- Network infrastructure. Ensure a 100Mb network is in place that emulates production. In most cases, this would thus imply the need for a public network segment as well as a back-end network for dedicated SAP Application server–to–DB Server connectivity. Ensure that the network reflects any load-balancing or performance-enhancing options used in production as well (e.g., port bonding, where two network switch ports are logically "bonded" together to provide a faster single connection).
- Disk subsystem infrastructure. Ensure RAID sets are carved up consistent with production-level RAID sets, including the same number of spindles per disk group, same disk controller cache settings, same load-balancing algorithm, and so on.
- Server and OS infrastructure. Validate that paging files are configured appropriately (both in terms of size and in terms of the number of spindles used). In the case of Windows-based systems like this, ensure that the OS is set to maximize throughput for network applications. Ensure local disk controllers are configured identical to production. Also, ensure that service packs and OS patches are applied as consistent with production, unnecessary services are disabled (identify services that actually *need* to be running for each SAP instance), and so forth.
- Database layer. Ensure that SQL Server is configured in the same manner as found in production, in terms of the following: dynamic versus fixed memory size, maximum worker threads, which processors will host SQL, whether Windows NT fibers will be used, service pack level, location of logs, TempDB and data, and all sp_configure and SQL Server Enterprise Manager settings.

- SAP application layer. Validate kernel patch and support packages release levels, other update releases, configuration of work processes across application servers (including how batch, online, and update work processes or dedicated servers might be distributed), all three profiles and their individual settings, and so on.
- SAP ITS AGate layer. Validate the entire stack as it is implemented on this layer, which often consists of one or two servers to maybe six or eight servers. This especially includes the disk subsystem (which likely consists of only a few drives—optimize this environment for the fastest write performance possible, to speed up end-to-end SAP transactions)—and OS layers already noted. I recommend 8kb allocation units for Windows-based ITS servers, as this blocksize represents an excellent trade-off between the superior read-ahead performance associated with large blocks and the smaller amount of disk fragmentation inherent to smaller blocksizes housing many small HTML files.
- SAP ITS WGate layer. Like its AGate counterpart, you'll need to at least tune the disk subsystem and OS layers, along with Web server–specific tuning parameters.
- WebGUI Client Access layer. If you leverage physical desktops for stress testing (especially common in single-unit stress-testing projects), you'll want to maximize network performance (optimize binding order and remove unnecessary protocols) and eliminate all nonessential services, applets, and so on running on the desktop.

Of course, if your particular test implementation includes third-party applications, other mySAP applications, or special infrastructure like that associated with Citrix MetaFrame, you'll need to include details relevant to each of these solution stacks, layer by layer. Doing so might sound time-consuming now, but in the end, it'll save you countless hours of time and also help you avoid the panic and general uneasiness associated with troubleshooting future performance problems when you're not 100% clear on how well you tested a change, simply because you never started with a known baseline configured in a repeatable manner.

Testing individual components or layers of your particular SAP Technology Stack in this way is also referred to as *system-level testing*, or *systems testing*. I like the term *component testing* better, though. The idea is to ensure that the individual solution stack layers and components operate well in a standalone manner before trying to tie everything together into a complex system. When things run smoothly in this standalone manner, you will then be in a position to more intelligently optimize the entire end-to-end technology stack, ultimately creating a cohesive solution of integrated components and technologies.

8.8.   Next Steps

Before we move on to Chapter 9, which discusses characterizing workloads, nailing down test mixes, and more, it's important to set the stage in terms of basic input, processing, and output requirements—a kind of Data Processing 101 refresher. That is, let's step back and look at the big picture again relevant to testing before jumping back into the details of testing and performance tuning.

8.8.1.   Input—Test Mixes and Workloads

An essential component of performing any kind of process regards *input*. Input in the context of stress testing includes the customer-specific data necessary to complete the "data entry" portion of SAPGUI or other front-end screens, and the master and other transactional data behind the scenes necessary to actually execute a business transaction. Thus, things like organization and customer numbers, material numbers, storage locations, plant codes, and the like represent key input parameters. Other things like user accounts, appropriate authorizations, other security parameters, and so on also represent input. So too does the number or range of items, like the number of materials ordered in an order entry transaction, or the range of purchase orders reviewed in a "PO display" transaction.

Of course, stress testing can be performed "beneath" the application layer. Disk subsystem testing might require batch input files, configuration or parameter files that indicate the mix of reads to writes, for example, and other similar data necessary to execute a test. All of these input data may then be combined into different collections of test mixes: read-only test mixes that do not make any net incremental changes to a mySAP database, mixes focused on exercising a disk subsystem's throughput capabilities, mixes designed to emulate daily loads or peak transactional loads, and so on.

Different randomization or pseudorandom algorithms for selecting the input to be used by a particular virtual user in a particular test run also represent critical stress-test input. This input, or workload, is critical to emulate as closely as possible and to repeat across different tests in as identical a manner as possible. Controlling when a user commences a test run, the type and number of business transactions he or she runs, and for how long are also important input parameters. The subject of input alone is so important to effective stress testing and performance tuning that it warrants its own chapter—Chapter 9.

8.8.2.   Processing—Execution Checklists and More

Once all of the necessary input has been assembled, and its use has been determined, the actual execution of a stress-test run or TU can commence. The time spent in executing the run is generically referred to as processing, of course, and represents the initial goal of stress testing—to actually simulate a business process or some kind of load on either an entire system or simply a component of a particular SAP Technology Stack. How well this load is emulated—how well it maps to simulating the environment described by the goals of the test at hand—is measured afterwards. Because we need to create a repeatable and predictable load on the system, the use of automated test tools, automated processes, and easy-to-follow execution checklists is highly encouraged. Such tools help us to ensure that different test runs are, for example, the same in terms of the amount of time they execute, the number and mix of users simulated, the quantity of orders created and processed, and so on. You can read about all of this and more in Chapters 10, 11, and 12.

8.8.3.   Output—Monitoring Considerations

Once a test run has executed for an appropriate amount of time or has otherwise completed its objective, its output must be collected, measured, analyzed, and brought together in a meaningful way to illustrate the results of the change that was tested. But remember that monitoring and test-run analysis involves much more than a post-run snapshot of a system's performance. A test run needs to be monitored *throughout* its execution. More to the point, the performance observed relevant to *each layer of the SAP Technology Stack* (or the significant layers, in the case of component-specific or systems-level testing) needs to be observed, noted, and later analyzed. Output will include the processing load borne by a server's CPUs and RAM, the network load created within the system, the disk queue lengths or total processed I/Os associated with the database, the number of orders or other post-transaction deliverables processed during the period, and so on.

Output also includes the following factors: any errors or warnings; the number of virtual or physical clients that "died" or otherwise became unavailable during the execution of the test run; whether a transaction completed successfully, partially, or at all; and much more. Even seemingly simple things like the stop and start times of a test run, or total execution-versus-think time of a particular virtual user, represent key output data. The monitoring and analysis of test runs are covered in depth throughout Chapters 12 and 13.

8.9.   Tools and Approaches

The tools and processes we covered in this chapter were largely unlike those discussed in previous chapters. That is, most of the key tools are actually paper-based logical processes rather than strictly software-based utilities. These preparation-oriented processes include simple paper-based project plans, execution checklists, and so on. Despite their low-tech nature, though, the value these processes bring to the table is unquestionable, so much so that I created custom versions of the following "tools," which may be downloaded from the ftp site:

- A sample strawman project plan, or reusable general template for stress testing and project planning
- A sample customized test plan template, specifically customized for a particular testing project or TU
- A sample execution checklist template, useful in executing the necessary step-by-step processes inherent to a repeatable stress test

Now, onward to the next chapter, where we take a closer look at the kinds of input necessary to pull off a successful stress test!

CHAPTER 9

Determining a Suitable Test Mix

Finally, we are in a position to give attention to one of the core matters surrounding testing and tuning: determining a suitable stress-test business process or other "input data" test mix. After all, it is the mix of activities, transactions, and processes executed under your guidance that ultimately simulates your financials' month-end close or helps you understand the load borne by your SAP customer-facing systems during the holidays or other seasonal peaks. And it's the test mix that brings together master data, transactional data, customer-specific data, and other input necessary to fuel a business process from beginning to end. You've certainly heard the phrase "garbage in, garbage out." It applies without question here, because poor test data will never allow you to achieve your testing and follow-on tuning goals.

Beyond SAP application-level data, though, input data can also consist of the scripts, batch files, configuration files, and so on required of lower level testing tools, like those associated with testing the performance of your disk subsystem, network infrastructure, and so on. As you know by now, sound testing of your SAP Technology Stack encompasses much more than strictly business process testing.

The goal of this chapter is therefore to help walk you through the challenges surrounding data: how to select appropriate data, what to look for, and what to avoid. In this way, you'll be that much closer to conducting stress-test runs that not only "work" but also truly simulate the load planned for your production environment.

9.1. Overview—What's a Mix?

What exactly is a test mix? In true consulting fashion, the right answer is "it depends." The next couple of pages provide a high-level overview of a test mix, followed by more detailed discussions on this subject. For beginners, note that all test mixes must include a way to control timing, or the time it takes for a test run (or subtasks within a run) to actually execute. Sometimes this factor is controllable via the test mix itself or a test-tool configuration file, whereas other times it's left up to test-tool controller software or the team executing and monitoring the test runs.

Timing is not everything, though. Test mixes also typically allow the number of OS or other technology stack–based threads or processes to be controlled, another key input factor relevant to multiuser stress testing. In this way, the very load placed on a system may be controlled, making it possible to vary workload rates or individual users or processes without actually changing the absolute number of users or processes.

Unfortunately, we must also keep in mind that the assorted tools and approaches we have examined thus far differ greatly in terms of their fundamental execution and goals, and therefore their specific data-input-mix requirements. On the flip side, test mixes tend to adhere to a set of general rules of thumb, too. But rather than trying to lay down a dictionary-style definition, let's instead look at test mixes by way of example, working our way up the technology stack, as follows:

- For network infrastructure testing, a test mix consists of factors like the number of data transfers or other network operations performed, the size of those transfers/operations, the use of configuration files that define the two end points necessary for testing (i.e., server-to-server testing), and even the protocols that may be tested (although for SAP testing, there's usually little reason to test anything other than TCP/IP-based RFC, CPIC, and ALE network activity).

- For disk subsystem testing, a test mix defines the number of reads and writes to be executed (either as a ratio or an absolute number), the types of operations to be executed (sequential versus direct/random, or inserts versus appends), data block sizes, and even the number of iterations (rather than leveraging timing criteria, a test mix might instead specify the number of I/O operations each thread, process, or test run will execute, such as 1,000). And the number of data files or partitions against which a test is executed is also often configurable, as is the size of each data file. For instance, I often execute tests against six different data files spread across six different disk partitions, each 5GB in size, thus simulating a small but realistic 30GB "database."

- For server testing, a test mix might include the number of operations that specifically stress a particular subsystem or component of the server (e.g., the processor complex, RAM subsystem, system bus). Server testing often is intertwined with network infrastructure and disk subsystem testing, too, and therefore may leverage the same types of data input as previously discussed.

- At a database level, a test mix must reflect operations understood and executable by the explicit DBMS being tested. Thus, SQL Server test mixes may differ from Oracle in terms of syntax, execution, and so forth. But, in all cases, a database-specific test will reflect a certain type of operation (read, write, join) executed against a certain database, which itself supports a host of database-specific tuning and configuration parameters.

- A single R/3 or mySAP component's test mix will often reflect discrete transactions (or multiple transactions sequentially executed to form a business process) that are executed against only the system being tested. I call these "simple" or "single-component" tests, because they do not require the need for external systems, and therefore CPIC-based communications, external program or event-driven factors, and interface issues stay conveniently out of scope. (Note that CPIC, or SAP's Common Programming Interface Communication protocol, allows for program-to-program communication.) The input necessary to drive these simple tests is transaction-specific, therefore, and relatively easy to identify: all input data that must be keyed into the SAPGUI (anything from data ranges to quantities to unique transaction-specific values like PO numbers, and more) and any master, transactional, or other client-specific data must be known, available, and plentiful. User accounts configured with the appropriate authorizations and other security considerations also act as input. The right mix essentially becomes a matter of the proper quantity of high-quality input data versus the amount of time a test run needs to execute to prove viable for performance tuning.

- Complex R/3 or mySAP component test mixes, on the other hand, necessitate multiple components or third-party applications to support complex business process testing that spans more than a single system. Even so, the bulk of the input data may still be quite straightforward, possibly originating in a single core system. But like any complete business process, the *output* from one transaction typically becomes the input to a subsequent transaction. Cross-component business processes therefore require more detailed attention to input data than their simpler counterparts, because the originating system (along with other supporting data) must be identified as well.

Many of these examples are discussed in more detail later in this chapter. Suffice it to say, though, that a single TU or stress-test run can quickly grow complex from an input data perspective if several technology stack layers or systems are involved, especially in light of the many stack-specific test tools that might be used.

9.1.1.   Change-Driven Testing

It's important to remember one of the fundamental reasons behind testing—to quantify the delta in performance that a particular change or configuration creates. I refer to this generically as change-driven testing, and believe that most if not all performance-oriented testing falls into this big bucket. But it's impossible to quantify and characterize performance without a load behind the change. In other words, things don't tend to "break" until they're exercised. The strength and robustness of a solution remains unproven, just like the maximum load a weight-trainer can lift, until it (or he or she) successfully supports or lifts it. The "it" is the workload, in essence the manipulation or processing of input data. Thus, it only follows that a good performance test depends on a good mix of data, data that has been identified and characterized as to their appropriateness in helping you meet your simulation and load-testing goals. Not surprisingly, stress tests executed without the benefit of adequate test mix analysis, or workload characterization, often fall short in achieving their goals.

9.1.2.   Characterizing Workloads

Given that the workload a test run is to process is central to the success of stress testing, characterizing or describing that workload is paramount as well. Workloads vary as much as the real world varies, unfortunately, so there's no easy answer. Key workload considerations as they pertain to the SAP application layer include the following:

- The mix or ratio of online users to batch jobs, reports, and other similar processes, reflecting a particular business scenario.
- The mix of functional areas, such that the resulting mix reflects a sought-after condition (e.g., month-end closing for the entire business) or state (e.g., an average daily load).
- The pure number of online users, batch processes, report generators, and so on leveraged to create a representative load on an SAP system.
- The predictability of a workload, so that apples-to-apples comparisons may be made against subsequent test runs—in other words, avoiding true randomization when it comes to input data is important. True randomization needs to be replaced instead with pseudorandom algorithms that are at once "random" *and* repeatable.
- The quantity of data. Low quantities result in higher cache hit rates as more data may be stuffed into hardware- and software-based caches, therefore exercising the disk subsystem less than the workload truly would otherwise.
- The quality of data. Only unique combinations of customers, materials, plants, and storage locations "work" to create a sales order, for example. Other combinations result in error messages in the best of cases, and more often in failed or simply incompletely executed business processes.

The configuration of the system itself in relation to performance also represents "input" to some extent as well, though I prefer to keep this separate, under the guise of configuration or current-state documentation as discussed in the previous chapter.

But how do you determine what a representative workload or data mix looks like? In the past, I've spent most of my time speaking with various SAP team members to answer this question. Functional leads are your best bet, because they know the business as well as anyone else on the SAP technical team. But SAP power users representing each of the core functional areas are also valuable sources of workload information, as are management representatives of the various functional organizations found in most companies.

Outside of people resources/team members, you can also determine the "Top 40" online and batch processes through CCMS's ST03 or ST03N, both of which display detailed transaction data over defined periods of time. That is, you can drill down into the days preceding or following month-end to identify precisely the transactions that are weighing down the system most in terms of CPU, database, network, and other loads, along with relative response-time metrics. Particularly heavy hours, like 9 a.m. to 11 a.m., or 1 p.m. to 4 p.m., can be scrutinized closely as well. These "top transactions" can be sorted in any number of ways, too: by the total number executed, the peak hour executed, and even by greatest to least impact (highlighting the transactions that beat up the database or CPU or network the worst, for example). And, because CCMS since Basis release 4.6C allows you to globally view ST03 data across an entire SAP system, the once time-consuming job of reviewing individual application servers for your production BW system, for example, is no longer necessary.

Once you understand the particular transactions and business processes representative of a particular workload or regular event/condition, you must then consider how you will represent this workload in a stress test. To make the process of workload characterization as flexible and manageable as possible, I like to create "packages" of work. Within a package, the work is typically similar in nature—online transactions that focus on a particular business process or functional area, batch processes that execute against a particular set of data or for a similar period of time, and so on might make sense for you. Besides maintaining a certain functional consistency, I also chop up the packages into manageable user loads. For example, if I need to test 600 CRM users executing a standard suite of business activities, I'll not only create a set of business scripts to reflect those activities, but I'll also create perhaps six identical packages of 100 virtual users each, so as to easily control and manage the execution of a stress-test run. If the workload needs to be more granular and represent five core business activities, I might divide the packages instead into these five areas (where each package then reflects unique business process scripts), and work with the business or drill down into the CCMS to determine how many users need to be "behind" or associated with each package. Even then, if one of these granular and functionally focused packages represents many users, I would still be inclined to chop it up further as just mentioned and as shown in Figure 9–1. More details regarding the creation and divvying up of test packages are discussed later in this chapter.

9.1.3. Don't Forget to Baseline!

Beyond baselining and documenting the configuration to be stress tested, each test mix also needs to be characterized by way of a baseline. The baseline serves as documentation relevant to a par-

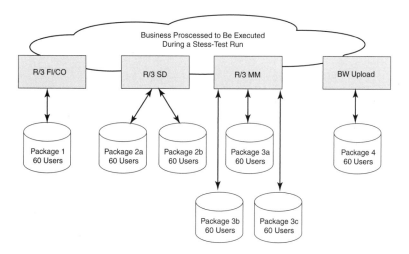

Figure 9–1 Once your workload is characterized and sorted by tasks, functional areas, or business processes, it makes sense to further divide the workload into smaller and more manageable packages, each reflecting a representative user mix.

ticular state—the configuration of the system in relation to the workload that it can support—so that future changes to either the technology stack or workload are not only easily identified but also specifically quantified in terms of performance. In my experience, these initial performance baselines tend to multiply rather quickly. For instance, I'll often begin initial load testing by working through a number of specific configuration alternatives, testing the same test mix against each different configuration in the name of pretuning or to help start off a stress-test project on the best foot possible. Each alternative rates a documented baseline, but only the most promising end-results act as a launch pad for further testing and pretuning iterations.

Once a particular configuration seems to work best, I then move into the next phase of baselining, called *workload baselining*. This phase is very much test mix–centric, as opposed to the first phase's configuration-centric approach. The idea during these workload characterization and baselining processes is to maintain a static system configuration (i.e., refrain from tuning SAP profiles, disk subsystems, etc.), so as to focus instead on monitoring the performance deltas achieved through executing different workloads. All of this is performed by way of single-unit testing, of course, to save time and energy. The goal is quite simple, too: to prove that a particular workload indeed seems to represent the load described by the business, technical teams, or CCMS data. The work of scripting a true multiuser load followed by real-world performance tuning comes later, then, after you've solidified your workloads and executed various stress-test scenarios as depicted in the next few chapters.

Baseline testing is useful from a number of different perspectives. For instance, it's useful even when it comes to testing a non-Production platform, like your Development or Test/QA systems deployed prior to building, configuring, and initially optimizing the Production platform. That is, you can still gain a fair bit of performance-related knowledge testing against a non-Production system, both in terms of single-unit and multiuser stress testing. And this knowledge can pay off simply by helping you create a faster development experience for your expensive ABAP and Java developers or by creating a functional testing environment for a company's unique end-user base. This is especially true prior to Go-Live, when the production environment is still being built out, but the need for initial single-unit or "contained" load testing is growing ever more critical. The same goes for any change-driven testing as well, however, such as that associated with pending functional upgrades, technical refreshes, and so on.

9.2.   Real-World Low-Level Technology Stack Test Input and Mixes

Although we have looked at a number of input data and test mixes at the highest application levels, the insight only made possible from real-world low-level examples should help lay to rest any lingering questions as to the value of your input data in executing a stress test. The next few sections detail specific stress tests from an input data perspective, identifying goals and how specific stress-test tools help achieve those goals along the way.

9.2.1.   Input Required for Testing Server Hardware

Many testing tools designed to validate the performance of your server platforms require little if any formal input. CheckIt requires nothing other than installation on the local machine, for example. But if your goal is to compare one Windows-based SAP server platform to another in terms of CPU performance, CheckIt allows you to "save" the testing results yielded from one platform's test as comparison or baseline data against which other platforms may be measured and compared. Thus, the output of one test acts as input, in a manner of speaking, for subsequent tests.

Other tools offer a bit more granular control, however, and not surprisingly, support additional data input metrics. If your goal is to measure how well your memory subsystem handles operations of different sizes, or differing random or sequential accesses, Nbench is an easy solution. It features the ability to customize some of your input, specifically the following:

- The size of various operations. Thus, you can test operations that reflect what your SAP server does (or will do) in production, rather than rely on arbitrary hard-coded values assumed by other tools. You might test your DB server for large values, for example, while you focus on smaller values for applications and Web servers.
- Execution thread count. Again, this gives you flexibility to emulate the expected level of multiprocessing that occurs in (or is expected of) your unique SAP environment, specifically regarding the disk subsystem.
- Values associated with integer, floating point, and memory operations.

Other input values unlikely to require customization include the access width of the memory bus (tested at a number of different levels), timing/control information, and the performance of both random and sequential operations. Other mainstay general hardware test tools, like IOzone, even go so far as to set processor cache size and line size to particular default values, though both of these settings and much more may be changed through command-line or switch settings.

9.2.2. Disk Subsystem Test Mixes

Disk subsystem test mixes, like those associated with using SQLIO, Iometer, IOzone, and others have quite a few things in common. First, the period of time a test will be executed is controllable through switch settings or manually through the standard "control-c abort" sequence. Second, the size and location of one or more data files (representing one or more "database" files) is configurable as well, as is the mix of reads to writes and ratio of sequential operations to random/direct operations. These tools also allow you to control the number of processes or threads utilized by the OS to execute the test, in effect allowing you to control the disk queue lengths that must eventually be processed by the OS and its underlying disk controllers and drives. Finally, this and the settings for many other switches can be saved in a single "input" configuration file, useful in ensuring consistency between iterative tests executed against different hardware or software configurations.

Of course, if we step back and analyze the need for input at all levels, the fact that a particular disk stress-test utility may only support a specific OS version, patch level, or similar operating environment factor reflects core input data as well. And if the output is only provided in a particular format, the installation of special readers or a specific version of Microsoft Word or Excel may be warranted, too. Along the same lines, if a particular subset of output data is also de-sired—like the CPU and system utilization performance metrics that can be captured and shared via SQLIO—the appropriate switch needs to be manually set (in this case, the "-Up" switch).

9.2.3.   OS Testing and Tuning

Performance testing the configuration options available to a particular OS often boils down to making specific utility– or command-line–driven changes and executing before and after test sce-narios that indeed help quantify any change in performance. For example, I've done extensive test-ing in the past on pagefile sizing for SAP R/3 Windows-based database and application servers, ranging from release 3.0F through 6.20. SAP's recommended guidelines changed quite a bit in the days just before Basis release 4.0 was made available, and continued to change somewhat over the last two years as well. My goal was to determine which configurations made the most sense from both financial and performance perspectives. To this end, I leveraged different hardware con-figurations (e.g., disk controllers, use of RAID 1 versus RAID 5, use of multiple disk spindles ver-sus a pair of drives) as well as different pagefile sizes, distribution models, and so forth. At the lowest levels, I used the Compaq System Stress-Test tool (once known as the Thrasher Test Util-ity) to force paging operations and therefore establish a baseline reflecting the relationship of I/Os per second for a particular memory range to the level of Windows paging that resulted. In a sim-ilar way, I also tested the impact that the "maximize throughput for network settings" Windows setting had on the memory subsystem and OS in general. In both cases, the tools I used for appli-cation-layer testing were nothing more complicated than custom-developed AT1 scripts. To cre-ate and drive a repeatable and consistent application-layer load, I simulated 100 users with minimal think times executing a suite of simple though typical R/3 transactions (e.g., MM03, VA03, FD32, and others that only required a single SAPGUI input screen). I could then compare the low-level thrasher results with the high-level SAP application-layer results, and extrapolate how different workloads would impact memory management in general and paging in particular.

9.2.4.   Test Mixes and Database Tuning

At the simplest levels, a database stress test begins with read-only queries that preferably execute against a copy of your actual production database (though a copy of a development or test client or even a small sample database may suffice, depending on your goals). Unless you want to bring in the entire application layer of your SAP system, you should consider a number of testing al-ternatives. For instance, tools like Microsoft's SQL Profiler allow SQL 7 and SQL 2000 database transactions to be "captured" at a low level, and then replayed against a point-in-time database snapshot at a later date, all without the need for SAP application servers, an SAP Central Instance, or anything else that is SAP-specific. This type of approach is perfect for stress tests where an or-ganization assumes (and rightly so most of the time) that potential application-layer performance issues can generally be solved either by adding more application servers or by beefing up the ex-isting servers. That is, performance at the application issue is moot and can therefore be pushed out of scope simply because SAP supports a robust horizontal scalability model in this regard.

So the test mix for a pure DB-based stress-test scenario simply involves the use of record and playback tools—database-specific tools capable of capturing the SQL statements executed during a certain timeframe by a representative group of end users. You might choose to capture the busiest day of the season, for example, or maybe the 4 hours during which the heaviest batch job load is being processed. The queries, table scans, joins, and so on captured during this time period become your repeatable set of input data, to be played back for the DB server—you need not concern yourself with your SAP instances.

These types of tools are necessarily database-specific, of course. That is, Informix administration tools simply cannot support Microsoft SQL Server, nor do SQL Server–based tools support Oracle. But the value of these record/playback tools is unquestionable—they're generally quite easy to learn and easy to use. And, because they tend to support the ability to play back the captured transactions in the exact timeframe they were recorded, or compress or stretch out the timeframe as you see fit, their value in terms of capacity planning and what-if analysis is great.

Case in point, as I mentioned before I used SQL Profiler to record the real-world transactions of one of my large R/3 customers that was preparing for an acquisition that would double the number of its online and concurrent users. The company was comfortable with the scalability of the application server tier of their current solution, but needed to better understand the impact on the DB server. To be sure that this SQL Profiler approach to testing would be suitable, I first went through a sizing exercise, analyzing the current mix of users (via transactions ST07 and AL08) in terms of the total number of users as well as the functional areas in which they were heaviest. I then analyzed similar data provided by the organization to be merged into the first, and found that the mix was close enough to warrant no further analysis—within plus or minus 10%, each organization supported about the same number of SD, MM, PM, FI, and CO users. I used these real-customer data to tweak my SAP sizing tools, to better reflect the weight of their as-configured functional areas (rather than relying on default weights provided by the tool), using data gleaned from Basis transactions ST02, ST03, ST04, and ST06. This allowed me to size a new DB server, which I then procured from our seed unit pool (a pool of gear used for the express purpose of customer demonstrations and proof-of-concept engagements). After loading the OS and database, configuring the server, and then working through a restore of the customer's 400GB SAP R/3 database, I was finally in the position to do some testing.

It was at this point that the value of SQL Profiler really sank in—because the number of users would double in the new environment but the mix of users would stay pretty much the same, I simply sped up the playback of my previously recorded transactions 2× and then sat back and observed how well my newly architected and deployed demonstration DB server handled the load. In this way, I was not only able to nicely simulate the customer's actual expected load, but I was able to validate our user-based sizing as well. In the end, after making some calculated processor and RAM upgrades to the currently deployed application servers (to account for the additional logged-in users), and installing a new DB server identical to the one I tested back in the lab, the customer's acquisition went off without a hitch. This database-centric approach to testing and tuning should appeal to any SAP test team focused on saving time and money when the other tiers of a technology stack can be ruled out and it's determined that full-blown end-to-end stress testing is simply not required.

Beyond these basic database-level test mixes, where only the raw SQL code is executed on a DB server, lies the ability to execute application-driven SAP transactions. Such transactions must be commenced on an SAP front-end and executed by an SAP Application Server, of course. But this incremental complexity gives you the advantage of testing the impact that your test mix places on your end-to-end solution. And, by varying this test mix, which might range from light-impact financial and material-based transactions to multicomponent and truly solution-intensive monster batch transactions, you can exercise various solution stack layers with near pinpoint accuracy. Detailed test mixes and the challenges a team faces in identifying and using them are covered in detail near the end of this chapter.

9.3.   Testing and Tuning for Daily System Loads

Load testing the average daily expected workload is perhaps the most fundamentally overlooked type of performance testing I'm aware of. The companies that embrace performance testing and tuning tend to focus instead on high-water peak stress testing or saturation-level smoke testing, or spend their budget dollars tweaking and tuning the disk subsystem. Certainly, these other areas are critical, but the first question that comes to *my* mind is "How often do you see the loads associated with seasonal peaks?" followed by "How truly important is it to know precisely at what transaction load your system breaks?" when it has never even been tuned for the mundane daily workload processed 99% of the time.

Tuning for your anticipated daily transaction load should represent the starting point for SAP application-layer stress testing, and used, as depicted in Figure 9-2, as a launch pad for in-

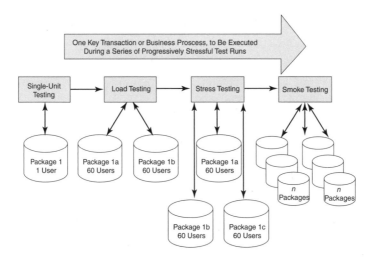

Figure 9–2 Use single-unit load testing as a springboard for daily load testing, peak stress testing, or high-water smoke testing.

cremental load, stress, and smoke testing. Specifically, you should have a series of TUs or test packages that, when combined, can emulate the typical online and batch workload seen Monday through Friday, 9 a.m. through 5 p.m. In this way, subtle changes to your workload or configuration alike can be quickly simulated, providing the kind of rapid feedback necessary for supporting sound change control processes. And the tuning made possible will benefit you 99% of the time, huge by any measure, because your system is optimized for a relatively steady workload. Finally, understanding and capturing your daily system load pays big dividends when it comes time to perform a major upgrade, add or remove a significant component of the workload (acquisitions and divestitures), or simply build on the load in support of testing and tuning for various business peaks, covered next.

9.4.   Testing and Tuning for Business Peaks

Though the tuning made possible by daily expected workload testing will benefit you 99% of the time, you must still work through an ROI exercise designed to determine whether it's financially advisable to stress test the remaining 1% of scenarios. To an outsider, 1% might seem trivial, but if the 1% represents any of the following scenarios, the financial impact associated with planning for, setting up, configuring, executing, monitoring, analyzing, and tuning might easily be justified:

- If you bring in a significant portion of your revenue via seasonal peaks
- If you must process a time-sensitive workload in a particular execution window (e.g., 2 hours start to finish), such as payroll checks or tax-return data, the failure of which would produce financial or other significant losses
- If specific SLAs are in place that penalize you significantly for "missing" key response-time or throughput metrics
- If your business peaks represent an opportunity to compress financial cycles or make it possible to gain an edge on the competition in terms of insight into product sales, order fulfillment, inventory turns, and so forth.
- If customer satisfaction is impacted beyond what is otherwise grudgingly acceptable

Business peaks vary nearly as much as the companies that endure them. As I mentioned before, almost every organization must suffer through some kind of seasonal peak workload—testing and tuning for this peak can mitigate much of the suffering. Similarly, working through issues surrounding weekly, month-end, and quarter-end financial closings, warehouse inventories, payroll runs, HR benefit update windows, and so on will not only help you avoid self-imposed or externally driven SLA penalties but also provide a competitive long-term advantage. And like the value of knowing your daily load, understanding your business peaks positions you that much better when it comes time to perform a major functional upgrade or technology refresh.

Data input required for your business peaks should not be that difficult to identify, because it's almost always associated with a particular business activity or functional area, as we have already seen. But it's all about *quantities!* The key is to ensure you have *enough* data to do the job of stress testing, along with access to the proper number and mix of virtual or physical users that truly represent the concurrent online or batch load you seek.

9.5.   Identifying Key Transactions and Business Processes

As I said before, there are many ways to identify the key transactions and business processes representative of a particular condition, event, or state. The opinions and experience of the end-user community that actually conducts much of this work is an obvious source of knowledge, albeit an imperfect and not necessarily holistic source. Regardless, I still recommend that you speak with your business representatives and functional experts. Indeed, for systems that have not gone "live" yet, there's really no alternative. But for precise and historically accurate information that reflects the load borne by your production systems day in and day out, week after week, month after month, I strongly encourage you to leverage the abundance of transactional and performance data sitting in CCMS. In this way, you can have insight into the whole picture—the most popular online transactions, the heaviest batch processing jobs and execution windows, visibility into the mundane repetitive tasks collectively responsible for much of the load, and so on. Month-end closes, seasonal peaks, and other high-water loads can be clearly understood in this way, and beyond this, how all of the various functions intertwine and come together to create the lifeblood of an SAP system—its workload—becomes clear as well.

Prior to following the steps outlined in the sections that follow, you need to determine the scope—typically by looking at an entire collection of application servers servicing an SAP system—and then the timeframe you wish to analyze. That is, SAP CCMS will allow you to look at the last "X" minutes or, probably more applicable for our purposes, a particular time period. I often start with analyzing the load of what I'm told is a "typical week" by plugging in start and end dates that reflect 7 full days (usually Sunday at 3 a.m. until the next Sunday at 2:59 a.m., though the timeframe you select may be different). I like somewhere around 3 a.m. because it's often the quietest time of the evening—backups are usually completed, the system is back up and available, but scheduled early-morning batch processes have not yet commenced, and few online users tend to be on the system. I try to avoid capturing only a partial business process or workload—as much as possible, I want to capture the entire week's work the moment it begins, without cutting anything off in the beginning or the end.

From this starting point, I then work to identify peak days within the week, and even peak hours within particular days. The term *peak* is subjective, of course, but most often involves first uncovering and sorting the quantity of transactions executed. Next, I'll change tack and look at all the transactions sorted by database load, CPU load, and so on. In this way, I can begin to understand the load placed on the various hardware components that underpin SAP. After this detailed analysis, I'll often take a look at an entire month's worth of data as well, just to be sure I didn't miss a particular processing peak not easily seen otherwise. And, in some cases, I might even drill down into a particular application or batch server, especially if capacity planning is one of the goals of the stress testing. In the sections that follow, we will walk through the exact steps necessary to uncover the specifics that come together to create your workload. To help you apply this process to all SAP systems, I will only draw on CCMS, as opposed to SAP Solution Manager or third-party systems-management applications and other tool sets which you may or may not have at your disposal.

9.5.1.   Online User Transactions

To determine the mix of your peak online user transactions and how they interplay to create a load on your SAP system's hardware components, log on with a user ID capable of executing core basis transactions to the system being tested, and perform the following steps (if you prefer the newer ST03N, keep in mind that a certain amount of modification to the listed steps will be required. The changes are quite intuitive, fortunately, and for experienced SAP administrators or Basis consultants will present few problems, if any):

1. Execute transaction /nST03 (the Workload Analysis screen is displayed).
2. Click the "Performance Database" button.
3. Select timeframe.
4. Select the "dialog" button—in this way, only online transactions are analyze.
5. Select "detailed analysis."
6. Select a column to sort by, such as CPU, and double-click it. Transactions will now be sorted by those that consume the most CPU time. Record the top 40 transactions.

9.5.2.   Batch Processing and Reporting

Follow a process similar to that outlined previously, though changed to reflect batch processes:

1. Execute transaction /nST03 (the Workload Analysis screen is displayed).
2. Click the "Performance Database" button.
3. Select timeframe.
4. Select the "background" button—in this way, only batch processes are analyzed.
5. Select "detailed analysis."
6. Select a column to sort by, such as database response time, and double-click it. Transactions will now be sorted by those that are most disk-intensive. Record the top 40 transactions.

9.5.3.   Most Popular Transactions and Other Workloads

Using ST03, the process to identify the most popular transactions (i.e., those that aren't necessarily the hardest hitting but represent the bulk of activities performed on the system) is as follows:

1. Execute transaction /nST03 (the Workload Analysis screen is displayed).
2. Click the "Performance Database" button.

3. Select timeframe.
4. Select the "total" button—in this way, all transactions are analyzed.
5. Select "detailed analysis."
6. Select a column to sort by, such as CPU, and double-click it. Transactions will now be sorted by those that consume the most CPU time. Record the top 40 transactions.

9.5.4.   Mixed-Bag Testing

With the step-by-step processes outlined previously, you should now have an understanding of the key online, batch, and noise transactions hosted by your system. At this point, you need to bring this knowledge together to create a "mixed-bag" workload—in effect, your workload to be emulated through scripting. Your workload mix will vary based on the goals of your test. For example, if you wish to test the benefits of a new server platform, you'll probably want to focus on the transactions that drive the heaviest CPU load. Similarly, if an updated disk configuration or brand-new virtual SAN is potentially in your future, you'll probably wish to create a workload that beats up the disk subsystem in the most representative manner.

Refrain from only focusing on a single type of transaction, though, if time and budget allow. Variety should be your mantra. For example, when it comes to disk subsystem testing, I suggest that you combine a number of hard-hitting online transactions and reports along with key batch processes, rather than simply going with easily scripted batch loads (easy because once you do one type, others tend to follow similar patterns or allow for cookie-cutter scripting approaches). In this way, different disk access patterns will be represented, which in the end will also best represent the real world. And I suggest tossing in a few noise scripts as well simply to keep a certain level of constant activity in the background, again representing the real world of most SAP enterprise solutions. At the end of the day, a mix of perhaps 50% batch processes to 25% online transactions and reports and 25% scripted noise activities will serve you well in stress testing and tuning your SAP disk subsystem. And the same argument can be made for testing other subsystems or technology stack layers, too—variety is desirable as long as your budget can absorb the incremental time necessary to perform the requisite business process scripting.

9.6.   Real-World Access Method Limitations

Although I've focused on test mixes from an application or low-level technology stack perspective thus far, another area that needs to be considered relates to the front-end SAP client. SAP offers a number of access methods or alternatives: the classic SAPGUI, which is available for a number of "desktop" platforms is the most prevalent, of course, followed by the HTML-based WebGUI and the newer JavaGUI. Generally speaking, though, the following challenges relevant to input mixes and access methods apply across the board:

- Not all test tools support all front-end client interfaces. Thus, test input quickly becomes a moot point if your goal is to perform virtual multiuser SAPGUI-driven testing but the available tool does not support the SAPGUI. The same holds true if you wish to leverage the WebGUI, but your preferred tool is incapable of driving Web-based content.

- Similar to the previous point, the specific development tool and mySAP component-specific SAPGUI snap-in may or may not be supported by a particular testing tool.
- Not all business transactions are supported by all user interfaces, especially those outside of the classic SAPGUI. This is not nearly the problem today as it has been in the past, where a small percentage of a business's key transactions simply could not be executed via the WebGUI (because of the absence of HTML-based transaction equivalents of the standard RFC-based transactional data and screens).
- Not all access methods are hosted directly by a client PC or laptop. For instance, a number of my larger SAP accounts have standardized on Citrix MetaFrame solutions for hosting and controlling the SAPGUI. Although the benefits are huge in terms of standardization, lower desktop software upgrade and maintenance costs (it costs an average of $40 for IT just to "touch" a user's PC—that is, to upgrade the SAPGUI), and extending a user community's PC lifecycle, the costs to replicate the necessary Citrix server infrastructure in a test environment can be prohibitive.
- Not all functionality is available on particular releases of the SAPGUI. For example, only the latest SAPGUI releases support some of the newest business and Basis transactions. And, even previously, the use of OCX controls and other GUI features were only supported on the SAPGUI releases provided after the "EnjoySAP" initiative.

The lesson here should be clear—take the time up front to determine how well your goals and success criteria affect the technology stack that is being tested. And then perform some basic front-end testing to ensure that what you envision is indeed possible with the tools, time, and expertise you have available.

9.6.1. Other Front-End Components and Interfaces

Front-end user interfaces outside of those previously discussed can come into play as well. The SAPGUI snap-ins mentioned earlier may or may not be supported by your favorite virtual testing tool, for instance. In fact, the interface you need to use in support of a specific TU may be completely foreign to SAP. Compuware's TestPartner is a good example of a tool that can prove helpful in these cases—not only is it a great WebGUI test tool but it also allows you to test a variety of user interfaces outside of those dependent on Internet Explorer or similar Web interfaces.

In these cases it is important to look beyond what is perceived as immediate front-end needs, and instead take a quick look at alternatives. Perhaps your testing can be driven without the need for a GUI—SAP eCATT can "talk" directly with SAP behind the scenes; or maybe part of the access-enabling technology that sits in front of your SAP system represents an unnecessary stumbling block, something in the way of your testing goals. If you need to test the online user load your R/3 system can handle, but EP represents the primary access vehicle to R/3, perhaps it's not absolutely necessary to keep EP in the testing loop, so to speak. In other words, to make things simpler you might consider forgoing the inclusion of EP into the solution stack to be tested back in the lab, and use the simpler direct method of access allowed by virtual SAPGUI connections. In this case, you won't be in a position to test the ability that your particular system has to support single sign-on (SSO), nor will you be able to validate any high-availability or other performance or scalability metrics. The same limitations hold true for SAP's older portal product, Workplace, as well as other legacy tools and utilities that help make SAP system access possible. Bottom line, though, if your goals don't require it, you can make your test infrastructure and test runs that much simpler by keeping only the infrastructure and components necessary to meet your test's goals or success criteria in scope.

9.7. Best Practices for Assembling Test Packages

With regard to breaking down and assembling good test packages, I've already mentioned a number of key approaches I often use. Four of these are worth more discussion, however, and are covered next.

9.7.1.   User-Based Test Packages

A simple method of controlling the amount of "noise" or any other functionally derived activities you introduce in a stress-test run is to directly control the number of users tossed into the mix. With this approach, you're not concerned about the load placed on the system per se, you're more concerned with the number of users hosted, and whether each user is executing consistent and repeatable work. I've mentioned elsewhere that I like to create packages of 100 users. One hundred is a nice number simply because it's a round number; its size is significant enough to allow me to build up a test run into a "large stress test" very quickly and in a highly controlled manner.

Load becomes an issue only if a group of 60 or 100 users (or whatever number you choose) overtaxes a system, invalidating the stress-test run. An obvious example might involve executing custom Z reports—if you toss 100 of these into a system configured for only half as many batch processes, you'll simply create a queue of work that monopolizes all batch work processes and completely destroys most DB servers. A better number in this case might be 10 instead. Experiment to find the best number for you.

9.7.2.   Functionally Focused Test Packages

Although controlling the pure number of users participating in a stress test makes sense, taking this to the next level and controlling a group of 100 SAP R/3 SD users, for instance, or 10 BW custom InfoCube reporting users, makes even more sense. Of course, you'll need to be careful to ensure that the mix of users (e.g., or batch processes, or reports) adheres to the mix you need to emulate in support of your test's specific success criteria. And your test tool needs to support both the high-water number of users you wish to simulate as well as the ability to create and control multiple packages.

9.7.3. Another Approach—End-to-End Business Processes

Building on the previous approach, this next approach is both intuitive and in many cases simply necessary. That is, because a business process by definition feeds off one transaction (the previous transaction's output data, actually), and then goes through a processing phase only to hand off newly created or processed data to the next transaction in line, the idea of bundling these transactions into a single package seems logical. Beyond this, though, it saves time and effort in scripting, too, because a common set of fewer variables can be leveraged. And a straightforward input-output approach to scripting lends itself to making even cross-component business processes more easily controlled than is otherwise possible. Finally, the granular control made possible through this method makes it easy to quickly ramp up the user count of a stress-test run while simultaneously ramping up the number of complete business processes to be executed.

9.7.4. Tips and Tricks—Making Noise with Noise Scripts

One of my favorite approaches to SAP scripting and stress testing involves the creation and deployment of *noise scripts*. As I said earlier, noise scripts capture and help represent the background processing or "noise" common in all SAP production systems. I typically create a variety of noise packages, some focused on general functional areas (e.g., MM or FI, where many lightweight transactions are common), whereas others might be focused on SAP Basis activities (to represent the load that monitoring places on a system), specific batch or report jobs, and so on. The key is to create a consistent baseline of user or batch-driven noise behind the scenes, and then quantify the per-package load to establish a tier of potential baselines, as depicted in Figure 9–3. Does this ancillary load represent 10% of the typical production workload? Or 20%? What is the impact of the load on your test hardware (that is, the HW hit)? Consider what many of my colleagues and I deem to be best practices as follows:

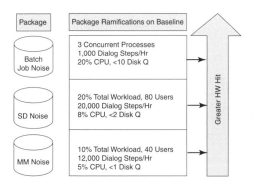

Figure 9–3 Noise scripts are useful in providing the fundamental underlying nonprimary transaction load underneath all productive SAP systems.

- Baseline just your noise scripts, to ensure they do the job you envisioned for them. Baseline not only SAP application-layer performance, but lower levels as well. Eventually, I recommend that you settle on any number of online users, batch processes, and so on that create an easy-to-measure load on the system, like 10% CPU utilization or disk queue lengths of three per disk partition or drive letter.
- Keep the target baseline utilization numbers small, so that it's easy to add incremental measurable load to a stress-test run—simply throw another package into the mix, for example, to add another 10% load on the CPU or perhaps another 40 users or three concurrent processes (whatever measurement you judge most valuable).
- Ensure that your noise scripts are pseudorandom. As I mentioned earlier, they need to be repetitive enough that they maintain a consistent load on the CPU, while random enough to encourage physical disk accesses. In other words, you don't want to create a noise script, or any script for that matter, that executes at different speeds every time it runs, or processes significantly different data between test runs. Make it repeatable!
- Ensure that you track the number of iterations executed, along with the specific number of discrete noise transactions executed within your noise script or scripts. This is useful after-the-fact, when you're seeking to understand and analyze a stress-test run—I suggest leveraging a counter of sorts within the body of your scripts (e.g., and publishing the counter's value to your output file), or simply dumping the script's output into your output file, to be counted in more of a manual manner after the run.
- Finally, if sound test management dictates that you should group your noise scripts together, you'll logically want to go to the trouble of creating one or more noise packages that either complement the core load being tested (you may create a noise script that effectively mirrors many of the transactions that represent core activities) or act as a "gap filler" and instead "round out" a test load (e.g., adding batch noise to a primarily online-user–based stress test).

One of the simplest methods of generating noise within a test run is to execute every core T-code twice—not the entire transaction, just the T-code associated with the first transaction in a business process. This kind of incremental and predictable load on the CPU is ideal when it comes time to measure overall performance, because the transaction is always executed from cache the second time it's executed. In this way, it not only does not ever disturb the system's buffer contents but it is easily scripted or added at the last minute in an iterative fashion if you need to bump up the CPU hit on a particular stress-test run.

9.8.   SAP Component and Other Cross-Application Test Mix Challenges

For each particular SAP application, component, or solution, there tends to be a special set of circumstances or limiting factors that complicates creating a repeatable, consistent, or adequate test mix. The following list identifies key problem areas I've run into in the past, and what I did to work around these issues:

- R/3 business processes range from one-offs to multicomponent, highly complex sets of transactions. But, for most companies, R/3 activities tend to focus on discrete transactions run repeatedly by many users throughout the day, alongside a subset of core batch processes. I suggest focusing on a few key business processes, like order-to-cash, to take advantage of the input/output nature of the underlying transactions. In this way, obtaining input data is a simple matter of leveraging the previous transaction's output. And the first transaction—a sales order—can originate in any number of other systems and be easily completed if core customer, material, and plant data are available and abundant.

- APO includes both online users and batch-oriented business processes. The real load borne by the system is represented by the latter, though, especially with regard to demand or production planning runs, or Available to Promise (ATP) processing. Online user activity is negligible in comparison. From an input data perspective, the number of key figures that reside in your liveCache server, the number of characteristic combinations (properties) that describe an object, the number of periods (measured in weeks) against which these processes will run, and of course the number of sales, purchase, planned, and other orders transferred from R/3 to APO are all important.

- BW and SEM activities range tremendously, so it's no surprise that input data ranges are equally wide. In the past, I've started a BW stress test by kicking off an R/3 data extraction process, or simply by pulling data from the ODS to create and populate a cube. These are certainly important functions, but may not represent your most important goals. Instead, you may wish to run queries against one or more standard or custom InfoCubes. The key will therefore be the cubes themselves—if it matters little how the data move through your SAP system landscape, make it easy on yourself and start with a fully populated set of cubes.

- CRM data hail from a number of systems within the CRM system landscape, including the TRex Server, Multi-Channel Interface Server, InQMy Application Server, and potentially a Workgroup Server and Communication Station, not to mention the CRM server itself. As such, it can be one of the more complex SAP solutions to stress test. As a starting point, I suggest that you concentrate on the core user type your system hosts (probably a Mobile Sales or CIC user, though others exist), and determine the input necessary to support the top five or so key user transactions. For your Mobile Sales users, you might focus on managing opportunities or activities, creating customer orders, performing service-related transactions, or managing customer, product, or project-specific data, for instance. If you host CIC users, you might instead go with the transactions and activities outlined in the SAP CRM benchmark kit, for example, and focus on transactions relevant to managing incoming and outgoing CIC calls

- EBP (the core component of SRM) is quite complex, especially from an input perspective—data originating from Requisite BugsEye (an online catalog), R/3, BW, and EP complicate executing core EBP business processes. But that's not all! There are other

SRM components that need to be considered as well, like the SAP Bidding Engine and SAP Supplier Self Services. Given all of this, a seemingly straightforward shopping-cart–driven procurement business process will have many touch points, will pull data from many sources, and will generally represent a whole lot of scripting and coordination effort.

- EP has evolved significantly over the last few years and today represents one of the fastest growing products in SAP's line-up. It's also potentially one of the most important products a company will implement, in that all users could conceivably (and, it is hoped, will) leverage its single sign on capabilities to gain access to all other SAP systems and many third-party resources, creating a potential high-availability and performance nightmare should the EP technology stack lack scalability. Thus, stress testing EP will only grow in importance as it continues to be deployed across the globe. Fortunately, stress testing can be conducted quite easily. Sure, many systems represent potential integration points, but an effective load test could very well consist of accessing only local resources.

- PLM supports users responsible for managing product, asset, and process information at any point in the product lifecycle, from selection and purchasing through production ramp-up, installation, operation, engineering changes, maintenance/repair, retirement, and more. From a data input perspective, then, you need to understand the precise functionality being implemented and what then needs to be tested—everything from Life-cycle Data Management and Asset Lifecycle Management to core functionality like Program and Project Management, Quality Management, and Environment, Health, and Safety (or EHS) can come into play. Plus, because PLM is implemented as an enterprise portal solution and is tied closely with CRM and likely APO, the business processes that can result may be complex indeed. I therefore suggest going after either the biggest couple of functional areas to be implemented (in terms of transaction counts or user counts), or instead the most critical functional areas, and script core transactions rather than full-blown business processes.

The world of SAP has grown considerably over the last year, though—well beyond the components and solutions just highlighted. The SAP XI, xApps, and other products represent additional systems that may be tested individually or as part of a larger SAP solution. For example, simulating the number and size of the messages that the XI Integration Server processes represents an excellent method of testing XI without all of the integration points necessarily in the picture.

XI offers some exciting capabilities when it comes to viewing collaborative cross-application SAP business processes. For example, business processes that span your R/3, APO, and CRM systems can be tied together via synchronous and asynchronous messaging defined by and maintained within XI. You may then leverage XI to enable true cross-application business process stress testing, regardless of whether heterogeneous system landscapes have been deployed—test cases would initiate from one of the core SAP systems tied together in this manner, of course. And test execution would be seamless, because XI would handle moving the output from one transaction into the proper component, where it becomes input for the next transaction in a business process. Beyond this awesome timesaving by-product of XI integration, XI also allows you to visually depict and manage SAP components as well as other enterprise applications from Baan, Broadvision, JDE World Software, Oracle, PeopleSoft, Siebel, and more. In this way, the inclusion of SAP and third-party enterprise applications may all be tied together into a cohesive virtual system. More to the point, these complex systems may be managed as a single entity rather than as a bunch of individual systems, which further simplifies testing.

Mainstays like SAP's ITS also continue to thrive. From a data input perspective, I suggest you focus on common transactions supported by back-end systems like R/3. Because all (or nearly all, in the case of older releases of R/3) SAP screen content is maintained in HTML on the ITS server, testing ITS amounts to testing the speed and throughput of Web connections. Fortunately, tools abound that support this input type, as we reviewed in Chapter 6, and scripts of this nature are fairly easy to write and maintain. And the best news of all is that you'll find that your ITS users tend to execute the same transactions as their SAPGUI-enabled colleagues (though exceptions exist—I've got a customer that has pushed the bulk of its HR and ESS workload on ITS, for instance, whereas other modules and functional areas are accessed via the traditional SAPGUI). So once you've established the core transactions executed by a particular SAP product or component, you're well on your way to using this information in support of ITS testing, too.

9.9   Tools and Approaches

Although there are few formal tools that help you analyze your input requirements, the approaches discussed throughout this chapter can save you time. I suggest that you document step-by-step processes (e.g., those pertaining to ST03 herein) specific to your TU, in effect documenting how you arrived at your determination that a particular set of input was both appropriate and adequate. Take a screen shot as well, and file this in your documentation repository. It may again prove useful as you iteratively execute various new tests, tune your system, and then return to testing.

Finally, take care not to assume too much when you find yourself implementing new SAP components or technology stacks because much of the documentation floating around is not necessarily applicable. For instance, with the advent of commodity 64-bit computing from Intel and AMD, there is a need for basic pagefile and OS memory/caching testing, along with database tuning as I described earlier in the chapter. This is the case because the rules are changing before our eyes, and the optimal configuration for some of these new platforms relevant to hosting high-performance SAP solutions has yet to be determined. So minimize your deployment and upgrade risks by testing and iteratively tuning early in the game and reap the rewards.

Automating a System Load

If we return to the input-processing-output analogy to stress testing I spoke of in the previous chapter, the work of automating a system load falls within the realms of both input and processing. Of course the workload itself, furnished with valid and plentiful data, lies at the heart of stress testing. But without a mechanism for automating this workload— for driving it in a fairly unattended but highly regimented manner and doing so in a way that reflects the appropriate number of concurrent users or processes—your stress-testing efforts amount to little more than inconsistent stabs at single-unit load testing. Automating a system load allows the following:

- It frees up human resources, both end-user- and technology-focused.
- It ensures a repeatable testing process is built, which in turn creates not only good baselines but good subsequent test runs that may be compared to the baselines.
- It mitigates Go-Live and change-driven risks.
- It saves money across the board, from people- and process-centric dollars (compared with manual stress-testing procedures) to the money inherently saved as a result of a solution being technically validated prior to deployment.

This chapter is dedicated to helping you make the most of your limited time and resources by focusing on effective workload automation. My own experience in real-world scripting and other automated techniques is highlighted here: approaches, lessons learned, tips and tricks to crisply and rapidly craft scripts that work, and more. And I identify a few alternatives to automating a test load, too, which will not only get you thinking but may also prove useful as sales tools should you find yourself in the position of having to justify or "sell" these automation techniques to your team, your boss, or perhaps even a steering committee.

10.1. Automation Fundamentals and the Big Picture

Automating a system load—the load emanating from your carefully constructed test mix, as discussed in Chapter 9—is all about doing more with less, and doing so in a repeatable, consistent manner. Automated testing approaches should allow you to:

- Leverage virtual test suites to make it possible for a couple of "human resources" to drive a stress test of perhaps thousands of users
- Leverage automated test tools to create, manage, and execute complex business processes subject to zero errors in execution
- Leverage various utilities or approaches to find a few core data combinations that can subsequently yield hundreds of additional valid data combinations
- Leverage a small number of multiprocessor servers to host what appears from an SAP perspective to be hundreds or thousands of end-user desktops
- Drive test runs from the same SAP interface utilized by your end users, making it possible to reuse and customize stress-testing scripts for other purposes, like functional and regression testing

SAP load testing implies much more today than it ever has in the past, though. No longer are interfaces to other systems handled exclusively through Application Link Enabling (ALE) or Electronic Data Interchange (EDI) technologies; instead, more and more systems are being linked leveraging SAP XI, or similarly robust and Internet-enabled approaches like Tibco, BizTalk, and other message buses, proprietary middleware products, Internet services, and popular protocols like http, XML, and SOAP. SAP NetWeaver by virtue of XI is especially compelling in that by embracing both Microsoft's .NET and Java connectivity/interoperability across the board, it's positioned to quickly become the de facto standard for extending and integrating diverse systems into tightly linked cross-application solutions.

Thus, the final reason to automate a system load is to ensure that these tightly linked, typically mission-critical systems perform well together. Luckily for us, there's no need to be an expert in low-level protocols and initiatives, nor necessarily in the systems and products that these protocols bring together. Instead, once we identify the right mix of business processes to be tested, partner with the "owners" of these processes, and then focus on populating each business process with valid and abundant data, we should find ourselves in a position to kick back and monitor the progress of our TU runs as our business processes execute to completion and everything generally falls into place.

But not so fast. Automation takes time, requires testing, and is anything but free—and automation may still require a certain amount of up-front coordination and other work simply to tie individual processes together that don't necessarily execute concurrently or sequentially (the latter two of which can represent excellent methods for generating heavy loads or long-running loads, respectively).

The fact is, in the front end of a performance-tuning/stress-testing engagement, I spend much of my time with both the business and technical teams at my various client sites identifying functional process flows and work flows, often followed by another chunk of time focused on finding enough valid data to support the stress-test project. Next, after installing the best scripting or other tool for the job on my laptop or customer-provided equipment, even more time is spent creating scripts or TUs that functionally work; like programming, script development is subject to development iterations, including fixing coding bugs, tacking on standard subroutines for error handling and reporting, and so on. Creating scripts is not as simple as it sounds either—even when I understand the business task to be scripted (e.g., the steps involved with creating a sales order), I typically run into issues regarding valid data combinations, data fields that are required in some cases but not others, data that generate unusual errors, warnings, or unexpected screens, and more.

Even the process of recording a business process is fraught with errors: scripting tools may fail to capture certain conditions, field values, or the fact that I double-clicked the mouse in a specific cursor position during a business process script "recording" session. In addition, the initial script that is created from a recording session is far from ready to be truly useful for stress testing. For example, hard-coded data-entry points (e.g., distribution channels, company codes, or customer numbers) usually need to be converted to variables, which in turn must be reflected in the scripts. And any variables created must typically be defined in terms of whether the data is numeric or text, the length of the variable, whether it should be maintained as a private or public variable, and more. Bottom line, recording only gets you halfway there—capturing each SAP transaction, keyboard entry, mouse-click, and so on executed via the SAPGUI (or WebGUI, Java-GUI, etc.) only serves to create a glorified text file. A true business process script is formed, on the other hand, only once your basic text file is edited to reflect variable input, to run in virtual-user mode, to open input files and capture output data, and so on.

Don't worry too much about this scripting process just now, though—we'll go into the electrifying details of business process scripting later in this chapter. Instead, let's first revisit the three key methods of generating a system load, and why custom application-layer scripting tends to provide the most value at the end of the day.

10.1.1. Level One Testing

Level One testing, also called component-level or system-level stress testing as discussed in previous chapters, is the most fundamental of testing approaches. Level One focuses on tuning discrete technology subsystems, testing the impact of a discrete process, or conducting other typically "single-unit" testing. Exceptions exist, of course, but by and large this type of testing does not generate the load typically supported by a system servicing thousands of end users or hard-hitting batch processes, and thus is mainly of value from a "pretuning" perspective. Remember, Level One testing is inherently accomplished through the use of a single "user," be it at the SAP front-end client level, the SAP application layer, or nearly any of the technology layers underneath these top-level layers.

Many disk subsystem test tools represent a key exception to this single-unit rule of thumb, in that multiple processes or threads may be leveraged to simulate realistic multiuser workloads. The same can be said of any test tool that can spawn multiple processes, threads, or similar multiuser constructs. But, even in these cases, great lengths must be taken to assemble a workload that resembles the workload generated by a diverse user community or complex batch job scheduler. And, in the end, even in the best of situations you could wind up with a tool that created a wonderfully representative disk I/O load but did nothing to address the network, CPU, and other hardware or database system component loads naturally driven by higher level application-layer tools.

10.1.2.   Level Two—SAP Standard Benchmarks

Driving an application load can be accomplished in a number of ways, including through the use of a standard SAP benchmark kit (made available primarily to SAP hardware partners). Creating such a load for different mySAP components can be quite demanding, though, from three perspectives. First, you need to consider the learning curve that must be conquered relevant to executing an SAP benchmark, by no means a trivial task. Next, only specific versions of select SAP components are covered—the particular version of BW you have deployed may simply not be available, for example. Finally, the skill sets needed by the team responsible for BW testing may find itself short on core testing expertise germane to BW, a shortcoming simply not addressed by a benchmark kit. Suddenly, the very reason you wished to leverage a standard approach to rapid benchmarking would have deteriorated considerably. And that's just the beginning.

Thus, be careful not to misunderstand the role of the benchmark kits published by SAP. I'm a big fan of them myself, but they take time to learn and to master. More to the point, they were never intended as tool sets or scripts waiting to be refined and deployed in the name of customer-specific benchmarking. Not to say this isn't possible, but the real value of a standard benchmark is derived from the fact that it is *standard*. Take away the apples-to-apples comparison value and you're left with only the shell of a basic testing approach. So refrain from going down this road unless you seek only platform deltas. And, by all means, avoid fundamentally changing or modifying the contents of a benchmark script or data—otherwise, you lose the ability to compare your results with real-world published benchmark results! And finally, if you run into benchmark execution problems (as so many of us have in the past, myself included), you can be confident that SAP has probably already seen your particular issue and has tweaked or changed the customized configuration delivered with the benchmark kit via support packages or an updated set of scripts. I suggest a quick SAPNET search, creation of a SAP Note, or phone call to your SAP Competency Center to help you resolve your issue quickly. Or, on the flip side, if you enjoy tweaking AutoIT scripts and generating new Perl code, getting down and dirty in the code may be just the thing for you—you wouldn't be the first (I certainly wasn't). Besides, there's a certain amount of satisfaction in sharing benchmark kit script bug fixes with our colleagues in Walldorf, assuming you're working against a leisurely test schedule. But at the end of the day, take care not to change the nature of the scripts or data itself!

10.1.3.   Level Three Custom Application-Layer Testing

The bulk of this chapter addresses Level Three testing, which includes customized and customer-specific load testing by leveraging high-end SAP-aware scripting test tools from companies like AutoTester, Compuware, and Mercury Interactive. Also called *Proof-of-Concept Exercises or Customer-Specific Benchmarking*, as discussed in Chapter 4, this type of load testing is the most difficult to conduct and unsurprisingly the most valuable. Think about it—driving the application layer via your actual business processes against a copy of your actual SAP database or databases is perfect for characterizing the impact that a specific load has on your unique system in terms of performance. And, though it's not always possible, doing so in an environment that closely mimics what you run in Production makes the whole process that much more relevant—for good measure, we'll also cover a number of approaches short of creating a copy of the production environment.

10.1.4.   Other Real-World Approaches to Load Testing

In the overall scope of stress testing, if you do not automate your test load through software-based means, you must nonetheless find at least a marginally consistent way to drive your workload— even if it's by way of trained monkeys pressing the Enter key on queue every 30 seconds in a test lab filled with 1,000 desktops you personally loaded and configured using a stack of CD-ROMs and floppy disks. There are many ways to do this, some of which are discussed later. I am not a fan of any of these approaches but feel like this chapter would not be complete without painting a worst-case big picture. Maybe this will help you sell the value that an SAP API–aware or other load-testing tool alternatively provides.

The first of these approaches, the "monkey method" alluded to previously, is not actually that far-fetched. Typically, it entails bringing in the system's end-user community, though, rather than real monkeys. The challenge (beyond getting these resources to show up somewhere on a weekend or after hours, given that they have real work that needs to get done during the week) is to encourage these users to execute at your command the various business scenarios and processes deemed important enough to warrant a prechange or new-implementation stress test. Problems are plentiful with this approach, as noted in the following:

- End users are expensive, because they already have a 40-hour work week to look after; any incremental time can be expensive in terms of actual costs (e.g., time-and-a-half pay for more than 40 hours).
- End users are just people, subject to getting bored, making mistakes, and taking long lunches and untimely smoke breaks. All of this manifests itself in a multitude of ways, the most important of which involves poor consistency in test execution and therefore low value from a run-comparison perspective.
- From a logistics perspective, bringing together the infrastructure necessary to execute a stress test from a central facility is unlikely. The alternative—keeping everyone where they are (which makes sense at many different levels)—has its own set of problems, though, especially surrounding test execution, coordination, and communication in general.
- End-user-driven tests take longer to execute than their software-automated counterparts.

Of course, to rectify some of these issues, a customer might choose to leverage detailed checklists and other process documents, along with long-running conference calls attended by functional leaders for each area or department. But overall, this approach is far from being a best-in-class approach.

Another marginal approach to load testing involves using tools that are not SAP API–aware. For example, my colleagues and I once executed a stress test that consisted of six core R/3 transactions executed by 300 physical desktops, driven by a basic Windows GUI driver (Visual Test 4.0, if you're curious). Besides the pure cost associated with acquiring such a large number of desktops, a huge amount of work was required, as follows:

- Each desktop had to comply with strict GUI standards, so that nothing "external" to the SAPGUI got in the way of successfully executing the scripts. Thus, standard monitors and screen resolution, font size, consistent naming conventions, and so on all became critical success factors.
- The scripting language itself was subject to flaws in execution—for no reason, desktops would lock up unexpectedly, script windows would "lose focus" and stop executing, and so on. Actually, it's not fair to point the finger solely at Visual Test, because NT 4.0 was probably to blame for at least some of these issues.
- Managing the start of a test was a big feat in itself, as best practices required a reboot (to clear cache, re-establish SAP client connections, and generally re-enable failed/locked desktops), followed by remotely executing the appropriate business transaction on the appropriate desktop.
- Stopping a particular test run was also difficult simply from a controller perspective (for those interested, the controller was a home-grown NetBIOS Extended User Interface, or NetBEUI, application created by some very bright folks at Compaq Computer Corp in the mid 1990s). And when test runs went awry, we could count on an hour of dead time before the next run would be positioned to execute again.
- Collecting data was a bit of a logistics nightmare—in the end, I had to create a batch file that established a connection to the local drive of each desktop, copied the contents of any output files to a shared drive, renamed the output file to reflect the originating desktop's name and test run, and then appended all data into a single file to be later manually analyzed via Microsoft Excel.

As mentioned before, a third method of load testing without the benefit of an automated test tool involves using an SAP benchmark kit. Executing SAP load tests by running a standard component-specific SAP benchmark kit might help prove that one technology stack outperforms another but does nothing to prove that a particular business process change performs better or worse than expected. And load tests that are focused on a particular component of an overall SAP solution are useful from a discrete perspective at best.

Finally, a fourth load-testing method that I've used in the past involves installing SAP's Internet (formerly International) Demonstration and Evaluation System (IDES), which is a full-blown system in and of itself. IDES contains all of the configuration, user, and master data required to execute end-to-end business processes, albeit none that are germane to your particular environment. That is, IDES is built around a fictional company created for demonstration purposes by the folks at SAP AG. So, finally, a certain amount of scripting work is still required to gain any benefit from this approach, and even then it's not specific to your company. But as a couple of my own customers can attest, it's still a good way to compare computing platforms against one another.

10.2. Approaches That Really Work

Back in the SAP labs at HP, there are plenty of ways to generate loads useful for stress testing. Much of the type of activity that drives this testing, as you would expect, tends to be hardware-specific or SAP benchmark-specific. This testing is certainly useful to anyone in a broad-brush kind of way, but not of much use to companies that seek to mitigate risk associated with a proposed SAP functional upgrade or other application-layer change unique to their Production systems. Instead, a method of testing that reflects core business activities—like the business processes impacted by a proposed functional change to R/3 SD—is in order.

Unfortunately, it's rare to find hordes of business process or functional experts just hanging about in your IT department with time to spare to dedicate to your nice little load-testing project. As discussed back in Chapter 5, it's not exactly commonplace to maintain a full-time stress-testing staff at all. Thus, practices and approaches to stress testing that require little functional knowledge can prove invaluable to the T3, even if the team consists of only one or two people responsible for stress testing in addition to fulfilling their other day-to-day duties. The approaches outlined in the next few pages have proven themselves in the real world—as such, it shouldn't surprise you that they're not quasi-Basis-specific or some other type of non-business-related methods (e.g., the approaches I spoke of previously). Instead, as we see next, these approaches drive core SAP business processes, providing the greatest load-testing value possible in a stress test project. And, because they can shorten your overall project timelines, my hope is that you'll find many of these approaches valuable when you're pressed for time, unable to identify specific business processes' testing requirements, or when you simply need to work your way through an SAP application-layer test quickly.

10.2.1. SAP Benchmarks—Classic Business Processes

One of the fastest paths to application-layer load testing leverages the appropriate SAP benchmarking kit as a *starting point*. The idea is not to even execute the actual R/3, BW, APO, or other benchmark kit, but instead to treat the scripts found within the kits as a template for creating custom scripts that must then be customized for your own SAP system. This is perfect for T3s pressed for time and unfamiliar with the transactions that make up an SAP functional area (e.g., SD, MM, or FI, each of which is covered by an R/3 benchmark kit). As I've discussed previously, simply taking a look at the business processes executed by the R/3, BW, APO, or other SAP benchmark kit gives you great visibility into at least a few key business transactions. And the beauty of the benchmark kits is that they tend to string together a number of component-specific key transactions, like those identified in Figure 10–1, so as to build a beginning-to-end business process (in

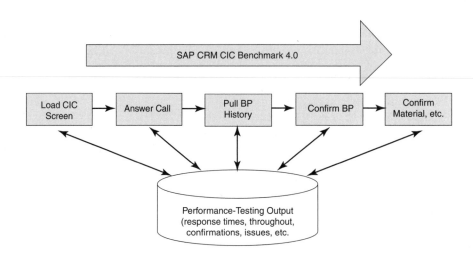

Figure 10–1   The transactions of the SAP CRM CIC benchmark kit, like those of all SAP benchmarks, string together key functional transactions into a end-to-end business process.

this case, relative to the CRM activities of a Business Partner, or BP). If you have little time to an-alyze which business processes to use for driving a stress test, or little time to script and other-wise prepare for executing a stress test, but have great flexibility in terms of *what* you test (i.e., you have the liberty of testing whatever application-layer business processes you'd like, such as the same business processes that the folks at SAP AG decided to put into their benchmark kits), this kind of approach is an excellent way to go. Nonetheless, there are a few things to keep in mind:

- This approach in no way leverages the scripts or data provided with the SAP bench-mark kit—you only benefit from visibility into *which* transactions may be executed and *how* the transactions follow one another to create a full-fledged business process. Thus, you still need to come up with the requisite data germane to each script and your partic-ular SAP system, customize and test scripts that map to your particular functional im-plementation (again, leveraging the benchmark kit's scripts as a template), and so on.
- This approach is limited to a very few number of transactions (those already scripted in the benchmark kit), perhaps none of which might be representative of your business! So a bit of top-40 due diligence is still required at minimum—identify your most popu-lar transactions via ST03, as explained in Chapter 9, to qualify the usefulness of SAP standard benchmark transactions within your unique environment.
- This approach is very much oriented to single-component testing. That is, you won't find cross-application business processes in the benchmark kits. Today, SAP bench-mark kits are monolithic in the sense that they do not span multiple SAP systems or components.

As long as you meet the core criteria outlined previously, you're well on your way to conducting rapid SAP stress-testing exercises. For those T3s in a weak position to select the functional areas and business transactions to be tested, perhaps a better method lies in what is described next.

10.2.2. Stringing Together the Top 10

Along the same lines of due diligence surrounding your top 40 online, batch, RFC, and other transactions, there is great value in simply scripting your 10 most popular business transactions—your top 10. The top 10 for a particularly short timeframe will vary considerably, of course, because business tends to be cyclical and dynamic in nature—business processes and the transactions that underpin them will vary to some extent day to day, hour to hour. But if you look at your system over the course of a month, it should become quite apparent which transactions are executed most frequently (again, ST03 will clearly illustrate this) and which of these place the greatest strain on the database server.

Don't get too hung up on identifying the top 10 transactions. Maybe there are 15 transactions that drive much of your system load overall in your case, or maybe only 8 or 9 core transactions—I use the term *top 10* here as a guideline, rather than as a hard and fast rule. Regardless of the specific number of transactions you decide to test with, I suggest creating a transaction "mix" that not only encompasses online transactions but gives weight to key batch processing or RFC-based transactions as well. For example, many of my clients identify seven or eight key online transactions and two or three key batch jobs in their top-10 mix.

As you may have already guessed, such an approach to application-layer load testing is far from true end-to-end business process–focused testing. Rather, a top 10 test mix tends to reflect a variety of key transactions that simply play important roles in various diverse business processes, as seen in Figure 10–2, not necessarily the transactions that start and finish an end-to-end business process. In other words, such an approach does not reflect taking an order and mov-

Workload: Transaction Profile Report

Long/short names ▶ Graphics Aggregation... Text

Instance			
SAP System		First record 10.01.2003 00:00:05	Period Month
Server	TOTAL	Last record 10.30.2003 23:59:47	Start 10 / 2003
Instance no. *		Elapsed time 29 days, 23:58:59	Task type Total

Sort: DB req. time   Entries: 4040

Program or Tcode	Background job	Dialog steps	Response time total (s)	Response time avg (ms)	CPU time total (s)	CPU time avg (ms)	Wait time total (s)	Wait time avg (ms)	DB time total (s)	DB time avg (ms)
TOTAL		4,797,333	13,520,277	2,818	1,670,517	348	115,813	24	4827,068	1,006
RFC		575,272	739,705	1,286	63,387	110	2,216	4	325,863	566
Z_SD_RR_REQ_	Z_SD_RR	30	788,558	26285276	25,609	853,619	0	0	198,762	6625,415
ZSNA	Z_INVOICE_P	85	605,500	7123,534	7,835	92,177	0	0	184,743	2173,449
KE30		8,402	186,298	21,964	10,478	1,235	16	2	175,333	20,671
VA01		609,152	341,475	561	120,901	198	7,261	12	160,795	264
RBDAPP01	Z_W	2,692	153,030	56,846	8,372	3,110	0	0	142,884	53,077
VA03		121,866	199,042	1,633	22,951	188	178	1	142,431	1,169
ZMMX2STAR	SAP	30	160,269	5342,312	6,515	217,159	0	0	130,141	4338,043
VA02		237,555	235,329	991	70,821	298	7,654	32	127,735	538

Figure 10–2 Top 10 mixes are useful in that they can reflect the online and batch business transactions responsible for the greatest load on your SAP database over time.

ing it through the system to picking, shipping, invoicing, and cash, or creating a new material and distributing it throughout your core distribution channels, plants, and storage locations. But given the pure volume of activity this top 10 approach reflects (e.g., if sorted by dialog steps), or the load placed on different subsystems (e.g., if sorted by database time or CPU time), it's often the cheapest, simplest, and most effective method of providing the core processing load necessary to quickly drive a realistic load or stress test.

10.2.3.   Batch Processing, Triggers, and Noise

One of my favorite methods of late for performing hard-hitting disk-focused application layer stress testing leverages SM36 and SM37 (to define and release batch jobs) along with SM64 (to define event triggers), or I leverage SE38 to execute any number of programs or reports. Either way, I can basically control a complex stress test through only a very limited number of actual scripts, taking advantage of the SAP batch scheduler to execute batch jobs one after the other. In effect, the completion of one job triggers the release of the next. Such an approach makes it quite easy to create a very intensive yet predictable load on a database server and is therefore perfect for validating new or updated SAN configurations for my SAP customers. Why? Because batch jobs can be set up as "periodic" so that they run every time a certain external event occurs. Such an approach lends itself to repeatable testing—once a job is released in this manner, it will run to completion and then be automatically re-released after the triggering event occurs again.

I can run program *sapevt* to monitor an event—like running a custom ABAP report—or to drive or control the further execution of a stress-test run. Or, I might instead execute *sapxpg* to run an external command, the results of which may be checked by my scripts to drive decision-based execution (e.g., whether to continue processing a test run or to quit). Jobs may also be defined to execute only after another job has completed (and, in fact, the status code of the previously executed job can be checked to validate that it completed successfully). This makes for repeatable testing as well—one batch job can be set up to release another, and so on, until a full suite set of test scripts is executed to completion. And of course batch jobs can be scheduled to execute at a particular time, which can also prove useful in purposefully staggering a significant load across both time and multiple batch application servers.

Scripting this type of stress-test load to be repeatable basically entails scripting only SM37 to do what it does best—release a specific set of jobs based on your particular requirements, events, or other conditions. It is unlikely that you'll need or want to script SM36, however. I recommend instead that you manually create the jobs to be executed (which, after all, should be a one-time event). Be sure you take a backup of the database afterwards, too, and make this backup the version of the database to be restored and used for subsequent testing.

10.2.4.   Noise Scripts

The use of "noise" scripts represents an excellent method of testing as well, especially when you have many test clients or need a background of activity against which to run a specialized test case. The contents of your noise script can vary considerably, of course, but I tend to go with transactions that are simple to script and easy to execute. Display-only transactions fit the bill nicely. Noise transactions that I have scripted for R/3 stress tests in the past include VA03 (display an order), MM03 (display a material), PA03 (display an employee record), MB03 (display material document), ME53 (display a purchase requisition), ME23 (display a purchase order), XD03 (display a customer), and quite a few other read-only transactions.

Similar to read-only noise scripts, I've also been pleased with executing a predefined set of long-running queries or reports "behind the scenes" using transaction SE38. A customer's custom Z reports can prove beneficial in this regard, for instance, while providing an excellent foundation for exercising your SAP system. And because so many programs and other reports exist, it's quite easy to find and automate a mix that's right for you.

Yet another method of generating noise involves simply executing a transaction multiple times, one after the other. For example, in the process of executing VA01, you'll go through three or four screens that need to be filled in with input data and then processed. At the end of the transaction, an order will be created. To generate a bit more load, I suggest simply running the core VA01 transaction again, after the order is created, only this time without going through the additional screens. Instead, immediately after executing VA01 and arriving at the first screen, execute a "/n" to return to the main SAPGUI screen, and then return control to the body of your script (repeating the VA01 loop again, this time completely, or executing some other transaction as you normally would). The end result is that the load on the system is increased in a regular and repeatable manner, without introducing new or unusual transactions or disturbing and displacing an SAP Application Server's cache.

Other noise loads are just as easy to generate: for really basic hardware-centric load tests, especially in cases where a system has not been fully customized, it's possible to gain a respectable amount of value from stress testing by executing a set of scripted *Basis* (as opposed to functional) transactions. Comparing system performance to a baseline can be easily accomplished in this way by measuring the total number of dialog steps processed by a test case, calculating the average response time over a 30-minute period, or simply monitoring the number of times a particular loop of transactions has been executed. Easy Basis transactions that may be readily scripted even before any developers have ever touched the SAP system include the following: ST02, ST04, ST06, ST07, OS01, SM04, SM50, SM51, SM66, DB02, DB13, AL08, AL11, RZ10, RZ20, and a host of others.

10.2.5.   Client Copies and Client Exports

I'd be remiss not to touch on the stress-testing value a good old-fashioned client copy or export can provide. True, executing a client copy (SCCL) or client export (SCC8) does not correlate in any way to executing a business process, but, like noise scripts, it can nonetheless play an important part of a larger stress-testing effort. Why? Two reasons:

1. I know of few companies that enjoy the luxury of performing client copies strictly during off-hours. On the contrary, the performance hit inherent to a client copy tends to be

a commonplace occurrence round-the-clock for many organizations, and therefore warrants being modeled and better understood as a real-world background or noise process.

2. The performance hit itself is significant, in that the disk subsystem must perform both massive reads and writes simultaneously. Because of the size of most SAP clients, the number of writes will well exceed a disk subsystem's posted-write caching ability, too, which means that the system performing the client copy will become I/O bound soon after the copy commences. In short, a client copy represents an awesome measurement of a disk subsystem's performance, and in the case of a client export, the underlying network infrastructure as well.

To be complete, I suggest including the process of creating an empty client as well (by executing SCC4, running "ANZG" or pressing "CTRL+F4" and then selecting the "New entries" button) in your scripts or test plan—this makes for a nice end-to-end process that requires very few input data to begin creating a load. So for those of you who are really seeking to emulate the real world for many companies that have adopted SAP, or who are simply looking for an easy-to-repeat load-generation mechanism, client copies can be an excellent load-generation device.

10.3.   Scripting Preparation

Before a single line of code can be written, or business process recorded, you need to make a few key decisions regarding whether physical- or virtual-user types are required, the specific tool sets to be used, and to what degree you require a certain subset of your stress-test environment to be "built out" so as to begin initial script development and testing.

10.3.1.   Pros and Cons of Physical Users

Consider the following. If you ever wish to execute a business process more than once (e.g., in support of quarterly test runs), and do so in precisely the same manner every time, scripting saves the day. Why? Because scripting makes the business process or task that much more controllable or schedulable, and therefore eminently repeatable. Scripting the simplest of tasks makes that task much more error-proof—you'll always execute the same job using the same variants, for instance. And scripting serves a dual role in that it is documentation in the most basic of forms. For these reasons, I've never been a big fan of anything other than automated enterprise testing.

But despite my admonitions against most forms of manual testing, I must admit that there will be times when the up-front cost of automated testing will exceed manual testing. Some of your batch process test cases, for example, may simply not be worth automating or scripting if there's not much other need for automated tool sets. In these instances, it might make more sense to keep things simple and leverage a number of physical desktops to provide end users access to the system via a physical (rather than virtual) SAPGUI session. Examples include launching a Manufacturing Resource Planning (MRP) run or other potentially complicated one-off business process, as long as coordinating such a launch is not problematic. Another example is the basic steps involved with generating low-level background noise through launching a couple of long-running reports or batch jobs. In these instances, the time and expense necessary to automatically launch each of these processes through a scripted scenario may be too hard to justify. If budgets are tight and a simple manual checklist may be utilized to provide practically the same level of control as an automated process, at next to no cost, then by all means take at look at this alternative. Consider the other benefits of using physical or "real" users:

- Factoring in the cost of software licensing will make it apparent to everyone whether the savings are still significant in the long run. To this end, I suggest that you consider sacrificing the ability to easily test many users running SAP API–aware scripts. Instead, look to manual processes or a low-end scripting product that may be used to drive the SAPGUI or WebGUI simply because these GUI products can be had as natively inexpensive Windows- or Java-based applications.
- By default, a physical user logging into SAP as a single user can execute up to *six* SAPGUI sessions simultaneously, making it easy to execute a number of business processes or discrete transactions simultaneously (note this default number of six may be changed via a profile parameter setting). For example, I've worked with a company that directed a roomful of financial analysts to each kick off a number of long-running reports and FI batch processes in one SAPGUI session, while they concurrently worked their way through a set number of various online transactions in a second SAPGUI session.
- Physical users also hit the ground running fast, so to speak, because they generally know the business processes for which they are responsible inside and out. This saves the time and effort necessary for a scripting resource to learn the business, or a business person to learn scripting (the latter of which is becoming easier and easier, but nonetheless takes time).
- Physical users can be easily adapted when things go awry or plans change at the last minute. Scripts, on the other hand, take time to revise and test.

To be fair, let's also take a look at the downside of using physical users for our testing and tuning endeavors, part of which I've glossed over previously. For example:

- The cost of paying overtime rates for real users—people—to come into the office after-hours or on the weekend can add up quickly, making a virtual testing tool look cheap in comparison. The cost depends of course on whether you need to bring in salaried employees versus those that might be coming in from the factory, distribution center, and so on. Do the math.
- Lower morale can result because of the long and unusual hours associated with testing. This lack of enthusiasm can manifest itself not only in mistakes and coordination issues during testing, but also in lower productivity during *normal* working hours as well. And I have seen such an approach negatively affect the attitude surrounding an SAP system's deployment or maintenance, too.

- Managing and controlling a significant number of networked and SAPGUI-enabled desktops is by no means cheap either, unless you've already invested in training facilities or a well-equipped war room. A good manual process needs to be highly coordinated, which implies a central meeting and execution place, not a "show up at the office and we'll do everything over the phone" approach.
- As mentioned earlier, end users are simply human, and therefore make mistakes, grow bored, get distracted, need to eat, become sleepy, need more coffee, and inevitably visit the restroom. Do you really want to coordinate restroom breaks?
- Finally, end users are simply not as "manageable" as their virtual counterparts—they may balk at coming in early, need to go home to feed the kids, and generally take issue at putting in long hours *outside of their core job responsibilities* for weeks at a time. At least without a nice bump in pay or promise of a decent bonus, neither of which you may have any control over. And even with pay or extra incentive, after a few weeks many folks still lose interest in putting in a lot of time after-hours.

So much of the manual-versus-automated testing argument falls back to price. People cost money, infrastructure isn't cheap, and the tools are not free by a long shot. I find it especially compelling then that companies like AutoTester allow its partners (HP Consulting and Integration Services, and others) to lease their software licenses at a fixed price, making this an option worth pursuing for discrete or one-off stress tests. In these cases, the customer walks away with the value provided by the stress test, as well as the scripts and data coming out of the testing, at a fraction of the price necessary to purchase testing software. In fact, only the software underpinning the stress test's execution is not theirs to keep, which, granted, makes the business scripts useless outside of serving as core documentation; however, all in all this represents an excellent way to go for the most price-conscious SAP stress-test projects.

10.3.2.   Benefits of Virtual Users

If you need to show the impact that more than a few end users or business processes have on a system, at some point it will become neither practical nor cost-effective to conduct load tests using physical desktop or laptops, each running a SAPGUI session manned by a real person. Instead, investing in an SAP testing utility that supports virtual users will represent the most cost-effective way to go. Virtual users look exactly like real- user sessions to an SAP system, with each one maintaining an API-based link to the system. The virtual SAPGUI sessions are simply executed behind the scenes (in most cases, anyway), making for an interesting twist—the actual GUI is not always required to be displayed by virtual users, freeing you from procuring hundreds of physical desktops. Why? Because the business process scripts executed by virtual users attached to most SAP systems don't actually need to enter data into the fields of an SAPGUI screen. Rather than tabbing between different fields and keying in input, virtual users instead drive business processes by referencing the SAPGUI's German field names via an API. Everything, from data-entry screens to drop-down boxes, radio buttons, and so on, is referenced in this way—no visible GUI required.

Tools that support these powerful virtual capabilities are not cheap, of course, ranging from a few thousand dollars for single-user developer licenses to perhaps a few hundred thousand dollars for the privilege of emulating thousands of SAPGUI-enabled end users. Despite their price, these tools tend to pay for themselves once you need to simulate between 30 and perhaps 100 real users. Given that even the most basic of application-layer SAP stress tests involves hundreds or even thousands of users, you'll find it cost-effective to leverage these powerful tool sets fairly soon in your load-testing efforts.

10.3.3. Selecting the Best Tools

My dad has an awesome set of tools, and freely shares them with me. But they are of little worth until I reach the point where I fully comprehend the *kind of work* I need to perform, or until I understand how to properly use a particular tool. So it is with testing and tuning—only once I understand my project's goals, tempered by real-world constraints, can I select the best tool set. And even then I still have some work in front of me: I need to learn how to make the most of the tool in light of my IT/business problem. If, for example, I want to capture business processes executed by SAP WebGUI clients, and am eager to manage all of my test cases using a single repository like that provided by SAP's eCATT product (built into Web AS), Compuware's TestPartner probably makes the most sense. On the other hand, if I'm strapped for cash, have standardized on SAP for the bulk of my enterprise application needs, and require the best SAP automated testing tools for the money, I'll lean toward using AT1 for scripting and AutoController for virtual load testing. In the same way, if I've got a bit of cash stashed away and my enterprise encompasses solutions from many of the top enterprise application providers, and I need arguably the best monitoring and postrun analysis tools on the market, I'll look to Mercury Interactive's products.

10.3.4. Real-World Stress-Test Preliminary Infrastructure

At this point, some degree of infrastructure will become necessary to conduct basic script development and testing in support of a Level Three custom proof-of-concept. But it is not necessary to build out the entire testing and client infrastructure just yet—that comes later (and is detailed in depth in the next chapter). For now, consider the following:

- To best automate a load, you'll want to begin leveraging at least a subset of the total testing infrastructure to be deployed as soon as possible, just to ensure that your automated approaches indeed scale well or perform as expected under an initial test load. In other words, you'll want the ability to start small, prove your ideas, and grow from there.
- On the other hand, you'll be pressured to create the multitude of business process scripts you'll need for the stress test, and focus on getting each to run successfully from start to finish.
- Likewise, you'll also be pressured to test how well each of the scripts executes concurrently with other scripts, in something like a mini-load test after each script is written and debugged.

Which do you do first? Finish all of the basic business process scripting or take the time after each script to ensure it can run with other scripts under load? The answer of course depends on a number of factors, many of which hinge on the availability of business process experts or other functional folks to help you identify and assemble well-constructed, accurate business processes. If you have dead time between working with different functional experts, you'll be inclined to perform a certain amount of concurrent-user testing. But, in my experience, time will work against you when it comes to working outside of the core scripting/script-testing loop you find yourself in at this point. In other words, you'll want to verify that scripts actually work as soon as possible.

Probably your best bet, then, is to set up a small combination virtual/physical test infrastructure environment initially conducive to single-unit load testing by virtue of executing your Automated Test (AT) scripts, as shown in Figure 10–3. In other words, single-unit testing will keep you busier than you imagine for now. Working through any issues running these tests in virtual mode will help you make use of the dead time between scripting and coding individual tasks and business processes, too. But hold off on building out a more complete test infrastructure that supports full-blown multiuser testing just yet.

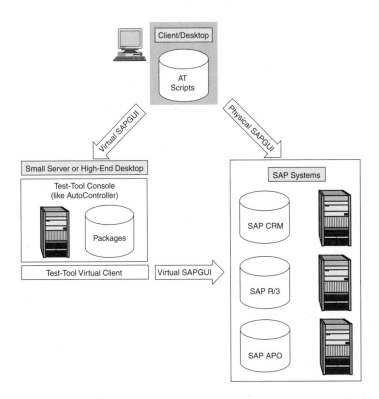

Figure 10–3   A relatively simple test infrastructure like this is perfect for conducting initial single-unit load testing from both virtual and physical perspectives.

Of course, if you're one of the lucky ones working for a company that embraces SAP load testing, you may already have at your disposal a mini-stress-test environment. One of my customer sites did a great job of creating a basic load-testing environment by simply deploying 10 or so fairly robust desktops, all identically imaged and loaded with WinRunner client software. And an 11th box—an inexpensive server—played the role of controller and file server, making initial multiuser stress testing both possible and quite economical (though ongoing input-file, script-version control, and output-file administration was complicated a bit given the number of physical computers involved).

Other customers of mine have simply added a number of four-way and eight-way servers to act as load drivers in their SAP Technical Sandbox or testing environments—even a single four-way server can emulate many hundreds of virtual users, and do so cost-effectively and with little need for incremental administrative time. And for stress-test environments where the SAPGUI must be displayed (e.g., for visually testing how well scripted business processes run before executing them in virtual mode without the front-end, or to execute business processes on any of the latest mySAP components that simply do not support hiding the SAPGUI), using VMware in conjunction with large servers can make the deployment of virtual machines, each capable of hosting multiple physical and virtual clients, possible and economical.

10.4. Sound Script Development Practices

I encourage all of my SAP testing customers to use a template or framework of sorts to help give structure to their scripts. Like following good programming rules, scripting is more easily performed (and scripts are more easily maintained!) when a common format and consistent approaches are used during the script development phase. One of the most common development practices that will save you time while helping you stay organized is to create a standard SAP login process, for example, which is covered in depth later in this chapter. Other general development considerations in creating a useful template include the following:

- Always leverage the ability of a script to send a *message* explaining the progress of the script to the user interface. I use this constantly during script development, and then simply "remark" the messages out prior to running scripts in stress-test mode. In this way, I have a better understanding of what's going on in my script—input being processed, the results of calculations, error messages, and so on.
- Create methods of addressing error handling. I typically approach this in a dual manner. First, I include an ERROR subroutine within the body of each script, useful in handling issues that aren't necessarily catastrophic but instead warrant restarting script execution from a known checkpoint (or even the beginning of the script). Second, I define an ERROR script that may be called in the event of a serious issue—this script breaks the SAPGUI connection and does what it can to capture and log the underlying error condition.
- Include a standard approach to acquiring input data. Often, this involves code that opens one or more text- or spreadsheet-based input files and then reads the "next" line

of input. I've also become a big fan recently of what I call *inline data input*, where all possible data combinations are provided within a subroutine of a script itself (instead of in an external file), and a particular slice of data is selected based on pseudorandom logic or other repeatable test criteria.

- Perform all pseudorandom calculations prior to execution of the body of the script, and write out the results of these calculations to your output log. This is especially useful to prove that your pseudorandom calculations not only work as you expect but are indeed "repeatably" random.
- Include a standard approach to capturing response time and other performance metrics. For instance, I like to reset and then capture application server response time into a unique screen-specific variable, so that I have it available to review online after the script completes, despite the fact that I also capture and dump the contents of all variables into a run-specific output log. This allows me to troubleshoot and quickly verify a script's execution.
- Build a run-specific output log, as just mentioned, and populate it with everything germane to the script's execution—input data, error messages, values used to drive randomization techniques, performance and other statistics or metrics, and any output generated by the business transaction (e.g., a purchase order number, sales order number).
- Wrap the entire script in a loop, such that it may be "called" by other scripts and executed in its entirety, or simply pass control to another script.
- Wrap the execution portion of the body of the script inside an if-then loop and include a method of checking within this loop whether the script should stop execution or move on to the next set of data and execute again.

Beyond creating a structure or template that encourages sound script development, like that illustrated in Figure 10–4, there's a lot more to take into account. The business transaction itself needs to be scripted, first and foremost. At this point, you should have a clear understanding of the exact workflow to be recorded in your script, through information gleaned via conversations with functional experts, power users, developers, or anyone else in the know. Once the basic script has been recorded using your tool of choice (probably the easiest part of scripting), it then needs to be tested to ensure that it actually runs to completion using the initial data provided by the functional experts tasked with assisting you. Just achieving this fundamental level of functionality is often more of a challenge than it rightly should be. Too often, I've been provided with data that worked one day and failed the next after configuration changes were made to a system or support packages were applied. Other times, data would work in the development client earmarked for scripting, but because of functional discrepancies (again, simple SAP support packages can make all the differences), not in the particular system or client to be used for stress testing.

Once a basic script is fully operational, it needs to be changed to be "SAP aware"—even the best recording tools don't necessarily replace all of your keyboard and mouse input with the special SAP-aware commands that make executing the script in virtual mode later possible. Fortunately, this updating is easily done. For example, in AT1's development environment I'll set the

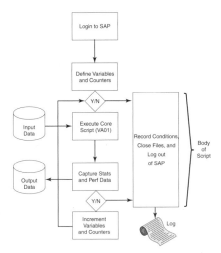

Figure 10–4 Here, a template or model of the primary subroutines within a scripted business transaction shows the level of effort potentially involved in scripting.

script to execute in virtual mode with the command "SapSetDirectMode On" and then I'll replace generic scripted commands like "Type" with "SapInputFieldValue" or "SAPSendKey" SAP-specific commands. To capture messages generated by SAP that indicate an order has been processed successfully, or to simply capture errors or warnings that might be displayed at the bottom of the SAPGUI, I'll also add commands like "SapRetrieveEntireMessage" (to capture the entire message and log it to my output file) or perhaps "SapRetrieveMessageSegment '1'" (which captures only the first part of a message, like the order number itself for example). These commands are discussed in more detail later in this chapter. Once I create any pertinent variables, I again test the script to ensure it still executes to completion, though now in SAP-aware mode rather than simply by driving the SAPGUI Windows user interface.

Next, the job of data collection becomes important. Years ago, I would request valid data combinations from the functional experts I worked with, because they had the best understanding of the business processes at hand and therefore the best combinations of data. Over time, though, it has gotten easier and easier for me to identify the data necessary to drive a particular business transaction. Some of that just comes with experience, but understanding the business behind the transactions has really made the difference. For example, knowing that only specific customers may order specific items defined in a particular sales group, or that only specific materials are associated with certain factories, plants, warehouses, and so on has made it easier to find valid data combinations. It's all about the rules surrounding various business processes that makes stress testing (and functional testing, for that matter) challenging. So although not absolutely necessary, a certain amount of functional knowledge can really make the difference. And by freeing up more of my customer's functional folks' time to return to their already busy day, this experience has helped me add more value in my own consulting engagements.

Next, comprehensive testing of these newfound data is necessary, followed by tweaking and tuning relevant to each core subroutine of the script—its input and output subroutines, error handling routines, and so on. Once a script performs well in single-user mode, it can then be tested to validate that it operates just as well when 10, 50, or 100 users are executing the same script (against different input data, to be realistic). All of this testing still falls within the realm of script development, as it is not uncommon to have to rewrite certain portions of code or include more error and other routines useful in addressing the unknowns of multiuser stress testing. For example, certain users or conditions may generate Information windows (e.g., SAP's common "Consider the subsequent documents" information message) or require additional input data (if defaults don't apply). Some of the more prevalent subroutines in my own experience are dealt with in the next section.

10.5. Building Standard Real-World Subroutines

Whether by your own work, or the work of others, leveraging a suite of standard scripting subroutines will not only save you time up front but will help you ensure that nothing is missed, and more important, that coding mistakes are minimized. To this end, I recommend building a library of subroutines covering each of the core component or template areas. For instance, build and save scripts that allow you to start an SAPGUI session by specifying either an application server/central instance or a SAP logon group. Create another set of scripts that opens input files in both text and Excel formats. Circumvent administrative and timing/business closing issues with a script that covers all date and calendar permutations, and another that creates a comprehensive yet standard output log, too. And then take care to cover everything in the middle as well, like the various screen-scraping commands, logic constructs, and so on, as shown in Figure 10–5.

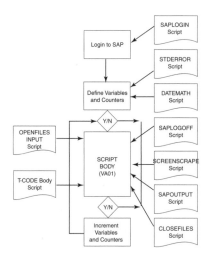

Figure 10–5 Standard subroutines play a key role in scripting and saving development and troubleshooting time, while easing postdevelopment maintenance as well.

Alternatively, if you're working with AT1, download the samples I've provided on my ftp site, and save yourself the time!

10.5.1.   Sample Scripts, Variables, and Input

When it comes to scripting, one of the most time-consuming chores is getting a handle on the proper syntax for creating, populating, and simply referencing variables. I'm talking about the actual coding found in a script, not the effort that goes into determining whether a variable should be text or numeric, specifics in terms of length, and so on. Just converting lines of a script, for example, to change hard-coded data-input items (e.g., the data that populate a newly recorded script) into code that references a variable can be a lot of work. I therefore recommend that you create a sample script that contains examples of how to manipulate data, reference variables, and so on. By having a standard block of code, you can quickly turn to that reference's SAPGUI fields, pull values from SAPGUI controls, validate that text exists in a particular screen location, select toolbar or menu item options, and so on, and you will avoid countless future scripting hours.

When it comes to collecting and centrally storing input data, although text-based files are easy to work with, I actually prefer Excel formats—this input type is much easier to manipulate than its text brethren, despite the fact that it's more difficult to initially set up. Excel-based input files make it easy to cut and paste data, insert additional columns (e.g., if additional input data are deemed necessary after you test your scripts), create number ranges (e.g., customer number 100,101,102) through an $n+1$ formula rather than by typing in a thousand different customer numbers, and to generally organize input data in a manner that's easy to read and simple to maintain.

To test the validity of *all* of a script's potential input data (an important but often overlooked quality assurance process), I create a simple and temporary loop within the body of my script, and inside this loop I use a log or output command to write the pass/fail nature of each line of input into a log/output file. In this file I also include the input data being tested as well as any errors or warning generated. I may then start the script and walk away, because the success or failure of each combination of data (as laid out in the input file) is captured and noted in the output log file. In the end, I have a list of good data combinations to use for the real stress tests later on. And just as importantly, I have a list of data or data combinations to avoid, too.

10.5.2.   Improving Virtual Capabilities

Fine-tuning or adjusting a script's virtual capabilities gets to the heart of the scripting matter: Will you be able to drive the proper number, and proper mix, to make all of your time worthwhile? It's therefore important to validate that the changes you made up front (swapping basic keyboard commands with SAP-aware commands, building basic what-if routines, and replacing hard-coded data with variables) meet your virtual-user requirements. Thus, script syntax and commands must be updated, necessitating more single-unit testing after these changes are made. For example, the name of SAP screens using AutoTester's SAPLookWindows command should probably be shortened and appended with an asterisk to support wildcard characters. Otherwise, variations in the expected screen name will cause your script to halt—some screens are named in a standard manner but then append a customer-specific name or number, for example, or insert a material number or some other unique value somewhere in the name, making it potentially unique every time the script is executed, and therefore more challenging to script.

Along the same lines, you need to plan how the script should react if the expected screen is never displayed by the SAPGUI when it is "supposed" to be displayed, and how to get around this through if-then logic (in this case, I like to look for the screen name for 60 seconds, and if I haven't found it by then I execute an error routine that logs the name of the current screen along with the name of the screen I was waiting for). The same is true of expected fields, drop-down boxes, or radio buttons; if the screen does not happen to have what you're looking for (e.g., because a certain subset of materials doesn't support a particular property, or was never sold during a particular timeframe, which are business process issues more than technical problems), this needs to be programmatically handled lest your script fail when these same particular materials are used during stress testing. Alternatively, stay away from using such input data, focusing your initial script testing efforts only on data combinations that consistently work across the board (a great idea, by the way, but not always representative of the real world and therefore perhaps not a great idea in your unique circumstances). You might find that default values found in various SAPGUI screens will cause problems with your scripts, too, as oftentimes a field is initially blank and then the next time screen is executed you find certain default values have been established. I suggest disabling these defaults when you can. Otherwise, work around them programmatically by virtue of your scripting. And while you're at it, set your SAPGUI cursor to "overwrite mode" to avoid some of these issues, and your visual design to "high contrast" to make for better screenshots (from most any SAPGUI screen, press the Alt and F12 keys at the same time—termed "ALT+F12" —to make these changes).

You'll also want to make sure you give your scripts enough time to find the window or screen name they're waiting on. I typically change the default value for this number to something like 60 seconds instead of the default 10 or 30. The neat thing about the way AT1's "SAPLook-Window" command works, for example, is that it does not force you to wait 60 seconds before proceeding—if the expected screen name is displayed in only 1 second, the script continues on its merry way. On the other hand, if your stress test is really stressing the system, it won't be uncommon to have a few transactions take quite a bit longer than the average—it happens, just like real life. If a default of 10 seconds is specified, though, and the screen is not displayed in time, the transaction and entire script will abort. My take is that I'd rather allow the script to continue processing, and know in turn that a certain percentage of screen name lookups in my scripts ran long (as clearly identified in my output log file), than to lose the virtual clients because of aborted scripts. Besides, as I mentioned before, since I take advantage of if-then "timeouts" to drive logic based on whether a particular screen failed to display itself, I'll know which screen names were particularly troublesome.

In short, then, take care to ensure that commands like the following are updated to reflect their SAP-aware or otherwise improved-on counterparts. The following example uses sales order transactions scripted in AT1:

- Replace */nVA01* with *SapTransaction "VA01"* or better yet *SapSendOKCode "/nMB1C."*
- Ensure all *SapLookWindow* commands are coded for 60-second wait times, rather than the default of 10 or 30 seconds.
- Replace *SapLookWindow "Display Order Status for 19000192" wait 60* with something that removes the order-specific data out of the screen name, like *SapLookWindow "Display Order Status*" wait 60.*
- Replace non-SAP-aware coding like Tab, Tab, Tab, Down Arrow (or anything along these lines) with the appropriate *SapInputFieldValue* command.
- Replace *SapInputFieldValue "VBAK-VBELN::Order::SAPMatch(1)" "383998"* with *SapInputFieldValue "VBAK-VBELN::Order::SAPMatch(1)" SD.VA03INPUT* (that is, replace hard-coded input data with variables that you have specifically defined).
- Replace Tab, Tab, Tab, mouse-click (or anything similar) to *SapClickCheckBox "RF02D-D0120::Control data::SAPCheckBox(2)"*—in this way, the precise box is clicked consistently, regardless of where it might be found on the SAPGUI or whether it is visually apparent (i.e., the click check box may be off-screen or may simply be unavailable when running in virtual mode behind the scenes).
- Replace any hard-coded keyboarding followed by data-entry values, or values associated with moving within the SAPGUI via the mouse and keyboard, with *SapSendOKCode* or *SapSendKey* commands—these commands are SAP-aware and let you take advantage of "sending" shortcut function key combinations to the SAPGUI, rather than driving a transaction through keyboard commands and mouse clicks.

Finally, to get the most out of your SAP-aware tool set, I recommend that you leverage the various errors, warnings, and other informational data displayed in the SAP Status Bar (the horizontal line running across the bottom of the SAPGUI) during and after a transaction's execution. For example, I like to verify that an order was indeed created when I script sales order transactions. To do so, I capture the sales order number displayed after the order is saved (and then I dump this information into my output log) using *SAPRetrieveEntireMessage* (to scrape the entire message like "Order 5100981 was created"), *SAPRetrieveStatusBarItem "1"* (to scrape just the order number itself) or *SapVerifyMessageSegment* (to compare the displayed message to what I expected to see), or a similar command. I also suggest you take advantage of commands like *SapVerifyFlag "SAPCheckBox(2)"* to validate whether a particular condition has been met in your script. This becomes very important once your SAP end user's custom defaults are "learned" by the system, because it means you won't necessarily have the same boxes checked off every time you run a transaction. Instead, the first time you might have all check boxes blank, though subsequent iterations of the same transaction will "remember" your preferences and check a particular box for you by default.

10.5.3.   Administrative Subroutines and Practices

Good programming or scripting focuses on creating reusable code, like useful subroutines that can be accessed as or when needed. Over the years, I have developed a cadre of simple subroutines that seem to prove themselves over and over again when it comes to performance analysis, stress testing, or even basic system administration and monitoring, as follows:

- Random, unique, or other input-data number generators. For one of my customers, for example, I needed to provide a unique value for a configure-to-order (CTO) product. The customer's business rules required a unique serial number for each manufactured product, so I created a variable that concatenated the year, month, day, hour, minute, second, and the virtual client's unique number. Just like that, I had a serial number that would never be duplicated, ever, no matter how many virtual clients ran the CTO process, whether today or 5 years from now.

- General error routines. Instead of passing control to a different error-handling script (discussed later), it's often advantageous to simply stop trying to process the current batch of input and instead move on to the next batch. I also try to "back out" of a currently stuck business transaction through standard functions like F3, F12, and so on. In both cases, I write code that directs the script to fail its current loop. In doing so, I force it to write an update to my output file for that particular transaction or business area indicating that the combination of data failed, and then I force the script to pull in a fresh combination of input data and start over. It's by programmatically addressing these error conditions that I often avoid running my special error subroutine (which kills the virtual SAP session and therefore aborts the virtual user as well).

- Specific error routines. I reference transaction-specific subroutines that cover things like explicit error conditions and warning or other status-bar-generated issues. By scraping these conditions out of the SAP Status Bar and then using them in a basic if-then statement, I can not only better control the script but also capture the kind of data important to analyzing my test runs after the fact.

- Do-while constructs. Sometimes, my customers request that a particular set of input files be used to feed the business processes I've scripted. If-then conditions must therefore be understood and set up to determine when the end of a file has been reached (in which case, I typically reopen the input file and start from the beginning). Similarly, when a virtual user establishes a session with SAP, it makes sense to execute a business process over and over again instead of logging in, executing the functional piece of the script, and then logging out. So a do-while loop (essentially if-then logic) is built around the entire business process in this case as well.

- Input file seeds. For reading input data, I also use the virtual client's unique number as a "seed" to help stagger where a particular client begins reading data sequentially in an input file. Thus, I stay away from true randomization if my input files are large (I do this for overhead reasons—it can take 10s of seconds or longer to go through a large input file). For the best staggering, I multiply the virtual client's number by 100, so that client 1 starts reading data at line 100, client 2 at line 200, and so on—in this way, each client is given its own range of 100 guaranteed-unique items to read (change the multiplier for larger ranges, i.e., for long-running stress tests). If staggering or randomization of some kind is not performed, all virtual clients will read and use the same input data at the same time (which does not reflect the real world in terms of user activity, while falsely increasing cache hit rates to make disk subsystem and database performance appear better than it really should be).

- Response time statistics. This involves capturing response-time data between screen changes in a transaction or business process. For example, if a test user presses Enter to advance from an initial VL02 Change Outbound Delivery screen to a Delivery Change Overview screen, I capture at minimum the associated SAP Application Server response time for that particular virtual user as it moves through executing that particular transaction. This is done by executing AT1's "Stamp on reset" command before pressing Enter, followed by capturing the value held in the $RESPTIME system variable and then executing "Stamp off." Sometimes, I might also capture the wall-clock time, or the amount of real time that has elapsed in a particular business process.

- Finally, I capture all of these application-layer response-time data, status bar messages and other error messages generated previously, and any other important information captured through variables, and pipe all of this out to an output file designated for the transaction or functional area.

I also try to avoid opening and closing too many files (a file management nightmare, primarily), while balancing the need to avoid using too few files (which then introduces too much potential for file contention or locking, as scripts seek out their input data or wish to write output log data). At one extreme, then, every client driver is given its own set of input and output files to read to and write from, while at the other extreme all clients access a shared set of input and output files. Your goal should be to find the *right* balance, one that minimizes administrative headaches without causing locking issues—a quick round of trial-and-error testing is about the only method I'm comfortable with.

When both scripting and associated single-unit testing are completed (including finding more last-minute data, which is not as uncommon as it sounds), the script is ready to be tested by multiple virtual users running concurrently. The exact number of virtual users is up to the T3 who should in turn seek feedback and buy-in from the business, e.g., the system's end users who own the business processes being tested. This important cog in the stress-testing wheel ultimately involves understanding just how many virtual clients will be needed to emulate the Production (or other) environment to be tested, specifically which functional areas should be tested and how many real users will be equated to virtual users. That is, there is not necessarily a one-to-one correlation between real users and virtual users. On the one hand, virtual users can run business processes many time faster than a real user. On the other hand, "wait times" may be easily introduced into a script so that it executes a business process much slower than its human counterpart.

10.5.4.   Leveraging Utility Scripts

Like standard subroutines, I've also created a number of utility scripts that prove useful over and over again. This library of scripts can function in a standalone manner or be incorporated within the body of a larger script, if so desired. Sample utility scripts include the following:

- SAPLOGIN, which allows me to log in to the SAPGUI and establish a virtual session
- SAPLOGIN_STAGGER, which provides multiple virtual users the logic necessary to log in sequentially with a specific amount of maintained between each login
- SAPLOGOFF, which logs out of the SAPGUI
- RANDOM_NUMBER_GENERATOR, a random-number generator, which I tend to copy and build into my scripts
- UNIQUE_NUMBER_GENERATOR, which is excellent for creating unique PO numbers, one-off serial numbers for CTO components, and so on
- SAPGUI_SCREEN_SCRAPE, which is perfect for capturing error and warning messages or basic informational messages like "credit limit for customer 9800060803 changed"
- COMPARE_ROUTINE, which is a simple script that provides different methods of performing if-then logic
- READ_TEXT_INPUT, which provides the commands and syntax necessary to open a file, read it, and restart as required
- READ_EXCEL_INPUT, which is similar to the previous script, though customized for reading a Microsoft Excel workbook (where workbook sheets must be taken into account)
- OUTPUT, which is a reporting and performance metrics/statistics-capturing subroutine, useful for concatenating multiple output data (e.g., input data used, client name and number, end-user name, date and time executed, test-run name/number, error messages related to the particular test run, pass/fail criteria, and output data created by the test run)

10.5.5.   A Special Utility Script—SAPLOGIN

I created the aforementioned scripts long ago, including the SAPLOGIN script, and focused on writing code that could be easily modified to reflect different login requirements. Today, my SAPLOGIN has grown quite large and has evolved over time to support new features and capabilities. In most cases, I "remark out" unnecessary lines of code, of course, leaving only the lines that establish a session with a particular SAP server and its system ID (SID). If a customer has used logon load balancing, I'll instead point to a logon group (which are easily identified via transaction SMLG) instead of a hard-coded application server. Either way, anything that is server- or login group–specific is defined as a variable in the SAPLOGIN script, so that other scripts may pass values to SAPLOGIN, thereby controlling how a particular functional script logs in to an

SAP system. Note that the core functionality of this script amounts to executing a command like *SapEstablishSession "server_name" "instance" front*, where *server_name* is the variable name of the application server or central instance, *instance* is the instance ID variable (e.g., 00), and *front* directs the script to display the SAPGUI screen rather than hiding it. In a similar manner, if a virtual connection to an SAP logon group named MARKETING is desired, I would instead customize the SAPLOGIN script to execute *SapLoadEstablishSession "TST" "message_server_ name" "/H/" "MARKETING" front groupconnect.* Note that "front" tells the code to run the SAPGUI executable in the foreground, so that the SAPGUI screen itself may be viewed real-time while a script is being executed. This is obviously handy for script development and initial load testing. And as I mentioned before, it's actually required by newer versions of the SAP Web AS's SAPGUI API—running in virtual mode behind the scenes is not currently supported in these cases.

Another core line of code in the SAPLOGIN script identifies the client, user ID, password, and language to be used for logging in to the appropriate SAP Application Server or login group. For example, once the session is established with the SAP system to be tested, you can then automate the rest of the login process through a scripted command like *SapLogin "020" "anderson" "pass" "E,"* where "020" is the client, "anderson" is the user ID defined for use in this particular client, and "E" designates the English language. Your password can be saved either in encrypted form or as plain text (in the previous example, the password is simply "pass").

In addition to virtual-user support, establishing an SAP session in the manner just described is what makes screen-scraping possible—error messages, values associated with a radio button selection, contents of any field, name of a particular screen, and much more can be pulled out of the SAPGUI because a virtual-user session was established. And, as I mentioned earlier, it's this feature that may be used programmatically to drive if-then logic. For example, if a particular warning message is displayed during the execution of a transaction, or an unforeseen condition causes an unusual SAPGUI screen to be displayed, the script may pass control to an error routine, call another program, force a "write" to a log file for tracking such circumstances, abort a particular subroutine, end the script and break the SAPGUI connection, and so on. But without a doubt, the greatest benefit of using SAP-aware commands in establishing a session in this manner—rather than scripting a process that logs in by simply driving the SAPGUI by clicking an icon or driving the Windows GUI, followed by logging in with the SapLogin command—is that once you start recording business processes to be saved as scripts, many of the SAP-specific commands rather than the general Windows GUI commands are automatically recorded. We've seen this situation already in many of the examples found in this chapter. Instead of executing a mouse-click followed by Down Arrow, Down Arrow, Tab, Tab, Tab, and then typing in a customer number, using the SAP-aware commands makes it possible to go directly to a particular field (by referencing what SAP AG calls its "German field name") and enter the data. Further, the SAP-aware commands do not require the SAPGUI screen to actually be up and available (again, unless the underlying version of Web AS requires it), making it perfect for conducting virtual-user stress testing. Of course, it's this virtual capability that we ultimately wish to leverage—not at the moment, perhaps, but later, after we have completed developing and testing our scripts.

10.5.6.   Staggering the SAPGUI Login

Establishing a virtual-user session is a bit more involved than it seems. If you just send off 500 virtual users on their merry way, they will all try to log in at nearly the same time—some will fail, others may hang and perhaps lock up system resources, and some will actually log in. To control the ramp-up of a stress test such that all users actually have the opportunity to log in successfully, the users need to be logged in over a period of time. Alternatively, if your script development package allows you to stall all logged-in virtual end users until the last one has logged in, you might simply be able to reactivate them to run the body of your stress test.

At one time, I simply created small AutoController packages, and then manually released these in a controlled fashion, thereby executing the AutoTester scripts within each package in a controlled fashion as well. But I always admired the way that the SAP benchmark kits could log in a new benchmark user every second and, in doing so, thus automatically control login behind the scenes. One of my best friends and colleagues, Fazil Osman, and I finally developed a programmatic "staggering" approach for logging in AT1 virtual users, a process I call the *Staggered SAPGUI Login Approach*. As discussed earlier, the core logic behind this approach is to manipulate the unique number assigned to each virtual user. Because this is held as a system variable, it is available for use even before a script is initialized or a variable file is identified (unlike user-defined variables, which, by their very nature, require a variable file to be defined).

Before making a virtual connection, it's good practice for the virtual SAP end user to check whether it is already logged in to an SAP instance—if so, no other effort is required, and the real work of the script can commence (e.g., displaying a purchase requisition, creating a sales order). Check the status of this by comparing the value of $SAP_SESSION against the value "0"—if 0, there is no connection. In this case, the virtual end user is not logged on, and therefore the staggered login script must be executed (after which the body of the script may execute). Thus, if the value of $SAP_SESSION is 0, I must next display and compare the value of the system variable $MACHINE (explained in detail later) to the word "Machine." This is because the machine variable is only set to something other than "Machine" when running a script virtually through AutoController. So if the variable is simply "Machine," that tells me that I am obviously not running a stress test and therefore none of this staggered login code is required. However, if the variable is something other than "Machine," then the meat of the SAPLOGIN staggered approach comes into play. For instance, I might execute SubString $MACHINE 17 2 LOGIN.COUNTERTXT, which simply means I want to extract the value of the last two characters in the virtual client driver's name, and save these into a variable. For example, if you installed the AutoController client-driver software with the remote virtual client name of "HPS" then virtual client 321 would have a full name of "HPS.VIRT.USER.0321." Performing the SubString function "17 2" would extract the last two characters "21." Similarly, "16 3" would extract the last three characters "321." Note that the SubString function operates from left to right, counting to the character position indicated by the first number in the command and extracting the equivalent number of characters specified by the second number in the command. Because these are alphanumeric characters, I assign the value to a text variable like LOGIN.COUNTERTXT.

Once the text variable file is assigned, I can then manipulate the data in any way I choose, including converting them to a numeric value against which I may perform calculations, as shown in the following code:

```
>Assign LOGIN.COUNTER = LOGIN.COUNTERTXT
>Message LOGIN.DELAY wait 1
>Delay LOGIN.COUNTER
```

The LOGIN.COUNTER variable is a numeric variable that can subsequently be used in comparisons, or as a starting point in a countdown, or used in a simple Delay command as depicted in the preceding example. Note that the Message command is optional—I like to see for myself during script development and testing that the staggered SAPLOGIN subroutine actually worked as I expected it to work. But I remark out this line of code in the actual script finally used for load testing for two reasons. First, it's simply not necessary. Second, and more important, this kind of video activity is detrimental to a system's performance, because it consumes a great amount of video resources on the client-driver machine. Think about the screen refreshes necessary for 400 virtual users running on a single client driver simultaneously, for example, and you'll begin to understand why it's a good thing to comment out message boxes.

It's important that this scripted staggered login subroutine be executed *before* you log in to SAP (i.e., before you execute the core SAPLOGIN code that established the session). Why? Because you are executing this subroutine to control when the SAP login process should commence! I recommend executing this logic in the beginning of the SAPLOGIN script or as part of an "umbrella" script used to log in and then execute multiple discrete transactions as part of a larger business process.

10.6. Data Considerations When Scripting

Although we looked at input-data considerations at length throughout Chapter 9, it's at this point in time in your stress-testing project that you must make a few very important choices with regard to scripts and data. I assume by now that you have already identified the workload that must be executed, and therefore understand the input requirements of this workload. Next, you need to

- Take into consideration from where you will obtain the best data and how you will get these data to the test environment. For example, do you need to take a tape backup of the system of record? Or can you simply perform a file copy from a staging area across the network? Are the data small enough to be burned to a CD-ROM? You may even consider leaving the data where they are, in the system of record, and simply make them accessible in one form or another to your test environment (an unlikely solution in most situations, as the system of record often represents a hands-off Production system itself, but worth considering). More often, you'll find yourself staging the data in a "holding" area, like a locally attached disk drive or network-attached file share. Or you

might perform a restore of sorts into a particular file system or database every time you
plan to execute a test run.

- Account for any data-formatting issues. This is critical, because there will be times
  when the data you require for a test run will not be available in the format required by
  your test tool. In these cases, you'll need to add a "data conversion" process to your
  general test plans. This might include converting database dumps or long lists of match
  codes into Excel or text formats, and may require manual manipulation (e.g., ensuring
  the data is in a tab-delimited format) or even manual typing of data into an input file!
- Determine how you will actually get enough good data for stress testing. Valid data are
  crucial, of course, but quantity is equally important. Exactly how much is enough,
  though? The right answer is simple—get enough so that you never use the same core
  input data *twice* during the execution of a test run. In this way, you will avoid artificially skewing the results with the benefits of caching, and you'll avoid some of the
  locking or data contention issues that can otherwise arise.

Although it's probably not obvious at first blush, access to the *right data combinations* is
as important a consideration in your overall stress testing as is selecting appropriate business
processes. In fact, a script is essentially worthless in the realm of load testing if only a few combinations of data are available—because after the data are used the first time, they remain in memory or are cached at a number of different technology stack layers. These include the hardware
cache in your disk subsystem, the database server's RDBMS cache, and the SAP Application
Server's cache. Thus, if you choose to leverage previously used data combinations over and over
again, the next time the same transaction is executed in your stress test these data will be immediately pulled from cache rather than the disk subsystem and will therefore drive next to no physical load on your disk subsystem. If you recall, to truly drive your disk subsystem is often a major
goal of load testing, because it represents the primary future bottleneck for most enterprise applications. And, of course, it will certainly be exercised in the real world! By running transactions
from cache, you will artificially inflate how well the system really performs, and miss the boat
completely. When it comes down to it, you'll be lucky to get any value out of your stress-test runs.

Exactly how can you go about determining whether you have enough valid data for a stress-
test run, though? Opinions vary, certainly, but the following four-step approach has proven successful for me in the past:

1. Take into consideration how long the test run must execute end to end. Do you need 30
   solid minutes, with perhaps a preceding 15 minutes for ramp-up? If so, my target would
   be to supply enough data for a bit more than 45 minutes' worth of processing. Further,
   if I am not planning on a graceful shutdown of my scripts afterwards (and instead will
   simply abort them), I need to give myself at least 5 minutes *after* the body of the test
   has completed, too. This extra time will help ensure that all users executing during the
   body of the script have an opportunity to write data back to the output logs (aborted
   users, on the other hand, behave erratically, in that some occasionally continue processing while others abort mid-transaction).

2. Determine how long a script takes to execute end to end. And think beyond the basic timeframe the body of each script takes to execute, including think time and all subroutines. If we take a relatively fast transaction like an FD32 credit check (followed by a credit line increase) into account, and then factor in a typical think time, it would be safe to say that the entire business process should consume less than 1 minute of wall-clock time. Therefore we could process 60 of these in 1 hour on every machine running the script.

3. Next, do the math. If the goal (as directed by the business) is to simulate the 20-member financial team's peak load for this particular transaction, we would need to process 900 credit checks/updates throughout the stress test (45 minutes $\times$ 1 $\times$ 20). In the best case, then, it's necessary to have 900 different customer numbers on hand, so that the same customer information is never pulled up twice. Add 20% to this figure "just in case."

4. Finally, ensure that any kind of ramp-up/staggered login approach has been taken into account. If you want to create a single input file to be logically chopped up and used by five different client drivers, for example, you'll need to ensure that you have 4,500 unique entries (stagger where each client driver starts reading its particular chunk of these data by advancing multiples of 900 reads "into" the input file).

This four-step method can prove effective for all transaction mixes or functional areas. But it gets a little cumbersome as the numbers get really large. For example, if my 20-member financial team became 200 people strong, I might be hard-pressed to dig up 9,000 customers that have even been set up in the system, much less able to be given credit increases. My suggestion is to work with the business to determine what is real. Do your best to simulate the real world with the data available to you. And, whenever possible, encourage the T3 and the business/functional experts to identify business processes that inherently enjoy a large array of easily obtainable data. Alternatively, embrace testing methods that are based on business processes which build their own data as they go, or that rely on few input data from the get-go; these and other approaches to scripting and executing test cases are discussed and analyzed next.

10.7. Best Practices in Script Writing and Testing

Creating functional scripts that not only work but provide elegant solutions to the challenges surrounding testing, executing, monitoring, and analyzing results is as much an art as it is a science. Like writing in general, no two people will approach scripting in exactly the same manner. Ergo, no two people will wind up with identical scripts—variances in approach, technique, and so on ensure this. However, in my travels I've been lucky enough to work with some folks who are truly gifted in scripting (which is fortunate, given that I'm not one of those people!). These experts seem to hail from a programming background, for the most part, and sincerely enjoy their work— a number of the consultants from AutoTester and Compuware and a number of my own HP colleagues naturally fit into this category. Their scripts make some of my brute-force scripting solutions look sad in comparison. Fortunately, over the course of our various consulting engagements or internal projects together, they have shared with me different approaches and general best practices that make their business process scripts really stand out in one form or another. The best of these are covered in the next few sections.

10.7.1. Capturing Critical Data and Statistics Real-Time

Without sound data collection and statistical processes in place to ensure that the right post-test-run data were collected consistently, the act of scripting would be futile. That is, it would be a waste of time. Because this subject is so important in the overall context of scripting, I approach output statistics from a number of different perspectives. All of these scripting other management approaches work hand-in-hand to provide a complete performance picture. First, I ensure that the fundamental hardware and OS layers are being automatically monitored at a hardware subsystem layer, using OS-level tools or simple infrastructure management applications like HP Insight Manager or Dell OpenManage. Next, I look to the testing tools themselves to provide valuable data, many of which are often consolidated into high-level results files while still making it possible to drill down into the various transactions executed, virtual users started, and even the lines of code used.

But at a more granular and script-specific level, I also use a highly concatenated output file stuffed with valuable data that can then be written to an output log a line at a time (e.g., after the completion of a "loop" within the body of a scripted transaction). The following shows how such a concatenated output script is written to capture and log output data for a basic R/3 Financial transaction, FB03:

- Assign RESULTS.SCREEN = "FB03-Display Document "
- Assign RESULTS.OUTPUT = FI.FB03INPUTDOC
- Assign FI.OUTPUT = $MACHINE
- Assign FI.OUTPUT = FI.OUTPUT + ", "
- Assign FI.OUTPUT = FI.OUTPUT + $TESTCASEID
- Assign FI.OUTPUT = FI.OUTPUT + ", "
- Assign FI.OUTPUT = FI.OUTPUT + LOGIN.SAPSERVER
- Assign FI.OUTPUT = FI.OUTPUT + ", "
- Assign FI.OUTPUT = FI.OUTPUT + RESULTS.SCREEN
- Assign FI.OUTPUT = FI.OUTPUT + ", "
- Assign FI.OUTPUT = FI.OUTPUT + $RUNNAME
- Assign FI.OUTPUT = FI.OUTPUT + ", "
- Assign FI.OUTPUT = FI.OUTPUT + $DATE
- Assign FI.OUTPUT = FI.OUTPUT + ", "
- Assign FI.OUTPUT = FI.OUTPUT + LOGIN.STRTTIME
- Assign FI.OUTPUT = FI.OUTPUT + ", "
- Assign FI.OUTPUT = FI.OUTPUT + LOGIN.STOPTIME
- Assign FI.OUTPUT = FI.OUTPUT + ", "
- Assign FI.OUTPUT = FI.OUTPUT + FI.RESPONSE

- Assign FI.OUTPUT = FI.OUTPUT + ", "
- Assign FI.OUTPUT = FI.OUTPUT + RESULTS.OUTPUT
- Assign FI.OUTPUT = FI.OUTPUT + ", "
- Assign FI.OUTPUT = FI.OUTPUT + RESULTS.ERROR
- Log "s:\ATWCS\outputFI.txt" FI.OUTPUT

Collecting data in this manner serves two purposes: it provides for a single repository of output data and "backs up" other methods of data collection that may or may not at the end of the day provide the data you seek in a consistent or reliable manner. Note that any data can be collected in this way, too—you simply "add" the new data, be they a numeric value or alphanumeric string, to the end of the list. There is a slew of useful system variables and other input, processing, and output details that could prove useful in your case. For example, AutoTester supports the *transaction* command, which lets you define the start and stop of an arbitrarily defined transaction, and then report the wall-clock time consumed in its execution.

I've also become a big fan of scripting CCMS transactions that can help me automatically gather test statistics for a particular period of time. Tools like transaction ST07 and AL08 can prove valuable while the system is under stress. The classic ST03 transaction, on the other hand, is an excellent tool for gathering post-test-run response time and throughput metrics associated with a particular test run. In the past, I've coded ST03 in combination with SM51; using SM51, I can select a specific application server (e.g., the first one in the list). I then follow this up with an ST03 to gather specific dialog steps processed for the run as well as average response time, wait time, load time, roll time, database request time, enqueue time, and so on. After collecting this application server–specific data, I simply run SM51 again and choose the next application server in the list. In all, these are just the kinds of data that truly prove an SAP system is ready for prime time, or that one SAP system outperforms another.

And rather than using commas to delimit the various data points, you might choose instead to go with tab-delimited spaces or other characters (I actually use both a comma and a space, as you may have noticed in the sample output script, to give me maximum flexibility). You can also set up the output log to dump directly into an Excel spreadsheet, making data analysis that much easier. Keep in mind, though, that if you use a number of client drivers or use different output logs for different groups of scripts, and need to eventually collapse a number of these files into a single file, you may want to stay with basic text-mode output data. A simple batch file can then be written to map a shared drive to each computer housing a log file, to copy and rename the file to a central location, and essentially to append each file to a master test-run output file.

10.7.2. Additional Coding Tips and Tricks

Throughout the years, I have come across a few additional scripting tips and tricks that should prove helpful to you. For example, in the case of simple hardware delta stress tests (where I want to compare the throughput of one SAP Technology Stack to another), one of my favorite practices is to avoid running transactions that *create* anything. Instead, I execute a read-only test case. In the long term, you'll still want to characterize the performance of other types of tests, like cache-only and 90% read/10% write situations. And it's still very important in some manner to eventually characterize write performance of the database and underlying disk subsystem, too (perhaps by executing transactions that make updates to sales orders, purchase requisitions, customer credit limits, and so on). But by creating a test case that purposefully avoids changes or inserts, you avoid growing the database and therefore eliminate much of the need for restoring the database to a known state before each of these types of stress-test runs.

This practice will speed up your overall test times tremendously, too. In a nutshell, read-only stress tests make for a much faster test cycle, from script development through managing input data through actual test execution—this read-only practice saves a lot of time on quite a few fronts! The biggest savings is in execution, though, because you don't have to devise a process for warming or populating the database prior to a stress-test run, nor do you have to take up time restoring the database to a known state before each test run.

For test runs where the previous read-only approach is not feasible or simply not desirable, you'll want to put together a process that's still as fast as possible to execute and re-execute. In these situations, the key is to determine how to reset quickly between stress-test runs because, bottom line, you need to refresh the database back to a known state after committing inserts or otherwise writing data, lest the comparison results be questionable. One hardware-centric method is to use clones or business continuity volumes to "snap off" a copy of your baseline database, and then resync from that clone once you need to get back to a known state. Other similar methods exist at OS and database layers as well.

I've also learned to use the random-number generators that ship with different load-testing tools and, more important, create my own pseudorandom generator. Some of these tools are quite good, in that they generate a different number or seed as expected. Others tend to generate the same sequence of numbers, which is therefore not random in my eyes, but may be used to create predictably unique sequences (which is always preferable to none at all when you seek true randomization). I highly recommend that you develop your own random-number generation process, too. Like the serial number example I gave earlier in this chapter, a random number can be easily created by simply concatenating many values that change constantly. I often use the virtual client's unique number (which is really the key) along with the numbers associated with the current time and date (which may be the same for many thousands of virtual users executing concurrently) to create a repeatably random number.

For scripting tools that are not SAP-aware, another useful practice is to drive the SAPGUI using keyboard commands as much as possible, instead of performing mouse-clicks. That is, if you can navigate via the keyboard to the button you need to click, or the radio button you need to click, you tend to get a more reliable script. And because many of the screens in the SAPGUI support function keys as well as "mousing," it's not too difficult to find keyboard shortcuts. While scripting, right-click the background of the SAPGUI to see the available function key shortcuts for that particular screen. And keep in mind that not all shortcuts are displayed in this way. In fact, one of my favorite shortcuts is not displayed at all—the key combination used to save or commit the results of a transaction, "CTRL+S," is not supported in Virtual mode by AT1 running new versions of SAP R/3. However, the "old" F11 function key used in the past to save these changes still works! You'll be hard pressed to find this noted anywhere, though, even if you right-click the background of the SAPGUI.

Another handy trick I picked up a few years ago involves using the number of seconds in the current time (0–59) as a way to randomly determine which transaction of many should execute. This is useful in umbrella scripts that essentially execute other scripts based on a set of criteria (generally improving script management and execution in the process). I use umbrella scripts and information provided to me by my customers to set up test mix distributions. For example, if my customer tells me that 10% of all scripts should execute FD32 and 30% should execute VA03, I set up if-then logic in my master umbrella script like "if time = 00 through 05, then execute transaction FD32." This represents 6 of 60 possibilities, and therefore 10%. Similarly, "if time = 06 through 23, then execute transaction VA03." This represents 18 of 60 possibilities, or 30%. As you can see, this method is granular enough to handle widely varying percentage loads. And if you create AutoController packages of 60 virtual clients each, you are assured of getting an excellent distribution (assuming you use the staggered SAPLOGIN approach I explained previously).

Finally, another method for ensuring that a script executes a specific number of times per time period, and *only* that number of times, revolves around using the clock as well. First I determine how long the script takes to execute under the load it'll eventually be required to run under. For instance, if I've been asked to execute 1200 MB1C transactions (to enter goods receipts and move a shipment from one place to another) per hour, followed by creating a transfer order (LT06), then this equates to 20 MB1C/LT06 business processes per minute. In the midst of a large-scale test with thousands of users, I must determine the slowest acceptable pace MB1C can run. For our purposes, let's say that even under the harshest of systems loads, MB1C and LT06 can run to completion within 60 seconds, with the typical time closer to 10 seconds. Therefore I need 20 virtual users, each executing MB1C and LT06 every minute, to meet my success criterion of 1200/hour. If I capture the minutes and seconds counters (system variables) before a virtual user commences execution, I can then use these numbers to control precisely when the next MB1C and LT06 will run again (this assumes I have scripted these transactions to run in loop fashion—over and over again). The key is to set up a loop after the body of the script to compare the current time to the time captured when the transaction started. Specifically, if MB1C started at 10:33:21a.m., the loop I set up after the body will be looking for the next time the value of 21 seconds (or greater, in case I miss it!) shows up in the seconds counter. Until 21 comes around again, the script simply loops through this counter, effectively creating a controlled delay. Once the counter hits 21 again, though, control is sent back to the top of the body of the script where MB1C is executed another time, followed by LT06, and so on. If I need more granular control, I can leverage both the minutes and seconds counters (i.e., to launch a new business process every 2 minutes, or every 4 and ? minutes, etc.). Proving that your scripts work as intended is as simple as reviewing your output logs, too, as the start time of each script should reflect that indeed the transactions executed by each of the 20 virtual users are staggered 1 minute apart.

10.7.3.   Regular Communication

Although I have focused primarily on the technical side of scripting, it's probably appropriate to wrap up the chapter with a discussion on communication. Regular communication is a huge plus in any endeavor, and scripting SAP business transactions is no exception. For example, I've been left in the dark myself before by well-intentioned clients, only to surprise them a few days before test week with my "take" on what they needed or wanted. It's not where I want you to be a few days before you're expected to demonstrate the value of everything I cover in this book, so please read on.

Throughout my own script development experience, I have found that at least a twice-a-week 30-minute to 2-hour status review meeting is a good way to ensure that everyone is (still) on the same page. So much can change in a few days, especially in a new SAP implementation or in the wake of a planned upgrade, that going any longer than a few days is simply too risky in my opinion. Most of the time, these meetings should be used to focus on the status of different technical or business-related challenges inherent to business process scripting, like the following:

- Review of the business transactions or business processes
- Status of the basic scripts to be written for each core functional area or business process
- Status of basic input-data requirements—where the data are coming from, how they will be obtained, and how much will be available
- Input approach—data-formatting issues, and how the development of text, Excel-based, or inline data files is coming along
- Script modifications regarding virtualization
- Status of error routines, if-then logic, and do-while logic
- Status of special randomization or similar needs
- Output approach—what's being collected and how it will later be analyzed
- General and specific script issues
- Test infrastructure build-out
- Status of packages and the review of software configuration necessary to execute scripts in a multiuser virtual manner
- Status update on the knowledge repository's growth, including what has been currently added to it and what's expected to be delivered to it near-term
- Data-contention issues, both in general and from a multiuser perspective

Thus, these regular meetings or conference calls typically revolve around both technical and business process folks—the technical team seems to be more involved in the middle of the scripting effort, whereas the business folks are more involved up front and then again at the tail end of the project. For projects lasting more than a month, I also like to include my project sponsor perhaps once every other week or so in these meetings. During our get-togethers, I work to ensure that all testing assumptions still hold true. In addition, I share status updates related to scripting in the various functional areas, identify issues or problem areas, give special attention to data or technical scripting issues, and share successes. If something is in the process of changing, or already has changed (e.g., a script development client refresh wiped out master or configuration data I depended on, or the new client no longer includes data previously used), we discuss what this means to the project overall, and the near-term timelines in particular.

Fortunately, some of the tasks associated with a stress test can be performed concurrently, including the following: working through the final test goals and success criteria, determining ways to validate success criteria, making revisions to the test plan and refining a testing methodology, working with the business units or functional teams to understand business processes or verify transaction flows, and actually test-executing each transaction. This gives the T3 the opportunity to *crash the project schedule*, a project-management term that implies throwing more bodies at a project to achieve milestones faster; in some cases, one or more of my colleagues have assisted me with data collection and script development, allowing these tasks to be completed faster than I ever could have completed them alone. On the other hand, tasks that cannot be crashed imply things that must occur sequentially, one task after the other. A good example of this is testing a script for bugs or other issues—each script must be recorded and then set up to run in virtual mode leveraging the to-be-tested variable input before any real bug testing can take place. Sharing updates like these helps to ensure that the project team stays on track, and the business process scripts, data, and supporting infrastructure and methods all make it possible to achieve an organization's testing and tuning goals.

10.8. Tools and Approaches

Suffice it to say here that due diligence in automating scripts and performing data testing is time-consuming in and of itself. Indeed, even the scripting approaches themselves benefit from automation. In terms of tools and approaches, I believe that the most valuable insight provided by this chapter surrounds coding practices, tips, and tricks that either improve this automation or reduce errors. To that end, the sample scripts included or discussed in this chapter illustrate much of what we have discussed herein. Although written for AT1, each script nonetheless provides an excellent source of technique that should be useful for creating scripts written for other scripting tools or load testing suites.

Preparing for Test Week

As we near "test week" or simply get closer to the time set aside to perform our load testing and tuning, there are a number of activities that first must be concluded. A more complete test infrastructure needs to be installed and configured, for instance, as do the testing and monitoring tools that will be used. Valid data (or harder yet, data combinations) may still need to be mined. Test scripts written to this point still need to undergo progressively intense multiuser testing prior to locking down individual test cases. And the processes and configuration surrounding execution of the test cases themselves need to be completed, including finalizing the execution checklist. Eventually, the entire gamut of load-testing resources, ranging from test infrastructure to data/scripts to the processes leveraged in executing and monitoring test runs, needs to be locked down and documented, too—everything from how you deployed your client-driver strategy to the precise step-by-step tasks outlined in your customized execution checklist. And through all of this, the team still needs to stay focused on meeting the business goals driving the testing, within the context of well-defined success criteria established long ago in the early stages of your project.

11.1. Reviewing Your Test Plan and Goals

Before the team members bury themselves in preparation, it makes sense at this point to go back and revisit the original test plan as well as the goals that drove testing in the first place. In particular, the team needs to ask itself the following questions:

- Are we positioned to actually meet our goals?
- Are our success criteria still valid?
- Are we testing the right things—the right business processes, within the right test mixes, against the right data?
- Does the state of our test infrastructure help or hinder us?
- Did we select the right testing and monitoring tools?
- Overall, what kind of course corrections do we need to take to stay on track?

I suggest taking the most candid approach possible in evaluating and truthfully answering these questions. If you're off track, or things have morphed into something much different than what was envisioned, step back and re-evaluate. For instance, if you couldn't script the real business processes you hoped for, and instead had to go with "plan B" transactions, make sure this truly is acceptable. Similarly, if you had problems replicating your Production environment and had to make compromises in your test-bed, ensure these changes are also acceptable. And, if you haven't done so yet, get the necessary buy-in from all stakeholders—the business representatives, senior business and IT management, and so on—to again verify that you're not wasting everyone's time before moving forward.

Next, concentrate on the tasks remaining to be completed, most of which are discussed in the balance of this chapter. Even though I depend on a real project plan about half the time at this stage in a load-testing project, I still like to put together a custom checklist that reflects each remaining task and timeline—this helps me stay focused. And my simple checklist is easy to share, is easy to stay on top of, and makes for a great way to hold razor-sharp in-and-out meetings. Finally, by using the checklist to capture and document status updates, it becomes the de facto method of sharing updates with others as well—with the technical team, business groups, IT management, and more.

11.2.   Implementing a Real-World Client-Driver Approach

By this time, you've already selected and thoroughly tested your client-driver approach. By client-driver approach, I'm talking about the software and processes necessary to create a load on the system. Thus, for single-unit or single-user testing, the client-driver approach is inherently simple, because it relates only to a single client connection—whether that connection is physical (likely in this case) or virtual (less likely, given cost constraints). But for multiuser testing, the method selected to drive hundreds or thousands of users represents one of the biggest decisions made thus far.

11.2.1.   Installing Core Client-Driver Support Infrastructure

Because it is one of the most critical keys to success, the client-driver installation and configuration also plays a key role in regard to the scripting software selected early on for recording and playing back business processes. That is, the two software layers are interlocked in that only certain packages will support certain scripting languages. The client-driver approach with which I'm most familiar leverages AutoTester's AutoController, driving AT1 scripts in virtual or physical mode. AutoController and its SAP API–aware counterparts can do much more than simulate a bunch of SAP users—they can drive the exact business processes, screen by screen, scripted by you or your team. But like its Mercury and Compuware counterparts, AutoController still requires some level of infrastructure to pull off a multiuser load test. And that is where this section comes into play—not only must the client-driver hardware and software infrastructure be set up but it must then be configured and optimized in its own right to support those thousands of users. Consider the following:

- Client drivers may physically consist of anything from 10s of desktops or laptops, to perhaps a few large servers.

- Depending on the release of Web AS, you may need to use physical client drivers rather than virtual ones simply for technical support reasons—the API used by the virtual toolmakers like AutoTester and Compuware has changed, and the old one is simply no longer available.
- Client drivers vary in terms of how well they execute on multiprocessing platforms, with a certain memory configuration, or leveraging the latest and greatest network infrastructures.
- Beyond simply installing the client-driver test infrastructure, it must also be configured to be useful. In the case of AutoController, this means that packages of business scripts need to be established, user counts need to be determined, data need to be made accessible and in the format necessary for input, and so on.

Assembling the client-driver portion of your load-test infrastructure is not trivial! As I mentioned previously, it is rare for a customer to have enough desktop or laptop front-end clients, network infrastructure, and time necessary to actually pull together a mock client environment—this is precisely why virtual direct-testing software products were created in the first place. In place of all these physical assets, though, at minimum you'll find yourself installing perhaps three to five servers to provide the client load on your quasi-Production system. On top of that, you'll need one or more computers to control these client drivers, too. In the world of AutoTester products, both of these functions are performed by different components of AutoController. The Auto-Controller *Virtual Client* product handles the virtual load-driver tasks, whereas the *Auto-Controller Console* addresses the latter. Before these products can be installed, though, the following must occur:

- The client load-driving infrastructure must be "sized." For client drivers, I typically recommend running no more than 100 virtual users per processor, running at 1-second think times. This rule of thumb varies according to the software package deployed as much as the processor speed, of course. But fortunately, since think times are not "built in" to this rule of thumb (which can be as much connection-oriented as anything else, depending on the platform), there is plenty of room left to extrapolate custom user-to-processor ratios. In the past, I've actually supported the equivalent of thousands of 30-second think time standard users on an eight-way server. So extrapolate as necessary, based on the type and number of servers you have available and the number of users you need to model—you can do quite a bit with a few four-way servers.
- Sizing the console is also required. Again, this is a connection-oriented process. But factors like MB RAM per user and processing cycles required by user make the biggest impact. I generally say something in the neighborhood of 300 to 400 virtual users may be supported per processor. But RAM varies considerably—products like Auto-Controller drive the front end and therefore require memory adequate enough to do this—perhaps 8MB to 16MB per user. Other products drive more of a server-based load or generic load and require much less. So do the math, and don't forget to add some-

thing like 128MB to 256MB of RAM to cover the OS, other overhead, and the needs of the controller product itself—do everything you can to eliminate all but the unavoidable fraction of a percentage point of requisite Windows paging-in from your pagefile.

Once the two layers of the client-driver infrastructure have been sized, install the underlying hardware infrastructure, including the network layer. I recommend at least a 100Mb switched infrastructure at minimum, simply to keep network latencies or similar performance considerations out of the picture; 100 Mb is more than enough bandwidth to handle many thousands of SAPGUI users, even at 4kb per average transaction.

11.2.2.   Client-Driver OS Installations

Next, install the server or desktop/laptop hardware and each system's OS. Strive for OS consistency to keep troubleshooting installation, configuration, or load-related issues to a minimum. For a 1,000-user virtual test, it's not unusual to have two four-way client-driver servers and a single console—three computers total. For smaller systems targeting specific types of loads, I'll typically install both the client and console pieces on the same server, an eight-way if available (to provide additional CPU horsepower should it be needed later, like during the what-if portion of the load-testing project). Depending on the processing platform you're deploying, I recommend going with the most capable OS for which you are licensed. For example, if you've got eight-way servers or find yourself with computers housing greater than 4GB of RAM, ideally you'll be in a position to install Windows Server 2003 Enterprise Edition or Windows 2000 Advanced Server (if supported by the testing application!) to take advantage of all of your processing power and support for the extra RAM. In other cases, you might be forced to go with Windows 2000 Professional or Windows XP.

Regardless, configure your OS in a manner that maximizes its performance as a load generator. Like the servers in your test environment running SAP, refrain from executing other applications or services on your test infrastructure. And run only the network protocols necessary for testing, typically TCP/IP. Finally, stay away from /3GB and /PAE memory management unless your software products specifically support these options, and don't forget to "maximize throughput for network applications." Finally, for systems that will be required to display the SAPGUI real-time, or display status messages generated by the testing application, ensure your video subsystem is up to snuff (and think about how video intensive hundreds of clients can be when real-time status messages are being displayed!).

11.2.3.   Client-Driver Installation and the SAPGUI

Once the hardware and OS are configured, install the appropriate version of the SAPGUI, taking care in the installation process to include the option to also install the SAP development tools. Be sure to copy both the services and SAPMSG.ini file from one of your SAP applications servers to your client drivers and console. These files are required to resolve central instance IP addresses or locate SAP-specific services and will likely be required by the actual load-testing software to be installed shortly (unless you go with pure IP addresses in your SAP login script). And keep in mind that you'll need to perform some amount of due-diligence client infrastructure testing regardless of the hardware and software components installed, especially in light of the new API leveraged by Web AS 6.20 and higher. Because the SAPGUI must be displayed when testing implementations based on these later Basis releases, as touched upon in Chapter 10, the importance of client-driver sizing takes on a whole new dimension—video requirements, the need for incremental RAM, and more add up quickly. In fact, you might instead begin to consider ways of leveraging virtual machine products to get the most out of your big servers. Products like VMware could come in handy in terms of virtualizing some of these front-end client requirements (though you'll still need to install the same number of OS, SAPGUI, and client-driver instances—the benefit will simply be less hardware to manage). I recommend that you therefore take a close look at your test suite's documentation or its main Web site, like AutoTester's *www.autotester.com,* for more details relevant to what is supported, which approaches might be limited, and any suggestions for overcoming the latest SAP AG–derived limitations. And then turn your attention to the next big hurdle—actually installing and configuring the virtual-testing software.

11.2.4.   Client-Driver Software Installation

Without exception, I've found that all of the major SAP-aware test-tool vendors put together a nice installation package for their virtual-testing packages. AutoTester's AutoController is no exception. I've outlined the key steps germane to most installations, based here on AutoController 5.02. Ensure you take into account the following factors:

- Ensure your OS is up to snuff. That is, only install your controller products on machines running a supported OS, which today typically includes Windows 2000, XP, or NT 4.0 with Service Pack 5. Note that support for Windows 2003 may be lacking for some products, and anything less than Service Pack 5 on NT 4.0 is generally not recommended.
- Prior to installation of the AutoController console, ensure the machine has an adequate amount of RAM. For the much-improved version 5 of AutoController, AutoTester recommends at least 1MB of memory for every 20 SAP virtual users executing concurrently.
- From the Windows control panel's System icon, create a pagefile equivalent to two to three times the amount of physical RAM installed in the machine. If this would result in a pagefile larger than 4GB on a single disk, create two or more pagefiles across multiple disks.
- Also from the System icon, set the foreground performance boost to "none" or set it to adjust performance for programs rather than background services.
- Enter a valid license key. After working your way through the requisite introductory and license screens, you'll be required to enter a valid license key—this is unavoidable. I know of no SAP-aware test-tool vendor that provides trial licenses to anyone but its hardware and software partners. That is, customers typically need to pony up some dollars.

- Next, select the low-level component you wish to install. AutoController allows you to install the AutoController console, a virtual client driver (remote virtual instance), or a physical client driver that supports distributed load testing, as shown in Figure 11–1.
- Select the network protocol, keeping in mind that virtual client drivers require TCP/IP connections, whereas other options can leverage either a NETBIOS or TCP/IP connection.
- Specify where reports will be kept, whether to install Adobe Acrobat (to peruse the read-me files, which I highly recommend), and so on.
- Initialize the AutoController client. Once the AutoController client in particular is installed, it still needs to be initialized. Specifically, I've found that if you limit the number of characters in the Remote Virtual Client Name field to three, you'll make things easier on yourself in the long run. This is because the virtual name associated with each virtual test user generated by a particular client driver uses this virtual client driver name within its virtual user names (it's appended). Longer or shorter names, therefore, change the length of the name of each virtual test user, and will therefore affect any script written to leverage this unique number (e.g., my staggered login approach which pulls the two or three unique virtual client digits from within the larger complete name).

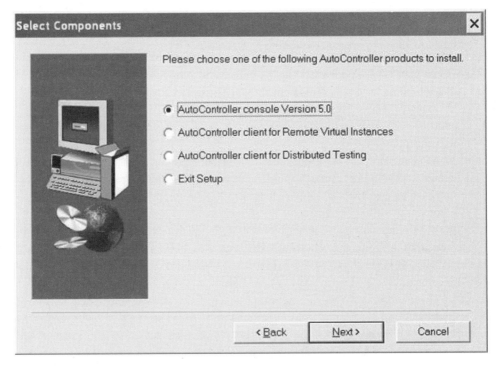

Figure 11–1   The AutoController installation process allows you to install not only a full-featured console but both virtual and physical (Win32-based) client-driver utilities.

With the client-driver and console installation behind us, we can finally shift our focus to the world outside of your client-driver infrastructure, as we examine a number of "external" tools and systems that, while already installed, need to be configured or tweaked as well.

11.3. Stress-Test Infrastructure Configuration

In my eyes, your stress-test infrastructure pertains to everything that will actually be *tested*—the servers, disk subsystems, OSs, and application/software stacks relevant to your SAP servers, system landscape, and the entire mySAP component suite deployed to emulate your Production environment. In the best of worlds, you'll get to run your stress test on your soon-to-be-deployed actual Production system, in fact. This approach is always preferred to any other test platform alternatives but is not always possible for reasons that should be pretty obvious—copies of Production are expensive. In most cases, then, a near-identical staging or DR system, or something cobbled together that truly *represents* Production, must suffice.

But simply having the SAP system available for testing is not enough. You'll need to ensure the following is seen to as well, prior to pulling the trigger on test-case execution:

- Document the entire stress-test infrastructure's current state, using tools and approaches like those discussed in Chapters 6 and 7.
- Baseline the configuration to be tested from a hardware perspective, too, especially in regard to disk subsystem and CPU performance.
- Run through the processes necessary to stock your system with data. This might simply mean performing an SAP client copy (where the client being copied already contains the necessary master, transactional, and other data needed by your test cases). On the other hand, you may need to run through scripted or batch-input processes that create data to then in turn be used by the stress test.
- Work through whatever process needs to be performed to back up your SAP client— perhaps this means performing a complete backup to tape (or a disk copy). On the other hand, you may choose to leverage your disk subsystem's capabilities to create snapshots or clones which will be used later as a master copy against which you will resync your database.
- Set up the SAP MMC or any other tools that will help you start and stop SAP quickly and in the correct order—you'll find yourself doing this often, so it makes sense to set yourself up to do this as easily as possible.

Let's now return to the client and console test tools, where a final bit of configuration needs to be performed.

11.4. Configuring Your Client-Driver Tools

Next, your client-driver tools must be configured—beyond simple installation, you need to set up the tools to be useful. Remember, the key at this stage is to focus on creating a great "test-case execution environment" rather than a Production-ready monitoring solution at one extreme or a hodgepodge of disconnected tools at the other. It is at this stage that you need to consider the final details relevant to how you will set up specific "packages" of scripts to be executed. That is, within the AutoController product or its equivalents, you may define packages that will execute previously developed individual scripts or sets of scripts. There are a number of ways to approach this, though, and other questions to consider as well:

- How will the scripts within the packages log in to the SAP system to be tested? That is, will a subroutine be called to stagger login, or will all packages log in and then "wait" to execute business process scripts at a later time (effectively creating a manual login process)?
- Should scripts or test cases be organized into functional groups, such that all R/3 SD scripts are contained in one package, R/3 MM in another, and so on?
- Should scripts be organized by business process, where each package equates to a single business process and therefore potentially contains a mix of functionally diverse individual scripts?
- Must certain scripts run sequentially, or is there a specific execution order that needs to be maintained?
- How many users should each package host? In other words, regardless of how functionality is divided between or maintained within packages, should a standard number of users be associated with a package, or should this vary to meet business goals (or emulate actual business conditions)?

11.4.1.   Creating Test Packages

Once the previous questions are answered, each package of scripts must be created and then tested. Initially, you will want to test each individual script in a package configured for a single user, ensuring that all options regarding tracing virtual- or physical-user progress or monitoring line-by-line transaction activities are enabled (see Figure 11–2). This is easily accomplished by creating a package in the AutoController console, and then right-clicking the package, clicking Properties, clicking the Communications tab, and selecting the option "Receive line-by-line status while processing." In this way, if you double-click the icon associated with a virtual or physical user while it is executing a package, you'll be able to see the actual lines of scripted code the package is running. As you can imagine, this is a great method of troubleshooting code—you can tell in an instant if your script is "hung" in a particular place, or if a particular line of code seems to be responsible for unexplainable aborts.

Once you validate that each of your scripts within each package runs to completion or as expected, you have accomplished a major milestone—single-unit testing. That is, at least until a change to the script or data forces you to go through the same iterative single-unit testing process again. Keeping things simple at this stage will help you iron out the little issues that tend to pop up at the last minute with data, scripts, or the infrastructure itself. And this practice helps you uncover any unique or unusual testing-application-specific issues. For example, AutoController 5.03 does not support directory names as lengthy as those supported by its updated counterpart, AT1 3.04.

Next, perform the same sort of virtual testing as before, testing each script within each package to ensure it runs to completion. Then begin ramping up user counts to identify issues related to data locking, script error, or infrastructure shortcomings. I like to bump up a test from 1 to 10 users, and then again to 60 (if using a staggered login method that leverages the current number of seconds in the current time) or perhaps 100 users. It's testing like this that lets you uncover the really interesting issues that would otherwise bring things to a halt during test week. For example, one testing observation in particular that I've run across, which seems to be fading away but still needs to be verified today, regards how well a client-driver application uses the processors at its disposal. Specifically, it has been very common for stress-testing client-driver utilities to appear single-threaded in the past; indeed, some have actually been single-threaded and could therefore execute only against a single CPU. But in the case of versions of AutoController prior to release 5.x, this only *appeared* to be the case. In the past, I had to regularly open the Windows Task Manager, navigate to the Processes tab, and find the *vatwrun* process. Then I would right-

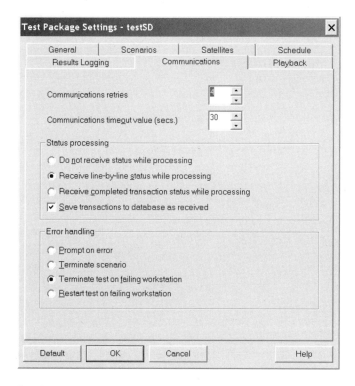

Figure 11–2 Single-unit testing in virtual mode is made quite easy through enabling a communications option that allows the actual lines of scripted code to be observed as they are executed by a user.

click this process and select the option to change processor affinity—only the first processor was selected by default. Simply clicking on all of the available processors would remedy this, though, enabling the vatwrun process to execute on all processors as it needed to (an operation that could be performed "on the fly," in fact). The jump in performance was unsurprisingly dramatic, increasing two to three times nearly immediately.

Today, the newest AutoController versions executing against SAP 4.6x and greater Basis releases feature a client utility that can be configured for better granularity, control of processes, and so on. These versions execute well on multiple-CPU machines, without the need to manually tweak or change anything, and in the process, they create a fairly even workload distribution across all available processors. With one less thing to worry about, and no loss in performance or functionality, it's a nice win-win situation for everyone.

11.4.2. Details Relevant to Ramping Up Real-World Loads

As I stated previously, once a single user can run in virtual mode, I like to first increment the packages I create in the AutoController console to execute 10 virtual users; executing one package therefore starts 10 identical scripts, each running the tasks associated with a single virtual user, single batch process, or whatever has been scripted. I verify that the input data used are indeed pseudorandom, ordered, or as specified by the project team or business. And then I resolve any issues related to locking/contention (usually by revising a script to check for new "warning," "information," or "error" messages generated by the SAPGUI session and simply not seen before). If changes have been made to a particular set of scripts, I then must fall back to single-unit testing, of course, and ramp up to 10 users again.

After 10 virtual users run their scripts to completion successfully, I jump to the maximum required per the test plan, or to 60 or 100 virtual users, whichever reflects the plan. In an Auto-Controller package responsible for starting many virtual users, timing is critical. And more than whether logins are staggered comes into play. In other words, the distribution of think times, built-in delay times (e.g., those surrounding message/status boxes), other hard-coded "waits," and so on need to be carefully reviewed after a package is tested for a great number of users. Why? Because the load itself will change the speed at which a transaction executes (no surprise—that's why we're stress testing!). So built-in or hard-coded delays used to ensure that you only execute a specific transaction rate per hour need to be modified. And think times may even need to be decreased if a targeted transaction throughput number cannot be otherwise achieved (though it would probably make more sense to increase the number of virtual users executing that transaction instead).

In my experience, if something like 60 or 100 users can run the same transaction or business process concurrently, leveraging different data but the same script, and the script successfully runs to completion (or successfully loops, as is more often the case), then many more users can probably do the same. I therefore halt most of my pre-test-week multiuser testing at this stage, confident that things will go well during test week. Like single-user and 10-user testing, I perform this final level of concurrent-user testing for each package and script, to ensure that no functional area, business process, or transaction goes untouched under load. And I complete my testing by running the various packages or scripts in the appropriate mixes to be run during test week—in this way, nothing that I do during test week will be "new and different." By spending the time now to ensure that the mix of online and batch transactions to be executed during test week still fulfills the test's goals, I'll save myself countless additional headaches in what will still probably amount to a stressful week of stress testing. So if, for example, I need to execute a mix of CRM, PLM, and R/3 transactions executed by 1,600 users, such that R/3 represents half the user-count load and the remaining two components represent the other half, I'll go ahead and do the math so that I can begin planning the construction of the appropriate packages now. Further, if R/3 needs to be distributed to reflect a certain mix (e.g., 800 users, broken down into 40% SD users, 20% WM folks, 20% FI analysts, and 10% PP users), I'll actually go ahead and construct those packages, creating perhaps five packages for SD, two or three for WM and FI each, and a package dedicated to PP. And, if there's a requirement to host an additional 400 background-noise users behind these core transactions, I'll create those packages as well and assign perhaps 100 low-activity users to each, depending on the requirement.

11.5. Locking Down the Test Platform

Although it would be enormously convenient, it's unreasonable to expect that everything relevant to a testing and tuning engagement will remain static throughout the project. It is more than likely that nothing will stay the same, actually. Systems and data change, SAP configurations and screens change, and therefore scripts and the test infrastructure used for testing are also subject to change. My approach to managing this change won't impress you with its fresh insight or unique vision—I simply deal with it as best I can, and put in the hours necessary at the last minute to ensure everything still works as it should—but I've learned a few tricks and techniques that might be helpful. Without exception, my favored technique revolves around letting my customers make whatever changes they need to in exchange for their assurance that I will be allowed to keep them from making any changes—locking down the entire project's assets, in effect—at some point close to test week. And because of my initial hit-and-miss experience trying to lock down SAP systems that screamed out "change me," I learned that locking down data, script, and infrastructure changes, in that order, was the best way to go.

11.5.1.   Data Collection Cut-Off in the Real World

You might wonder why locking down data before scripts and infrastructure changes are made makes the most sense up front. The answer is easy—the data drive script development, which in turn drives the infrastructure. When data change—the input necessary to execute your scripted business transactions or processes—the scripts will almost certainly break, and do so in a big way. Of course, good if-then conditions will catch much of this (hopefully!), but eventually your goal is to execute business scripts, not a series of if-then statements that fail to process any real data because either the data are invalid or the scripts can't handle the data. I've been there, done that. It wasn't the goal, and didn't add a lot of value at the end of the day.

Thus, at some point in time, it will become necessary to put a stake in the ground, so to speak, and end your data collection or data-mining activities. I call this point in time the "data collection cut-off" and in the best of worlds it should precede test week by a month or more. In the real world, though, you'll be lucky to get at minimum 1 or 2 weeks to test the impact that updated data have on your scripts, which is covered next.

11.5.2. Final Script Development and Testing

With data locked down, script development and testing can finally conclude as well. If you're like most of my customers (and me), you'll find yourself tweaking code up until a few days before test week. Much of this is historically driven by troubleshooting, but real issues should have been resolved by now. Instead, data issues—bad customer numbers, materials that don't "fit" in a particular default storage location, nonexistent purchase requisitions, and so on—consume your time today. Beyond removing the offending data, which may not be an option if that severely impacts the quantity of data left for testing, you are faced with building grand if-then logic around much of your scripting. This becomes particularly troublesome if you're forced to build many nested if-then loops that seek to verify the expected SAPGUI screen name (using the SapLookWindow command, if coding in AutoTester's scripting language), each of which may take different actions based on what is discovered.

And the changing data may impact how well a script performs under load, too. You might find, for example, that data relevant to activities within a particular company code tend to result in more locks and therefore more script aborts. Updated master data may cause a script to fail completely, too, if values or properties have not been considered, resulting in additional script aborts. Thus, only once data are locked down may scripts undergo the final levels of single-user and multiuser testing. Then, based on these results, a functional expert or business representative should help refine your timing decisions before moving on to the next step: locking down your servers and storage.

11.5.3. Locking Down All Hardware Components

Locking down each one of your test servers, client-driver boxes, database-related and other data structures, network infrastructure, and so on is usually a much bigger job than it sounds. Sure, it's easy (though time-consuming) to walk your way through each server's individual technology stack layers in detail, from infrastructure and hardware through OS, database, and SAP updates and other releases, capturing salient configuration details and recording them somewhere. But how do you do this quickly? And what can you do about other mySAP components? More important, how do you keep others from introducing changes to your carefully constructed solution stacks? And finally, how should you go about limiting and controlling access to these resources so you can conduct a repeatable stress test? My ideas are as follows:

- Communicate the fact that the stress-test system is now "locked down" widely across the team and organization as a whole.

- Once everyone understands the system is locked down, reiterate your goal of achieving a Production-like environment. Remind them of your initial goal: to replicate (or nearly so) your Production environment consisting of all of the various firmware, software, kernel, and other updates that you (or an enterprising colleague) otherwise might be inclined to update—changes are strictly off-limits for the moment. Perhaps you'll pursue some delta testing or change-driven testing at a later date, but for now promote the fact that your "static" environment is just that—static—because your Production environment happens to be locked down for the time being as well.
- Just to ensure nothing changes without your knowledge, I suggest taking a "snapshot" of the technology stack every day for 2 to 3 weeks prior to test week. Leave your digital camera at home and instead use current-state data collection tools like GetConfig, Survey, Enterprise Auditor, and so on (described in Chapter 7). In this way, it's easy to prove that a particular configuration has been changed or that it in some other way deviates from what is expected. And most such tools make it easy to determine *when* the update occurred, helpful in creating an audit trail to hunt down the approver or perpetrator, as the case may be, of a last-minute change.
- Control physical access to the gear through secure data-center practices like keeping it behind lock and key, requiring the use of security cards, and limiting all levels of access on a need-to-know basis. I highly recommend avoiding "standard" passwords, too—administrator or root are commonly guessed, database user accounts like "sa" and SAP* and DDIC passwords need to be changed from their defaults, and any "standard" accounts your IT team has standardized on over the years need to be set up with a non-standard difficult-to-guess password. Finally, all passwords then need to be held in close confidence within a very small subteam of need-to-know individuals. Refrain from changing these passwords once you start your project (primarily to avoid issues with people not being able to get their work done), but take care to audit these accounts on something like a weekly or biweekly basis. While you're at it, lock down remote access to your systems as well, unless it's required to conduct the tests in the first place—products like PC-Duo, Windows Terminal Services, Citrix Metaframe, and so on need to be considered.
- If systems-management packages or utilities are loaded on your servers, take care to change default passwords along with default behaviors. For example, the default option for a number of packages allows you to reboot a server remotely—if your SNMP community string is easily guessed (stay away from *public!*), you risk someone seriously interrupting one of your stress-test runs down the road.
- Baseline the individual system components of every machine involved in the test at least once, especially each computer's disk subsystems, CPU performance, and network performance. In this way, even if a change was never overtly applied, you'll still be able to catch performance deltas manifesting themselves because of impending hardware failures or passive events (e.g., network or CPU overhead related to other activities).

It's worth reiterating that you need to ensure everyone on the team is aware of what is taking place with your test system, and when. I can't remember the last time I ran into a problem days before a stress test was to commence that did not start with "I didn't know." Limit any opportunities for anyone to use this excuse. Communication via regular e-mail distribution blasts, team meetings, team Web-site postings, and even strategically placed "notes" firmly attached to your test infrastructure will go a long away in making test week run that much more smoothly, and your already long nights of work that much shorter.

11.6.   Stress-Test Monitoring Considerations

If you've ever run through a series of performance tests only to discover afterwards that you failed to gather the right performance data to quantify whether your system's performance is improving or deteriorating (oh wait, I'm the only one who has ever done that), you already understand how important it is to assemble and then execute a sound monitoring strategy. I've been in this situation more times than I care to remember. But it helped solidify in my head long ago the need to formally approach how I monitor stress-test runs or performance-improvement projects. And out of this experience came a multipronged approach to monitoring that essentially mirrors the SAP Technology Stack while adding a few "management-tool" overlays for good measure. My approach boils down to the following:

- Leveraging data collection and monitoring utilities like those covered in Chapter 7, to make for a consistent and comprehensive testing process at the hardware layers of the stack
- Manually gathering certain pieces of data in real time during the execution of a stress-test run, using SAP CCMS and other tools that allow for snapshots in time
- Automating the collection of other performance data both real-time and after the fact, again leveraging CCMS and more
- Using a systems-management package (though only if the team responsible for performance tuning and testing already uses this tool, or the other tools being used fail to cover a layer in the stack)
- Wrapping the previous points together in a repeatable manner, using a simple execution checklist

The next few pages detail each of the aforementioned points and look more closely at systems-management packages that may be used for monitoring.

11.6.1.   Real-World Manual Data Collection Details

As you execute your stress test, there will naturally be some areas that demand real-time attention. Why? Because it only makes sense to ensure that an individual test run is actually progressing as expected (i.e., that the number of users or processes or machines you expect to see are actually busy creating a load). Thus, as long as you're "required" to review how well different areas or technology stack layers are performing as your test progresses, I suggest recording what you observe in either your execution checklist or a specially created output form. I suggest doing so at a regular interval, like every 2 or 3 minutes during the execution of each test run, and make note of multilayer statistics or conditions as follows:

- Using AL08, take a snapshot of the *total number of users* connected to the system and validate that you are within acceptable logon load-balancing test constraints.
- In a similar manner, use ST07 to take a snapshot of the total number of concurrent users, users actively using a work process, and perhaps functional mix data (e.g., if this mix is important to "prove" that a particular test run reflects the expected functional load distribution).
- With SM66, capture the number of concurrent (active simultaneously) work processes. Many of you probably already know that this transaction only provides a snapshot of activities. You may wish to execute it three or four times in quick succession to get a better feel for the average number of concurrent work processes—it's what *I* do. And you may wish to optimize SM66 via the Settings button to show or hide certain things (such as removing your own connection and work processes used to execute SM66 itself from the display, or avoiding making RFC connections to other servers if you truly only want to view activity on the local application server).
- At a hardware or OS layer, capture the current disk queue length and MB/second throughput numbers for the drives housing the database. I'll do the same for the log volumes, too, if the test is specifically geared toward understanding and optimizing holistic database performance. Note that I tend to use hardware-specific utilities if they're available (e.g., DSview); otherwise, PerfMon is an easy way to gather these data for Windows-based servers.
- Also using PerfMon or a similar Unix utility, track current and peak pagefile utilization, RAM utilization, and both current and peak CPU utilization. Other key performance statistics include average and peak disk queue lengths for your data drives (and log drives, if necessary), details relevant to the mix of reads to writes, and basic network throughput figures. Note that I normally set up PerfMon to capture statistics and dump them into a log every 10, 30, or 60 seconds—the timeframe depends on the length of the test and the level of granularity desired. And remember, more monitoring impacts performance!
- If you run into problems with a virtual or physical user, and the connection between AutoController and SAP seems to persist even after a user's script or package aborts, execute transaction SM04 (see Figure 11–3). SM04 allows you to end a particular session without impacting the rest of your stress-test users. Remember to annotate your notes or execution checklist, too, if you find yourself ending SAP user sessions during a test run.

Figure 11–3 SM04 is invaluable when your script aborts or your SAP test tool's user loses its connections and therefore "awareness" to your SAP system.

I'm a big fan of minimizing the number of tools used in my monitoring endeavors. Thus, if your test requires detailed network or low-level database information, for example, consider using PerfMon to record these values as well. Many other tools are available, however, a few of which are discussed here:

- The Windows MMC is Microsoft's built-in OS management tool. SAP AG has created a powerful MMC snap-in, giving Microsoft solutions for SAP an edge in terms of both basic and quite detailed monitoring capabilities. The SAP MMC snap-in, which is loaded on the central instance, database server, and all application servers during an SAP installation, allows you to manage the OS, database, and any number of mySAP components all from a single console. Even better, though, SAP AG has put together a simple checklist to allow you to install the SAP MMC snap-in anywhere, like on a machine dedicated to managing your stress-test runs. It may then be configured to manage and monitor multiple SAP instances in this way, making it very easy to monitor the entire SAP system supporting your cross-application business processes. For Windows 2000 and WS2003 environments, the installation is a snap; no prerequisite software is required (unlike NT 4.0 environments, where minimum versions of Microsoft Internet Explorer 4.0, Microsoft ADSI, and the core Microsoft Management Console version 1.1 must be installed first).
- A slew of Unix command-line utilities may be leveraged to support SAP systems management of stress-testing and performance-tuning engagements. One of the most common utilities, *vmstat,* lets you monitor the run queue, swap file details, paging daemon scan rate, CPU status, and more. Another common utility, *w,* displays process usage in that it monitors load averages over 1, 5, and 15 minutes, similar to a Top Sessions report or ST06 data. For a comprehensive CPU activity report (among other system details), I recommend executing *top* regularly. Other utilities like *collect* and DCPI (Digi-

tal Continuous Profiling Infrastructure) provide excellent performance-oriented data, too. Finally, for swap file performance measured as a percentage of swap space utilized, *swapinfo* is valuable.

Many other utilities and tools that give you a real-time picture of your system's performance are available as well, especially across the various Unix and Linux flavors. Thus, I suggest you refer to your OS's administration guide or contact your hardware vendor for details specific to your OS release. Most of the time, though, I think you'll find the utilities previously mentioned more than adequate.

11.6.2. Automated Processes, Utilities, and Scripted T-Codes

Although regular snapshots represent a surefire way to validate that your test run has not completely bombed (along with providing the data for a nice activity bell curve when everything falls into place during your test run), you really need access to highly detailed data collected throughout each test run, data that must be analyzed afterwards because of their volume, interrelationships, and potentially complex interdependencies. Because these kinds of data are inherently granular and buried deep inside CCMS or your systems-management tool, collecting them may unfortunately represent a time-consuming proposition. At the most basic level, if you use an SAP-aware systems-management application like HP OpenView or BMC Patrol, I recommend that you determine the performance metrics most important to your test, and then create a custom report that captures the salient details. Run this report to collect data specific to each test run's execution time period.

Without an HP OpenView or BMC Patrol at your disposal, though, the process of drilling down into CCMS and pulling out relevant data is certainly more troublesome. To combat this, I developed a number of automated scripts that would turn my own postrun analysis into a relatively fast and exceedingly consistent undertaking. The effectiveness of these scripts lies in using SAP-aware scripting tools capable of screen-scraping, like Mercury Interactive's WinRunner or QuickTest Pro, AT1, and so on—the same tools you used to develop your automated business process scripts. Without the ability to scrape data from the SAPGUI, a live person would have to track and record the data being displayed, and these scripts would certainly be less valuable, not to mention time-consuming. Thus, long ago, before the days of RZ20 or the SAP Solution Manager, I scripted transactions like the following to provide real-time system performance snapshots that could be accumulated throughout a test run, providing excellent data for analysis after the fact:

- ST02, to capture buffer details like that related to the use of extended memory, the status of roll and heap memory, program and screen buffer hit rates, and much more
- ST04, for database details like data buffer and shared pool cache hit rates, reads versus writes, total reads versus those that had to access physical disk, the relationship between user calls and recursive calls, and so on—these can prove invaluable in rationalizing disk activities observed at other solution stack layers, as seen in Figure 11–4.

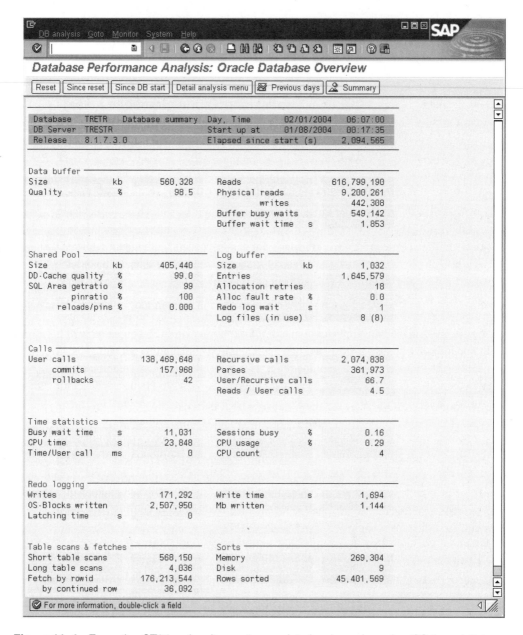

Figure 11–4 Executing ST04 makes it easy to correlate hardware-based or OS-based disk statistics with activity borne by and seen at the SAP application layer.

- DB02, to validate to what extent the database is growing, broken down by table size and index size if this level of granularity is required
- ST06, the OS Monitor, which provides details like the number of processes waiting on the CPU, CPU user utilization versus system utilization versus idle time, pages in (important to monitor for Windows-based systems) and pages out (important for Unix systems), and much more
- ST07, which makes it easy to track how a particular test run ramped up, leveled out, and then ramped down in terms of total logged-in users, active users, users in a work process, and so on
- AL08, to provide per-application-server statistics related to the number of active users on each server, as well as total users
- SM50 for each application server, to determine whether a work process entered PRIV mode, indicating it needed to access heap memory
- ST22, to simply track the growing number of ABAP dumps for the day (which helps validate that your stress-test transactions executed successfully to completion)
- SM12, to record whether a long-time table lock existed during a stress-test run
- SM31, for very specific requirements related to the contents of a particular database table (this represents one way to verify a database update was indeed made)
- SM66, to provide a global work process overview (displays the number of concurrent work processes across all instances of the system)
- ST03 or ST03N, for workload details relevant to a particular time period, including total dialog steps processed for each type of work process, data transferred per transaction, and response-time specifics
- SU53, to display any failed authorization checks for the currently executing virtual or physical user (e.g., which might then explain why a transaction failed from a security perspective—a last-minute change to authorizations made way too often in the real world)

To be honest, I still find myself using some of these scripts even today—once they are scripted, they are easy to modify for use in a new SAP system or stress-test/performance-tuning project. In the case of long-running stress tests, for example, I find that SM66, ST07, and AL08 are perfect for verifying in real time the load I expected to generate, especially in the context of logon load balancing and using realistic think times (e.g., 30 seconds or so). As a reminder, transactions SM50 and SM66 allow you to display the status of dialog, update, and other work processes, the latter of which is arguably one of the most powerful cross-application T-codes available. That is, SM66 is perfect for monitoring multiserver mySAP systems by monitoring active work processes across the *entire* system—it leverages an RFC connection to take a quick peak at each application server in your system, so as to provide a holistic view. Remember what I said previously, though—if your system is so busy that SM66 doesn't have the time to establish these RFC connections (as in the case of a smoke test), you can disable this feature via the Settings button, and instead view only the local application server's load.

11.6.3.   The Power of ST03N

Before we move on, a quick note regarding ST03N is in order. Take care in using this latest iteration of the classic ST03 transaction (which is no longer available on the newest SAP Web AS–based SAP products). ST03N is as powerful as ever, but it defaults in a new installation to collecting data only for 2 days (and then rolling this up for 2 weeks, and then 2 months). You'll want to change this default for your testing project to something like 60 days, 20 weeks, and 14 months—providing you with plenty of performance data should you ever need it after the fact (assuming the system has not been restored, of course). Make this change by getting into Expert mode (click the top-left button named Administration, until it toggles to Expert), and then click on the Collector and Performance DB icon, then the Performance Database icon, and finally the Reorganization page (or Collector and Reorg page, depending on the version of the Basis layer). From here, I suggest that you update the retention times for standard data, and then click the Save Values button before exiting. Although a bit involved, the process described here is not nearly as difficult to follow as it might seem. Refer to Figure 11–5 for an illustration of a sample Collector and Reorg page—note that the 2-day/week/month defaults are shown here.

Although these scripts are easy to develop and use, and nearly as simple to maintain, over the last 1 or 2 years SAP AG has given us some of the greatest monitoring tools ever produced out of Walldorf. These products—specifically CCMS Monitoring and the SAP Solution Manager—are discussed next.

11.6.4.   CCMS Monitoring and Alerts

Frankly, I failed to capitalize on the value that the CCMS Monitor Sets (accessible via RZ20) could provide until early in 2003. RZ20 supports cross-application monitoring and management, much of which is either overkill or inappropriate for stress testing. But there are some really compelling reasons to consider using this tool for monitoring performance-oriented test runs, like the ability to

- Leverage definable thresholds. This can make for very straightforward success criteria, because either a test will "stay green" or fall away in the yellow or red zones.
- Leverage a great number of CCMS monitor templates. Many predefined templates are available by default, from performance- and workload-oriented templates to templates that drill down into dialog activity, the OS, and even the entire system.
- Create very precise monitors, or on the other hand, very broad ones.
- Specifically monitor many different mySAP components, like EBP, CRM, and much more.
- Leverage the ability to monitor interfaces to non-SAP Basis systems as well, like ITS.

See *service.sap.com/systemmanagement* for more details.

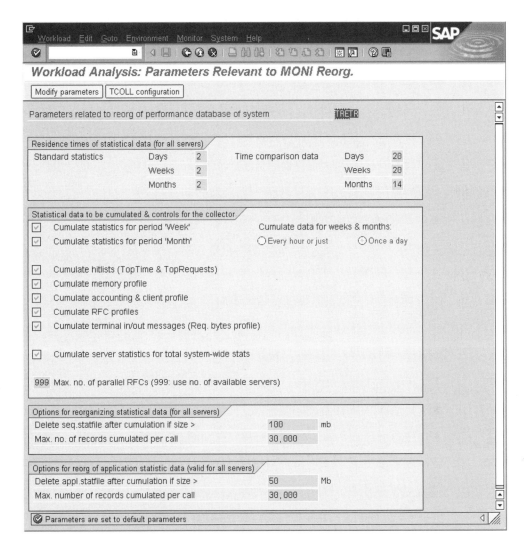

Figure 11–5   Default data collection parameters of 2 days, 2 weeks, and 2 months should be changed and saved prior to executing any test runs.

11.6.5.   SAP Solution Manager

Use the Solution Manager to display the kind of data available via RZ20 in a business process–oriented context. To this end, Solution Manager's *Optimization Services* are ideal for testing and tuning engagements and support continuous improvement through capacity planning, configuration management, system upgrade/migration services, and, more to the point, performance optimization.

Solution Manager is simple to install—it's an add-on (e.g., similar to an industry solution) and therefore is installed via transaction SAINT. Out of the box, it supports application and system monitoring, technical monitoring of your mySAP.com solution (including the availability of interfaces, individual system components, service-level reporting, and complete business process monitoring). And it provides a graphical alert monitor. All systems that are to be monitored must be defined with a graphical tool. Keep in mind that at least one system must be defined in the graphical tool so that you can take advantage of the Service Level Reporting function. Just add the system's SID, the installation number (for SAP systems), and the system type (e.g., R/3, CRM, BW), and you'll be in business.

11.6.6.   Finalizing Your Execution Checklist

With all that has been covered in this and previous chapters, it should be clear by now that there are many steps that must be executed over and over again for each test run of a stress test. You should have already created a strawman execution checklist. Now, as you begin to go through pre-test-week test runs, tweak and customize this checklist to reflect the individual 30 or so steps necessary to execute a consist and repeatable test run. Beyond the more obvious steps found in such a checklist, ensure you take into account the following steps as well:

- Start all monitoring tools—include everything across the SAP Technology Stack, from PerfMon logs and hardware data-capture utilities, to the database-specific Enterprise Manager, SAP CCMS scripts, the SAP MMC or other systems-management utilities or applications, and so on.
- Note timing—include any timing requirements for commencing scripts or other activities. I suggest automating this as much as possible, of course, but regarding how often you might execute manual monitoring tasks, it usually makes sense just to record how often this must occur in your checklist (every 2 to 3 minutes is typical).
- Validate CPU, RAM, disk, network, and other core hardware subsystem performance on a repeatable basis.
- Capture the number of active work processes, users, and sessions to later correlate this with the workload being processed.

A completed execution checklist is available for your review on the ftp site.

11.6.7.   No Breathers in the Real World!

With all of the tasks outlined in this chapter behind us, it only seems right to take a breather before test week. After all, the time and tasks related to everything that has been accomplished over perhaps the last few weeks or even months hasn't left much room for half-day Fridays, Aloha Wednesdays, and long lunches. On the contrary, developing the business process scripts to be executed during test week and setting up the infrastructure necessary for single-user and multiuser load testing alone probably made for some really long nights.

Unfortunately, your schedule won't be getting much better anytime soon. Not to say that all of your preparation and planning won't pay off—it will, and in a big way. But just like a real-world complex enterprise system, problems will tend to crop up at the last minute and things will tend to "break" at the most inopportune times. For the folks engaged in supporting test week, it may seem at times like no matter what level of preparation is taken up front, test week will represent more work than any other period of time.

In fact, although I like to label the period of time spent executing and monitoring test runs as "test week," it's important to understand that I use the term pretty loosely. For discrete testing activities, you might be looking at a day or two of actual testing. As I've said elsewhere, though, it's not unusual for this "week" to actually run 2 calendar weeks and maybe longer in the case of large-scale Go-Live tests . You can gain a lot of real-world knowledge with load testing, after all, and 5 to 7 days come and go quickly. Some of the extra time spent in test week will probably result from interesting twists or opportunities that present themselves and simply offer too much compelling value to ignore. For example, I've been asked to broaden the scope of perhaps half of the stress-test projects I've worked on simply because my client suddenly recognized the value of ramping to a user count or batch process load greater than we originally planned on, wished to test the kind of impact a mass Central User Administration update might have in a test environment, or wanted to measure the delta between the in-place network infrastructure or server platform and something new that walked in the door that week. We'll cover many of these value-adds—squeezing the last bit of value out of all the time and energy spent in preparing for and executing our test runs—in the final chapter of this book. But first, on to test week!

11.7. Tools and Approaches

We're almost ready to begin testing. I suggest you take a closer look at the following items, however, to gain a clearer understanding of how each of these fits into a testing and tuning preparatory role. Download my samples from the ftp site and fine-tune these for your own purposes, too:

- A completed execution checklist.
- A checklist identifying the steps necessary to install the MMC and SAP snap-in on a machine of your choosing. I install this as part of my core monitoring infrastructure, making it easy to collect a certain amount of systemwide performance data. In addition, it provides the ability to start and stop instances, review real-time status and errors, and more.
- Sample Basis monitoring scripts, recorded in AT1.

Executing and Monitoring Stress-Test Runs

Finally, the big event has arrived! Whether it's a full week, a couple of weeks, or maybe just a couple of days, the start of your official stress-test runs marks a significant milestone in your test plan. But to successfully pull off stress "test week," many things must come together, just as they did in the days and weeks preceding test week. This chapter is dedicated to covering those things, in effect walking you through an actual stress test and helping you deal with the trials and tribulations that are common along the way. Thus, how I leverage my own custom execution checklist as a tool for establishing and managing predictable test runs plays a big role in this chapter, as does how I monitor individual test runs both up front and throughout each run. For the best general level of consistency and the broadest degree of relevance, I focus on executing my stress test primarily on the Wintel platform. However, because something as complex as monitoring the performance of complex business processes spanning multiple mySAP components often touches more than one platform in the real world, I highlight other tools and approaches that have proven useful to my colleagues and me in the past. Likewise, because multiple platforms usually necessitate more than one performance-monitoring utility, I reach down deep into my tool bag to leverage some of the many technology-stack-specific performance-monitoring solutions. Doing so is often the only way to gather a broad base of performance data, which will in turn be analyzed (in the next chapter) to be subsequently used in iterative performance-oriented test and tuning runs.

12.1. Repeatable, Repeatable, Repeatable!

Before I dive into test-run execution, discussion of a couple of high-level housekeeping items is in order. First and foremost, my mantra now and for the remainder of the testing and analysis stages is "consistency"—everything I do must be repeatable, predictable, and completely documented. If I make a change, regardless of how slight—to my test infrastructure, a script, a test package used to execute a script, the data, or even processes I will use in starting, ramping up, executing, monitoring, and ramping down my test run—I *must carefully document this change*. In a perfect world, close attention to test-run documentation would be unnecessary, because there would be no change to a test environment or test data throughout all of test week. Perfection is all that's required . . . or a miracle. But given that only two men have ever walked on water, and

I didn't make that list, one thing I'm sure of is that I will encounter problems along the way. I'll be forced to deal with those problems and will likely do so by making changes in my test environment, however small or insignificant these problems might seem at the time. Perhaps I'll need to add more test client drivers. Maybe one of my business scripts will fail to run to completion. Maybe my data will prove flawed in certain business cases, cases I failed to test thoroughly enough. Maybe I'll need to change the timing I use in ramping up virtual SAP users because the system is not capable of handling the load I expected at the rate I expected to introduce it. And maybe I'll simply be the victim of a tripped circuit breaker, and find myself restoring databases instead of executing test runs. Regardless of the reason, if I fail to capture these problems and track their resolutions, or forget to explain why a particular situation caused me to make a change to the test plan, these seemingly innocuous changes could have quite serious ramifications, such as discussed in the following:

- Each change represents a window of opportunity to impact a test run's end results; in the end, any change may positively or negatively affect response time or throughput metrics, making future apples-to-apples comparisons suspect at best, useless at worse.
- An undocumented change makes re-creating a particular configuration, scenario, or situation impossible, and makes a future apples-to-apples comparison impossible.
- At the end of the day, the real value of the testing becomes questionable.
- More important, undocumented changes increase the risk that a future Production system's availability will be compromised, or SLA targets missed.

All of the aforementioned points are important, but the last one is arguably the most important because it speaks to the uptime a system may fail to provide. For example, the application of even the most trifling of firmware updates, OS patches, or SAP support packages constitutes a fundamental change to a system. If the change goes undocumented, and your stress-test runs ultimately result in promoting a new solution stack model into Production, chances are good that you'll miss the update that was tested during test week and actually wind up promoting a solution stack into Production unlike the one that was tested. The end result? You'll have introduced unknowns into Production, and will unwittingly live with the risk inherent to these unknowns. A robust checklist-based testing method, one that yields repeatable and predictable results, will keep you out of all of this trouble, plain and simple.

12.1.1.   Establish the Baseline

Early the first day of testing, once I get my hands on a Diet Coke and whatever other vending machine fodder is around to get beyond the "I'm still not a morning guy" thoughts I tend to have before noon, my goal is clear: to do what I need to do to establish a test baseline. It's during this first day of testing that I hope to work through 99% of the miscellaneous issues that are sure to crop up, and walk away that evening with at least a baseline test run. The importance of a baseline might seem obvious, but consider the following:

- A baseline gives me a starting point, so that I can treat changes to my test plan, scripts, data, and so on as simply "iterations" in testing. One of these iterations might even become my "new" baseline.
- A good baseline must, however, be repeatable. I need to be able to essentially follow the same method and, in doing so, obtain the same results, a feat that's a bit harder than it sounds.
- In the same way, a baseline must not only be repeatable from an execution perspective, it must also be repeatable in terms of the processes used to collect quantifiable performance data.
- Without a baseline to quantify the initial performance characteristics of a particular configuration, all subsequent testing is for naught, because there's nothing to really compare future tests against.

Baselines are interesting—you need a baseline from which to measure changes to your system's performance down the road. But you also don't want to put too much stock in a single baseline test run. That is, "one version of the truth" (as one of my newest and favorite customers in New York likes to say), though generally a good idea, has no place when it comes to baselines. So multiple baseline runs, averaged to remove statistical outliers, have always been my preference. This process allows you to "prove" that your baseline is inherently repeatable, too, at least within an acceptable margin of error (5%–10%, though greater or smaller margins may be acceptable or even mandatory, depending on your situation). Creating more consistent baselines, and making them repeatable, is discussed next.

12.1.2.   Not Once, but Twice

After working through any issues I've faced up front, and finally completing what I consider a baseline test run, there's still more work to be done in terms of ensuring the baseline itself is consistent and repeatable. This is especially important early in test week, because the methods, tools, and processes used in the beginning need to stay reasonably the same throughout the week. So once I execute a baseline run to completion, I need to turn around and do it all again, and, it is hoped, realizing nearly the same results. Every test will be conducted in the same manner—not once, but twice. For my most risk-averse or skeptical customers, I adopt a "three-times" approach (or more!).

At the end of each pair of runs, a bit of quick analysis is in order to ensure the results are indeed consistent. In a perfect world, it would be nice to see identical results, of course. But as is much more often the case, a variance of plus or minus some percentage needs to be established instead. Results within this variance—like 5% or 10%, as I mentioned before—usually equate to a consistent test, whereas results outside of an acceptable variance suggest the following:

- An inconsistent test case, package, or even script startup, execution, and shutdown processes (i.e., the time necessary to ramp up, level out, ramp down, and so on).

- Package inconsistencies in terms of options enabled (e.g., the ability to see real-time the steps executing within a script) or configuration details (e.g., whether results logging, or the myriad of details pertaining to this, is enabled). Changing these kinds of configuration settings in a test tool will change how quickly a test case executes.
- Inconsistency within the scripts or test cases themselves. Perhaps the randomization techniques being employed are simply "too random," resulting in wide discrepancies between test runs.
- Inconsistency in terms of the workload generated, from a logged-in user or business process perspective, to the scripts executed within a particular package or test case.
- Data inconsistencies, leading to execution inconsistencies (e.g., customers or materials associated with particular company codes may invoke differing behind-the-scenes checks or other processing).
- Inconsistent monitoring processes that result in less than accurate measurements test to test.

It's important to note that test results outside of an established variance may still embody some of the inconsistency problems just described. So I also use the checklist just described to help me review and refine tests that appear consistent and successful. Perhaps my variance was simply too wide, or I made some changes and failed to capture them in my documentation.

On the other hand, I've used variances that were too narrow as well—for example, customer-imposed requirements (the desire to select random sales orders from a list of thousands, many of which were quite dissimilar in nature) made it impossible to execute a test run that only varied 5% in terms of response time. In these cases, it was necessary to establish up front the fact that individual test results would vary, and therefore that many test loops would be required to create a pool of results which can then be averaged and analyzed as a group, rather than as individual test runs.

12.1.3.   In the Real World, Make Only One Change at a Time

An essential characteristic of any test—functional, stress, regression, whatever—is that subsequent test runs only allow a single factor to be changed between test runs. This is true whether we're talking about changing configuration details specific to the test run or infrastructure itself, or more commonly, application-level iterative tuning (e.g., SAP profile maintenance) that's taking place, or tuning the technology stack layers below SAP itself. In the first case, a change to the test itself creates something of a new baseline, which might be a goal in itself. For example, I've often run through tests where I had to change the order or speed with which my test run ramped up, simply because the technology stack did not scale as I expected it to prior to tuning. And, in the same manner, I've had to increase the amount of RAM in a database, reconfigure SAP profile parameters, add SAP application or client-driver servers in support of database smoke testing, and so on. These changes fundamentally changed the system being tested, and therefore each one represented a new baseline of sorts.

More often, though, I've been tasked with increasing the performance of the system being tested without fundamentally changing the technology stack—classic "tweaking." This kind of testing is more about hardware and software reconfiguration, a zero-sum kind of approach where nothing is really added or removed but instead simply changed. In these cases, the goal was to tune a customer's platform to maximize throughput or reduce response times. Sure, after the system was optimized I would often be asked to add and then test the impact of additional hardware resources (e.g., to provide incremental bandwidth for unexpected peaks or provide more just-in-case performance headroom). But without completing the iterative testing and tuning to maximize the platform's performance as it was initially configured, my customers would never have known exactly where the line was, and therefore at what load "capacity planning" became a critical-path necessity. In short, none of this tuning-derived value would have been possible without methodically testing the platform one change at a time.

12.2.   Pre-Test-Run Preparation

Before an individual test run or test case is executed, a number of activities may need to take place, and specific conditions may need to be satisfied. To be sure that I don't forget to perform one of these pre-test-run tasks, I make sure my execution checklist reflects even the smallest of details, discussed next.

12.2.1.   Prepare Your Execution Checklist

Given the execution checklist's dual roles of encouraging consistency and promoting good test runs by helping to ensure nothing is missed during startup, ramp up, execution, and ramp down, it should be no surprise that I keep harping on the value it provides. In the previous chapter, I walked through customizing this checklist to fit a specific stress test's needs. At this point, it's finally ready to be put to the test and actually used. A couple of steps need to be taken prior to every new test run, though:

- After ensuring your previous test run is indeed completed, file each checklist away in a safe place. That is, ensure you got everything you needed from the last test run, and get it all down on paper (physical or otherwise), as you prepare to start fresh on a new one.
- Update the electronic template of your checklist as required with any notes or changes that will *now* be required for the remainder of the test runs (e.g., if you've altered the starting sequence of your stress-test packages or in some other way fundamentally changed something that will likely remain changed throughout the remainder of testing).
- Print off a fresh copy of the checklist, or prepare a new electronic copy of the current template to be used for the next test run. I'm a big fan of keeping things on the laptop and avoiding paper when I can, but in the case of test runs, I still prefer the paper— maybe it's because there are so many other monitors and computers involved already, or because things are moving fast and paper allows me to quickly jot down notes along

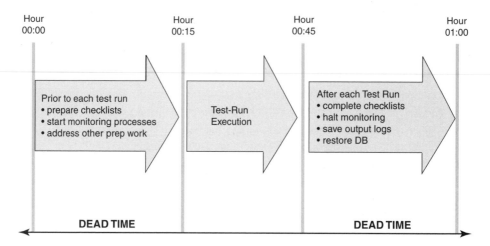

Figure 12–1   The time consumed actually executing stress tests consists of both test-run time and a substantial amount of preparation or "dead time."

with the data being captured. Regardless, it's comforting for me in some kind of way to do the paper-and-pencil thing as I move from task to task, and monitor to monitor. Later, I'll dump this information into Microsoft Word or Excel anyway.

• Label (or name) the current checklist with the date, time, and the test-run name appended with a number (e.g., R3_CRM_PLM_daily_load_001). Do this for every test run, even the unsuccessful ones—trust me, it makes things easier later on when you're sifting through performance logs and other information trying to correlate results with specific test runs.

If you're beginning to think there's a lot to do *in between* test runs, you've been paying attention. "Bravo, bravo," my 5-year-old daughter, Ashley, would tell you! This "dead time" between test runs can easily consume more clock time than the tests themselves, as shown in Figure 12–1. The next section covers a few ways to maximize your time, helping you speed through dead time between test runs without inadvertently introducing time-consuming errors or oversights.

12.2.2. Reducing the Time between Test Runs

The fleeting moments spent actually executing test runs, combined with the time necessary to prepare for each new run, add up fast. Because the test run itself is fairly well locked down in terms of time and is therefore inflexible, I do what I can to minimize the time spent both prior to and after each run. The biggest obstacles to overcome are those related to tasks like restoring one or more SAP databases, restarting systems, and going through a prelaunch checklist of activities that, in theory, should set the stage for a successful test run.

Just as important, after each test run, it's imperative to rapidly collect the minimal performance data necessary to prove you've completed a good test run. This does not necessarily mean capturing and filing away the complete record of performance statistics associated with the run—that step tends to come later, after the bulk of test runs have been completed. But a subset of these data needs to be pulled up and quickly analyzed just to ensure I've indeed had what appears to be a successful test run. Only then can I really begin the test-run process again (more on how I cover this process can be found later in this chapter).

Suffice it to say here, though, that if you take too long to gather data, or fail to prepare adequately up front, the number of test runs you can successfully complete in an 8-hour period will shrink accordingly, and the days associated with test week will therefore grow very long indeed, perhaps stretching into test weeks. Beyond simply executing very few runs per day, you might face an even worse fate if your preparation process is flawed—you might find yourself spinning your wheels, essentially tossing out many invalid test runs as you seek over and over again to complete a single good test run.

12.2.3.   Database Consistency: Leveraging Database Restores, Clones, and Copies

Most of the time, a baseline database restore is required prior to executing a new test run. The restore brings my test back to a known point in time, where all stock is plentiful, orders are ready to be delivered, customer accounts have credit to burn, and so on. Just as important, a known database state represents a specific technical state against which other tests can be measured. That is, the database is set at a particular size, each table consists of a known number of rows, and so on. Thus, as each test run executes and "internally" changes the database by virtue of inserts and appends, the effect on performance can be measured consistently—no particular test run enjoys an advantage over another simply because the database was a bit smaller or a table was less populated or consisted of fewer extents.

I've led or participated in a number of stress tests that did not require my team to make time for database restores. Although certainly not the norm, these tests were unique in that they consisted of read-only transactions that never even made a change to a database. In another project, the tests consisted of simple read- and update-based scripts that would only commit minor changes to a database (rather than inserts or appends), like updating a customer's address or material's description. In both cases, a zero-sum gain resulted and the database could therefore remain as-is throughout each test run, changing a bit over time in the latter case but never in a fundamental way that necessitated restoring the database to a known baseline.

Given that insert- and append-intensive stress tests are more real-world in nature and therefore better represent the world of SAP enterprises (of course, a heavy read-only load needs to be brought into the mix as well), it's more common in large testing efforts to be faced with a seriously time-consuming dilemma between test runs: How can the baseline database be quickly restored so that another test run can commence? The issue at stake is how to achieve rapid database consistency between runs, or how to quickly fall back to a known state. I have used, or seen used, the following approaches:

- Tape-based backup and restore of the entire database. Although one of the more universal solutions to this dilemma, it is nonetheless the most time-consuming and thus has, in the last 5 years, given way to the next approach.
- Disk-based backup/restore, which is faster than tape solutions but may still present a challenge for very large databases (for starters, you need twice the disk space originally planned). Essentially, the solution is to save a copy of the database at a file-system level (via a simple file-system copy command or OS utilities), and then use this copy from which to restore, prior to the start of a new test run. Because many shops don't stop at a single copy, choosing to maintain multiple copies for historical backup purposes, this gets expensive too!
- Software- and (more commonly) hardware-based mirrors. All OSs support mirroring in one manner or another, and beyond this, all SAP-certified hardware platforms support RAID controllers as well. The idea is to "break off" and therefore save a baseline copy of the database, to be used again only after resynchronizing the changed database back with the original disk volumes or physical disk drives, so that both "sides" of the mirror again represent the original baseline database. The potential for overwriting the baseline database with the updated version makes creating a repeatable process for resynching very important.
- Taking the previous approach to the next level, most enterprise-class disk subsystems support clone sets or business continuity volumes (BCVs), which are basically just a third set of mirrored drives that can be easily broken off and resynched through hardware-specific disk utilities. This removes some of the process-related dangers inherent to hardware-based mirrors, and is the fastest method of restoring a database to a known state. It takes only minutes to break out the clone set, and huge throughput speeds can be realized during the resync process, given that each disk may be concurrently written to (though this feature is hardware-specific—check with your own vendor for ballpark figures).

Other backup/restore solutions tend to be tossed around as well. One of the most exciting lately involves taking a snapshot of a particular database or disk volume, and then tracking only the changes made to that volume to a new Logical Unit Number (or LUN, which essentially maps one or more physical disk unit numbers to a logical unit number, which in turn is recognized as a physical disk by the OS) or set of disks. The benefit to this snapshot approach is that "breaking off" or creating the snapshot is nearly instantaneous. However, resynching such a snapshot may range from very simple to relatively complex—again, check with your hardware vendor to determine the tools available and costs required to support snapshots, and do your homework to verify that the time and potential complexity are worthwhile. This can be a wonderful solution overall! Beware of products that use RAM only to track the delta between your baseline database and the updated one, however, because power losses and other conditions put your data not yet physically committed to disk at risk. In these cases, the snapshot product may still be a great way to go—simply make a traditional tape- or disk-based backup for just-in-case purposes, and reap the benefits of snapshots.

12.2.4. Restarting All Systems

I'm often asked if it's *really* necessary to restart everything in between test runs. At the risk of sounding facetious, are you *really* interested in adopting stress-testing best practices, or do you prefer to waive consistency in favor of the even later hours you'll put in reactively troubleshooting future performance issues? Restarting your systems is all about providing a clean and consistent starting point for each test run and is more than just a little important. Consider the alternatives:

- If you opt not to restart your SAP Application Servers prior to each test run, the cache of each server will be empty the first time you execute a test run—and that test run will execute relatively slowly as SAP programs try to run from cache, determine the cache does not contain what is needed, and then are forced to access the database server and its disk subsystem. Thus, on the first test run, all programs will be first compiled from disk, a time-consuming process. However, subsequent test runs will benefit from the programs now sitting in cache and, comparatively speaking, will scream.
- Each change to your test—scripts, data, timing, and so on—will impact the mix of data found in the cache, too, causing inconsistency and introducing doubts as to how well a particular test run actually executed compared to its counterparts.
- In the same way, if you fail to restart the SAP database server, its data cache and procedure or other caches will also be empty on first starting, but will be filled otherwise with data last used by the most recent test run.
- Even the OS-based and hardware controller–based caches will suffer the same condition, because each will be empty after a restart and full of "hit-rich" data otherwise.

The problem at hand really becomes one of consistency versus availability versus time. If you are sure you won't experience the requirement to reboot your systems often, you might be able to afford the time "wasted" in executing test runs after the occasional reboot, and the time necessary to refill the caches at the different layers in the SAP Technology Stack. On the other hand, if you expect to live through the typical stress-test blow-ups, system meltdowns, locked-up client drivers, and occasional human errors that make system restarts a reality once or twice a day (and performance testing/tuning that much more interesting!), it makes a lot more sense to require such a restart prior to every single test run.

The level of restart necessary in your particular case is debatable as well. As I said in the previous list, even the hardware or OS-based caches are impacted by a test run. If you're more concerned with measuring the performance a particular solution stack provides after a certain amount of time has elapsed, or after a certain load has been supported, you might be able to get away without rebooting the entire test and client-driver infrastructure. That is, perhaps restarting the database and SAP Application Server instances will be "good enough." On the other hand, if your test includes a repeatable ramp-up, execution, and ramp-down component, or in any way includes monitoring and measuring performance at the layers beneath SAP, a full restart is the best way to go by far. Remember that, in the end, the greatest level of consistency mandates clear caches across the board, and therefore complete power-cycling. If in doubt, play it safe and, before executing a new test, restart *everything*.

12.2.5.   Real-World Prelaunch Systems Check

Beyond executing a database baseline restore process followed by a complete reboot of all infrastructure and test systems, many other tasks of a "prelaunch systems check" nature remain to be completed. I equate this stage of the preparatory process to the steps NASA takes prior to launching a rocket into space—without a repeatable list detailing the minutiae that must be performed or managed, something would be missed and accidents therefore would become quite common. The most typical examples of these real-world, important minutiae include the following:

- Restarting each system in the proper order, such that nothing gets in the way of bringing up the SAP test infrastructure or client-driver infrastructure.
- Verifying all systems are up and available after each system has been restarted, utilizing tools like the SAP MMC, service applet, and CCMS and transactions like SM51 to validate that a landscape is available and SM59 to check RFC connections, and so forth.
- Quickly reviewing event, error, and system logs prior to commencing a new test, to help ensure an otherwise undetectable issue with the potential to skew your test results has not surfaced.
- Starting client software components. For example, AutoTester AutoController's client components must be started prior to starting the Controller component.
- Starting any other special "lab test tools" as well. Tools like eTimer, AutoShutdown, and others serve a great purpose in that they help you achieve a repeatable test within strict management guidelines. These are not monitoring tools (which are covered in more detail later) per se; rather, these are simply tools that make conducting a test run much easier than is otherwise possible.

Next, the actual packages configured to execute a test case or test run must be reviewed again prior to initiating a new test run.

12.2.6.   Validate All Packages

My final act prior to kicking off all monitors, commencing the virtual-user login process, and releasing everything to execute is to verify that all AutoController (or similar) test packages are good to go. Remember, each package contains the scripts that will execute on a system, scripts that drive end-user logins and then execute the business processes that provide the "load" of a load test. This means that I need to do the following:

- I must edit each package to reflect start times, if I've elected to use this feature to automatically start my stress test at a prescribed time. For tests of more than, say, 100 users, it makes sense to stagger logins as well. I might therefore configure five different test packages, each set up to execute 100 virtual users, to start their respective SAP login or execution scripts 2 minutes apart, for instance.
- I need to ensure all communications settings, status processing (e.g., that related to receiving real-time line-by-line script status updates), virtual- or physical-user counts, and so on are set as they should be—consistent with other test runs. This is usually only a problem after a test run has bombed and, for example, I've changed things around for troubleshooting purposes.
- I also tend to rename the test packages in between test runs, reflecting the name and iteration of the test run to make it easier on me during the data analysis phase. This adds work in large testing efforts, though, to the point where you might prefer to sort things out after the fact (e.g., based on date/time stamps).
- If I'm using a staggered login approach, the virtual-user number becomes important and needs to be considered prior to kicking off any test runs. For example, if I've got a license for 500 virtual users, and use the number of the virtual user as a countdown timer, then user 500 will wait 500 seconds prior to logging in. If I've had to make any adjustments to login times, or the order in which functional packages are released, my timing will be off. Thus, it might be necessary to reallocate virtual users to packages at that time (which in itself might mandate a new baseline, depending on what I'm testing).
- If I'm in the midst of a series of tests that increase the user counts per package, now is the time to make those changes as well. Alternatively, I might need to create new test packages as well.
- Finally, if any scripts have undergone a revision, I have to change the script name as identified in the Scenario tab of a package (because I "version control" my scripts, as I recommend that everyone do).

After validating all test packages are ready to go, I'm now in a position synonymous with the final stages of a countdown.

12.3.   Ready . . . Set . . .

We're getting close—just a few more steps to complete before packages may be released and workloads may finally get underway. As I review the steps remaining in the execution checklist to be sure nothing has been missed, I need to take the time to note any problems thus far, or identify potential problems (e.g., the fact that a client-driver's connection seems flaky or a script is having trouble reaching its peak user load). And most important, I need to stay relaxed—this is no time to rush through anything. That is, my methodical approach to stress testing only really pays off in the next few minutes, and then only if I continue along the same path and carefully work my way through starting all of the various monitoring tool sets necessary to capture performance data that can later be analyzed.

12.3.1.   Gentlemen, Start Your Monitors!

Depending on the kind of test I'm executing, my project's success criteria, and the tools I've been granted, I may need to start only a single monitor (e.g., Microsoft's PerfMon or, in other cases, SAP's CCMS Monitor, RZ20) or I might need to start a slew of technology-stack-specific monitors. Of course, because I would have already been through all of the pretesting described in Chapter 11, at this point I'm keenly aware which monitors are required, and I know not only that the data I seek are indeed collected by these monitors but *how* to collect these data as well. So depending on my needs, I may start any or all of the following monitoring tools:

- Network layer. Any number of hardware-based sniffer products (or Microsoft Network Monitor) are intrinsically valuable to testing that must characterize the load between a front-end client and the SAP Application Servers (especially if slow links are in the picture). The same holds true for application server to database server traffic, too, or the traffic between ITS/Agate servers and their SAP Application Servers.
- Server hardware and OS layer. These tools are server- and OS-specific. For Windows-based solutions, I nearly always lean on PerfMon to provide a broad base of performance statistics (from network activity up through the OS to the database), configuring it to dump performance snapshots to a log file. Sometimes, I'll capture all statistics, though more often than not I'll narrow this down to specific hardware subsystems or OS constructs. For Tru64 or Digital Unix systems, *collect* provides just about all of the value I need in a monitoring tool while requiring only a very small fraction of a system's horsepower to execute (certainly not true for all Unix versions).
- Disk subsystem. For classic Digital- and Compaq HSG80–based and similar SANs, I depend on *vtdpy* or its GUI-enabled counterpart *DSview* to provide the raw MB per second throughput numbers and I/Os per second data points valuable to many stress-test exercises. These tools also provide detailed information related to the average blocksize, load on individual physical or logical drives, and more. A connection to the particular disk subsystem in question is required to use either of these tools. With newer HP/Compaq Enterprise Virtual Arrays or HP's Virtual Array (VA) product line, however, I need only a browser pointed to the system's SAN Management Appliance.
- Database layer. I typically do not need to start a database-specific monitor, because the data I need are readily available in part through the OS and in more detail via SAP CCMS (ST04 and DB02, in particular).
- SAP application layer. CCMS transactions executed in real time during the test run and via scripted Basis monitoring transactions started before the run commences form the foundation of my SAP-specific monitoring. In addition to the slew of transactions covered later in this chapter, I might also start RZ20 for "daily load" stress tests (after having cleared all events so that the CCMS monitor I am executing starts "green"), because this allows me to visually monitor the real-time status of buffers, workloads, response-time thresholds, and more.

- ITS layer. The ITS Administrator serves as the backbone for monitoring transaction-level activities and how they correspond to server loads.

Outside of these stack-specific tools, I might be inclined to execute one or more generic utilities or applications as well. Sometimes, the application depends on my customer's environment. For example, my customers that depend on BMC Patrol or HP OpenView may already have a set of monitors and monitoring criteria that could prove useful to me in a stress-test run. Indeed, they might even require using these tools to leverage standard or custom reports with which they are already familiar.

Other times, the decision to use a general systems-management tool may rest solely in my hands, rather than as an absolute requirement requested by my customer. For example, given my background with Compaq Computer Corporation, I often found myself running Compaq Insight Manager (CIM), not as a primary data collection tool but instead as a secondary way to gather network-, disk-, and CPU-related load and performance data. CIM acted as a "backup" to my primary data collection tools, helping me essentially to corroborate the data yielded from these other tools and approaches. And, because I've used it for years, issues with learning curves are minimal. In the same way, I've used PerfMon even when there's been no requirement to provide OS- or database-level performance statistics—the numbers still prove useful in validating throughput metrics pulled from ST03, ST04, ST06, and other SAP CCMS transactions.

As I mentioned before, another tool I use in monitoring a test run is a utility like eTimer, which is especially handy when it comes to executing a countdown and helping track when a particular milestone occurs (e.g., the login of the final SAPGUI client, signaling the start of the actual business processes). For a particular test run, I might set eTimer for a 40-minute countdown reflecting a 5-minute login period, a 15-minute ramp-up period, a 15-minute execution period, and a 5-minute cool-down period. I might use two or more timers to track multiple events, too, like the start of different functional scripts or after achieving a certain workload factor. And for test tools that support it, like AutoController, I might use both AutoController and eTimer to help me manage timing—I'll use AutoController to automatically launch a stress test at a prescribed time and use eTimer separately to track key events or milestones like those already discussed.

12.3.2. Log In to SAP

With all of my monitors up and running, and eTimer set for a countdown of perhaps 35 or 40 minutes, I'm at a point where the users may log in to SAP. I usually script this as a subroutine and use my staggered login approach to get everyone logged in as quickly as possible. However, I might choose instead to simply log in each virtual user and then have them all wait until I'm ready to commence the actual ramp-up or execution of a test. Thus, I might simply wait for the prescribed time established in each AutoController package to start the business process scripts, or I might manually release these test packages based on a set time tracked by eTimer (e.g., releasing a package exactly every 2 minutes until all packages are released). If I choose to manually release test packages, I try to choose a nice round clock time (e.g., 10:15 a.m. and 0 seconds precisely) to make calculations a bit easier going forward. Because the SAP login process itself is so resource-intensive and potentially time-consuming, it is important that I carefully note the start time of each login cycle, because I will also want to later ignore any performance statistics associated with this typically irrelevant phase of a stress-test run.

12.3.3.   Go!

When the time is right and either all users automatically start logging in or executing or I manually control this by releasing the test packages myself, the stress-test run has finally commenced. At this point, it's critical that I maintain strict control over timing. Why? Because everything from this point on is tightly linked to timing. If I allow a portion of a test to go too long, or foul up the timing and release a test package too soon, the following will occur:

- The load will be skewed, and therefore the test run will not faithfully reproduce the details associated with the baseline's load.
- The amount of work done, or throughput, will also be skewed, because more or fewer front-end clients will be involved and therefore the potential to create more or fewer sales orders, for example, will exist.
- Response times will accordingly differ from what they otherwise would have been (too great a load will naturally cause each business process to execute more slowly than it should have, for instance).

In effect, then, mucking around with the test run's timing represents a variable or change to the execution of the test run itself (in addition to the change or delta being tested in the first place), therefore breaking the cardinal rule: only one thing may change at a time. And the test run would therefore need to be tossed out and re-executed. This explains why I take extra precautions like using checklists, automating the release of test runs, or using timers—one less thing for me to worry about makes it that much more likely I won't screw things up. And maybe I'll make it home in time for dinner that night, too.

12.4.   Validating a Good Test Run: Initial Data Collection

Once the test run is underway, it would be nice to kick back for 1 or 2 minutes and reflect on what a great job I've done so far. Yeah, that would be nice. But there's really no time for that yet. For one thing, there are plenty of real-time monitoring details to attend to. But more than that, at this initial stage in a test run it is important to simply validate that I'm on my way to a successful run, and not a nightmare that will need to be aborted shortly. And, if possible, I'd prefer to make this determination sooner rather than later. So in my execution checklist I include performing a few tasks like the following: check that the scripts are indeed executing to completion, determine that the load (in terms of user counts and/or concurrent processes) seems to be heading in the right direction (typically up, at this point), check that the output from my scripted monitoring transactions seems valid, and, finally, determine that the test tool itself is not reporting any errors.

12.4.1. Inline Data Collection Output

For those of you who have already forgotten, let me remind you that my "practically patented" inline data collection subroutine is one of the coolest and most effective ways to collect performance-related and other data—data that validate how well a test run is executing. And it removes dependence on controller-related or postrun CCMS analysis. I execute an "inline data collection" subroutine after every loop in my scripted business transaction or process, such as after every successful completion of MM02 or VA03. The subroutine simply appends a lot of important data and other information useful in later proving I met or missed my success criteria and tosses these data out to a log file as a single line of comma- or tab-delimited text (which may then later be easily sorted or analyzed via Excel). Examples may be found on this book's ftp site.

With regard to validating that I'm on my way to a successful test run, though (before I get in too deep and waste lots of time), *manually* checking the output log file generated from this inline data collection routine makes good sense. I peruse this output at the file-system level, using something as simple as a text editor like SAPpad or Microsoft Notepad to view the output data. If the log doesn't exist, I've obviously got big problems—the scripts must not be running! Beyond this, though, if the log shows I'm not successfully completing a particular transaction (even though I've programmatically set up the output logic to do so) or displays errors or warnings regarding a transaction (like I've run out of stock, or hit a credit limit, or somehow uncovered a bad combination of data that never showed itself in single-user testing), I might need to stop the current test and go back and perform some troubleshooting before starting over and continuing on.

12.4.2. Scripted Monitoring Transaction Output

In addition to checking how well the inline data collection routine is running, I also take a quick peek at the output logs generated by any scripted monitoring transactions I've put together. Unlike business process transactions, these special monitoring transactions execute for the sole purpose of collecting data—things like how many users are logged into SAP, the load on the database server, and so on are all valuable metrics useful after the fact during the data analysis phase. Most often, I script one or more basic transactions like ST07 (the Application Monitor, the output for which is displayed in Figure 12–2) or AL08 (which displays currently active users, and helps you prove that logon load balancing is indeed distributing the load) to quantify how well ramp-up proceeds and, perhaps more important, whether I achieved my target active-user goals. In the past, I've also scripted SM66 to give me an idea as to how many concurrent processes are executing at a particular point in time across an entire system—another excellent indicator that a stress test is progressing normally. And a scripted ST06 can provide excellent data as to how busy a particular server is, in terms of CPU activity, memory and pagefile/swap utilization, and so on. In each of these cases, I set the scripted monitoring transaction to execute at a certain interval, like once every 10 to 30 seconds in the case of user counts, and once every minute or so for average concurrent processes or CPU snapshots. This method provides an excellent history of a test run from start to finish and provides excellent data with which to compare the output from database-, OS-, and hardware-based monitoring tools.

Application	Number of users			Sess.per	Appl.
	LoggedOn	Ative	In WP	User	Server
Basis Components	188	10	6	1.57	5
Controlling	9	1	0	1.44	3
Cross-Application Components	10	1	0	1.30	3
Financial Accounting	49	12	0	2.47	3
Logistics - General	34	4	0	2.18	3
Logistics Execution	46	4	2	2.63	3
Materials Management	96	13	2	2.07	3
Plant Maintenance	75	11	1	1.75	3
Production Planning and Control	16	2	0	3.19	3
Project System	5	2	0	1.40	2
Quality Management	2	2	1	2.00	2
Sales and Distribution	43	9	2	2.40	3
Other	37	5	1	1.86	3
Total	610	76	15	1.97	5

```
🗒 st07-output.txt - Notepad                                                                                    _ □ X
File  Edit  Format  View  Help  defax
X, ST07,, ST07 Output, Test, 4/2/2003, 11:54:09 AM, ResponseTime=, 1.802, LoggedOn=, 279, ActiveUsers=, 182,
UsersInWP=,      15, AvgSessions=,      1.99, NumberOfServers=,      7,
X, ST07,, ST07 Output, Test, 4/2/2003, 11:55:15 AM, ResponseTime=, 1.642, LoggedOn=, 299, ActiveUsers=, 188,
UsersInWP=,      14, AvgSessions=,      1.99, NumberOfServers=,      7,
X, ST07,, ST07 Output, Test, 4/2/2003, 11:56:08 AM, ResponseTime=, 1.703, LoggedOn=, 308, ActiveUsers=, 200,
UsersInWP=,      13, AvgSessions=,      1.98, NumberOfServers=,      7,
X, ST07,, ST07 Output, Test, 4/2/2003, 11:57:14 AM, ResponseTime=, 1.703, LoggedOn=, 316, ActiveUsers=, 212,
UsersInWP=,      23, AvgSessions=,      1.98, NumberOfServers=,      7,
X, ST07,, ST07 Output, Test, 4/2/2003, 11:58:08 AM, ResponseTime=, 1.732, LoggedOn=, 339, ActiveUsers=, 277,
UsersInWP=,      36, AvgSessions=,      1.98, NumberOfServers=,      7,
X, ST07,, ST07 Output, Test, 4/2/2003, 11:59:14 AM, ResponseTime=, 1.632, LoggedOn=, 376, ActiveUsers=, 295,
UsersInWP=,      44, AvgSessions=,      1.99, NumberOfServers=,      7,
X, ST07,, ST07 Output, Test, 4/2/2003, 12:00:03 AM, ResponseTime=, 1.753, LoggedOn=, 401, ActiveUsers=, 299,
UsersInWP=,      46, AvgSessions=,      1.99, NumberOfServers=,      7,
X, ST07,, ST07 Output, Test, 4/2/2003, 12:01:11 AM, ResponseTime=, 1.010, LoggedOn=, 490, ActiveUsers=, 341,
UsersInWP=,      56, AvgSessions=,      1.99, NumberOfServers=,      7,
X, ST07,, ST07 Output, Test, 4/2/2003, 12:02:04 AM, ResponseTime=, 1.722, LoggedOn=, 500, ActiveUsers=, 399,
UsersInWP=,      70, AvgSessions=,      1.99, NumberOfServers=,      7,
```

Figure 12–2 ST07 presents key real-time data as to how many users are logged in and actively executing transactions in a test run.

You may have noticed that the ST07 and SM66 transactions previously mentioned are "global" in nature. That is, they reflect the load placed on an entire system, not just a single application server. What this means is that they leverage an RFC connection to other nonlocal hosts, however, which in turn consumes test-system resources. Unfortunately, if the stress or load placed on a system is great (as is often the goal), it may be impractical to get timely systemwide updates. All work processes might be busy, for instance, especially if the test mix includes long-running dialog-based transactions (and if I've changed the default dialog timeout value from 5 minutes to perhaps 1 hour). So checking the output logs generated from monitoring scripts like these may prove only that the monitoring transaction has not executed in a while, presumably due to a lack of available work processes. In these cases, executing the same monitoring transaction in real time will yield no real data either, because the transaction will *still* remain unable to connect to other systems, again, due to a lack of available work processes. For this reason, then, it's helpful to take advantage of a monitoring approach that is neither SAP-specific nor tied to a particular technology stack—it's time to rely on the test tool's standard and advanced monitoring capabilities, discussed next.

12.4.3.   Real-Time Test-Tool Feedback

All SAP-aware testing tools provide some kind of real-time feedback during a test run's execution. AutoController, for example, provides an intuitive color-coded interface that makes it easy

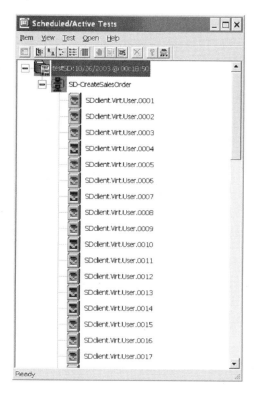

Figure 12–3 AutoController's use of color-coding and special icons makes it clear which test packages are executing and which virtual users are still successfully running.

to determine if a virtual user is actively processing or having problems doing so. It also displays users that have started and subsequently stopped (blue on the screen) versus those that are still executing (green). The use of additional colors and specially shaped icons makes it easy to organize different test objects while highlighting potential issues, too, as seen in Figure 12-3.

And beyond the Schedule/Active Tasks window, AutoController provides real-time feedback as to when a test run started and stopped, the name of the log file relevant to a particular test package, and the name and directory location of additional "logged" data. Status information relevant to each virtual user and its specific start and stop times, elapsed test time, completion status, and whether detailed results are available may all be accessed via AutoController, too, as shown in Figure 12–4.

12.5. Real-Time Use of SAP Monitoring Tools

So much to do, so little time. You're in the middle of a test run, and before you know it, your stress-test run will be over. It's critical now more than ever to carefully monitor the remainder of the test run. I use a combination of approaches to watch over SAP application-layer test runs, consisting

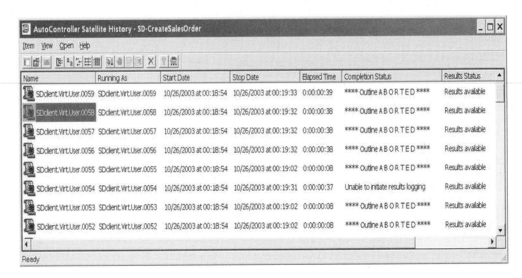

Figure 12–4   AutoController provides a comprehensive window into the status of your stress-test run, valuable in helping to pinpoint the reasons a test run failed.

primarily of SAP CCMS performance-oriented transactions and, more recently, RZ20—the CCMS Monitor.

12.5.1. CCMS Alert Monitoring via RZ20

As I mentioned earlier, RZ20 has been around awhile but I personally only started using it over the last year. It's a powerful transaction in that it provides a standard set of SAP monitors—screens or views customized for a particular set of activities or technical areas, like buffers, the change and transport system, the file system and database, and much more, as shown in Figure 12–5—while also providing the ability to specifically monitor mySAP components along with non-SAP interfaces. And because it covers SAP R/3 release 3x up through the most current Web AS–enabled solutions, RZ20 can represent a big part of the one-stop-shopping answer to your daily load-testing or change-control-driven testing prayers.

I find RZ20 most useful in monitoring whether a certain load exceeds a configuration's current-state tuning. That is, after tuning buffers, optimizing other profiles' parameters, and generally tweaking a system, RZ20 provides a straightforward method of measuring whether a particular workload runs well on the updated configuration or if more tuning is required. And it's all so easy—just execute your test run and watch in real time for buffer overruns, long-running work processes, long DB Request times, unusual disk queue lengths, poor front-end network response time, and so much more, as shown in Figure 12–6.

If you find a certain parameter setting acceptable, but find that it keeps displaying yellow or red in the monitor, simply change the preconfigured (or customized, whatever the case may be) CCMS Monitor threshold. All in all, RZ20 is one of the simplest to use and best holistic monitoring tools I've used for testing.

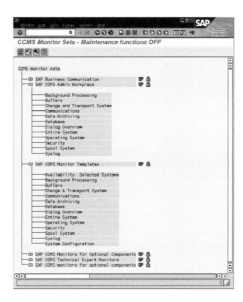

Figure 12–5 When it comes to testing that seeks to prove the viability of your painstakingly precise and iterative tuning (like that associated with supporting your daily average load), RZ20 is comprehensive enough to cover much of your SAP Technology Stack.

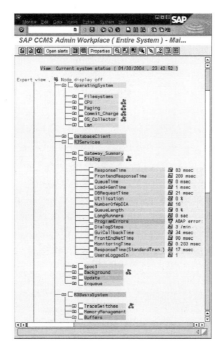

Figure 12–6 RZ20 provides real-time visibility into how well your tuning efforts pay off in a particular stress-test run.

12.5.2.   Discrete SAP CCMS Transactions

As an SAP Basis consultant for 7 years now, certain habits die hard. That is, I love the capabilities provided by RZ20 and the newer SAP Solution Manager, but I still find myself returning to
a core set of monitoring and performance-oriented transactions every time I support a customer's
performance-tuning and stress-testing project. I've covered a number of my favorites like ST07
and SM66 quite a bit already. These and some of my other CCMS favorites, discussed in more
detail here, include:

- STAD (formerly STAT) displays statistical details sorted by either date/time, detailed
  business transactions, or summarized business transactions. And because it also allows
  you to limit your searches to a particular user, transaction, program, or task type, and
  then further limit your search criteria by whether key response-time metrics have been
  exceeded, STAD provides great value when it comes to monitoring and later analyzing
  specific test-run results. This transaction is explained a bit more later in this section,
  and in great detail in Chapter 13.
- ST03 and ST03N, like STAT and STAD, provide insight into response times and other
  performance metrics, but they also allow you to delve into higher-level workload
  specifics.
- ST02, the Tune Summary, is useful in determining real-time how your various buffers
  are performing in terms of percentage utilization and color-coded to help identify potential issues quickly.
- ST04, the Database Performance Analysis Monitor, is useful in understanding the mix
  of reads to writes, sequential to direct operations, physical to logical disk accesses,
  number of changes/updates/inserts, quality and size of key database buffers, and
  much more.
- DB02 is another database monitor that lets you look into table and index details, including size and other space statistics (providing insight into how quickly a database is
  growing over time). And DB02 lets you display missing indexes as well.
- ST06, the OS Monitor, is perfect for monitoring CPU status in terms of the workload
  queued over the last 1, 5, and 15 minutes. ST06 also give you access to real-time and
  historical data related to memory swapping/paging, low-level disk access and disk
  queue details, and similarly low-level network access details.
- SM04, AL08, and ST07 provide insight as to the number of currently active or online
  users connected to the system. AL08 provides this information systemwide (or globally, by application server instance), whereas SM04 only allows you to view the users
  logged in to the application server instance you happen to be connected to. SM04 is a
  bit more limited, but also allows you to view the details regarding an end user's session,
  and terminate that session if desired.
- SM50 displays the status of work processes (both active and inactive) on the current
  application server. By clicking the clock icon, it's easy to tell how busy each work
  process has been over time and therefore whether any bandwidth exists for incremental
  work to be executed or processed.

- SM66 is similar to SM50 though with the difference (a very good one, in this case) that only active work processes are displayed by default. The snapshot of activity that SM66 provides is invaluable, however, in that *all* application servers are displayed (an RFC connection is made in real time to each server, as discussed in more detail in Chapter 11).
- ST09 (Network Alert Monitor), AL02 (Database Alert Monitor), AL03 (OS Alert Monitor), AL05 (Workload Alert Monitor), ST12 (Application Monitor), and RZ08 (CCMS Alert Monitor) are all valuable monitoring transactions, especially in older SAP releases (as was STUN, used for general performance monitoring).

Before we move on, I want to express a bit more of my appreciation for STAD. By default, a great amount of data are available—response-time statistics are broken down by CPU, database request, kilobytes transferred, and more. But some of the real power in STAD lies in the fact that you can customize its output by selecting what you wish to view from a long list of options (see Figure 12–7). From the main screen, simply click the F9 button (called "Select Output Fields") and click what you'd like to have included in your custom output screen, keeping in mind the limit of 255 characters per line that may be piped out to the display. In this way, it is easy to add otherwise isolated or hard-to-find performance metrics, such as the following: roll-in/roll-out details,

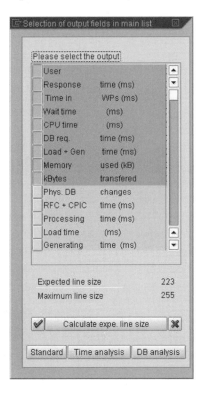

Figure 12–7 As a monitoring tool, STAD is superior to many others in that its output can be specified, configured, and customized.

sequential read details (including database rows read, physical reads, buffer requests, and more), similar details on updates and inserts, the terminal ID of the workstation creating the workload, the work process number used, whether the work process went into PRIV mode (private mode, which indicates it's using heap memory, and therefore will require a restart after the last user has finished its current task), the number of RFCs processed, the client used, GUI build time, and much more.

Other transactions prove useful as well if your stress test goes awry or if you simply need to validate or review a particular piece of technical configuration information. For example, the SAP system log may be reviewed via SM21, RFC connections may be validated via SM59 and monitored via SMQS (qRFC monitor for SAP), active gateway connections may be monitored via SMGW (gateway monitor), lock entries and updates may be reviewed using SM12 and SM13, respectively, and SMLG can be used to help you understand how current logon load-balancing groups are configured. Transaction SM51 not only allows you to connect to any server displayed in green but gives you the ability to establish a real-time RFC connection to another SAP Application Server in your system. Further, use RZ21 to set thresholds and other parameters used by RZ20, use RZ03 and RZ04 to display and configure or change "Op Modes," respectively, and use ST11 to review work process traces and similarly related error logs. Do you have any off-limit transactions that need to be locked down? Use SM01 to list (in alphabetical order) any transaction, and then lock it down in a few easy steps.

And in cases where I have used the SAP Job Scheduler to help me drive a stress test, using SM37 to review the current status or start condition of a job is helpful. I also tend to use SE38 or SA38 to execute manually jobs that have been scheduled, useful in troubleshooting problem variants or validating timing of a single transaction under no load. Sometimes I'll even script jobs to run using SE38 or SA38, simply to make their execution eminently repeatable.

For the deepest level of troubleshooting problem test runs, I suggest setting up and executing traces. SAP system traces may be conducted through ST01, whereas SQL traces can be executed using ST05. I often draw on the insight provided by ST22, too, because it provides a summarized cumulative update as to how many short dumps or ABAP runtime errors have occurred since the system was brought up, as well as the details surrounding each dump—this can help easily narrow down the problem transactions you might be running into in a last-minute stress test of modified business processes. And if you need to pull up disp+work traces or for that matter any other file (e.g., tpparam or another configuration file) at an OS level, use AL11. Finally, the System Administration Assistant (transaction SSAA) can be useful across the board in administrative circumstances—the color-coded output of SSAA allows you to track whether a particular operational task has been performed or whether a condition has been explored, for instance.

12.5.3.   Don't Forget the OS Monitoring Tools!

Beyond using PerfMon for viewing real-time and logged statistics on Microsoft's solutions, other OS-based tools are available and simple to use, too. And these tools, just like PerfMon, come with added benefits. For example, if the SAP system I happen to be testing is so bogged down with stress testing that I can't make much progress with SAP CCMS (perhaps because no work process is available), command-line tools like *sar* and *iostat* for Unix save the day. My favorites include the following:

- For HP-UX, I use *sar -u 10 180*. In this way, I can pull CPU statistics every 10 seconds for 180 periods (equating to 30 minutes). Details include the percentage of activity related to performing user computations, system (kernel) computations, I/O wait time, and idle time.
- Also for HP-UX, I like to execute *sar -d 10 180*, which for 30 minutes provides snapshots every 10 seconds related to disk activity—queue lengths, percentage of time that the disk was busy, number of reads and writes executed per second, average wait and service times, and more.
- For Tru64, everything I could ever want is provided by the Collect utility.
- For many flavors of Linux, *iostat -x 10 180* will provide extended CPU- and disk-related statistics. For example, the number of read or write requests merged per second that were issued to the device, sectors read from and written to devices, average size of these reads or writes, queue lengths associated with activity, time necessary for I/O requests to be serviced, the percentage of CPU time consumed in support of I/O requests (broken down by user and system/kernel), CPU idle time, and more are displayed by this handy utility.
- Sun Solaris and IBM AIX also support the *iostat* command, and provide similar results. Refer to their respective OS administration guides for details.

A quick note of clarification is in order regarding the CPU statistics *% Privileged Time* and *% User Time*, both of which are available on Windows and Unix boxes alike. The former measures the amount of time spent executing NT or Unix kernel commands, like those associated with SQL Server or Oracle I/O requests. On the other hand, % User Time indicates the amount of time spent actually executing applications like SQL Server or Oracle. So if the database I'm testing tends to find most or all of the objects it is seeking in the data cache, relatively little I/O is generated—this can result in a % Privileged Time as low as 5% to 15%. The amount of % User Time can easily climb to 85% to 95% percent in these cases, though.

On the other hand, if the database server's RDBMS generates a large quantity of I/O that must hit physical disk, then the % Privileged Time will be something greater than 30% to 40%, whereas the system's % User Time will be lower than previously discussed. In the end, analyzing both of these values provides great insight into how your system is performing. If the system is spending too much time doing I/O, I focus my efforts on the disk subsystem and what I can do to speed up I/O. And if I'm worried more about the database itself, I focus further on SQL trace activities to understand what's happening behind the scenes. This may include working with ABAPers and other developers to determine if it's possible to reduce the number of joins, provide better or updated indexes, change a table's buffering characteristics, and so on.

12.6. Winding Down Test Runs

Once eTimer, another timing mechanism, or a closely watched clock indicates that the majority of my test run is nearing completion, it's time to begin thinking about winding down or "ramping down" the test run. This is necessary because most of the time I set up test runs to execute indefinitely (for flexibility in where I later mark the start and stop times for that particular run) rather than for a set period of time or a specific number of loops. Note that I set up this ability to run indefinitely at the script level (through a logic-controlled perpetual loop) rather than at the controller level, because it lets me run the same script standalone or as a scenario/member within a larger package. A number of methods are available to ramp down a test, each with its own unique benefits and pitfalls.

12.6.1   Stopping a Test Run Gracefully: External Status Files

Back in 1997, I was exposed to what I believe still represents both the most elegant and the most useful approach for gracefully stopping a perpetually executing stress-test run. In a nutshell, the approach uses an OS-based text file like STATUS.txt—called a "status" file—and compares the contents of the single line of text within this status file with a "control" word like "stop" or "start." If "start" is found, the script's if-then logic either begins processing or continues to process; the loop of the script continues as normal. However, if the word "stop" is found, the script's if-then logic points to a subroutine within the script—or a completely different script, for that matter—that essentially closes all files, wraps things up, and logs the user off of SAP. The beauty of this approach is that it can be used with both network-based and local status files, the former of which make it easy to control the graceful shutdown of thousands of users from a single file. In addition, the content is not set in stone either—any word, any phrase will work equally well, and additional logic may be built around this content (e.g., building logic around the phrase "pause x" where "x" is a numeric value representing the number of minutes to pause).

As long as the STATUS.txt file can be opened and "read" by multiple users potentially simultaneously, this process works quite smoothly. In my experience, reading the contents is not a big deal. However, updating the contents of the file can be a challenge during a busy stress-test run simply because one of the virtual or physical clients always seems to have it opened for reading, and therefore locked. To get around this, I actually use a batch file that contains the proper word (start or stop) and simply copy a new STATUS.txt file containing the desired control word over the existing one.

Permutations of this STATUS.txt approach abound—rather than comparing the contents of a file, and therefore requiring the file to be opened and closed, you might instead simply "look" in a particular folder or directory for a file to exist. That is, your script might instead be coded such that if file c:\temp\STOP.txt exists, the script will begin the shutdown process. On the other hand, if the file does not exist, things would carry on as normal and the next loop in the script would be executed. And you can apply this to the status of a shared or global variable as well, as long as your test tool supports this and a method of updating the value of the variable is available during the middle of a test run.

12.6.2. Forced Aborts

When all else fails, you may need to simply abort a test run. Forcing a test run to abort should be considered only as a last resort, because it inherently impacts to some degree how well the test results are rolled up or collected—that is, the output associated with the tail end of a test run essentially becomes invalid. How is this possible? If a virtual user is only halfway through executing a scripted business process and then aborts, no performance data or workload data will be natively captured by the script (because I generally collect these data immediately after each loop in a test run), so the output logs generated from the script will be incomplete. Another shortcoming associated with aborting a test run is the fact that not all virtual and physical clients will stop executing at the same time; indeed, some may never actually stop executing at all. And in other cases, if you have hundreds or thousands of virtual users aborting simultaneously, they may or may not attempt to concurrently log their output to a shared output file, resulting in "missing" transactions that in reality were responsible for driving a portion of the load borne by the system. All of this needs to therefore be factored in when analyzing the results later, if indeed the test run was worthy of being analyzed—in most cases, it's not. Besides, because I usually abort a test run because of circumstances that would yield a poor run, the fact that the output log data are incomplete is not a problem.

An abort can be accomplished in a number of different ways or at a number of different "levels" in the SAP Technology Stack. Obviously, SAP testing tools represent the top of the heap, especially the controller application used to launch and manage test cases. Right-clicking an active AutoController package, for example, provides the option to abort it. Beyond using the test tool itself, though, test runs may be aborted at the database, OS, and even hardware layers. This becomes important if, for example, your test tool locks up or freezes, or one of the SAP components (e.g., an application server) is lost and you need to stop the current test to regroup. A number of SAP Technology Stack-specific methods are presented here:

- SAP. Using the SAP MMC or other tools to stop an SAP instance is a good way of ending a stress-test run. SM04 provides this ability in a limited fashion, too, in that you can at least end particular user sessions in this manner.
- Database. Bringing down the database or otherwise forcing a crash is an option, too. I don't recommend doing this unless you have to perform a restore anyway, and therefore have no risk of completely corrupting a database that must remain consistent for future test runs.
- OS. Killing the processes, or stopping the services, associated with SAP or the database is another way to go, albeit a rather risky proposition unless you're already planning on restoring the database and restarting the services for the next test run.
- Hardware. Bouncing or rebooting your disk subsystem along with your SAP servers and test infrastructure is a surefire method of aborting a test run. So is burning down the data center, as long as you're at it. Be sure this is what you want and that the potential ramifications are acceptable.

12.6.3.   Loop Counter Testing

If you prefer to control the number of iterations a test run cycles through rather than focusing on executing a test run for a particular timeframe, a method I call *loop counter testing* is available. This is perhaps the simplest method of ramping down a test run, because it leverages an uncomplicated loop counter within the body of each script. Once the body of a script has executed a specific number of times—like 15—it may then be directed to write out the final results, close all files, and gracefully end the SAPGUI session. This is easy enough to do of course, because any incremental or countdown loop logic may be used. And it's great if you have an idea as to how long a script tends to run and you still wish to execute a test run for a rough period of time. In other words, if the body of your script takes about 2 minutes to completely execute and you're shooting for 30 minutes of activity, a loop counter of 15 or 16 iterations is a good way to go. Keep in mind the following points, however:

- Your script will end prematurely if it runs faster than expected. This results in a "load" that was nonexistent through the final portion of your load-test period. The analysis performed afterwards would indicate a much lighter performance hit than expected, along with less work performed, and ultimately the entire test run might be of less value in an apples-to-apples comparison (if not completely worthless).
- Conversely, your script might take longer to run than you expected, turning a 30-minute test into perhaps a 45- to 60-minute test. The real downside of this is that you wind up getting fewer test runs completed in a day, and you have more pre-ramp-up and post-ramp-down test data to "throw away." If your success criteria hinge on achieving a certain transaction rate per hour, the whole test might need to be tossed in favor of executing a new one, too (presumably with updated "tighter" scripts). And for the bean counters out there, another real downside of this might be the fact that you have to keep people around later than otherwise required, adding up to potentially significant dollars.
- Using a hard-coded script-based loop counter reduces flexibility. If you want the ability to stretch out a particular test run, it's simply not possible without going back and changing the loop counter within a script and then re-executing the test run. In these cases, I first recommend using a counter function within your Controller software, rather than within the script itself. If this is not possible, though, I suggest converting your hard-coded counter into one that uses a variable (which may be changed on the fly—an input-file-based text variable like the contents of COUNTER.txt makes this easy enough). It's especially easy to use a loop counter variable when your counter counts "up" rather than executing in countdown mode, in that you can change the 15 in COUNTER.txt to a 20 on the fly, and the script will be none the wiser. It's quite a bit more troublesome to change a countdown counter on the fly, though. For example, if you're at loop 6 in a test and are counting down, and wish to execute another 5 loops, not only do you need to be aware of the fact that you're in loop 6 but you need to be

able to change the status of this counter to 10 within an actively executing script. On top of this, your output statistics would then reflect 2 runs of loops 6, 7, 8, 9, and 10, complicating data analysis later on.

The good news when it comes to using scripts that are bounded by a loop count is that there's realistically no chance of running out of materials or stock or running into other business process–specific supply-related constraints. That is, it's easy to plan for your specific input requirements, because you will know from the beginning exactly how many users will be executing each script and for how many iterations.

12.7. Tools and Approaches

Along with a number of scripts and text files discussed herein, on the book's ftp site I included screen shots for every transaction code covered in this chapter. My hope is that these screen shots may assist you in making sense of the kind of performance and throughput data available to you as you plan for and execute your stress-test runs, helping you collect the data you really need along the way. In the end, these data will either prove or disprove the success of your test runs; sound analysis of your test runs, as discussed in the next chapter, is only made possible by capturing the right data and turning them into quantitative information.

CHAPTER 13

How to Analyze Test Runs

A s I've said before, a well-executed and seemingly successful test run followed by anything but sound statistical analysis is just a waste of time. In Chapter 11, we worked through the preparation steps necessary to ensure a successful series of test runs. In Chapter 12, we finally kicked off a stress test and worked through the details associated with successfully monitoring a test run. Now, with output logs and other data in hand, it's time for the real fun—to bring everything together. Initially, this means analyzing the response times, throughput, and other performance metrics associated with each test run. It also means creating a custom set of spreadsheets, tables, charts, and graphs that explain these results in terms that clearly show whether the test's success criteria were met. Further, because the results of a test run may be shared with a variety of stakeholders or other interested parties, it's important to customize the output to a particular audience—some will prefer aggregate data, for instance, whereas others will be more interested in the details surrounding a particular set of test runs. I cover all of this and more in this chapter.

A test run might be considered a complete or final product in its own right, or it might play a smaller role in what amounts to iterative cycles of testing and tuning. In both cases, though, I believe it's imperative to analyze the data coming out of a test run as soon as practical after the test run is completed (or set of runs; e.g., in the case of a stress test that seeks to measure the performance inherent to different user or workload distributions). That is why I've inserted this chapter before a detailed discussion of iterative testing and retesting/tuning loops, which is presented in Chapter 14. In reality, though, the line where testing stops, data analysis begins, and testing starts again can be rather blurry. For instance, you'll likely find yourself performing a subset of the data analysis tasks described herein after each test run. But by the same token, if you're like most people, you'll save creating the "big report" for last, delivering it to your management team and end-user communities well after the last set of test cases has been executed. You may even embrace a phased approach to testing, data analysis, and tuning, alternating every few months between sharing detailed results with technical teams and high-level results with upper management. This approach makes the most sense when stress testing and performance tuning play a role in your change management processes, or if you're engaged in a long implementation or upgrade where you seek to quantify and refine performance deltas every few weeks or months as you near Go-Live, simply because your Go-Live platform or understanding of the workload to be hosted by this platform continues to evolve during this period.

Regardless, once you have executed a test run and worked through collecting your various technology-stack proof points, all of these data must go through a cleansing process of sorts, culminating in the cleansed data being dumped into an analysis tool. My analysis tool of choice is Microsoft Excel—it's easy to use, accepts data in many different formats, is widely available, and, when the need arises, can be used to feed more refined presentation tools like PowerPoint. I call this simple process "collect, cleanse, analyze, and present," and it forms the foundation of this chapter. In the bigger picture, this analysis method is but a piece of the "stop, analyze, and resume" process discussed in detail in Chapter 14. So with our focus firmly planted on the "analyze" portion of the big picture, let's take a look at the kind of data available at each SAP Technology Stack layer prior to pulling all of this information together in the name of "data collection" for an SAP stress test.

13.1. Overview—SAP Technology Stack Performance Data

First of all, there's really no such thing as a typical stress test for SAP—as you have read already, objectives differ, test tools vary, and success criteria range widely. Nonetheless, I've found over the years that the kind of data collected at different technology-stack layers tend to stay pretty consistent, even though the stack itself varies from customer to customer. The following list reflects the key data points or performance metrics germane to a performance-oriented test. Note the importance I place on collecting data at two different layers in the SAP Technology Stack— in some cases, this approach is only used to validate another layer's performance figures. In other cases, though, such an approach allows me to capture what I believe is the maximum performance a particular layer or component is capable of, and then compare this to what is observed at other layers to better understand bottlenecks or additional factors that limit performance elsewhere:

- Server hardware. Data relevant to CPU performance are the biggest key, and therefore it's important to validate from a hardware perspective how rapidly the CPU subsystem can process data when no bottlenecks elsewhere slow things down. I most often correlate these high-water data with application-layer response-time statistics observed via SAP CCMS (e.g., ST03 and STAD). Just as important, though, I'll use the CPU data points in comparative analyses to better understand the potential processing throughput deltas between different processor speeds, cache sizes, or 32-bit versus 64-bit architectures.

- OS statistics. The inherent overhead an OS incurs can be difficult to quantify and is really only practical (from an apples-to-apples perspective) on systems that support more than one OS. Thus, running a delta test between two identically configured HP Proliant servers, one loaded with Windows Server 2003 and the other with a particular version of SuSe Linux, can make sense. More often, this type of testing involves running CPU- or disk-based tests. Another key OS factor to watch is pagefile or swap file utilization. Your goal is to minimize the amount of paging, doing what you can to utilize physical RAM rather than the logical RAM that slow disk-based pagefiles or swap files represent. To that end, it's especially important to avoid "paging in" for Windows-based systems and any kind of paging for Unix systems.

- Disk subsystem. Understanding maximum MB per second and I/Os per second throughput are essential keys to achieving good disk subsystem performance. But these two metrics need to be captured in terms of sequential and direct/random reads and writes. And, to be real-world, a load should represent a realistic customer-specific mix of all four combinations of reads and writes, sequential and direct. This is all put into context when disk queues are taken into account as well. Finally, it also may make sense to try and understand which component within a particular disk subsystem is limiting performance—caching algorithms, controller load-balancing algorithms, the optimal number of disks per disk group or LUN, the storage infrastructure or "fabric" interconnecting disk storage systems with servers and tape solutions, and so on. All of these contribute to a disk subsystem's overall performance in both positive and negative ways.

- Database statistics. The maximization of cache hit rates for data and various buffers, the success of your database table buffering plan, the reduction of expensive SQL, the use of effective indexing, and the proper physical layout of the database in terms of data and logs all play key roles in maximizing database performance. So, too, does the selection of the optimal OS-level blocksizes, along with database-specific and hardware/controller-specific blocksizes.

- Interfaces and middleware. Network throughput and latencies, and the time spent waiting on a middleware component to do its thing and pass control back to SAP are key areas to monitor, measure, and tune. Thus, RFCs, ALE connections, and SAP CPIC times need to be considered, along with characterizing the performance of the network interconnecting everything. Once core latencies are understood, it makes sense to look at each middleware solution as its own technology stack, and accordingly optimize it layer by layer.

- SAP application layer. Characterizing online user and batch job response times, broken down by response-time specifics like those available in STAD and ST03N, is very important. So, too, is understanding workload metrics—throughput numbers, like the number of sales orders processed in an hour, give meaning to the previously described response-time numbers.

- Multiple systems and components. Like middleware components, when it comes to tracking a cross-application business process, it's important to understand the load borne by each discrete technology stack "island" along with the performance of the network infrastructure or system component (e.g., the SAP XI) effectively bridging these islands together. The islands themselves may include SAP ITS components, any number of mySAP Business Suite components, non-SAP/legacy enterprise applications, SAP enhancements or bolt-ons, firewalls, routers, and so on.

- Front-end client. At the end of the day, the speed an end user ascribes to a particular system is subjective. The response time observed after pressing the Enter key, for example, includes the time it takes the end user's request to traverse everything already described in this list, and then make the roundtrip back to the user—a lot of movement for a seemingly simple user request. The pieces often missing in this equation include lag time associated with the front-end network, however, along with roll-time and a factor known simply as "GUI build time," or the time it takes to create and update the SAPGUI or other user interface back at the user's computer.

Many more areas of configuration may be important to a particular test run. Note, for example, that I don't include characterizing RAM performance as a key metric at the hardware layer. Although RAM is obviously critical, and more RAM is always better than less, the fact that it's so fast generally removes the need for deep analysis in stress tests. On the other hand, in the past I've benchmarked different systems using different RAM technologies or system busses/architectures based on specific customer requests or the need to simply characterize new customer platforms. How to best divvy up RAM into the various buffers and pools used by SAP and its underlying database is another common test scenario, too. In the end, what to test depends on your situation.

13.2.   Real-World Performance Data Sources

If necessary to your unique testing endeavors, collecting all of the data mentioned in the previous section could require something like pulling the output or log files from six to seven discrete testing and monitoring tools. Or a single enterprise systems-management console coupled with the appropriate technology-stack-specific data collection agents can be configured instead. In addition, many of these data are actually available through SAP CCMS as well, or can be extracted from a test-tool console. So where's the best place to get your data, and why is one approach preferred over another in some cases? The answers can be found in the next few sections, where we look at the various data repositories or sources that might be available to support test-run-based performance tuning.

13.2.1.   Leveraging Your Test Tool

First and foremost, I leverage the tool I've used for testing as my primary data collection or performance feedback tool. Even the most basic of tool sets spit something back at you or otherwise share something of value; otherwise, they would not exist. The simplest tools tend to provide snapshot data—snapshots of system performance, which are basically one-off data points which may only be displayed on your screen and not logged to a file to be captured permanently and analyzed later. Other tools, like AutoTester's AutoController, provide both real-time status feedback and detailed user-specific postrun "results" files. In this way, such a tool serves an awesome purpose—as a real-time test monitor and as a historical data collection repository tool. And because this repository lies in a single place (typically on the system housing the test console), tracking the performance and throughput of cross-application test runs is made easily possible. Unfortunately, not all metrics or data points are tracked from all test-tool consoles in the first place, and therefore available for analysis. It is solely for this reason that other tools and approaches must be used to get the full end-to-end performance picture.

13.2.2. Data Collected through Observation

Although it appears simplistic (because it is!), the power of observation during a stress-test run can fill in many holes in your performance analysis plan. I use my execution checklist, for example, to help me remember when and what to collect, including what tool or system interface to use. In the past, snapshots in time of a system's CPU utilization, disk queue lengths in front of each data file or key table spaces, and globally active work processes have helped me plug in holes or provide a "second source" data point—good for validating performance results observed or collected elsewhere. These kinds of data are available across the board, from basic hardware and OS monitoring tools, to various SAP CCMS transactions, to the SAP CCMS Alert Monitor/RZ20, or to STATTRACE. Don't make the mistake of underestimating such an approach to data collection, though. The fact is that it's simple to conduct aids in collecting these kinds of observation-based data in the first place, and it serves as a great "backup" if you find yourself missing data normally provided by another automated tool or approach.

13.2.3. Automatically Collected Background Data

The most basic data points collected in an automated fashion require the use of tools that support historical analysis. In other words, the tool must be able to dump real-time performance data into a log or other repository, and then allow you to sort and sift through this after the fact. The most prevalent approach, using a tool like Microsoft PerfMon, the Unix *top* utility (which by default runs continuously), or other OS-based performance-tracking tools, can be easily "automated" such that the status of a particular test run is captured consistently, like every 10 seconds, and logged to an output file. Getting back to my execution checklist, I use this checklist to remind me to manually start the log collection process, set the collection interval, and name the test-specific log to reflect the date, nature of the test run, and an incremental run number. At the end of the test, my execution checklist also reminds me to stop and save the logs, and voilà I have a package of detailed test data with the ability to help me correlate hardware, OS, and even database performance trends against workload and other SAP throughput metrics captured by other tools during the test run.

13.2.4. Scripted Transactions: Output Data

Like the performance data I collect automatically through starting and stopping logs, special performance-tracking transactions that have been scripted to execute on a regular basis can also be started and stopped at the beginning and end of a test run. By doing this, I can turn a tool that is normally valuable only in terms of snapshots (e.g., SM66, which displays the number of active work processes at a particular point in time) into a tool that effectively provides historical value. And by scripting this Basis transaction (among quite a few others, as discussed in earlier chapters), the data collection method becomes not only regular (every 2 minutes) but also makes for a repeatable process that can be executed against multiple test runs.

I dump the data collected from such an approach into a text-based delimited file or even straight into an XLS format if supported by my scripting tool. If I've done my homework, I'll have regular data points that tend to coincide with and capture key places of activity within a business process or transaction. And because I typically script SAP-layer CCMS transactions, I'll also wind up having data that can be compared against hardware-, OS-, and database-specific test metrics, providing great insight into a test run from multiple perspectives.

13.2.5. Bringing Everything Together at a Global Level

Using automated and scripted data collection processes is a simple enough prospect for SAP stress-test runs that happen to hit against only a single SAP system. But how do you capture performance statistics relevant to business processes that span multiple systems? Part of the answer lies in regular collection processes—processes that are precisely timed to take a snapshot of multiple systems at the same time. In this way, the results may be plotted in a time-oriented table or graph, supporting cross-solution-stack analysis; the load may be correlated not only within different layers in each system's stack but across the various stacks as well. For example, I can observe how a sales order initiated in SAP CRM burdens that system until a call to R/3 for further processing is required. Then I can observe the CPIC wait time increase on one side as the load moves to the other side—all of this is made evident in regular snapshots of both systems' performance.

In the same way, STAD also gives me insight into the system load incurred by a business process. And ST03G provides aggregated statistics across multiple systems, which may then be manually correlated back to business processes. But it's not until I use a tool like the Operations portion of SAP Solution Manager that I can finally monitor the performance of a business process across multiple SAP systems, and do so natively. For instance, the Business Process Management service found in Solution Manager leverages the performance data collected on different systems (connected via RFCs) by SAP CCMS to track the physical data flow and subsequent performance impact from one system to another—true business process monitoring. And services like the SAP Business Process Performance Optimization and SAP SQL Statement Optimization offerings lend themselves to consistency and completeness.

13.3. Collecting More Data: Using SAP CCMS during and after Each Test Run

Beyond collecting SAP data real-time throughout a test run, there is much in the way of performance data inherently available long after the runs are complete. That is, CCMS is chock full of transactional, user-specific, and other performance data soon after a test run is completed. The trick is simply getting to it all, both during and after each test run, as discussed next.

13.3.1. User, Functional, and Application Server Distribution

From a user distribution perspective, it's important to achieve not only the target number of online and active users but also the proper mix of users. Further, I like to ensure that a customer's

Application	Dialog steps	Resp. time avg(ms)	CPU time avg(ms)	Wait time avg(ms)	DB time avg(ms)	Requested kB avg
Basis Components	60,890	1,389	251	23	696	130
Controlling	2,322	10,202	738	2	9,357	1,488
Cross-Application Components	1,686	3,255	577	27	1,756	429
Financial Accounting	44,686	1,717	190	8	470	136
Logistics - General	2,464	1,192	143	4	951	430
Logistics Execution	4,109	828	74	11	709	80
Materials Management	6,275	663	165	27	260	96
Production Planning and Control	41	21,218	3,329	0	16,725	2,999
SAP Media	1,516	269	76	1	148	57
Sales and Distribution	64,161	1,257	391	38	604	107
Treasury	784	67	22	1	36	21
Other	30,079	5,921	728	11	2,874	349
Total	219,013	2,105	344	22	1,009	168

Figure 13–1   The real-time snapshot data provided by ST07 become valuable historical data, making detailed response-time and throughput analysis possible when captured every 60 seconds.

logon load-balancing mechanism as configured via transaction SMLG is effective not only from the get-go but over time as well. All of these needs may be satisfied by executing ST07, AL08, and SM04 throughout the course of a stress-test run. However, because these transactions represent point-in-time snapshots in the same way that SM66 provides only real-time data, it is critical during the course of a stress-test run to regularly capture these real-time statistics. These statistical data can prove especially valuable in the case of ST07, where much in the way of details is available outside of the requisite "logged-in users" count, as shown in Figure 13–1. Later, this output file (sometimes called a performance log) may be analyzed back at the office.

13.3.2.   DB02—the Database Overview

Given that most test runs will require the database to be restored, some of the basic value surrounding monitoring database growth over many weeks or months will be unavailable—at the beginning of every test run, the SAP databases underpinning your test infrastructure will be restored and therefore begin life again at the same size. But because DB02 provides a real-time summary as to how data and indexes add up in terms of space used, as shown in Figure 13–2, it is useful to take a look at DB02 immediately following a test run. In this way, you can validate how much the database grew during the latest test run and validate that the load placed on the system was consistent between different test runs. For example, between test run A and B, you can verify that the 500 newly created sales orders associated with each run consumed pretty much the same amount of disk space overall. A basic apples-to-apples database-specific comparison is then made possible between different test runs. And with the added ability to check the growth of or use of extents by specific tables that may be of interest (e.g., MSEG and MARA!), DB02 can be an indispensable postrun stress-test analysis tool.

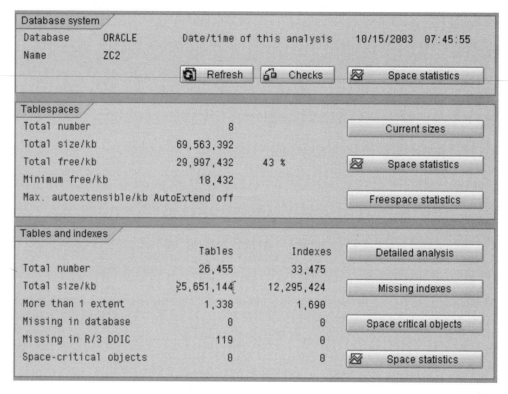

Figure 13–2   Using DB02, it's possible to validate to some degree that a load was substantially the same between two different test runs. The total database size should be nearly identical after different test runs have completed.

13.3.3.   Updates, Locks, and Disk Subsystem Performance

An understanding of how well updates are committed to the database during a test run, and whether lock entries are holding things up, can be accomplished real-time through viewing or, even better, scripting SM12 (Database Lock Entries, Figure 13–3) and SM13 (Administer Update Records, Figure 13–4).

But the ability to more completely analyze a database's performance relative to the load an SAP application stress test drives is available through ST04 (Database Performance Analysis). As shown in Figure 13–5, ST04 provides real-time insight into cache hit rate values, logical versus physical reads, and critical "buffer busy waits" values (which, along with database request time as provided in ST03, is critical to understanding load-driven database performance).

The real-time value of ST04 is complemented by the fact that these core performance metrics may be collected from a particular point in time (statistics "zero out" and start accumulating again when the Reset button is pushed). This represents a perfect way of analyzing individual back-to-back test runs in cases where the database is not restored between runs. And the Reset

Select Lock Entries

| List |

Table name	
Lock argument	
Client	400
User name	10013

Figure 13–3 SM12 makes it easy to identify locks related to a particular user, client, or table, and supports wildcards.

Shared Memory Segments in Workprocesses, sorted by Key							Date: 10.15.20	Time: 1	
Key	Size	Address	Fill	%	FillPattrn	OsKey	OsKey	Handle	Att Seg
1	304	05770040	0	0		1	00000001	644	0
2	1,987,104	05780040	0	0		2	00000002	652	0
3	13,059,200	05970040	0	0		3	00000003	656	0
4	536,672	08580040	0	0		4	00000004	964	0
5	4,096	03F60040	0	0		5	00000005	576	0
6	307,200,000	8DA00040	0	0		6	00000006	1,072	0
7	7,424	08570040	0	0		7	00000007	960	0
8	134,217,728	100E0040	0	0		8	00000008	944	0
9	268,435,456	60BA0040	0	0		9	00000009	940	0
11	500,000	0FEF0040	0	0		11	0000000B	1,016	0
12	6,000,000	1F4F0040	0	0		12	0000000C	1,064	0
13	20,141,728	1E1B0040	0	0		13	0000000D	1,060	0
14	4,400,128	07DC0040	0	0		14	0000000E	936	0
16	16,816	003F0040	0	0		16	00000010	568	0
17	2,678,944	08200040	0	0		17	00000011	948	0
18	525,344	08490040	0	0		18	00000012	952	0
19	50,000,912	0BE60040	0	0		19	00000013	988	0
30	29,200	0FF90040	0	0		30	0000001E	1,080	0
31	3,418,176	06600040	0	0		31	0000001F	676	0
33	10,240,016	0EE10040	0	0		33	00000021	992	0
34	4,194,304	208D0040	0	0		34	00000022	1,136	0
37	37,664	003E0040	0	0		37	00000025	528	0
41	6,989,568	0B7B0040	0	0		41	00000029	984	0
42	8,807,184	0AF40040	0	0		42	0000002A	980	0
43	32,484,272	08610040	0	0		43	0000002B	968	0
44	6,828,272	0A510040	0	0		44	0000002C	972	0
45	3,756,272	0ABA0040	0	0		45	0000002D	976	0

Figure 13–4 SM13 displays real-time database update activity.

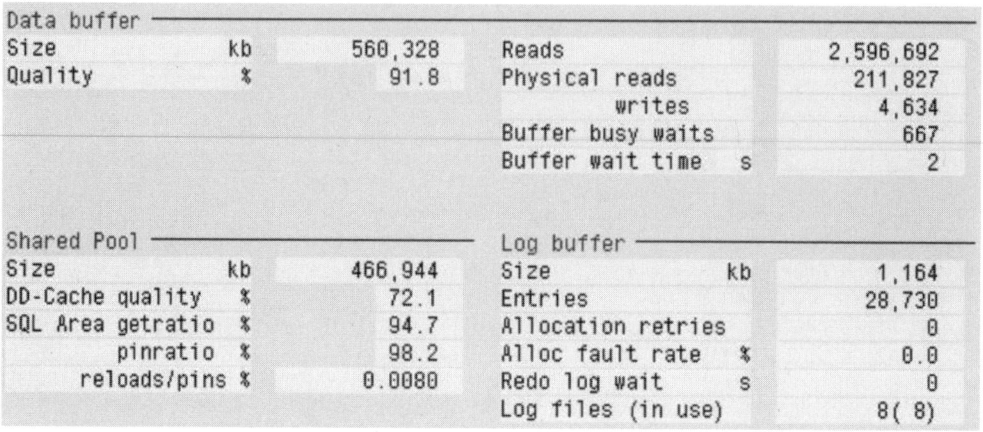

```
Data buffer ─────────────────────────────────────────────────
Size           kb        560,328    Reads                     2,596,692
Quality        %            91.8    Physical reads              211,827
                                            writes                4,634
                                    Buffer busy waits               667
                                    Buffer wait time    s             2


Shared Pool ───────────────────────    Log buffer ─────────────────────
Size              kb      466,944    Size              kb          1,164
DD-Cache quality  %          72.1    Entries                      28,730
SQL Area getratio %          94.7    Allocation retries                0
          pinratio %         98.2    Alloc fault rate  %             0.0
     reloads/pins %        0.0080    Redo log wait     s               0
                                     Log files (in use)           8( 8)
```

Figure 13–5   ST04 provides insight into how well a load is being handled by a database, including cache hit rate and buffer busy wait statistics, and the overall mix of logical to physical reads and reads to writes.

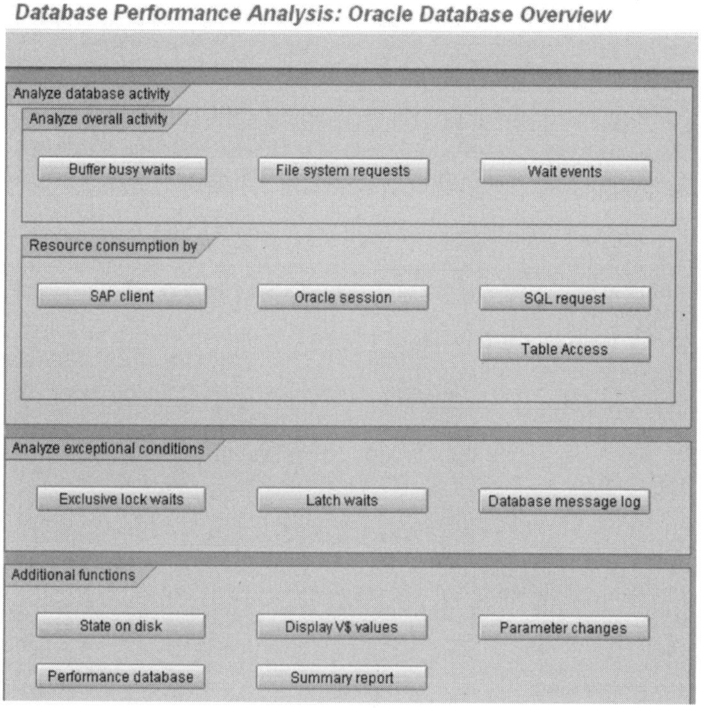

Figure 13–6   The Detail Analysis Menu provided by ST04 opens the door to further SQL request or table-specific analysis, as well as greater visibility into buffer busy waits, lock waits, latch waits, and more.

button acts as a toggle switch when its depressed again, defaulting back to displaying all database statistics since the database was first started (an excellent and appropriate method of analyzing a group of test runs). And a Detail Analysis Menu is available as well, as shown in Figure 13–6, making it easy to drill down into overall activity, exception events, resource consumption based on specific SQL requests or table accesses, and more.

13.3.4. Memory Management and ST02

ST02, the "Tune Summary" (or as I sometimes say "the red swap screen"), provides real-time snapshots of how well the various buffers as configured via the SAP profiles are performing under load (see Figure 13-7). Buffers that are improperly configured or simply not optimal for a given load executed on a particular application instance will be displayed with a red- highlighted value in the Swaps column Note that not all red-highlighted field values are really all that bad, though—a bit of swapping is pretty normal for Program buffers, for instance. But if you tend to constantly see a lot of red, or the values in red grow quickly, some iterative testing and buffer tuning would probably pay off.

ST02 also provides much more value outside of buffer management. Memory utilization aggregated to reflect an entire system is represented in the SAP Memory section of the display. Although all four of these metrics are important, I especially like to monitor the current utiliza-

Tune Summary (usr3prddb_PRD_00)

Current parameters   Detail analysis menu

System: usr3prddb_PRD_00   Tune summary
Date & time of snapshot: 11/04/2003 11:45:27   Startup: 11/02/2003 16:30:35

Buffer	Hitratio [%]	Allocated [kB]	Free space [kB]	[%]	Dir. size Entries	Free directory Entries	[%]	Swaps	Database accesses
Nametab (NTAB)									
Table definition	99.78	5,044	3,209	80.18	30,000	24,056	80.19	0	6,173
Field description	99.51	32,348	11,374	37.91	60,001	54,373	90.62	0	5,661
Short NTAB	99.91	4,848	2,164	86.56	60,001	57,972	96.62	0	2,829
Initial records	99.87	6,348	3,051	76.28	60,001	56,912	94.85	0	3,089
Program	99.83	350,301	5,822	1.66	87,500	80,436	91.93	2,015	27,318
CUA	99.59	5,000	2,448	54.75	2,500	2,022	80.88	0	480
Screen	99.10	19,531	13,021	60.73	10,000	9,566	95.66	43	1,572
Calendar	99.97	488	367	76.78	200	59	29.50	0	141
Tables									
Generic key	99.96	48,828	2,471	5.22	10,000	5,602	56.02	1	8,241
Single record	98.18	30,000	25,748	85.99	500	371	74.20	0	6,122
Export/import	94.10	20,000	14,040	88.97	20,000	19,181	95.91	0	0

SAP memory	Current use [%]	[kB]	Max. use [kB]	In memory [kB]	On disk [kB]	SAP cursor cache	Hitratio [%]
Roll area	1.73	3,816	6,392	220,000	0	IDs	99.84
Paging area	0.27	704	22,888	96,000	166,144	Statements	99.00
Extended Memory	5.60	88,064	327,680	1,571,840			
Heap Memory		0	0				

Figure 13–7   The Tune Summary details both memory- and buffer-related performance statistics.

tion percentage of Extended Memory, and validate that the use of Heap Memory is as minimal as possible.

13.3.5. Table Buffering: ST03, SE13, ST10, and DB05

Validating your table buffering strategy is another good use of stress testing. When tables are buffered optimally, performance across the board improves. The whole idea in analyzing how tables are accessed and used is to increase performance by filling the buffers with the most popular and best-suited tables (and therefore reducing expensive database and disk accesses). I suggest you analyze the ratio of database calls to database requests to give you a better idea as to how efficient your current table buffering is—at the end of the day, the fewer database calls that result in database requests, the better. To level set everyone, let's quickly review the ground rules for buffering:

- Tables set for read-only access or those that are not modified are great candidates for buffering.
- Other tables that may be buffered include those that are written to very infrequently— it's this word "infrequently" that may be quantified through real-world analysis.
- Only Pool and Transparent tables can be buffered; Cluster tables cannot.

I suggest using a process similar to the following step-by-step procedure to work through potential buffering issues:

1. Shortly after a representative stress-test run, execute ST03 (the Workload Monitor) and display dialog and update tasks. For each of these, click the Transaction Profile button and then sort the results by "response time."
2. Analyze the transactions or programs that consume the most database time (DB Request Time). Best practices generally indicate that DB Request time should not exceed 40% of the total response time, though exceptions abound.
3. For each of these transactions, analyze single records by executing transaction STAD and double-clicking the appropriate line. Look for buffer reloads that have occurred in a corresponding dialog step, and then select DB and check to see if the message "Tables were saved in the table buffer" was issued.
4. Many such notes indicate frequent buffer reloads, an unwanted condition that may be further analyzed through SE13 and ST10, discussed next.

Use transaction SE13 to review table buffering attributes, which range from "buffering not allowed" (because the table is changed too frequently, or programs require the most up-to-date data from the table) to "buffering allowed but switched off" to "buffering active." Then execute transaction ST10 to search and sort tables by timeframe, server, and the way in which they are buffered (see Figure 13–8).

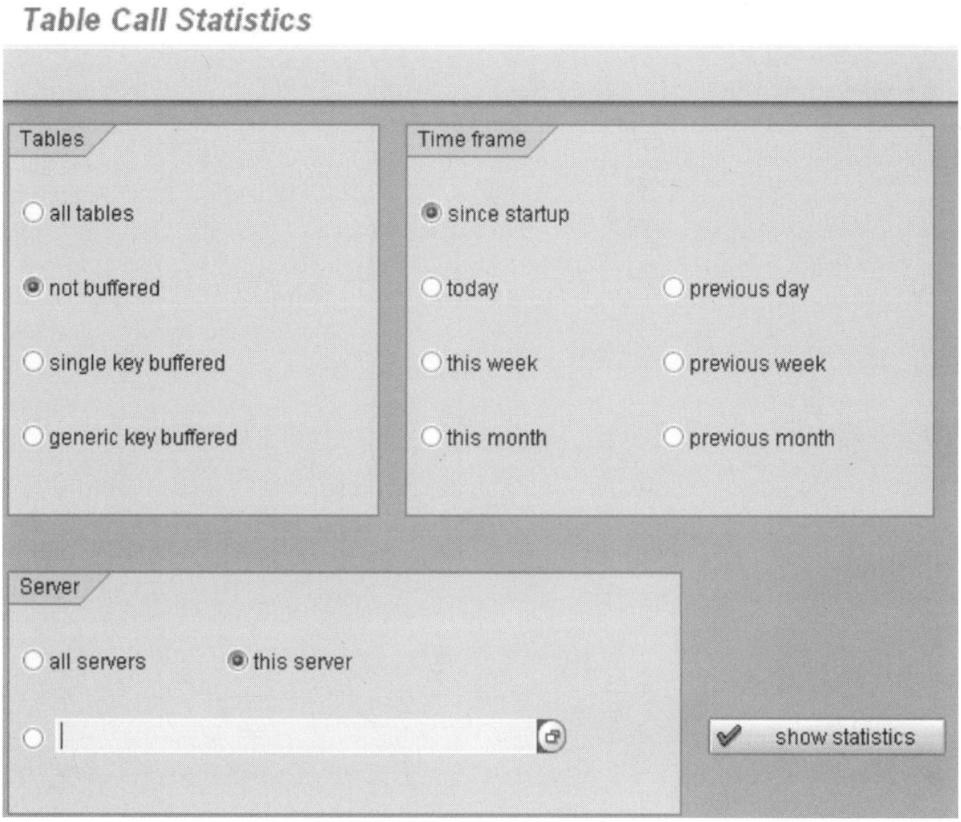

Table Call Statistics

Figure 13–8 The initial screen provided by ST10 is simply a front end used for searching and sorting through the thousands of tables in an SAP database.

I typically look for tables that are not buffered but need to be, or tables that are indeed buffered but are not good candidates because of their propensity to be updated. The Table Call Statistics screen shown in Figure 13–9 should give you an idea as to the types of requests or disk activities you may sort by—for instance, high direct or sequential reads make for good buffering candidates, as long as the number of changes made to the table is relatively low.

Next, if you double-click a specific table, like DD12L shown in Figure 13–10, you are made privy to detailed activity regarding this particular table.

Further, once you've determined the best probable tables to be buffered, you can pull more statistical data on each table in question by executing DB05. Simply type in the table name and press F8 to execute either a background job (the default) or conduct an online analysis of the table with regard to indexed fields. Once the analysis is complete, a screen like that displayed in Figure 13–11 provides data like the following:

- Number of rows in the table
- Requested bytes per row
- Bytes to be buffered
- The current buffering mode configured for the table
- Key indexed fields within the table, and how they're used to access the data

Table		ABAP/IV Processor requests				DB activity	
	Changes/ Total (%)	Total	Direct reads	Seq. reads	Changes	Calls	Rows affected
Total		25133,795	24227,911	735,699	170,185	1,500,872	125730201
DDNTF	0.00	21610,906	21600,403	10,503	0	21,003	10,503
DDNTT	0.00	2,433,696	2,433,696	0	0	27,095	13,547
D010SINF	0.00	299,872	5,330	294,542	0	305,244	299,873
D010INC	0.00	55,151	0	55,151	0	55,203	243,127
D010LINF	0.00	54,256	0	54,256	0	54,258	1,999
TPRI_DEF	0.00	14,970	0	14,970	0	29,970	0
HRP1001	0.00	9,885	0	9,885	0	10,000	7,162
DD02L	0.00	8,139	2	8,137	0	8,595	525,822
DD01L	0.00	7,790	0	7,790	0	7,899	29,600
DD08L	0.00	7,589	5	7,584	0	7,698	3,638
DD03L	0.00	7,550	0	7,550	0	7,614	49,711
DD04L	0.00	7,532	0	7,532	0	7,642	30,492
DD09L	0.00	7,285	0	7,285	0	7,302	1,464
DD12L	0.00	7,278	0	7,278	0	7,581	140,701
SMOHPUBL	0.00	5,884	0	5,884	0	5,945	19,509
SMOHMSGQST	0.00	5,856	2,928	2,928	0	8,974	64,440
TCP01	0.00	4,914	0	4,914	0	6	4,913

Figure 13–9   The Table Call Statistics screen with ST10 provides basic table details—use this to sort by changes, total requests, and so on.

Performance analysis: Table call statistics

Print

System:
Date & time of snapshot: 10/29/2003   09:20:55

Not buffered tables
System Startup: 10/24/2003 08:20:58

DD12L   R/3 S_SECINDEX: secondary indexes, header;

Table description	Buffered	no
	Type	TRANSP
	Application class	SDIC
	Client dependent	no
	Last modified	02.06.1998
	by	SAP

Operation Type	ABAP/IV Processor		Database Calls				
	Requests	Fails	Prepares	Opens	Fetch/Exec	Rows	Time [ms]
Select single	0	0	0	0	0		0
Select	7,278	0	23	0	7,558	140,701	0
Update	0	0	0		0	0	0
Delete	0	0	0		0	0	0
Insert	0	0	0		0	0	0
Buffer load			0	0	0	0	0

Figure 13–10   Detailed information related to how a table has been accessed is available deep within ST10, including the number of selects, updates, inserts, and so on.

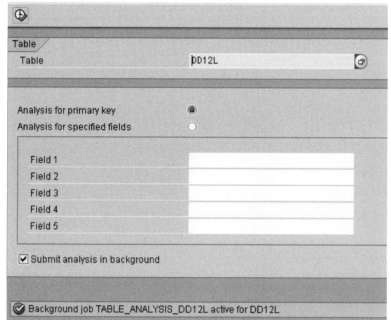

Figure 13–11 DB05 allows you to analyze the effectiveness of indexed fields within a table, like table DD12L shown here.

Change, test, and tune your table buffering strategy iteratively—this kind of tuning is relevant to a couple of profile parameters in particular:

- zcsa/table_buffer_ area: 60000000
- rtbb/buffer_length: 40000

After each test run, walk through the ST03/STAD process described earlier to validate that your changes made a positive difference.

13.3.6. ST06, the OS Monitor

The OS Monitor, ST06, is another SAP transaction that displays much in the way of real-time performance data; CPU utilization broken down by user, system, and idle, the CPU load count at 1-, 5-, and 15-minute intervals, and current-state memory/swap metrics all lend themselves to being collected over time and analyzed after the test run. However, ST06 is special in that you can access historical data, too. The Detail Analysis Menu provides access to a breakdown of historical data across all major hardware subsystems, as shown in Figure 13–12. This includes not only detailed data encompassing the last 24 hours (under the section "Previous hours") but also longer term data housed in the SAP Performance Database.

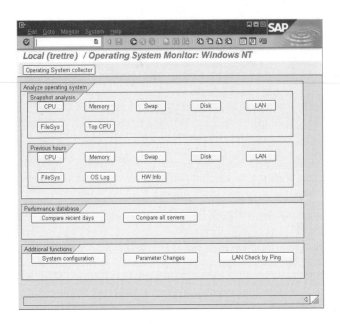

Figure 13–12   The OS Monitor, as ST06 is known, provides access to both real-time performance snapshots and historical data.

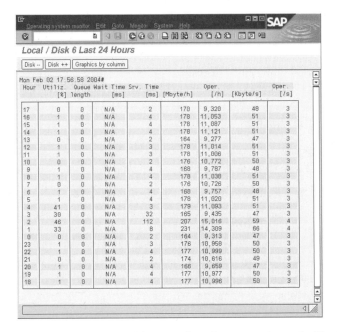

Figure 13–13   Historical data relative to disk queue lengths, percentage of utilization, MB per hour, and I/Os per second leave no doubt as to the per-disk activity borne by your SAP solution.

The historical data available from ST06 not only cover all of the major subsystems (CPU, memory, swap/page, disk subsystem, file-system specifics, and more) but, for our purposes here, help make stress-test monitoring and analysis much easier than otherwise possible. For example, the data displayed in Figure 13–13 are useful in correlating disk performance of a particular data drive observed at hardware, OS, and database levels with that observed by SAP (these data may be "rolled up" by toggling through the individual disk choices until you come to "Disk_Total"). Similar functions, like the ability to review hourly CPU load over the last 24 hours, make it easy not only to identify start and stop times of a particular test run but also to monitor and analyze CPU performance relative to throughput. In the same way, the hooks into the SAP Performance Database make it easy to launch additional serverwide or server-specific analyses from ST06.

13.3.7. STAD, ST03N, and ST03G: Response-Time and Workload Details

STAD and the various incarnations of ST03 (e.g., the newer ST03N and ST03G) make for powerful response-time and workload analysis. Truth be told, these tools form the basis of much of my performance analysis work, whether stress-test-related or not. With ST03, the response times of a particular period's top transactions may be easily determined, broken down by core CPU, DB Request, Wait, Load, Roll, and other components of response time. And, as shown in Figure 13–14, the ability to analyze only the load processed by batch work processes or, in other cases, dialog, update, or even total work processes makes for a compelling workload-specific analysis.

ST03N's approach is a bit different, in that all task types are displayed simultaneously in rows rather than individually, as shown in Figure 13–15. Each method is effective, albeit slightly different. Given that ST03 already has made way for the newer and more capable ST03N, and is no longer even available in the latest SAP Basis releases, the writing on the wall is pretty clear— get comfortable with ST03N.

ST03 and its kin (ST03x) also allow for identifying and analyzing the number of dialog steps processed by each task type, sorted by each server enduring the load. This allows for powerful delta comparisons between different application server platforms, or simply lets you prove that a particular load-balancing scheme indeed distributes the load well, perhaps better than a previous configuration.

In addition, ST03x makes it easy to measure the difference in performance between direct reads, sequential reads, and changes (database updates or commits, as they're commonly called). The average number of bytes requested per transaction is also available, useful in understanding the worst-case potential load that a disk subsystem might be required to support if caching mechanisms fail to work well. In this same screen, displayed in Figure 13–16, the mix of database requests (number of direct reads, sequential reads, and changes) may also be compared and analyzed, along with the overall ratio of database calls to requests; this makes it easier to characterize the load a particular disk subsystem should be configured and optimized to support. And its data complement those found in ST04, too.

Beyond pure response-time metrics, the Time Profile and Transaction Profile buttons available from ST03 allow you to quantify a system's load over a particular time period or based on a

Performance: Recent Workload

| Top time | Transaction profile | Time profile | Memory profile | Accounting profile | Task type profile | Applica |

Instance

SAP System	TRTRE	Date 02/02/2004	First record	17:52:31
Instance no.	*		Last record	18:06:31
Server	tressdb		Time elapsed	00:14:00

Workload

CPU time	77.1 s	Database calls	268,659
Time elapsed	840.0 s	Database requests	268,859
		Direct reads	245,226
Dialog steps	22	Sequential reads	23,518
		Changes	115
Average CPU time	3,504.4 ms		
Av. RFC+CPIC time	0.0 ms	Time per DB request	0.3 ms
		Direct reads	0.3 ms
Av. response time	6,477.9 ms	Sequential reads	1.0 ms
Average wait time	70.0 ms	Changes and commits	6.0 ms
Average load time	4.8 ms		
Av. Roll i+w time	0.2 ms	Roll-in time	0.0 s
Av. DB req. time	4,234.5 ms	Roll-out time	0.0 s
Av. enqueue time	0.0 ms	Roll wait time	0.0 s
		Roll-ins	5
Average bytes req.	3,214.8 kB	Roll-outs	5

Task types

| Current | Background | Others | Dialog | RFC | Total |

Figure 13–14 With its simple toggle buttons, ST03 makes it easy to view the performance characteristics of different types of work processes, in this case background work processes used to process batch jobs.

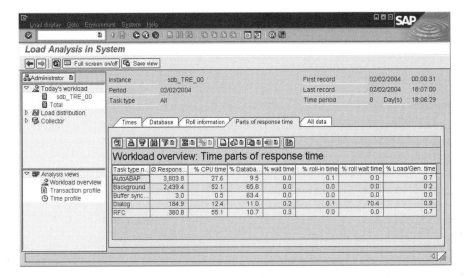

Figure 13–15 ST03N displays more work process–specific response-time data in a single screen than its predecessor ST03.

Database calls	568
Database requests	14,376
Direct reads	1,544
Sequential reads	12,708
Changes	124
Time per DB request	0.2 ms
Direct reads	0.0 ms
Sequential reads	0.1 ms
Changes and commits	8.0 ms

Figure 13–16 Disk subsystem tuning specialists appreciate the level of detail available from ST03x—the number and ratio of sequential reads, direct reads, changes, and more help to characterize the load for which a disk subsystem should be optimized.

particular workload—the top transactions responsible for placing the most load on a certain hardware component are easily identified in this way as well, as discussed in previous chapters. And with the ability to aggregate data at an "application" level, you can validate after a test run that the run indeed emulated the correct mix of functional workload desired from the beginning (something akin to a "historical" ST07).

Finally, ST03G offers new, previously unattainable functionality—the ability to view and analyze the load associated with external systems, as shown in Figure 13–17, and analyze generally the performance of systems underpinning cross-application business processes. This latest iteration of ST03 is the most powerful yet from SAP AG, and I imagine it will quickly become the de facto performance analysis tool for many SAP shops as they try to support more complex, extended SAP enterprises.

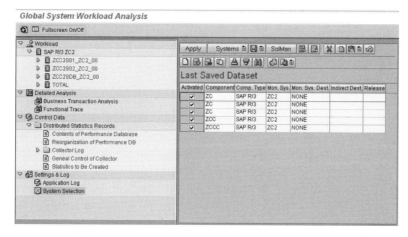

Figure 13–17 ST03G gives us the ability to perform global workload analysis covering both the "primary" SAP system and additional external systems, even going so far as to support a plug-in for the SAP Solution Manager.

13.4.   Collecting and Cleaning Real-World Data

In the last few pages, we have seen how to produce or find the data necessary to quantify the performance of a system. Now we must bring together all of these data pulled from different sources both during and after a test run, and clean them in a way that makes for meaningful configuration changes and improved performance tuning.

13.4.1.   Collection Preparation

If you've embraced my scripted approaches to collecting real-time data during a test run and to saving the results to an output log file, you'll be in good shape overall. Worst case, the output files simply will need to be delimited in some manner (if you failed to do this in scripting for output) so that the contents may then be poured into Excel. Depending on what you collected, too, you might want to build additional spaces before or after certain fields in your output data so that, for example, your columns line up nicely in Excel. Over the years, I've learned to keep my output logs pretty consistent in this regard, but I remember well what my first few pivot tables looked like, and the work necessary to clean up the input files behind them.

You might need additional preparation, though, prior to collecting historical data from CCMS. For example, in Basis releases prior to Web AS 6.20, where you're still using ST03 to analyze your workload and have a just-executed test run to analyze, you'll need to "build totals" first. From the main screen in ST03, simply click the Build Totals button, and select whether you prefer to conduct this operation in the foreground (real time) or background (through a batch process that will immediately execute without any further input). Once the operation has completed, refresh the ST03 display and you're in business.

For those with newer Basis releases or for those of you who prefer ST03N, a similar process is used—underneath "Today's workload" simply double-click "Total" as I've shown in Figure 13–18. A box entitled "Total data for today not available" will be displayed, like the one in Figure 13–19. Select Background or Dialog, and once the totals have been calculated, they will be available for display.

13.4.2.   Loading SAPGUI Screen Output into Excel

Capturing SAPGUI screen contents and saving them out to a file does not always require a tool capable of SAP API–aware screen-scraping. Some transactions, like the Workload screen in STAD, give the end user the ability to natively save the screen's contents to a number of file formats simply by clicking the Download button—unconverted (text), spreadsheet, rich text format, and HTML format are all at your disposal instantly. But one of the coolest things about the SAPGUI is that these four formats are actually at your disposal whenever you need to save list-based output locally, pretty much regardless of what kind of list you happen to be looking at—ST07, ST10, AL08, and anything else that generates a list can be manipulated in this way. To save screen-based output to a local file or mapped network share, simply enter the transaction %pc in

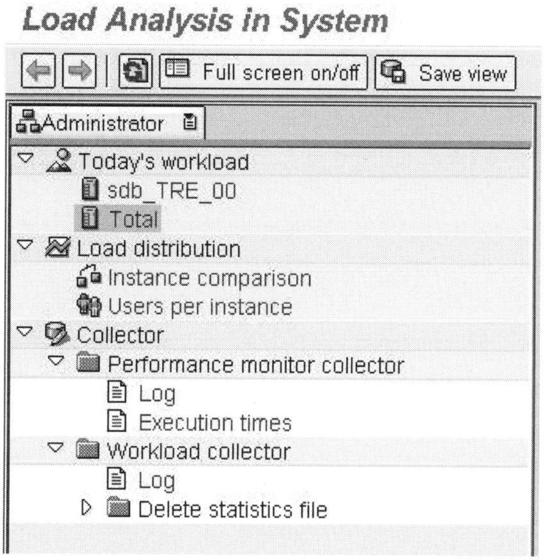

Load Analysis in System

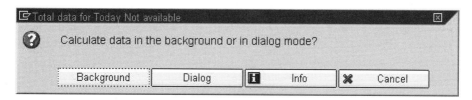

Figure 13–18 ST03N has no Build Totals button like ST03. Instead, double-click Total underneath "Today's workload" and follow the prompts.

Figure 13–19 To aggregate the most recent performance totals from CCMS, select either the Background or Dialog button, and the updated results will be quickly collected and displayed.

the same place you type in a T-code like /nAL08, and then press the Enter key. The same window you see in STAD after pressing the Download button (see Figure 13–20) pops up, and defaults to saving the screen's contents in unconverted file format. Choose the spreadsheet format (or any of the other three if you prefer, though XLS is surprisingly the most compact format, not to mention often the most useful). Then press Enter, browse to the desired directory path, type in the name of the output file you would like to create, and press the Save button to save the data to the file name you specified. It couldn't be much easier.

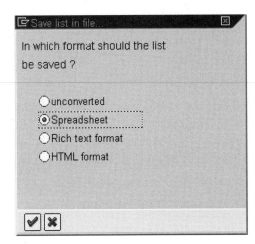

Figure 13–20 Use the %pc transaction to save a SAPGUI's screen-based output to a spreadsheet, text file, and more.

13.4.3.   Cleaning Up the Output Logs

Before the data found in an output log are pulled into Excel, they need to be cleaned up in what amounts to a two-phased approach. First, the data are visually analyzed for obvious outliers—for data that appear incorrect, duplicate data (often the result of variables that failed to be reinitialized), and so on. I don't automatically toss all of these data, of course. I analyze them and in many cases correlate them to data points collected at totally different layers in the SAP Technology Stack, to determine with more certainty what stays and what goes. I keep copies of all of the original output logs, too, because you never know what you might need to review again one day soon. After this first phase of data cleansing, the data must be further cleaned. I'll explain this second phase in the next section using a fish analogy.

13.4.4.   Chopping Off the Head and the Tail

I've never been a very good fisherman. Maybe it's because I'm not a morning person, and my grumbling, if I manage to get up that early at all, sends the fish off in search of a quieter spot. Or maybe it's because I just can't seem to get too excited about catching and eating something that takes hours to find and pull up, when it's so readily available at one of the corner grocery stores for less money than I'd pay in lost bait and Diet Cokes. Maybe it's because it's just fish. Give me a license to take down some Angus beef! Now that's something to get excited about. A large prime rib, an enormous porterhouse, a couple of New York strips—they're worth my time.

No matter, I get my share of fishing when it comes to cleansing data in preparation for pouring it all into Excel. Specifically, the performance data and other information found in OS logs, inline data collection output logs, CCMS postrun analysis screens, and so on all need to be pared down to reflect the steady-state or level-testing time period. As depicted in Figure 13–21, the raw

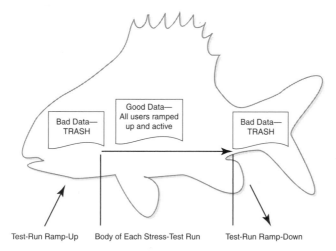

Figure 13–21   Here, chopping off the head and the tail of a test run in terms of the total collected output data is clearly illustrated.

data associated with startup and ramp-up, and then again with ramp-down and stopping, must be removed. Otherwise, the imprecise nature and timing associated with ramping up and down thousands of clients would affect the accuracy of any analysis.

The only part of a test run that should be analyzed (unless you're expressly testing for something else, like how long it actually takes to log in 1,000 users) is the body of the run—the period of time after ramp-up has completed and before ramp-down has commenced. It's during this time that all users are logged in, all workloads are at their peak, and everything is generally running smoothly. In a nutshell, the system is performing the real work of the stress test during this time. It is this precise time period that is to be measured and compared against identical time periods (e.g., 30 minutes) from other test runs.

13.4.5.   Dumping Other Output into Excel

With the raw data cleaned up, the bad data eliminated, and everything generally good to go, now is the time to import all remaining output and other performance data into Excel. If you were on top of things during scripting, you may have already set up many of your scripted CCMS monitoring transactions or inline data collection output-file routines for the XLS format in the first place. I typically create a single workbook with which to stage and measure all of my test runs for a particular stress test. If I'm running three very different kinds of tests, I'll create three different worksheets within my single Excel workbook, though, and stage multiple runs so that the same data occupy the same columns, thereby facilitating analysis. Note that because each worksheet gets its own tab (label), I take this opportunity to double-click the tab and rename the worksheet to something meaningful.

If you have some text-based output data that need to be imported into Excel, simply open or create your Excel test-run workbook, navigate to an empty (or appropriate, if you've used it before) worksheet, and click on the cell that will represent the upper left-hand corner of the location of the data you wish to import. Then from the tool bar, click on "Data" and then select the option "Import external data" followed by "Import data." Navigate through the file system until you find your data source, and then double-click it. The initial screen of the Text Import Wizard opens up, as shown in Figure 13–22. Ensure you set the "Delimited" option (assuming this is true), and then press Next.

Screen two of the Text Import Wizard opens up, where you need to ensure that the appropriate delimiter is selected (I usually go with comma delimited, though space- and tab-delimited output can be useful as well—it all depends on how you separated your output data's fields, and whether some of those fields already contain commas). Click the Next button again, and the final Text Import Wizard screen is displayed, as shown in Figure 13–23. Here, you have a final opportunity to manipulate data columns, tweak formats, identify the decimal and thousands separators

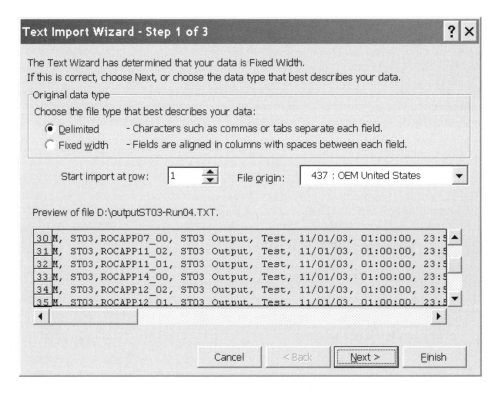

Figure 13–22   Be sure to select the proper file type that best describes your data, taking care to be as consistent as possible when importing multiple input files.

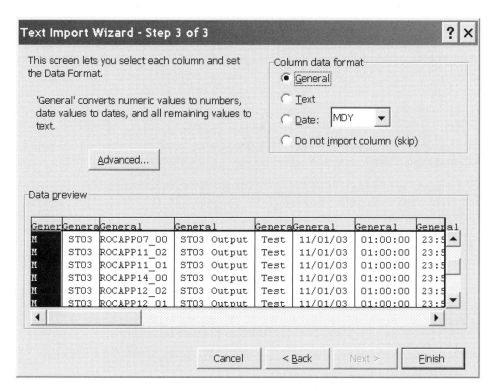

Figure 13–23   Once you've indicated the proper column data format and addressed any "advanced" items, select Finish to initiate conversion of your test run's raw output data into Excel.

(by clicking the Advanced button—very useful in case the default German values were never changed in your SAP test system!), and so on. Click Finish when you're ready, take the default in response to the question "Where do you want to put the data," and press OK. Your text-based output log will be poured into Excel, ready for further analysis.

13.5.   Data Analysis: Figuring Out What It All Means

If possible, I suggest you drop as much of your data into a custom Excel-based stress-test workbook as possible. Not only does this approach facilitate detailed and aggregate analysis but it serves as a great way to unite in one place much of the disparate data pulled from different tools and different layers of your unique SAP Technology Stack or stacks. Once this is accomplished, it then becomes very important to begin considering how you will best present these data, keeping in mind that different audiences prefer different formats, level of detail, use of charts and graphs, and so on.

13.5.1.   Know Your Audience

Well before I execute any test runs, I already have a good understanding of the kind of data points or results that a particular set of stakeholders will value, and the format in which they will most value seeing these data displayed. Technical colleagues will tend to want to see the details "behind the scenes" and will therefore appreciate the Excel workbook itself. IT management and project-driven team leads, on the other hand, will probably want to see rolled-up detailed data reflecting the final outcome of each test run. Senior management and executive teams will be more interested in looking through a relatively few slides regarding high-level technical results or business-specific proof points.

My point in saying this here is simple—know your audience. And lest you begin to think all people occupying the same chair at different companies or within different departments are the same, remember, they're not. I've run into many an executive who still appreciated a detailed graph now and again, for instance. Thus, my recommendation is nothing short of brilliant—the most effective way to meet a particular audience's presentation needs is to ask them what they want to see. And then give them what they want to the best of your abilities.

13.5.2   Turning Data into Information—Charts, Tables, and Graphs

There are some fine methods of presentation available that turn raw data sitting in columns of Excel spreadsheets into useful information. In the past, I've used the following methods:

- PowerPoint-based pie charts, bar charts, and similar constructs are simple to create, may be linked directly to your Excel spreadsheet (to avoid having to retype data from one Office application into another), and are effective at displaying high-level trends or results. For example, I like these kinds of tools when it comes to illustrating bottom-line response-time averages, disk subsystem throughput averages, and top 40 transaction loads. Pie charts and donut charts alike are good for breaking out the individual transactions comprising a complex business process, too, and illustrating which transactions consumed the most time, system resources, and so forth.
- PowerPoint-based scatter charts are hugely effective in comparing two test runs, two platforms, or two of anything else over time, especially when the two items are different in some key respects but from a distance tend to look very similar. This is often the case with two stress-test runs that only vary by the fact that a single profile parameter was changed—they will tend to look very similar at first blush but in fact will differ in one or two important ways. Scatter charts nicely highlight these differences.
- Excel-based three-dimensional line charts are a good way to compare multiple test runs or configuration options. I also think these are effective communication vehicles for comparing the different pieces of a particular test run (as long as the numbers are fairly close). For instance, tracking the big components of response time, like DB Request,

CPU, and possibly Roll or Wait time, can be done well using three-dimensional line charts. Even CCMS has some great three-dimensional charts—check out the excellent graphics available in transaction ST07, for example!

- Excel-based two-dimensional graphs are perfect for mapping different user loads (e.g., representing different test runs) against average response times, so as to understand how incremental user counts increase average response times. In the same way, mapping actual workloads (orders created, total dialog steps processed, and so on) to various user counts is done effectively in this way, too.
- Simple Excel tables that clearly illustrate subtotals, totals, and averages can effectively communicate how different test runs stack up against one another at the most granular of levels (e.g., the low-level components of response time). I also tend to use this format to compare iterative test runs against one another, because a basic format like this lends itself to comparisons where a single factor changed between test runs.

Spider web charts are another effective means of displaying results deltas between multiple runs. Regardless of the presentation tool, though, remember to clearly identify the baseline of a particular set of tests. For instance, if you are tasked with tuning a system's use of table buffering, remember to capture the baseline data points prior to executing any testing and iterative tuning. Without the baseline, your test results will look much less impressive than is otherwise possible! And, by the same token, take the time to quantify key performance metrics associated with different test runs as a configuration changes or morphs based on your tuning. This holds true regardless of whether certain changes resulted in worse results—tracking these changes, and then quantifying exactly how much worse off you were compared with the previous iteration, will help you avoid the same tuning mistake later on. In fact, these less-than-successful attempts at tuning will play an important role in your lessons learned, something we'll take a closer look at in the next chapter.

13.6. Tools and Approaches

As in the previous chapter, this chapter displayed many screen shots of the transactions we discussed, all of which are on the book's ftp site, too, along with sample output formats (text format and Excel spreadsheet) and presentation vehicles (two different PowerPoint formats, each geared toward a different audience). Combined, these materials should serve you well in terms of acting as guides or templates to help you understand what kinds of data are available and then how to present these data in a meaningful way. In doing so, you'll be better positioned for your own testing and tuning projects to be better understood by others, naturally promoting the perception that the overall effort not only was valuable but also represented a good use of company time and resources.

CHAPTER 14

Iterations in Testing and Tuning

If you have ever wondered how many iterations it takes to finish performance tuning a complex enterprise solution like R/3 Enterprise or those found in the mySAP Business Suite, you've come to the right place. The answer is simple—*many*—and you'll likely *never* find yourself putting the final performance-tuning touches on your system. If you're fortunate and stay heads-down, you might get close, but by the time you peer back up, everything will look different again, much like the way the stars can't help but move across the sky at night.

So instead of trying to achieve performance-tuning perfection, I subscribe to an approach that says you must draw a line in the sand that falls short of achieving 100%. A tuning or performance optimization goal of perhaps 90% to 95% is more realistic, representing the upper end of a range in that 1% might imply "out of the box/no explicit tuning" whereas 100% would represent the "completely tuned and optimized" nirvana that no one ever really attains for more than a few moments. The idea behind the line-in-the-sand approach to testing and tuning is to simply push as rapidly as possible toward the line, aware that you will eventually hit a point of diminishing returns where additional testing and tuning actually costs more to the organization than the potential value or benefit derived from it.

But there's good news. In my experience with tuning both productive and benchmark-oriented end-to-end SAP Technology Stacks, my colleagues and I tend to hit what we perceive to be 80% or so fairly quickly—maybe as soon as 1 to 2 weeks—consisting of three to five testing/tuning iterations at each core layer in the technology stack. Eighty percent should not be taken lightly, either—it's relatively easy to reach this level of achievement; indeed, it's practically within spitting distance of that 95% goal. And, in the big picture, hitting 80% is cheap! To take this level of optimization to the next level and hit 90% could easily be another 2 weeks of effort, in fact, depending on a slew of factors: technology used across the landscape, workload mix and distribution, load balancing, expensive SQL, poor coding in general, and more. And once this 90% level of performance is achieved, to again bump a system's performance another 5% might take another significant level of effort on the part of an entire team! Clearly, as we near 95%, the returns diminish quickly as the costs begin to escalate exponentially—each major iteration in testing and tuning costs more than the last, and often delivers less incremental value.

It's for this reason that effective tuning is all about iterative stress testing. In turn, iterative testing is about maintaining a can-do attitude and a high degree of dogged determination or persistence as much as anything else. Indeed, this latter statement is directly at odds with one of my favorite quotes from W. C. Fields, who said, "If at first you don't succeed, try again. Then quit. There's no use being a !&*# fool about it." Although it sounds like good advice to obsessive gamblers, if you quit early in the game, as Fields suggested, you'll be lucky to achieve 80%. But if you persist in conducting consistent and iterative test runs, you'll make progress, however small, and that 95% target, albeit down the road a ways, will be eminently achievable.

Beyond the technical, business, functional, and attitude challenges inherent to optimizing a complex enterprise solution, another real challenge everyone must deal with is that the concept of "good performance" is a moving target at best. Your end users may tell you that they're not happy with performance one day, but be pleased the next, even though nothing in terms of load or configuration has really changed. Your customers who are intent on getting their hands on their daily batch reports as quickly as possible may be completely satisfied most days, and unhappy with the turnaround time on other days. My point here is that *perceptions* will drive many a user's current definition of good performance much of the time, and genuine performance issues will drive the rest.

Outside of perceptions, though, the workload itself will morph over time, fundamentally changing how to quantify and characterize "good performance" simply because the baseline against which you're measuring is no longer valid. SLAs will change over time, too, based on what the business needs at the current moment in time to keep the *real* customers happy—the ones making it possible for all of us to pay our mortgages and keep two cars in the garage. One month, achieving a particular SLA will be business as usual, whereas the next month it may fail to impress. All of these conditions simply underscore the importance of consistent benchmarking, baselining, and testing. After all, what better way to ward off a potential performance issue than to catch it in its infancy? And what better way to fight perception than with the hard performance facts and response-time metrics that load testing can provide?

14.1. Stop, Analyze, and Resume

During an SAP stress test, it's quite tempting to simply execute different test runs back to back as hastily as possible, because the days grow long pretty quickly, and anything that looks like it can speed up matters often seems like a good idea. Although this approach isn't entirely without merit, my experience has shown me time and again that I actually burn up *less* time overall when I practice a testing method I call "stop, analyze, and resume." Consider the following:

- The word "stop" implies a definite end to the current test run. Scripts are stopped gracefully or otherwise, data collection routines or processes are stopped as well, and all of the supporting performance data relative to the run are collected.
- The key to this method lies in the next word, "analyze." I don't mean to say that the reams of hardware-based, OS, database, and SAP CCMS data need to be analyzed in their entirety; indeed, such an approach would unnecessarily waste time. However, a

basic postanalysis of the test run should be conducted simply to prove that the test run itself was executed and monitored in a valid manner, and that "good" data were collected from the run. Skipping this analysis—a step I believe to be crucial—only leads to rerunning test cases at the last minute (e.g., at the end of the day, or end of the week!), test cases which down the road may take an enormous amount of time to set up and prepare for again.

- Finally, the word "resume" suggests it's now appropriate to move on to the next test case or test run, though only after taking the proper steps as usual to ensure that the stage is set for another good test run, of course.

What exactly should be analyzed, you ask? It only makes sense to perform a high-level review of the data that ultimately *prove* the test run was executed in a consistent manner, and then to verify that something close to the expected results was obtained. Thus, the first thing I look at is whether the test's timing was consistent with goals or other test runs—did it execute long enough, ramping up, leveling out, and ramping down as expected? Next, I ensure that the monitoring processes—scripted CCMS transactions, data I collected manually, data available from the test tools and so on—were executed consistently. Do the monitoring data prove that the user load reached its expected point? Did I achieve a certain number of concurrent processes, execute a certain number of loops in a test run, or in some other way meet the objective of the test run? Finally, do the numbers *look* right? A few minutes spent poring over key success criteria metrics and then mapping these metrics back to the data just recently collected will help avoid going off on a tangent and basically wasting lots of time. This is especially true of iterative performance tuning test runs that tend to build on one another. For example, when tuning a disk subsystem for an SAP OLTP environment, there will be tasks associated with tuning the hardware that should be accomplished prior to optimizing the OS, database, SAP, and any front-end client software. Failing to verify that a test run is progressively showing better or faster test results, not slower, will pretty much invalidate all of your subsequent test runs. Instead of throwing away only the last 30 or 60 minutes' worth or work, you could easily toss out most of a day's worth of activities, in fact, and find yourself seriously behind schedule faster than you can say "We're gonna need another round of tall double-shot nonfat caffe lattes."

It should be apparent that *not* conducting a postrun analysis, however brief, adds up to significant time and money. On the other hand, validating a test case's results via a quick analysis is inexpensive in the long run and helps ensure that you probably won't need to fall back to a point in time (in terms of hardware configuration, SAP configuration, and so on) that may be extremely difficult if not nearly impossible to duplicate. Analysis therefore acts as the gateway for iterative and sound testing, in that an investment in creating a repeatable postrun analysis process makes it easy to justify moving to the next phase in a stress test.

14.2. Tracking and Evaluating Changes

Throughout this book, I've taken the position that changes—any changes—to a system, process, or workload, or to the infrastructure beneath a performance test, outside of the changes explicitly being tested, are frowned on, because these changes tend to make initial baselines worthless and therefore create more work for everyone. Some changes are much more manageable than others, though, so before we dive into iterative tuning, it makes sense to take a look at how to overcome or work through certain changes, especially those that seem to commonly crop up. And, by the same token, it's important to understand which changes are show stoppers—which ones require that a new baseline be established, for example, and which changes simply necessitate a bit of re-work.

14.2.1. Stress-Test Method Changes

Method changes may be acceptable either because they can be worked around or because they tend to yield a useful byproduct: additional information. But this information can come with a hefty price tag, because in changing the approach or methodology used to execute or monitor a stress test, you may in essence be creating a new baseline, a new test case, and a new set of test runs. Consider, for example, an R/3 stress test that requires 1,000 users to execute a range of business transactions. If the timing method used for ramp-up and ramp-down is inadvertently changed between runs, more or less work will be performed by the users logged into the system, resulting in different throughput values that have nothing to do with the platform-based tuning or configuration changes you really seek to test and understand. This change in method can be overcome, though, simply by selecting a known time period that is consistent across multiple test runs. For example, let's assume you are testing the impact that different buffer-related profile parameters have in a BW performance test of 25 minutes in duration. Your three test runs excluding ramp-up and ramp-down might range from 25 minutes for the first run, to 30 minutes for the second (perhaps because you got sidetracked with a couple of hot pizzas showing up earlier than expected), to an overanxious 24-minute final run. Your first inclination might be to execute the second and third tests over again, taking greater care to hit the 25-minute mark. Or you might approach it in this way:

- The first run will fit perfectly into the test criteria.
- The second test run can also be "made" valid, assuming you chop off the output results associated with the last 5 minutes of the test run. Failing to do this, however, will result in a test run that appears to get more work done with the same number of users logged in, therefore inaccurately portraying the effectiveness of the profile buffer change.
- The third test run needs to "fit" into the 25-minute test-run criterion. You might simply analyze the last minute of testing, and add these results to the test, making it a 25-minute test. Or you might extrapolate the average value of each of the 24 minutes, and add this to the total.

But another approach might be more effective. What if you just take the lowest common denominator—the smallest of the three values, or 24—and base the evaluation of all three tests on the results yielded by the first 24 minutes of each test run? This will make for a consistent stress-test period to be analyzed, while avoiding the need to extrapolate or otherwise manipulate data, the validity of which may later be questioned by others. Twenty-four minutes, while not the goal in the beginning, may actually represent a fine series of test runs, assuming your goal didn't absolutely require 25-minute test runs across the board! And if you did need to support apples-to-apples comparisons with previously executed test runs that all happened to be 25 minutes long, it might be just as easy to shrink them all down to 24 minutes instead.

But what if you changed your method for monitoring and failed to capture consist performance statistics across all three test runs? Or what if you never restarted the servers and disk subsystems between test runs, leaving precious data in caches to artificially boost the performance of the second and third test runs? These kinds of process modifications change the playing field and yield new test cases, plain and simple, making it necessary to start over. So, to reiterate, making a change to the process used for conducting or monitoring a stress-test run not only potentially represents a huge investment in time, and certainly additional work, but also may represent a new baseline in and of itself. If this is not the desired outcome, I suggest cutting your losses quickly, tossing the rogue test case out, and repeating the test run with an eye toward achieving greater consistency. Stop, analyze, take a break if necessary, pay closer attention, and resume.

14.2.2.   Client-Driver Changes

Probably the least important of all changes that must be validated or tracked in a test run are the changes related to the client drivers and other supporting test infrastructure. That is, most of the time, as long as you achieve the number of concurrent batch processes or online users, it matters little if the client drivers have been tweaked, tuned, or even replaced. But it is nevertheless important to track these changes, if any, because these can potentially result in unwanted impact to a set of test runs. For instance:

- If you tune or optimize your client drivers such that they are capable of ramping up a user load more quickly than before (and this process is not throttled by the test-tool software), you'll change the nature of any subsequent test runs. Perhaps the test runs will look like more work is being performed, or some other throughput measurement might appear out of whack, all other things being equal.
- If you reduce or increase the *number* of client drivers, you might similarly increase or decrease the load placed on your network infrastructure, which could in turn artificially limit the potential throughput of your scripted end users. In my experience, this won't be a problem for modern 100mb or faster networks. But it's worth considering if you're driving a significant load, especially if you're moving huge volumes of large data blocks (e.g., those associated with BW data loads or extracts back to R/3, database backup/restore operations, and so on).
- If you increase or decrease the throughput capabilities of your client drivers by introducing or removing CPUs, RAM, and so on, you risk impacting test throughput—some test tools may actually slow down or speed up in terms of active users and processes.

- Any software changes made to the client-driver technology stack may also result in slowdowns, speed-ups, and just plain problems. Patches to an OS, your test tool, and other software represent a greater unknown than hardware-based changes. I therefore recommend analyzing test runs with greater care than you otherwise might be inclined to do, even to the point of re-executing a previously executed test run to serve as a comparison; use this to "prove" that a client driver software update has not resulted in performance changes, and then resume testing.

With the method and client-driver infrastructure squared away and accounted for, we can now turn our attention to the reason a series of test runs is executed in the first place—to iteratively tune SAP.

14.2.3. Test Platform Iterative Updates

Testing your Production SAP platform or another system similar in design and deployment is what SAP performance testing and tuning is all about. For pre-Go-Live stress tests, I typically start my first set of test runs with the goal of proving that any preliminary tuning has paid off. With a large repository of test configurations and performance results behind me, I usually have an idea as to what kind of pretuning to conduct as a matter of course versus what kind of pretuning warrants its own set of test runs. Testing different disk subsystem configurations to find the best controller–cache drive–HBA combinations makes up the bulk of this level of testing, followed by running a couple of baselines against which future changes will be measured.

I'll then test any OS-level configuration changes, like the impact that different blocksizes has on throughput or the load incurred by running a particular set of management agents, third-party services or processes, and more. Changes to how RAM is addressed or handled, or optimized for buffering, drive more testing, as does testing the impact of new drivers, service packs, patches, or kernel updates. It's important to then perform a set of tests that holistically reflects the performance of the entire system—hardware and OS alike. This test set will serve as a baseline in the future.

Database-specific and SAP-specific configuration changes come next. With a whole slew of potential changes that may be recommended by either the database vendor or SAP AG themselves, this testing can consume quite a bit of time. I try to leverage my own experience and that of my colleagues, along with documented best practices as published by the respective software vendor's (or other partner's) SAP Competency Centers, to speed through this work. With the many settings recommended by SAP Notes, whitepapers, performance briefs, and so on, I find that it is pretty easy to arrive at a moderately well-tuned system in no time. As I said earlier, though, pushing the bar to achieve 80%, 90%, or better tuning requires exponentially greater investments in research, testing, and iterative tuning. And like the testing performed at hardware and OS levels, a set of tests that exercises the system holistically is required at this point for baseline purposes. On top of this, for cross-application business processes, a set of tests that exercises multiple systems will also be required. Thus, the key to good test platform testing, I believe, is to work your way up the SAP Technology Stack model, consistently applying a proven testing method and leveraging a static test infrastructure and client-driver environment. Such an approach lends itself to one-change-at-a-time testing—namely, that focused on testing changes to your SAP platform's configuration.

14.2.4.   Workload Changes

Tuning a system for a specific or unique workload might appear to be the end-all, be-all goal of many a stress test. But workloads vary according to the time of day (peaks at 10 a.m. and 2 p.m. are common), time of year (e.g., seasonal peaks, such as during the holidays or back-to-school season), and so on, and test runs must therefore vary accordingly if the goal is to tweak and tune for these different periods or occasions. I have often found myself executing stress tests focused on replicating the unique load associated with month-end processing for heavy finance and logistics, for instance. Assuming the time and budget are available, though, there's much to be gained by characterizing a system in terms of daily loads, quarter-end loads, and even fiscal-year closings. And for companies with seasonal peaks or other peak loads that may fall during the same timeframe as a month-end or quarter-end load, the knowledge that comes from testing and tuning for these combined test cases may pay off big-time down the road in terms of proactive capacity planning.

Workload changes might be much more subtle than replicating a month-end load, though. I've executed test runs in which I slightly varied the functional end-user test mix, for instance, to understand how a particular company's SD implementation would probably scale over the course of the next year, because it was expected to account for more and more of the workload mix. I've also introduced different functional areas into a "baseline" workload mix simply to understand at what point an application server's cache would give out as indicated by hit ratios that dropped below 90%; doing so helped a company craft a better logon load-balancing scheme.

In another stress test, I changed the ratio of batch jobs to online users, primarily to observe how user response times fell apart as batch loads (measured in terms of concurrent batch processes, observed via SM66) increased. In another case, I ramped up user counts in increments of 10 to see precisely where a set of performance thresholds was exceeded for a particular workload on a particular configuration. All of these cases lent themselves to iterative testing; indeed, workload testing naturally lends itself to this, so much so that I've dedicated more space to workload testing in the next and final chapter.

14.2.5.   Apples to Oranges? Starting Over . . .

If you've stayed with me over the last few pages, you've probably noticed how easy it is to veer off track and start going off on a new tangent or course of testing outside of what was originally envisioned. As I've tried to show in Figure 14–1, each new tangent starts as and represents a new baseline, and subsequent tests will almost surely be limited to being compared with this tangent's baseline, given that the value of comparing the run to the original baseline disappeared along the way. As I mentioned earlier, if these tangents are not providing new information or insight in the

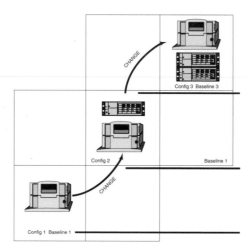

Figure 14–1   Changes to a system equate to tangents, which essentially drive test cases with their own unique baselines, making apples-to-apples comparisons to prior configurations impossible.

form of new baselines, they need to be tossed out—it's too easy and too tempting to try and use these test runs in some kind of comparative way. Doing so amounts to apples-to-oranges testing, which is clearly not desired in most circles. And this, in turn, leads to starting over.

14.3.   Tuning the Disk Subsystem, Database, and SAP Application Layers

At the end of the day, a well-tuned application running on a properly configured database can mask a multitude of hardware and OS shortcomings. But the opposite is true as well—oversizing a system is a common way of addressing unknown capacity-planning issues or dealing with un-clear peak demands. Oversizing is by no means cheap, either, as the term implies. I therefore submit that tuning is best accomplished by working consistently *up* the SAP Technology Stack, from infrastructure to hardware, OS, database, and then application and integration layers. I typ-ically use major and minor test iterations to stay both focused and on track. In other words, once I get the infrastructure squared away, I test and tune before moving on to the next layer in the stack, using tools and utilities discussed in Chapters 6 and 7. The same approach holds true for all layers, especially with respect to hardware (where misconfiguration can severely dampen your tuning efforts elsewhere). Once the hardware and OS layers are optimized, I then turn my atten-tion to the database layer, testing and tuning the layout of data files and tables, logs, temp/sort space, and more.

Next, I review and test configuration changes to SAP itself, being careful to never circum-vent SAP if my tuning efforts force me to make changes that impact the underlying database. That is, I never make changes to the database outside the control of SAP, because these changes cannot be tracked or validated by SAP, increasing the risk of error and misconfiguration along the way. What this means is that all database-relevant SAP system tuning is done from the SAP application layer—changes I might make in terms of creating or deleting indexes are a good example. Also, any changes made to buffering database tables must be done through SAP as well.

In the end, tuning an SAP system involves a lot of work as should be evident by now. Let's look at some of the common areas where iterative testing and tuning are known to pay big performance dividends.

14.3.1. SAN Fabric and Disk Subsystem Tuning

The two focus areas for testing and iteratively tuning disk subsystems today lie in the infrastructure associated with SANs and the layout and configuration of physical disk drives into larger disk groups, or LUNs, that use various RAID approaches. With regard to the former, if you find that you're pushing the limits of your disk subsystem in terms of MB/second throughput, you should go ahead while you presumably have the time and investigate the performance delta that additional server HBAs provide. But if your OS or hardware platform limits the number of HBAs you can effectively use, you have a problem. This is where other testing and tuning efforts must be leveraged. For instance, you might be tempted to investigate different SAN fabric configurations (assuming you have access to incremental SAN switches, if necessary). Different SAN designs can be assembled to give you more bandwidth per HBA or provide more ports for servers or more ports into the SAN itself. For example, the most commonly deployed configuration, termed *skinny tree,* provides more average "available" ports per switch than most configurations and affords a healthy though moderate cross-sectional data rate. It has a classic core/edge network design, leveraging a "trunk" of two or more switches connected on the right "side" to servers and on the left "side" to the SAN disk controllers. In this way, the trunk (which logically resides in the middle of the two sides, which are also called *leafs*) represents the bottleneck in the configuration. Additional trunk switches can be added, however, to increase the potential throughput of the trunk—and a good stress test will help you validate that the change indeed delivers the incremental performance you desire.

But what if the minor change to your skinny tree fabric fails to deliver the throughput that your SAP systems require? In that case, you might want to look into architecting and testing another popular SAN fabric configuration, called *fat tree*. Fat tree configurations are more expensive than their skinny counterparts, because extra hardware is required to provide the same number of available ports to what is presumably a fixed number of servers and SAN/disk controller ports. The "extra" ports lost between a fat tree and skinny tree are consumed by the fabric itself—more connections are made between the various switches, so as to provide the highest bandwidth rates available. The high relative number of total ports dedicated to interswitch links accounts for the incremental costs.

Regardless of the SAN fabric changes you make, this is where application-layer tuning can be most helpful in proving that such an investment is worth making in the first place. Think about it—if you only perform low-level disk-centric testing, you might prove that a fat tree design or "thicker" skinny tree trunk can indeed handle another 50% increase in raw I/Os. But what you *really* need to know is how that increased I/O capability maps to improved application-layer performance. For instance, if you have a bottleneck somewhere between the hardware and application technology stack layers, you'll never have the chance to take advantage of the increased capacity made possible by your SAN fabric reconfiguration. All in all, this is a good example of where iterative testing and tuning at a high level pays off.

Another area where iterative testing can help you maximize your investment in SAP is at the fundamental disk subsystem configuration layer—there might be good reason to investigate basic performance differences between different RAID configurations. For example, even though you already should have gone through the pretuning steps discussed in Chapter 8, your circumstances may have changed. Perhaps now you find yourself needing additional disk space but have run out of budget dollars—you may be tempted to convert your RAID 0+1 and RAID 1 disk sets into more spacious RAID 5 stripes. Before doing so, however, you'll want to validate that a RAID 5 configuration is actually capable of meeting your performance targets using disk-testing tools like those covered in Chapter 6.

The same holds true for converting RAID 5 volumes into something like a RAID 0+1 mirrored stripe set. Can you get by with less disk space? If so, what exactly is the trade-off in disk space buying you in terms of increased performance? Questions like these are easily answered with a quick delta test. And because the differences can range widely depending on the disk controller, version of firmware installed, and so on, the time invested characterizing different configurations is time well spent. This is especially true if you run into performance problems later—a baseline record of disk throughput metrics will help you verify that the disk subsystem still performs as well as it used to (at least from a raw I/O perspective), letting you focus your attention elsewhere in the SAP Technology Stack.

14.3.2. Database Tuning

Both database tuning and optimizing the application layer residing on top of the database are accomplished by making configuration changes. Such changes involve software-based updates rather than physical changes to a system. Configuration changes are discussed next in the context of how iterative testing and knowledgeable tuning can increase your system's performance.

When I'm asked to tune a database, I first focus on understanding the information provided in transaction DB02—the size of the overall database and indexes, the size of individual table spaces or particularly active tables, the number of missing indexes, and the enormous compilation of space statistics (especially regarding the growth or utilization of particular tables, table spaces, and the database in general). I also tend to execute a detailed analysis of the tables and indexes, using ST03 and ST04 to look for those data that represent the highest database access times as well as the greatest average response times. Once these data are obtained, I cross-reference them back to the number of dialog steps associated with accessing each table, sequential reads versus direct reads versus changes (information also available in ST03), and more, and then file this information away—it'll be more useful once I have a better handle on the database's performance compared to other systems I've work on. That is, once the current-state system information and other data noted previously are obtained, I can then take a multipronged approach to analyzing database performance, which includes comparing the system with similarly sized SAP accounts by reviewing the following:

- Database cache hit rates and I/O mixes (in terms of logical read to physical read ratios, and physical reads to writes), as identified in transaction ST04.
- ST04/Detail Analysis Menu, followed by clicking the File System Requests button. This step provides insight into how specific table spaces and even drive letters or mount points are accessed (reads versus writes, average access times in milliseconds, and more). I'm especially fond of "I/O per path" and "I/O per file" statistics, which reveal the load borne by each logical disk drive—in this way, I can compare a database's disks to validate that the underlying disk subsystem is balanced, as shown in Figure 14–2.
- Additional data available through ST04/Detail Analysis Menu. The resource consumption by "SQL Request" and "Table Access" helps me create a short list of potentially expensive SQL statements, including the tables/indexes used to access the underlying data along with the total number of buffer gets (bufgets), bufgets per row, the number of times the SQL statement has been executed as well as bufgets per execution since the database was started, and the total number of disk accesses. I usually toss out most SQL statements that have been executed very few times, require very few disk accesses, or represent a small ratio of executions to bufgets.
- More ST04 data. Because expensive SQL statements impact not only the execution speed of the statement itself but the speed with which other transactions may be executed, I'm inclined to invest the time necessary to identify the worst culprits. From ST04/Detail Analysis Menu, click the SQL Request button, then enter search criteria (e.g., >100,000 bufgets). At this point, a list of potentially poor SQL statements and the

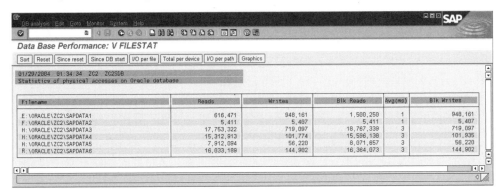

Figure 14–2 Clicking your way through ST04, Detail Analysis Menu, File System Requests, and then pressing the I/O per Path button make it easy to verify whether a disk load is balanced across logical drives.

programs that execute those statements will be listed. I look through the list to find statements that are executed often and drive a huge number of disk reads or bufgets per execution. Double-clicking one of these SQL statements then allows me to see how it's used and implemented in terms of the specific *select*, *from*, *where*, and other clauses or statements used, as well as how the SQL statement accesses data in the tables referenced by it (including the indexes used, how they are leveraged, the execution plan, and more). An expensive SQL statement is shown in Figure 14–3.

- Buffer hit rates, available through ST02, and application-specific buffer hit rates, available through ST07 after the SAP Buffer button is clicked. These rates help prove how well the Oracle System Global Area (SGA) or RAM associated with the database is performing, given the way it's chopped up into buffers and caches. In fact, iteratively testing different SGA configurations is about as common a test scenario as any when it comes to Oracle database tuning.
- Table buffering, revealed via ST10 (table call statistics) and, if necessary, DB05 (analysis of tables with respect to indexed fields).
- Database statistics, to ensure that the tables in question have undergone a recent "database statistics" analysis as performed by Oracle's cost-based optimizer, for example. I also like to review table *dbstatc* to verify that any tables in question indeed undergo some kind of regular update statistics process, and I then follow this up with a review of DB13 (the DBA planning calendar) to ensure the update statistics job is scheduled once a week or whatever is appropriate.
- Database request times for the top 40 or so transactions, as provided by ST03. I usually review these data aggregated over a period like a month, if I'm looking to quantify average daily loads, or over a smaller period (e.g., the few days surrounding a month-end close) if I seek to really understand the end-of-month transactions and tasks executed during this time.

In addition to the previously described analyses, databases like SQL Server and SAP DB (rebranded MaxDB as of the end of 2003) allow you to specify the number of CPUs in your database server dedicated to database processing. In this way, you can ensure that processing bandwidth remains available for other tasks, like those associated with hosting the SAP central instance (if a combined database/central instance is deployed), or for addressing network or other requirements. Before you run off and make these decisions, though, I encourage you to iteratively test a few variations. Worst case, your effort will serve as due diligence and therefore mitigate risk. On the other hand, you might prevent an otherwise lousy configuration decision, avoiding the need to bring the system down to reconfigure the number of processors used by the database.

In a nutshell, then, database tuning is very dependent on a number of areas: the number of CPUs configured; the quantity and impact of database requests on a particular set of tables; and how these tables are indexed, buffered, and otherwise managed to provide the greatest potential access to the data. If you're interested in more detail, I suggest that you pick up a copy of Dr.

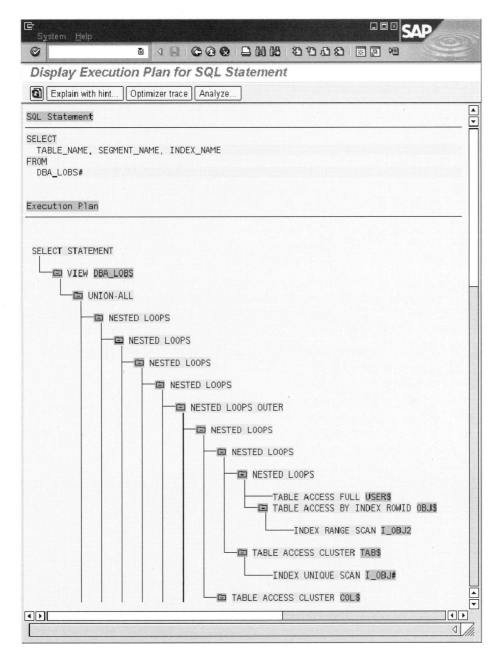

Figure 14–3 Because expensive SQL statements cause response-time issues not only for the programs executing the statements but for other programs fighting for limited hardware resources, iterative load testing is warranted, if not encouraged, to test SQL code changes.

Thomas Schneider's latest edition of the *SAP Performance Optimization Guide*. Published by SAP Press, it's one of my personal favorites and certainly the unquestioned authority when it comes to tuning databases for SAP solutions.

14.3.3.   SAP Profile Tuning

Much of the tuning germane to SAP can be accomplished by tweaking the *default* and *instance* profiles relevant to each application server and the central instance. These revision-controlled profiles, as well as the *start* profile for each server, may be accessed via RZ10. With regard to the default profile, which is shared by all instances within a particular system, it is worthwhile to iteratively tune the following profile parameters, among others:

- rdisp/bufrefmode
- zcsa/db_max_buftab
- max_wprun_time (for dialog, background, update, spool, and more)

And in regard to the central instance or any application servers and their respective instance profiles, you might be interested in testing and tuning the following:

- The number of configured work processes
- The amount of memory configured for each work process, including roll-first, extended, roll-extension, and heap
- Buffer sizes and buffer areas
- Many additional memory parameters, including "physical memory size" and a number of "heap-related" configuration choices, among others

Just keep in mind that although there are plenty of parameters to be tested, it still will prove worthwhile to keep track of each profile parameter as it evolves over time, noting how performance increased or decreased with each iterative load test performed on the system. It's no wonder why scripting is so valued in these cases—imagine the time spent otherwise walking through the various load scenarios while trying to maintain some level of "repeatability" in your load-testing process!

14.3.4.   Other SAP Application-Layer Tuning

Outside of the SAP default and instance profiles, other areas support iterative reconfiguration or some level of tweaking and tuning, the most important of which include the following:

- ABAP or Java coding and other development activities. These are performed primarily to minimize disk subsystem loads and maximize database performance. SQL traces (ST05) can be key in helping you determine the effectiveness of a particular approach over another.

- The creation of new indexes. This can provide more efficient ways of accessing table data (where the goal is to minimize the number of records that must be searched in a table to find what you're looking for). Again, leverage ST05.
- SAP Kernel changes and updates. The idea is to verify not only that the new version works as advertised but actually works *well* in your particular environment.
- The RFC configuration and performance relative to connections to other systems. Performance testing will help you understand whether these external links have inadvertently become bottlenecks to further performance gains. For example, a stress test can quickly prove that your newly upgraded and refreshed SAP system now floods other systems with requests beyond their ability to process quickly.
- Table buffering. Huge database throughput gains can be realized once you determine which tables indeed provide the greatest buffering bang for the buck in relation to the relatively small size of SAP buffers available to cache these tables, how often the tables are changed, and whether they tend to be read-oriented.
- Processes that update statistics associated with tables and how the data found in a particular table are best accessed. Statistics need not be generated for all tables, but for others must be updated often to provide the most value.
- Processes executed by SAP to monitor itself, like those associated with CCMS in general and RZ20 in particular. These can have a huge performance impact on the database and must therefore be controlled in terms of execution times (stay away from peak hours!), frequency of execution (refrain from *too* much performance monitoring!), and so on.

Use ST04, ST03, ST02, and the other useful monitoring transactions and approaches discussed in Chapters 7 and 12 to provide both snapshot and historical data to validate your tuning efforts.

14.3.5. SAP Front-End Tuning

Although front-end tuning is not usually the first thing to come to mind in a performance-tuning project, it can be quite important nonetheless. I suggest you pay attention to how the SAPGUI or other front end is configured, and test different options in your sandbox environment. The Customizing button in the far upper-right corner of the SAPGUI can be used to configure a number of parameters that ultimately impact SAPGUI *build time* and *front-end average network time*, both important performance metrics tracked by ST03 relative to dialog response times, as shown in Figure 14–4.

For example, you can change general settings, local cache sizes, the placement of this cache on your local system, trace modes (including the level of detail, and whether errors and warnings are tracked), and the visual design (e.g., high contrast is much better for collecting screen shots). In addition, the size of the fonts displayed and even the number of colors used can be customized, the latter of which is especially useful when you execute the SAPGUI real-time (rather than vir-

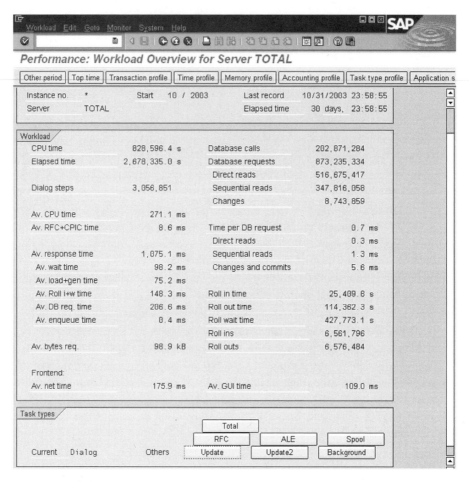

Figure 14–4   Settings available through the Customizing button found on the upper-right corner of most SAPGUI screens can directly impact build time and front-end average network time (found at the bottom of the ST03 output screen, dialog task only).

tually) and wish to minimize the load placed on your client drivers. And with the ability to throttle the SAPGUI in terms of EnjoySAP-initiated interface details, testing the throughput associated with slow network links is still warranted today.

14.4.   Lessons Learned in the Real World

During the course of my travels, I've had the privilege of learning from my customers as much as, if not more than, they have learned from me. The following section discusses lessons learned from years of iterative testing and tuning—I hope you find these beneficial and use them to avoid what can otherwise amount to very time-consuming if not just plain, old, expensive mistakes.

14.4.1. Server IT Consolidation for SAP

When I am involved with stress testing new server platforms to be eventually deployed to Production, I typically focus on delta testing. That is, I want to understand how the difference in CPU speeds, system bus architecture, RAM or memory subsystem architecture, and so on between different platforms provides additional processing headroom. In the past, I've made mistakes in the following areas:

- On more than one occasion, I've failed to verify (or set, in the case of new systems) the system configuration utility to the proper OS setting. This is one of those low-level settings in a computer's Basic Input/Output System (BIOS) that tend to impact performance more than you'd expect. For example, forgetting to change a BIOS setting from one that specifies Windows 2000 as the primary OS to one that instead specifies Windows Server 2003 initially resulted in an inability to access the 16th processor in HP ProLiant (affecting other Intel Xeon MP eight-way systems as well) using Intel's hyperthreading technology—now there's a performance impact!

- I've failed to take into account the fact that preproduction or *beta* servers (those made available before a platform is officially released by its vendor) may perform better or worse than their generally available production counterparts—system boards change, available processors change, and so on. This is manifested in different CPU revisions, CPU speeds, available cache settings, and more. The same idea applies to comparing the first new servers rolling off the assembly line to the same model 6 months later, too.

- I've failed to take into account that different CPU cache sizes make it a bit difficult to precisely estimate apples-to-apples performance deltas. For this reason, years ago, I became a big fan of Survey, GetConfig, and other current-state utilities that capture low-level hardware information, making it easy to validate later a particular hardware setting or firmware revision level.

- I've forgotten to take into account the difference in write performance (especially paging performance) of different onboard or built-in disk controllers. That is, some systems tend to ship with basic SCSI or Integrated Drive Electronics (IDE) disk controllers, whereas others ship with higher performance RAID controllers with read cache, and still others ship with write-cache- and read-cache-equipped RAID controllers. Being able to "post" pagefile writes to the local disk controller's cache rather than waiting on physical I/O yields a big boon in performance, especially when physical RAM is scarce or otherwise limited.

- I've simply failed to understand that consolidation issues go beyond that which is actually being consolidated, the testing of which can therefore generally consume a lot of time. A number of years ago, I sized and tested a significantly consolidated SAP Application server farm. I "did the math" properly but really didn't take into account the effective amount of RAM a single instance could access in a Windows environment, a novice oversight I hate even mentioning! Anyway, to effectively host the expected peak workload, I needed more RAM than could be housed or accessed in the new consolidated server environment. Thanks to pre-Go-Live testing, this amounted to an inconvenience rather than a nightmare.

- On another occasion, I failed to take into account the effective number of work processes that SAP would support on a single Windows-based SAP Application Server instance. My consolidation plans for a particular company looked really compelling until one of my on-the-ball colleagues realized the problem fairly late in the game—another round of test iterations I wouldn't mind forgetting.

A second pair of eyes can really make a difference here. I suggest enlisting the aid of your hardware partner's SAP Competency Center to validate your sizing efforts and consolidation approach prior to testing and deployment. Worst case, if you prefer to keep things "internal," briefly enlist the assistance of one of your colleagues to give your strategy and test-bed a once-over prior to kicking off your stress-test runs—you'll be surprised at how many basic misconfiguration issues or other shortcomings can somehow slip through the cracks.

14.4.2.   SAN Consolidation and Disk Subsystem Upgrades

Like server consolidation projects, implementing a SAN or another disk subsystem solution for your SAP environment represents huge opportunities to introduce unknowns into your solution. It's really easy, for example, to put way too many eggs in a single basket! Take care to avoid the following:

- Although a SAN is a great way to consolidate disk/data resources, unless you know what you're getting into, avoid consolidating your entire SAP system landscape into a single SAN! A few years ago, one of my customers initially designed a single SAN for its entire R/3 and BW environment, bringing together technical sandboxes, development and QA systems, and finally Production into a single SAN fabric with multiple storage cabinets. Had we not realized it during testing, they would have gone live with an environment in which testing firmware upgrades to the SAN fabric would have been impossible. A single fabric was planned to tie everything together, which unwittingly represented a single point of failure capable of bringing the entire SAP environment down if a future firmware upgrade failed to go well. The solution was to create a non-Production SAN (containing the sandboxes, development, and QA systems) and a dedicated Production SAN. In this way, fabric changes and upgrades could be thoroughly tested without impacting Production while still achieving a high level of consolidation.
- Take care to consider varying I/O patterns and peak workloads associated with combining different SAP solutions in a single disk subsystem. I've assisted a number of my customers with collapsing R/3, BW, and CRM Production systems into a single SAN, for example. Had we not taken the time to understand the loads placed on each Production database during particular time periods (daily, month-end, and so on), though, we would have inadvertently carved up the physical disks into logical disks unable to meet peak-load requirements. And, in some cases, controller cache configurations would

have differed, too, resulting in less than optimal cache hit rates during peaks, and less than maximum performance at other times.

- Test the throughput and I/O bandwidth a particular configuration is capable of, too, regardless of what you think you know about the performance of particular RAID configurations or controller settings. With today's high-performance virtual arrays and the ability to create a few high-performance stripe-sets consisting of literally hundreds of physical drives, or many smaller logical drives consisting of fewer drives each, iterative testing is a must. Different approaches to segregating varying I/O patterns need to be considered—should you deploy dedicated data-file drives, one or more for each discrete database? Can you combine all databases on the same set of physical drives? Do you need to consider a separate logical drive to house all write-intensive operations, like those associated with logs? And if the answer to the last question is yes, does it make sense to validate changes to the controller's write cache, so that, for example, you can post more writes than are otherwise possible using the controller's default configuration?

- By the same token, don't forget to conduct multiple-system concurrent stress testing on your proposed SAN design. That is, if you're combining R/3 and BW onto a single SAN, for example, you need to execute performance tests that drive loads on both the R/3 and BW databases *at the same time*. This is a truly valuable stress test, and should be performed at a hardware or OS level (using tools like Iometer or SQLIO) as well as at an application level (using custom business scripts to simulate workloads executing concurrently on each database housed within the SAN). Concurrent workload testing is the only way to effectively validate that your SAN design will hold up under the stress of the real world prior to actually deploying it. Finally, don't forget to iteratively test different OS block sizes (like 1KB versus 4KB for Oracle redo logs)!

Disk subsystem consolidation is still a huge area of activity for many SAP customer environments today—learn from the lessons discussed previously to hit the ground running while avoiding the most common reasons for going back to the drawing board. The downtime needed to make significant changes to a SAN can be hard to come by once everything is moved over and productive again. This is because you'll have traded the bit of flexibility you had when the individual SAP disk resources were left in their own little islands for greater density, resource utilization, increased performance, and lower TCO.

14.4.3.   Functional Upgrades

When I think of performing a functional upgrade, like most of you I automatically think about all of the functional testing that must take place to ensure that the business can continue to run on the new version of software to be deployed. But functional upgrades often include a certain number of infrastructure upgrades as well, given the historical tendency of SAP AG to require more and more hardware to support the same number of end users. Thus, testing how well these incremental updates support the new business solution needs to be worked into the functional upgrade's project plan.

Oftentimes, this simply means adding incremental CPU horsepower or RAM to a couple of servers. But in conjunction with your functional upgrade, you might decide to pursue a server consolidation or SAN deployment strategy. A best-practices approach dictates creating separate projects, of course, but in the real world of shrinking downtime windows and ever-increasing throughput capabilities, this might be impractical. I suggest at least mitigating your risk with a series of iterative stress-test runs, then, designed to prove as much as possible that the new configuration—at both hardware and functional levels—will deliver what the business requires.

Functional upgrades might take into account database software updates too. For instance, iteratively testing the impact an SAP functional upgrade has before and after a proposed database update (like the 27–49% potential increase in throughput relative to a Microsoft SQL Server 2000 upgrade from SQL 7) is of obvious benefit. Similarly, testing strategies for getting around 32-bit-SQL's 2.6GB procedure cache limitation when a database consolidation strategy is desired represents another good use of iterative testing. After all, a multiple SQL Server instance strategy (in which each instance automatically benefits from its own 2.6GB of cache) isn't the only game in town now that Intel and AMD have given us commodity 64-bit computing.

14.5.   Tools and Approaches

Iterative testing forms the backbone of sound testing. Use the content found in this chapter to help you craft a custom "iterative testing" checklist for your particular project. And to help you avoid re-creating the wheel completely, don't forget to leverage the documents available at the ftp site.

Don't Quit Now! Valuable Insight Is Just Around the Corner!

As someone anonymously once said many years ago, "No amount of planning will ever replace dumb luck." If you're one of the lucky few who seem to enjoy great system performance, more than adequate availability, and a perfect track record of meeting SLAs, I'm really happy for you. Really. Go ahead and get what you can for this book on eBay and enjoy the good life, you deserve it. For the rest of us, though, elusive dumb luck will have to take a back seat to something more concrete and consistent, like a well-planned methodology for load testing proposed changes or a repeatable process for iteratively tuning our SAP systems even while our underlying solution stacks, workloads, and end-user expectations continue to morph over time.

Actually, I don't really believe in dumb luck—things happen for a reason, whether overtly because of preparation and planning or inadvertently because of a lack of something else. Ray Kroc, the founder of one of my kids' favorite eating establishments, was probably thinking along the same lines when he said, "Luck is a dividend of sweat. The more you sweat, the luckier you get." So it is with stress testing and performance tuning. The more you work at creating an environment for repeatable testing and the more you embrace a pragmatic approach to testing and implementing change, the more likely you are to enjoy long, uninterrupted weekends and vacations with your family—yeah, the good life.

Of course, now that you have a load-testing environment and the requisite processes in place, why not use this to the fullest extent possible? That's where things really get interesting. The fact is, probably the neatest outcome in making this critical testing and tuning investment is that it can be easily leveraged to provide all kinds of incremental value to your organization. A well-put-together test environment, backed by proven processes and procedures and a skeleton team, makes for a great foundation when it comes to the following areas:

- Validating your high-availability solutions or processes
- Proving your DR or business continuity plans are effective

- Proving a proposed SAP Technology Stack delivers the required level of performance at a lower TCO
- Conducting capacity-planning exercises
- Testing how well your systems-management reporting processes, tools, scripts, and so on deliver in terms of an actual system load
- Testing new or unique consolidation approaches
- Testing new technologies
- Playing what-if in terms of supporting new workloads or varying online user mixes and incremental user or batch loads and so on
- Validating performance metrics associated with Web services, Web-enabling your current solution, and in other ways extending your implementation in support of constantly evolving business processes

In a nutshell, there's valuable insight just around the corner! And all of this extra knowledge and insight can be gained by leveraging your investment—a sunk cost, I might add—previously made in the name of performance testing. This final chapter focuses on extracting that last bit of value that may be obtained from performance testing. My goal is to take you to the next level and help you erect a bulkhead of strategic advantages between your IT boat and the waterfall a few hundred yards behind you, an undertaking simply not possible otherwise.

15.1. Determining True High Availability—the Second Pillar

Remember back when we covered the pillars of an SAP system? Nearly all of this book has been dedicated in one form or another to the pillar I labeled "Performance." But there's much value to be gained by testing and iteratively tuning your system to maximize how well you meet your organization's *other* core needs, namely those I described as the second, third, and fourth pillars of SAP: High Availability, Scalability, and TCO. Of special importance to everyone from the boardroom to the computer room, not to mention those in thousands of cubicles, shop floors, and warehouses, is high availability.

15.1.1.   Introduction to High Availability

A system that exhibits good high availability is one that is available when its end users expect it to be available. High availability is therefore a subjective term, driven by the needs of a system's customer base or users. Highly available systems meet the needs of their end-user communities through the use of sound technology, people, and processes, which in turn directly impacts SLAs, therefore making the business of conducting business possible. Looked at another way, high availability directly affects whether in-flight business processes have a chance of completing when things go awry, not so much from a functional perspective but rather in terms of creating a technical solution that remains "up" and performs well enough to remain "available" despite harsh circumstances. High availability makes it possible for end users to do their job and customers to be serviced in a responsive manner when the lights go out.

And, in one form or another, the lights are certain to go out eventually. Things simply don't work forever, or even in the way they're intended. Systems and networks fail, the power spikes or goes out completely, and people make errors. And, as I've said before, because we're talking about mission-critical systems driving core functions within an organization, simply waiting for the problems to work themselves out is rarely an option. This is where attention to architecting and implementing a highly available solution earns its keep—a high-availability solution can withstand component level and even more holistic systemwide problems because it has been *purposefully configured to do so.* That is, an organization has invested in what I call availability through redundancy (ATR) by identifying and eliminating (or simply mitigating, in some cases) single points of failure within a computing solution through building in n + 1 redundancy. With good ATR, the ability to continue processing sales orders and executing payroll runs is only interrupted momentarily, or perhaps not at all, even when the power goes out, a server dies, or the primary network connections between users and their applications fail.

At all times, the overriding principle is simple: at a certain point, an organization's level of downtime tolerance will eventually intersect its desire to put forth the dollars necessary to eliminate or mitigate its system's single points of failure and other risks. This point, shown in Figure 15–1, defines the organization's threshold of pain. Beyond this threshold, additional system availability would be nice to enjoy, of course, but the dollars necessary to ensure this availability would be beyond what the organization would be actually willing to pay.

For organizations seeking to best understand and mitigate the risks inherent to unplanned downtime, a test of *how well* their high-availability solution works is in order. Why? Because the technology necessary to provide a certain level of uptime can be complex, and misconfiguration will prove expensive—the organization will fail to enjoy what it's paid for, at precisely the time it needs it most. Beyond this, even when high availability is reflected in terms of redundancy and the many other safeguards built into a system—redundant network cards and switches, RAID arrays, clustered databases, redundant and load-balanced application servers, and so on—the degree with which a system successfully tolerates a failure will differ between high-availability

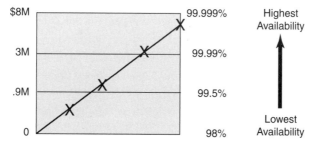

As downtime decreases, dollars increase...

Figure 15–1 Here, an organization's threshold of pain in regard to dollars versus downtime is illustrated.

solutions and approaches used. Even barring configuration issues, none of these solutions or approaches deliver the same level of availability. OS features and limitations, differences in database and hardware technologies, varying workloads, and so on all work together to create a unique
environment; why would this environment behave in anything other than a unique way in the
event of a failure of some kind? Will users be dropped because of lost network packets caused by
the presence or absence of a particular NIC or driver? Will batch processes fail despite RAID protected disk volumes because of other unforeseen configuration or business issues?

And finally, for organizations that seek the highest levels of availability, clustered servers
and other one-for-one redundant resources may be used to reduce the chances of system failure
that much more. Clusters take the concept of ATR to the extreme, in effect making an entire server
redundant. In this way, even beyond the ability to withstand in-the-box and similar server component failures, such a system could withstand the complete destruction of a server node. That is,
if it's configured correctly! In most SAP implementations, it's common to cluster a SAP database
server with its central instance, or an organization's Production system with its test system. And
the process of *failover* describes what happens when a Production resource fails—the services
initially available on the failed server node "move" or fail over to another available node in what
amounts to an invisible (or nearly so) process. So companies concerned with achieving the greatest levels of availability will test not only how well their unique ATR implementation fares but
how well their failover processes work under load as well.

15.1.2.   Testing Failover

From a testing and tuning perspective, the goal of "failover testing" is to understand the following questions:

- What constitutes a failure of your system, such that a failover is necessary?
- To what degree is failover automated, and what factors come into play that may impact
  this?
- What happens to in-flight user transactions and other business processes during and after a failover?
- What steps must be taken after a failover to ensure that the integrity of the system's
  data remains unquestioned?
- How will users and batch processes execute after failover? That is, will a certain degree
  of system degradation be acceptable, or must the system perform in terms of throughput and response times as well as it did prior to failover?
- How will daily support, systems management, and maintenance activities be accomplished after a failover?

As you can see, the actual level of high availability that may be achieved by a system is in
direct proportion not only to the high-availability solution used but also to the architecture of the
solution, the configuration of the solution components themselves, business- and technology-

driven failover criteria, systems-management practices/processes, the need to safeguard the system's data, and much more. Each of the previous questions can be used to craft system-unique success criteria, which may then be literally put to the test via a stress test that emulates a representative workload. And, by varying the workload, a series of iterative test runs may even be used to help characterize the performance of your high-availability system in response to daily workloads, seasonal or quarter-end business peaks, long-running batch processes like MRP, and so on (discussed in more detail later in this chapter).

15.1.3.   No Single Points of Failure (SPOFs) Allowed!

Ultimately, the goal of high availability in your enterprise SAP environment is simple: to increase the time that your SAP solution is available by decreasing both planned and unplanned downtime. In the end, the resulting uptime will meet or exceed your business-driven SLAs, and people will generally be able to get their work done. Before you ever reach the point of forcing a failover between servers or systems, though, my belief has always been that it's preferable to exercise whatever redundancy has been used "in the box" first. The reason is twofold. First, the risk of data loss associated with the untimely and unplanned failure of a database, and then the failover of database services to another node, is something to be avoided unless absolutely warranted. Second, the speed with which a failover may occur varies from seconds to many minutes, depending on the workload being processed and the need to roll back and roll forward a database's logs. Either way, these two factors represent unknowns that I would just as soon avoid.

So the first level of high-availability-focused stress testing I like to pursue involves proving without a doubt that no SPOFs *unknowingly* remain in a system. As SPOFs are uncovered, I work to eliminate or mitigate them, and in doing so, remove another potential failover scenario from ever playing out in the real world. Executing a repeatable series of stress runs (especially in terms of workload) makes for a real-world test-bed and a pretty cool method of validating that no SPOFs exist in your system to boot. Just how do you validate that your system configuration indeed is SPOF-free, though? You test it, and do so thoroughly! At an SAP technical conference a number of years ago, my SAP colleague and friend Fazil Osman and I demonstrated just how effectively a system could get around common SPOFs. We set up and shipped a highly redundant clustered R/3 system to the showroom floor, and every day over the 3-day conference proceeded to demonstrate over and over again the depth and breadth of both in-the-box and complete system failures our solution could withstand. We showed the power of ATR, along with good planning and plain common sense. Lacking something as nice as a table or counter in our limited booth space, we instead stacked piles of hardware, one on top of the other, on a chair next to the rack housing the SAP cluster to make our point. Our daily high-availability proof-of-concept demonstration went something like this:

- The entire SAP database/central instance clustered system was powered up, a SAPGUI was started on a network-attached desktop (providing the ability to manually execute a business transaction as well as run various CCMS transactions), and a command prompt was started on the desktop as well (to allow for a continuous series of network traffic aimed at the database server). In the latter case, the ping utility with the -t switch proved useful in displaying real-time that the system was connected and available.

- As the cluster was configured with mirrored and RAID-protected data, log, executable, and OS drives, we commenced the high-availability test by attacking the disk subsystem. This makes sense at many levels, too: disk drives represent the number one device failure in any computing solution, because of their moving parts. Thus, the first thing we did was to pop out these mirrored drives one by one, stacking them on the chair next to the servers. Then we removed a drive associated with the RAID 5 database volume as well. The system continued to run.

- Next, we "failed" one of the redundant controllers in the fibre-attached disk subsystem by simply unplugging it and tossing it on the stack. Sometimes, we would instead power off one of the redundant fibre hubs or remove a fibre cable.

- In the same way, we also failed a network card, typically by pulling out its network cable or powering off a redundant network switch (we momentarily enjoyed the thought of ripping out the PCI card from the running system, too, but thought better of it in the end).

- Yanking hot-pluggable power supplies or simply power cables was the next step, from each of the cluster servers as well as the disk subsystem.

- We then pulled out two of four hot-pluggable fans from each server, noting how large the stack of gear was growing on the chair.

- Next, we failed one of the application instances, watching the SAPGUI lose its connection and then later retry and successfully log back into its logon group.

- Because this was back in the days of CPU power modules, we also managed to wrestle one of these free in a cluster node, watching as the system failed over to the remaining node, while the first node rebooted automatically and then came back up with one fewer processors. The ping utility paused during this time but recommenced in short order once the server was back up—we did nothing but watch and smile.

- We then grew bored with the test, as the pile of hardware grew to a nice stack (maybe that's where I first started saying "technology stack") and forced a redistribution of the system's resources such that the cluster was again distributed between two nodes. Moving the central instance was accomplished so quickly that the SAPGUI connection at the desktop wasn't even phased. Moving the database between nodes, however, forced the SAPGUI connection to drop. It would happily reconnect at our command a few minutes later, though, after the database failed over to the remaining node and automatically rolled back and rolled forward.

All in all, we were told it was a nice show. At a minimum, it at least killed a good chunk of time on the showroom floor. And in all seriousness, it certainly demonstrated the viability of both ATR and clustering, showcasing what was then Microsoft's initial foray into this arena—MSCS version 1.0!

15.1.4.   Maintenance Windows and High Availability

As we've seen, at the end of the day high availability assists mission-critical business processes in executing to completion, safeguards the data supporting these business processes, and minimizes the risk and time inherent to otherwise withstanding a complete server failure. But high availability ultimately provides flexibility with regard to maintenance windows, too. This is true regardless of the OS or database that resides underneath SAP; as long as your SAP system is configured in a cluster, you can enjoy a certain level of maintenance window flexibility. And even outside of clustering, if you use a high-availability or disaster-recovery technique like database log shipping, for example, you may still benefit nonetheless. Many of my customers use the ability to manually fail over the processes associated with their database or central instance to free up the node for routine maintenance. For instance, you can take this opportunity to make changes to the following: the server's systemboard and local drive firmware; disk controller firmware and patches; OS kernel updates, patches, security updates, and service packs; and, in cases where the database executables reside on each node in a cluster, database patches and service packs, too.

Even more compelling, I've helped customers perform in-place server upgrades using this process, too. In one case, another friend and long-time colleague, John Dobbins, and I helped a customer completely replace the servers in its R/3 cluster with brand-new servers, using a structured "failover and evict" approach to make this happen. We tested and carefully documented the process in the lab, including the hardware/OS load and database backup/restore process, and labeled it a "SAP in-place cluster upgrade." With regard to performance tuning and stress testing, the point of all this is simple: realistic workload testing will help you identify and plan the precise steps necessary to pull off such a process whether the system is supporting 1,000 users during the middle of the day (not really recommended, actually, if you can help it) or merely a few users over the weekend (certainly a more risk-averse approach). The value is in learning what to expect, and then figuring out how to deal with the results *before* you potentially expose your Production end-user community to the same situation.

15.2.   Verifying Scalability—the Third Pillar

Beyond pure performance testing, or testing designed to prove your high-availability strategy works as expected, there is great value in validating the *scalability* of your Production environment (or a system configured to emulate it in a key way, like in terms of processing power or disk throughput). Scalability, the ability to address incremental workload needs or needs beyond what was originally envisioned, is at odds with cost. That is, a high level of scalability is easily achievable—it's easy to supersize your system—if you don't mind writing a big check for something you may rarely need. It's for this reason that I believe scalability testing is so vital. The concept is simple – it's better to understand the load a system can handle well *before* you might be required to handle that load.

Different kinds of scalability exist. The first, *in-the-box scalability,* speaks to the processing headroom (or other available bandwidth relevant to perhaps memory, network throughput, and so on) above and beyond what you absolutely need. Thus, scalability usually is not looked at as the solution for meeting regular month-end financial closes or other scheduled events; these events should have been planned for and taken into account from the beginning. Instead, I believe scalability is more often all about addressing *unplanned* workloads, and doing so in a manner that still meets the minimum response time and throughput metrics of the system's end users. This underscores what I've often said in the past—when deploying or upgrading SAP, it's crazy to buy exactly what you think you need at the time, because invariably a need will evolve later that was never understood or envisioned up front. I believe that scalability is therefore an integral part of sizing and should naturally take into account an organization's foreseen growth in workload as well as provide a certain level of scalability to meet unforeseen needs over the next 2 to 4 years. Traditional in-the-box server scalability approaches include the following:

- Buying a server with additional CPUs, RAM, or disks built in, essentially oversizing SAP *now* to address future workload unknowns. In doing so, the system will naturally benefit from better-than-required response time and throughput performance, though at a price of course.
- Buying a server *capable* of scaling or growing in terms of the number and speed of CPUs, RAM, disk capacity, I/O slots, and so on, but *forgoing actually purchasing these components*. In this way, the system is ready to grow with only minimal downtime required. The downside is that you may actually wind up buying a server that supports more in-the-box growth than you'll ever need—usually a minimal cost, but not always.

The second kind of scalability common in SAP environments is usually referred to as *horizontal scalability*. In a classic sense, this distributed approach to computing is seen, for example, when an organization chooses to purchase a large number of relatively inexpensive servers (or other components) rather than deploying fewer though larger and more expensive servers. An organization investing in 16 different two-CPU systems rather than one well-equipped 32-way server is taking such an approach to computing, one that implies that

- The different technology layers of the solution being deployed must therefore support horizontal scalability.
- A TCO analysis has indicated that it's the best way to go in terms of technology, people, and process costs incurred initially as well as over time.
- Perhaps a more consolidated approach is simply not possible; not all applications scale well in the box, for example.
- High-availability concerns might be driving the architecture decision; perhaps the high-level redundancy is preferred to mitigate the risk of one or few servers taking down an entire system.

Iterative load testing is a perfect fit for helping an organization determine which scalability scheme works best for it, as shown in Figure 15–2. To determine the best fit for a particular organization, I take into account an organization's high-availability requirements, application needs

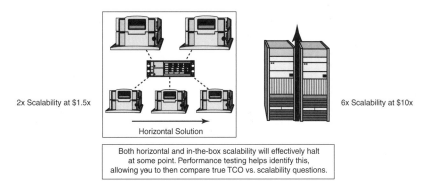

2x Scalability at $1.5x

Horizontal Solution

6x Scalability at $10x

Both horizontal and in-the-box scalability will effectively halt
at some point. Performance testing helps identify this,
allowing you to then compare true TCO vs. scalability questions.

Figure 15–2 Although both in-the-box and horizontal scalability options are viable in most situations, one approach tends to provide greater value than another based on the circumstances—iterative load testing helps solidify this value.

and constraints, unique workloads and the history with which these workloads grow and shrink throughout the year, any technology biases, general people skill-sets, and overall familiarity with deploying and maintaining distributed versus consolidated SAP solutions.

Scalability goes way beyond merely server hardware, too; the disk subsystem, OS, database, SAP application components, and middleware solutions all exhibit different levels of in-the-box and horizontal scalability. That is, you can buy more than you need of any of these technology stack components, in effect creating bandwidth on demand. Organizations that make the decision to purchase a more robust disk subsystem or more capable OS release without a current need for the capabilities inherent to these better than required versions are actually investing in scalability.

15.2.1. Baselining the Current State

I've harped on remembering to baseline your system prior to iterative testing. This is especially true of scalability testing, where the lack of a baseline makes it nearly impossible to later conduct apples-to-apples measurements between two or more system configurations. I also suggest that you baseline from a number of different angles; because you may not quite know what to look at up front, be sure to capture a variety of workloads, configuration settings, and so on.

15.2.2. Determining True Carrying Capacity

First of all, let me thank one of my newest SAP colleagues, Rolf Michelsen of HP, for sharing with me the term *carrying capacity.* I love this term, because it speaks clearly to both capacity planning and what I've in the past labeled *real-world smoke testing* (without the accompanying strange looks and questions about fire!). Carrying capacity is a fairly self-explanatory term that seeks to answer the following: What kind of load—online, batch, or otherwise—can a particular system configuration reasonably sustain in the real world? For example, given the desire to limit most CPU spikes to something below 70% and average RAM utilization to something less than 80%, how many users or batch processes may realistically be supported? That is, at what workload does the system exceed these self-imposed metrics? Working against a set of metrics to determine a system's carrying capacity is a great way to stay focused on the things that matter back in the real world—monitoring and managing Production response times and throughput rates to keep them from exceeding acceptable Production-like thresholds.

15.2.3.   Capacity Planning and Reverse Engineering

Have you ever been asked to show your management team concrete evidence that speaks to the capacity your system may possess after you complete a large merger or acquisition? Have you ever been told that you have no money to buy additional gear, but your system needs to support a new functional area and 500 more users by year-end? Like carrying capacity, these questions traditionally beg for an exercise in "sizing" to be conducted. But sizing is not an exact science, and an organization's uniqueness—its SAP customization, the layout and performance of its database and disk subsystem, and more—is often difficult if not impossible to capture and model in a reasonable time.

   For these reasons, many years ago, my colleagues and I at the SAP Competency Center devised a simple way of capturing the workload and performance statistics relevant to a particular company, so that we could then reverse-engineer the sizing process and ultimately understand a company's current workload-to-performance ratio. With these data, it was then possible to tweak our sizing and configuration tools, in effect customizing them to reflect the company's SAP implementation rather than a generic SAP sizing model. Finally, with a little bit of extrapolation it became possible to accurately size any number of what-if questions. And because the custom-sizing model had to take into account the entire custom solution stack deployed by the company, it was easy to determine a system's current-state carrying capacity as well. Bottom line, we were able to identify the precise bottlenecks that, left unaddressed, would artificially limit a system's potential throughput, while also pointing out when it made sense to add incremental in-the-box horsepower or incremental servers.

   At the end of the day, though, even a company-specific sizing exercise is not foolproof. It is for this reason that a "mini" stress test, like one focused on the performance or scalability of a key technology-stack component, can help validate the accuracy of a sizing exercise, and provide the concrete proof that many organizations require. And with the primary bottleneck identified via this exercise, a full-blown test is often not required. Instead, in my experience, I've seen delta tests provide all the proof a company needs to give it either peace of mind in its current solution or the ammunition it needs to justify incremental technology purchases.

15.2.4.   Smoke Testing

When the weight of the real world is not a concern, and you simply need to understand the maximum potential throughput a particular system is capable of sustaining without "melting" under the weight of its own workload, it's time to look into smoke testing. Another favorite term of mine, smoke testing, is near and dear to the true technologists and benchmarking fanatics among us. Smoke testing seeks to answer questions that are not often asked in the real world (e.g., "How many users can I actually support on an eight-way database server, regardless of CPU utilization?"). However, the answers to questions like this can provide valuable insight into where performance-limiting bottlenecks might crop up in a particular type of server platform, disk subsystem configuration, OS or database release, or even a particular SAP architecture or middleware component. Of course, whether or not to make such a technology purchase is not a question easily answered. During times like these, where financial decisions and business problems intersect, a TCO analysis can make all the difference.

15.3. Analyzing TCO—the Fourth Pillar

TCO has been a hot area for many years now. Even when many companies were flush with cash from investing in IPOs with neat products and lousy balance sheets, TCO still commanded quite a bit of attention. Lately, helping organizations understand their SAP environment's TCO consumes much of my time, especially those organizations on the verge of needing to sign new outsourcing contracts, considering renewing OS and database licenses, or looking to deploy new hardware platforms to support SAP functional upgrades or technology refreshes. Where stress testing becomes useful is when an organization wishes to validate the respective performance of two or more different SAP Technology Stacks, or key technology components, so that it can then compare costs and arrive at a TCO delta number between the different solution approaches. For instance, I've recently worked on customer-sponsored TCO studies for the following SAP environments: Windows/Oracle versus Linux/Oracle, HP Tru64/Oracle versus Windows/SQL Server, Sun Solaris/Oracle versus HP-UX/Oracle, and IBM AIX/Oracle versus Windows/Oracle or SQL Server. And I've worked on a number of hardware platform–focused analyses as well, like Unisys 32-way versus HP Superdome, Unisys 32-way versus HP ProLiant eight-way, Intel 32-bit versus 64-bit platforms, and AMD Opteron vs Intel. In most of these cases, the numbers spoke for themselves and the perceived or potential performance risk was well worth the dollars to be saved. In a couple of cases, though, an application-layer benchmark or stress test was called for to quantify and prove the performance numbers, tweak the TCO numbers, and subsequently generate an accurate company-specific TCO model.

TCO analysis is all about determining how much your SAP business solution really costs, taking into account the initial acquisition costs along with ongoing maintenance and support costs. Thus, it's more complex than simply determining the relationship between computing power and budgets (although this is a good place to start!). When you're faced with a question of TCO, and need to better understand the potential cost-benefit tradeoffs of one solution approach over another, I suggest you keep in mind the following:

- A TCO analysis usually first focuses on one-time initial costs, or acquisition costs, covering technology, people, and processes.

- Technology, people, and process costs need to be considered across the lifecycle of the solution, too. Sometimes these are called "recurring costs" and include the cost of SAP operations and management, annual maintenance and people costs, the business cost of downtime, and other day-to-day costs that must be factored in.
- One-time costs include both product procurement and product installation costs, including any migration costs necessary to move you to a new technology stack, along with the training dollars needed to support the installation or migration.
- Given that a TCO analysis must include technology (which is fortunately easy to quantify in terms of dollars), you should work your way through the SAP Technology Stack to help ensure nothing is missed.
- Don't forget to include systems-management costs—that is, any specific infrastructure, hardware, or software tools that must be leveraged to manage a technology stack, including the training and pilot or "demo" time necessary up front.
- With regard to people costs, don't forget to include the one-time requirements like hiring contractors or long-term consultants to install and deploy the system, provide training, perform onsite support, and so on.
- Try to quantify only the difference in administrative, operational, business, and other processes that one solution might enjoy over another, to keep things simple.

Remember to perform a TCO analysis of your current system as well as any proposed systems—I like to use a delta approach and only consider areas that will change between the two solutions. For example, if the data center will remain the same (i.e., there's no chance of outsourcing it), and the hardware server platform will remain the same, but the release of the database along with the disk subsystem are both being considered for replacement, I only focus on identifying costs associated with the latter two areas (assuming an incremental technology, people, or process upgrade is not required elsewhere). And before I quantify the current system's costs, I generally engage in at least a limited performance-tuning assessment project, designed to get the most out of the in-place solution to basically extend its life, returning to the company much-needed bandwidth in exchange for a few days of consulting, testing, and tuning. With this behind you, a more objective TCO analysis is possible, one that won't be questioned to the same degree or looked on as biased by proponents of the current SAP Technology Stack.

15.4.   Ensuring Your DR Solution Is Not a Disaster

Whether it's called DR Planning, Business Continuity Planning, or something else, the goal of disaster recovery is clear—to protect an organization's Production data and business processes from interruptions beyond what is deemed an acceptable threshold. The challenge is threefold:

- Determine precisely where the acceptable threshold for a particular business organization lies in terms of timeframes. Can the system be down no longer than an hour? A day? A few days? This is the organization's threshold of pain.

- Map the intersection of long-term downtime costs against what you can "afford" (the hit against revenue, or any other penalty, that your organization can withstand) to understand the organization's tolerance for downtime based on a set of customer-specific budget and risk variables. In other words, determine the dollars you are willing to invest to safeguard yourself against greater dollar losses.
- Mitigate the potential for system failures by investing in a proactive DR solution or method of safeguarding your data and business processes, including systems-management products and approaches, such that the Production environment is unlikely to reach the organization's threshold of pain.

A DR solution is simply insurance—you pay your premium and then take comfort that while you're spending dollars for something that you hope proves unnecessary, you're actually saving a great deal of money in the long run. The next few sections detail the role that performance tuning and stress testing play in the world of planning for and mitigating disasters.

15.4.1.   Disaster Recovery and Failover

I consider disaster recovery as the logical successor to high availability, the latter of which alone has little hope of addressing an organization's need for true disaster recoverability or disaster resilience. Where high availability might be concerned with addressing relatively small downtime outages that range from seconds to perhaps many hours, disaster recovery focuses on how to handle extensive potential downtime, ranging from many minutes or hours to maybe even days or weeks. Thus, whereas high availability might simply represent short-term failover solutions or incorporate tactical practices and system characteristics designed to increase general availability, disaster recovery speaks to how a company continues to do business in the aftermath of a disaster.

Also like high availability, a certain amount of failover is associated with DR solutions, though typically to a much greater extent. Why? Because a disaster implies that the source system is no longer available at all—because of fire, flood, hurricane, terrorist threat, and so on—and therefore all core services associated with a system must be rapidly migrated to another site, to be hosted and accessed from there. In terms of stress testing, the real measure of success for a company might involve executing a real-world load test, and then forcing a failover to the company's DR site in the middle of a test run, to answer the following questions:

- How did the systems on each side respond? Was the transition smooth? Did the receiving system behave as expected?
- How did the business processes hold up, especially with regard to multiple systems? Did each system maintain accurate "state" information to essentially pick up where it left off after the failover, or did the entire business process fail?
- Did the in-flight data and database in general successfully make the transition? Was anything corrupted? How long did it take to roll back/roll forward, if necessary at all?

- What was the impact on the users? How long were they without service, how easy was it to connect to the new system, and what was the status of their in-process transactions?

Depending on your particular needs, the answers to these questions could vary widely, but you could still meet your DR requirements. The idea is to simply test the DR process in a real-world scenario before you're ever forced to actually live and work through a failover . One less thing to worry about in the aftermath of a disaster makes good business sense to me, and because you can leverage the dollars already spent in the name of stress testing and iterative performance tuning, the incremental dollars should be easily justifiable.

15.4.2.   Proving the DR System Delivers

Like high-availability solutions, DR solutions are implemented by way of technology wrapped in processes, managed by people. Each one of these areas is subject to "fail" both during and after a failover. So, like testing whether the failover process works well in the first place, validating that the receiving system *performs* well also makes good business sense. What I suggest, therefore, is a full-blown load test similar to the testing conducted on your Production environment. Of course, if the DR system models Production identically, no test is really necessary. But because such perfectly replicated environments are rare, it might behoove you to characterize exactly how well your DR system performs compared to Production. Doing so will help you set your end users' expectations correctly, and make for the smoothest possible transition in using a DR system. After all, failing over to a DR site implies that your end users will be utilizing it for an extended period of time, presumably while the primary data-center site is undergoing repairs or rebuilding. For all of these reasons, proposing a mini load test as part of your annual DR test plan or review makes great business sense.

15.4.3.   Failing Back

It's not enough to be able to fail over to a DR site in the event of an emergency. You must also be able to "return" services back to the primary site as well! The final value-add of stress testing in regard to disaster recovery involves just that—testing and tweaking the processes related to failing back. Doing so makes it possible to identify and resolve any issues before you find yourself needing to do so in the real world—the same kinds of questions and issues described previously when failing over to the DR site. And because I propose doing so as part of a load test, especially troublesome areas related both to in-flight business processes and how user connections are handled will help you establish the rules surrounding fail back. For instance, can you fail back during normal business hours, or must you wait for a specially designated downtime window? And if you must wait, what kind of timeframe is required at minimum? Finally, are there processes that need to be put in place to make all of this happen successfully?

15.5. SAP Systems Management

To some folks, it might seem unlikely to lump "increased systems administration understanding" into the list of additional benefits made possible by a string of stress-test runs. After all, systems management itself does not appear related to performance testing (though monitoring a system is certainly taxing to that system, inherently impacting performance!). But I say there's no better way to characterize or prove that your systems-management processes, performance thresholds, alert mechanisms, and reporting processes work as expected than to do so while a load is placed on your system, as discussed next.

15.5.1. Systems Administration and Daily Operations

As discussed in Chapters 12 and 13, the key to successfully executing a load test lies just as much in sound monitoring and performance data collection as in emulating and driving the actual Production business processes. The knowledge gained in doing so can represent a huge windfall to the organizations ultimately responsible for day-to-day operations and general systems administration. Thus, just the ability to help these organizations understand what a "stressed" system looks like—how to identify performance issues, bottlenecks, and so on via CCMS's tools like RZ20 (CCMS Monitor), SSAA, ST02 (tune/buffer summary), ST03 (workload statistics), ST04 (database performance), ST06 (OS monitor), and much more—can be a huge plus! If you have the time, I strongly encourage you to at least engage in a certain amount of cross-training or familiarization training—bring these supporting organizations in, set them down, and let them watch how you execute and monitor a stress test. Even better, if they have their own budgets or can get funded out of a larger pot of IT dollars, you may wish to pursue a more "dedicated" form of on-the-job training. In my eyes, it's this kind of cross-team schooling and mentoring that in the long run will pay off big in terms of increased performance, better availability, and predictable scalability.

15.5.2. Systems Management Approaches

Like testing an organization's proficiency with SAP CCMS, SSAA, or similar transactions, stress testing can also prove useful in validating how well you have configured and used holistic enterprise systems-management applications or suites. For example, products like BMC Patrol and HP OpenView can be quite a challenge when it comes to setting up thresholds, monitors, alerts, reports, and so on—doing so is time-consuming and tends to be subjective as well. With a couple of daily-load test runs behind you, though, it should become quickly apparent which alerts are important to review or save, which can be tossed, and at what level an alert should be escalated. It's the emulation of a real-world business process load that makes this possible.

15.6. Testing Proactively and Playing What-If

With fundamental testing and tuning values applied to areas outside of strictly performance-oriented engagements, it's time to open the door a bit wider and see what else of testing and tuning value lies out there. The next couple of pages identify and address a number of key benefits that may be easily derived by standing on the shoulders of (load-testing) giants.

15.6.1.   From Transaction Processing to Business Processing

Once you've made the investment in simple single-system testing or basic single-transaction stress testing, it's an easy step to begin adding more real-world complexity. I don't often initially jump into complex business process testing myself, for instance, without taking similar baby steps—only over time do I add or factor in incremental systems or create more involved business processes by assembling and connecting simpler discrete transactions. Staying focused in the near-term on consistently executing and monitoring key transactions running on single systems improves success rates, plain and simple. Later, with the fundamentals behind me, I can more easily build on the existing scripts and processes to flesh out real-world end-to-end business cases or other specialized processing needs.

15.6.2.   New Technologies

Up and down the entire SAP Technology Stack, the opportunity to test and tune proposed changes to the stack exists. Many of these changes come in the form of updates to a particular hardware or software component; these make up minor changes and of course warrant change-control-driven testing prior to promoting these changes into Production. But on a regular basis, brand-new technology solutions or approaches are introduced to the SAP marketplace, creating huge opportunities for introducing critical problems into the stack. Of course, the flip side is that by embracing these changes and seeking to stay on top of change in general, the benefit inherent to new technologies can be more quickly realized by companies with a sound "test, adopt, and go" strategy. And this is where the real value lies in stress testing new technologies—to mitigate the risk associated with the "test" part of this strategy and thus avoid a "ready, fire, aim" approach to introducing new technologies.

Your new technology testing might be quite limited in scope, perhaps focused on simple hardware-based or OS-level testing. Or you might instead choose to run through a comprehensive application-layer test that by its very nature drives activity at all of the layers in your SAP Technology Stack. Regardless, companies in a position to leverage technology-enabled competitive advantages will tend to get new products to market earlier, close their financial books sooner, obtain a more accurate picture of their inventories and supply chains, and so on. And everything else being equal, they'll be more successful.

15.6.3.   Consolidation Plans

Although I covered "lessons learned" from some of the most common approaches to IT consolidation for SAP in Chapter 14, it's worth discussing how those and other approaches lend themselves to what-if performance testing and tuning. For example:

- It's rare that I hear of clients collapsing their network infrastructure, but it happens. If you're considering moving from a distributed multitier network to perhaps a flat network model, I recommend testing at three levels. First, validate that your back-end SAP Application Server to database server traffic is good to go. Then analyze the front-end traffic, too, paying attention to factors like dialog response times (specifically, front-end network time). Finally, consider all the other traffic that may be routed across either of these networks: print jobs, Citrix, workflow, e-mail/SMTP, ftp, other protocols (a little IPX/SPX, anyone?), other applications (Peoplesoft, Oracle eBusiness Suite, Siebel), and so on. And don't forget to factor in the lost bandwidth associated with collision-oriented networks like Ethernet—a 100Mb network segment is hard-pressed to effectively push more than 40Mb, for example, unless it's switched.
- It's important to test the impact that a proposed change to your SAN may have by driving the database via an application-layer stress test. Even three to five hard-hitting SAP transactions or batch processes can drive enough load to prove viable in this regard, as long as they are "DB Request" intensive (as measured via ST03).
- OS updates, like moving from Windows NT 4.0 Server to Windows 2000 Server to Windows Server 2003, naturally lend themselves to delta testing. I recommend creating a standard OS-based workload that hits both CPU and disk, and tracking the differences in throughput for each respective platform. I also find that it's important to track minor revisions as well, like those associated with security fixes, Service Packs, and other patches. Finally, if you're considering moving from one version of an OS to its more capable brethren (e.g., Windows 2000 Server to Advanced Server or Datacenter), one way to really prove you're getting the most out of the upgrade is to conduct a simple performance test. For example, a stress test that proves you really *do* benefit from the additional RAM made available to you by going with Advanced Server of Datacenter helps you set aside those kinds of questions once and for all.
- Like testing same-family OS updates or even completely different OSs against one another, server consolidation is all about workload delta testing. Create a baseline that emulates an appropriate workload—a representative mix of CPU, memory, disk, and network loads, for instance, all rolled into a single "test case"—and execute this in delta fashion against multiple server configurations and consolidation approaches. In cases where the OSs differ, to save time be sure to select a test tool that functions on different platforms—this is the easiest way to conduct apples-to-apples testing, too!
- If you're considering SAP's MCOD initiative, a load test conducted at the application layer is a must. Sure, SAP supports most any combination you can throw at MCOD today. However, if you don't perform the due diligence of load testing, you'll never quite know how well *your* SAP systems play together until the bearer of bad news walks into your office complaining of poor performance during month end closing.

- For my colleagues who like to collapse SAP Application Server instances or ITS instances, a workload test makes sense here as well, specifically at the application layer of course.

The potential benefits of IT consolidation for SAP environments are absolutely huge, dangling promises of something in the neighborhood of the elusive tenfold increase in performance or decrease in price that I talked about in Chapter 1. I'm a big fan of consolidation, but by the same token, I believe that all but the most basic of consolidation approaches warrant a certain amount of load testing to mitigate a good deal of the risk.

15.6.4.   Characterizing Changing Workload Mixes

One thing sure to happen to every SAP system in production today is that the current workload will change over time. Maybe new users will be added, or others removed. Maybe new functional areas or mySAP components will be introduced, or current functional areas will be changed to support new or extended business processes. Whatever the case, the changes will come in little waves, and over time they will tend to vary considerably in retrospect—it will be hard to compare year-to-year workloads, for instance, because both daily and peak loads will change significantly. Through all of this, there's no substitute for capturing a system's performance baseline and updating it every so often to reflect the current specific workload as it morphs throughout the years. In the end, you'll be able to look back at a set of data points (if you've captured the relevant low-level statistics) that reflects key SAP Technology Stack performance metrics.

In this way, that daily online user load you see somewhere between 9 a.m. and 11 a.m. most every morning, or maybe that hard-hitting batch process you run every month on the sixth workday, will serve as documentation of both the state of the workload and the state of the SAP system hosting the workload. These data points will let you identify changes in the top 40 transactions, help you track trends in growth, help you conduct regular capacity-planning exercises steeped in the realities of your end-user's work patterns, and help you extrapolate long-term system needs as well.

15.6.5.   Validating Execution Windows

Similar to the system-maintenance windows discussed earlier in this chapter, *execution windows* also represent and support a repeatable business requirement of a system: to provide a highly available, well-performing, and usually limited window of time to complete a particular activity. In new implementations, it's usually pretty easy to find a window of time for activities like payroll and MRP runs, critical batch updates, BW extracts/downloads to R/3, and so on.

As the system's workloads change and grow more complex and online users tend to demand more system resources and faster turnaround time, though, the remaining contiguous time left in a system to address the aforementioned "window-based" activities will continue to shrink. SAP IT shops that "follow the sun" (a term commonly used to imply that both users and support staff will be global in nature, coming and going in "shifts" around the world as the workday begins and ends every 8 hours or so) may be unable to sustain large execution windows. Because of this, I've been personally involved in a number of tightly focused performance-testing engagements designed to ensure that a particular process or task could either still be completed in the customer's allotted timeframe (e.g., in the case of a process that may have changed) or be completed in a shorter timeframe (typically because of improved coding or, more often, new technology). Moving forward, these kinds of tests will probably never completely disappear either; they're inherently useful, and, in light of their narrow scope, relatively easy to pull off.

15.6.6.   Looking Outside the Box

Outside of business and IT drivers that force companies to evaluate new technologies, or spend time analyzing SQL statements to maximize the efficient use of shrinking execution windows, leading-edge companies that have adopted SAP will continue to seek new ways to increase performance not only inside but "outside the box," too. Approaches include adopting new common/middleware software and hardware components, systems-management applications, improved firewalls and other safety tools, load-balancing approaches, or IT consolidation projects. And, in the end, the proactive organization that stress tests its assumptions and inferences will position itself to best meet the needs of not only its end users but ultimately its customers, vendors, and suppliers. This will in turn help promote sound change control, encourage planned technical refresh and functional upgrades, and mitigate a host of performance-related system risks—probably the best reasons for stress testing presented in this entire book!

15.7.   Conclusion—Me, Your Boat, and Three Little Rules

Do you remember the boat analogy I beat to death back in Chapter 1? Forgive me in advance but I feel the need to drag it back out and tie up everything I've talked about in this book. Probably the nicest thing about working with you, many of whom are already my SAP customers or colleagues, is that I get to enjoy all of the benefits of having a boat without actually having to buy one myself. It's *your* boat I'm referring to—your SAP system. I'm kind of like that friend who always manages to fit him- or herself into your Memorial Day weekend plans out on the lake, but can never be found when it's time to top off the boat's gas tank or perform some routine maintenance. I somehow get all of the fun of working on and around your SAP implementations, upgrades, and so on without any of the mundane responsibilities or headaches. Or the need to write the big checks.

So with that, as I've shown in Figure 15–3, I'll close with a simple "thank you" and share with you some wisdom recently passed on to me by one of my friends and clients, Jim Bonner. Jim wraps up our world of supporting SAP environments with what amounts to three rules. Rule number one is simply "Make it fun." Keep in mind that this is the first rule, not the last—despite the mission-critical nature of supporting an enterprise infrastructure, and the ramifications that go along with failing to achieve acceptable performance, scalability, availability, and TCO, the world of SAP is rewarding. Good people, interesting technology, plentiful changes, and challenging learning curves ensure good times.

Figure 15–3 Steer clear of those waterfalls!

Rule number two pertains to personal job satisfaction: "To be successful in SAP IT, you need to invest time, and you need to invest money. But you'll be twice as successful when you invest both at the same time." I couldn't agree more, and can point to many others who have successfully put that same philosophy into action. And finally, rule number three speaks to TCO and the financial ramifications of introducing major change into a mission-critical business/IT solution like the solutions provided by SAP AG: "To even consider a large change like an SAP platform migration, essentially changing the way SAP IT works, you should expect to receive either a tenfold decrease in cost or a tenfold increase in performance." Although a ten-fold change either way represents a huge delta, I must admit that I see the wisdom here quite clearly—a change must at least *look* compelling enough financially or in terms of end-user productivity (again, financially!) to warrant potentially disrupting business-as-usual, especially once you factor in all of the hidden costs surrounding change.

I'm pleased to say that Jim himself saw the fruit of performance tuning and testing turn a minor financial investment into a much greater than tenfold increase in performance. My friend I spoke of earlier, John Dobbins, and I helped Jim's organization realize a huge up-tick in system throughput by exercising a great number of principles (not to mention tools and processes) described in this book. At the end of a week-long systems review and performance-tuning engagement, we managed to decrease the replication time for Jim's Production SAP/SQL database from 2 days to just 1 hour. Similarly, the time necessary to work through a million rows in a particularly sticky database table contracted from 8 minutes down to 11 seconds. Like Jim said, "It seemed a little dramatic, but covered my ten-fold rule nicely!" I trust many of you will see similarly spectacular performance and availability results if you truly put into practice in your own SAP environment the contents of this book. In the meantime, remember rule number one! And thanks again! Even after all these years, you continue to make this more fun for me than I ever thought possible. I'll see you on the waters.

Index

Wouldn't it be great

if the world's leading technical publishers joined forces to deliver their best tech books in a common digital reference platform?

They have. Introducing
InformIT Online Books
powered by Safari.

■ Specific answers to specific questions.

InformIT Online Books' powerful search engine gives you relevance-ranked results in a matter of seconds.

■ Immediate results.

With InformIT Online Books, you can select the book you want and view the chapter or section you need immediately.

■ Cut, paste and annotate.

Paste code to save time and eliminate typographical errors. Make notes on the material you find useful and choose whether or not to share them with your work group.

■ Customized for your enterprise.

Customize a library for you, your department or your entire organization. You only pay for what you need.

Get your first 14 days FREE!

For a limited time, InformIT Online Books is offering its members a 10 book subscription risk-free for 14 days. Visit **http://www.informit.com/online-books** for details.

POWERED BY
Safari

informIT
Online Books

informit.com/onlinebooks

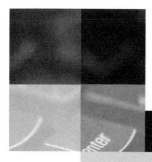

informIT

www.informit.com

YOUR GUIDE TO IT REFERENCE

Articles

Keep your edge with thousands of free articles, in-depth features, interviews, and IT reference recommendations – all written by experts you know and trust.

Online Books

Answers in an instant from **InformIT Online Book's** 600+ fully searchable on line books. For a limited time, you can get your first 14 days **free**.

Catalog

Review online sample chapters, author biographies and customer rankings and choose exactly the right book from a selection of over 5,000 titles.

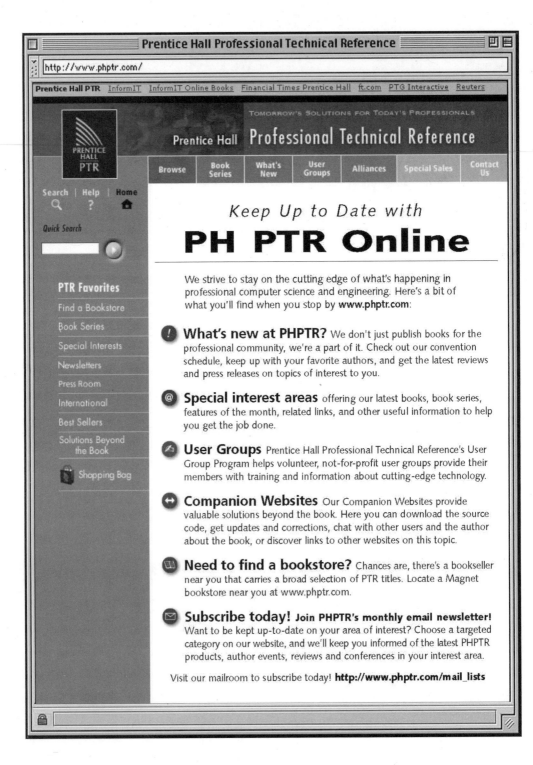